Why People Pay Taxes

Tax Compliance and Enforcement

Joel Slemrod, Editor

Ann Arbor

THE UNIVERSITY OF MICHIGAN PRESS

Published in the United States of America by
The University of Michigan Press
Manufactured in the United States of America

1995 1994 1993 1992 4 3 2 1

Library of Congress Cataloging-in-Publication Data

Why people pay taxes : tax compliance and enforcement / Joel Slemrod, editor.
p. cm.
Includes bibliographical references and index.
ISBN 0-472-10338-5 (alk. paper)
1. Taxpayer compliance—United States. 2. Tax evasion—United States. 3. Income tax—United States. I. Slemrod, Joel.
HJ4653.E75W45 1992
336.2′91—dc20 92-28163
CIP

A CIP catalogue record for this book is available from the British Library.

Preface

Tax evasion is a pervasive phenomenon in all societies. It is impossible to understand the true impact of a tax system without knowledge about who complies with the tax law as it is written and who does not. How the tax law ought to be enforced is as critical a problem for tax policy as is the structure of tax rates and the definition of tax bases. Yet it is only recently that academics have turned their attention to tax compliance and enforcement. When they did, it was quickly realized that there is little empirical evidence on which to base policy prescriptions.

In an effort to consolidate and expand our knowledge of these subjects, the Office of Tax Policy Research commissioned twelve studies on tax compliance and enforcement that were presented at a conference held on December 7–8, 1990, at the School of Business Administration of the University of Michigan, Ann Arbor. This volume begins with an overview chapter and then contains the twelve commissioned essays, each followed by commentary written by a participant in the conference. The essays investigate the determinants of tax compliance from several different perspectives. This interdisciplinary interchange of views brings out many new insights into this important and challenging set of issues.

We would like to thank the National Science Foundation Division of Law and Social Sciences and the Internal Revenue Service for providing the financial support for this project. The conference and this volume could not have been possible without the administrative and organizational support of Mary Molter.

Contents

Why People Pay Taxes: Introduction

Joel Slemrod

It is impossible to understand the true impact of a country's tax system by looking only at the tax base and the tax rates applied to that base. A critical intermediating factor is how the tax law is administered and enforced. What is apparently a highly progressive tax rate structure may, in fact, be proportional, or even regressive, if taxes levied on the wealthy are not collected. What is apparently a tax base finely tuned to reflect individual differences in ability to pay may, in fact, produce a capricious distribution of tax liabilities if the tax law is selectively enforced.

Stressing the importance of tax compliance and enforcement is not merely a technical point—it is a quantitatively important one. Tax evasion is a pervasive phenomenon in all societies, albeit one that is difficult to measure precisely. For the United States, the Internal Revenue Service has estimated that, in 1987, noncompliance with the individual and corporate income tax cost the Treasury $84.9 billion, comprising more than 20 percent of tax liability. Although comparable studies for other countries do not exist, anecdotal evidence suggests that the extent of noncompliance is even larger outside the United States.

Recognizing the importance of tax compliance and enforcement raises several fascinating policy questions. Foremost among them is the extent to which resources should be expended in enforcing the tax law, how those resources ought to be deployed, and what penalties should be imposed on detected evasion. In this era of annual deficits approaching $300 billion, a tax gap approaching $100 billion becomes a tempting target for policymakers, especially in view of the IRS claim that each dollar it spends on enforcement will be rewarded with ten dollars in collections, and because increased revenue from enforcement is not a "tax increase," an important distinction in today's political debate.

But these easy arguments are often misleading. From an economic perspective, it is not optimal to increase the IRS budget until one dollar spent returns no more than one dollar in revenue, because the expenditure is a real resource cost to the economy and the revenue is merely a transfer from private to public hands. Furthermore, increased enforcement of the tax system will have disincentive effects similar to an increase in tax rates and bases. Finally, the capacity of increased enforcement to raise much more revenue has recently been called into question. Getting sensible answers to these questions depends on reliable information on the determinants of tax evasion.

Unfortunately, there is very little known with much certainty about tax compliance behavior. But it can no longer be said that the subject has been ignored. There is now a burgeoning literature, both theoretical and empirical, by accountants, economists, lawyers, psychologists, and sociologists as well as scholars from other disciplines. But scholarly communication across disciplines is much harder than within disciplines.

Not only is there little hard evidence about tax compliance, but there is still much dispute about the proper conceptual model to use in addressing the issue. Economists have traditionally viewed the problem as one of rational decision making under uncertainty—cheating on your taxes is a gamble that either pays off in lower taxes or, with some probability, subjects you to sanctions. From this perspective, one would expect that noncompliance would respond to changes in both the likelihood that an act of evasion will be detected and punished, as well as the severity of the punishment. Social scientists from other disciplines have stressed the narrowness of this view and focused on the importance of peer pressure, civic responsibility, and other factors.

Because so little is known about the decision process that accompanies taxpayer compliance decisions, this volume begins with two essays that analyze data on taxpayer thought processes that was collected during the course of a tax filing season. Marco Steenbergen, Kathleen McGraw, and John Scholz analyze the influence on taxpayer attitudes and compliance intentions of: (1) tax reform's objective impacts on the citizen's self-interest, (2) discussion with other taxpayers, and (3) subjective evaluations of tax reform. They interviewed 359 taxpayers before and after the 1988 tax season, the first in which the main effects of the Tax Reform Act of 1986 came into effect. They find that the taxpayer's own tax situation had little effect on attitudes conventionally associated with compliance. Only subjective evaluations of the tax reform significantly altered attitudes and beliefs. The largest influence on taxpayer attitudes came from the social influence of discussions about taxes. The perceived attitudes of individuals with whom the respondents discussed taxes had consistently strong impacts on inhibitors and commitment related to compliance.

The essay by John Carroll explores the ways a decision-making perspective can be brought to the study of taxpaying. To do this, he investigates information collected from 100 taxpayers who kept daily diaries of tax-related thoughts and behaviors, and did their major tax preparation work in the presence of a research assistant, who recorded their thoughts as they "thought aloud." He finds that, of all tax-related statements, nearly 60 percent were regarding the likelihood of receiving a refund. Noncompliance by misrepresenting income was significantly related to lower income levels, more opportunity for noncompliance, reliance on a tax professional, and diary comments about time spent and fear. Noncompliance by misrepresenting deductions was significantly related to postseason tax knowledge, reliance on a friend or relative as a source of information in the prior year, receiving a better-than-expected refund, and diary comments about the unfairness of tax procedures.

The insights gained from taxpayer interviews can inform the systematic analysis of taxpayer behavior. As of now, there are three principal sources of quantitative evidence about the determinants of tax noncompliance: statistical analyses of historical data, statistical analyses of survey data, and controlled experiments in a laboratory setting. Each of these research strategies is represented in the next group of essays.

Statistical analysis of historical data relies on the fact that, either over time or across individuals or geographic areas, the determinants of tax compliance vary. By relating the differences in the determinants of compliance to measures of compliance and holding other factors constant, one can cull from the data an association between the factors that vary and the degree of tax compliance. Causality can never be decisively established, but in many cases the direction of influence is not controversial.

Unfortunately, as a leading tax expert once put it, statistical analysis of tax evasion is straightforward "except that you can't measure the left-hand side variable and you can't measure the right-hand side variables." This is a bit of an overstatement, but it also has the ring of truth. Tax evasion is notoriously difficult to measure precisely, and some of the potential influences on compliance, such as the perceived probability of detection and opportunities for evasion, are also difficult to measure.

For research about compliance with the U.S. income tax system, there is available perhaps the best data set in the world—from the Taxpayer Compliance Measurement Program, or TCMP. The TCMP is used by the IRS to help it to construct the formula it uses to select returns for audit—other things being equal, it prefers to select returns that are likely to exhibit noncompliance. Every three years it randomly selects about 50,000 returns for an intensive, line-by-line audit. The TCMP data set contains, for each return and line item, what the taxpayer reported and what the auditor determined was appropriate. This data has been made available to researchers on a selective basis.

Many of the important cross-sectional studies of tax evasion have been based on the TCMP data. This volume features three essays that make ingenious use of recent TCMP data. In the first of these essays, Kurt J. Beron, Helen Tauchen, and Ann Dryden Witte use taxpayer reports in 1969, aggregated to the three-digit zip code level, to estimate the deterrent effect of audits. They find that although audits stimulated compliance, the effect was not large and not statistically significant for all groups. Audits were more effective at inducing accurate reporting of subtractions from income than of income itself. The results suggested, however, that IRS activities other than audits do have significant compliance effects. Their work also has an important methodological message—that the estimated effect of education on compliance depends on the model's specification. For example, the estimated effect of education on compliance is negative when income is included and positive when it is not.

Brian Erard investigates the subsequent year reporting effect of an audit using IRS data sources on individuals who were the targets of an audit in one year and, by pure chance, were the subjects of a second audit two years later. His results indicated that a substantial proportion of taxpayers demonstrate improvements in compliance following a large prior year audit assessment. However, estimation of a statistical model reveals that once one controls for taxpayer characteristics and prior year audit selection rules, the results do not indicate a positive relationship between taxpayer compliance and prior audit experience. If, however, it is assumed that individuals targeted for a prior year tax return audit are otherwise more prone to file noncompliant returns in the future than taxpayers who are not targeted for such audits, then a significant deterrent effect of prior audits on subsequent reporting behavior is obtained.

In his essay, Eric Rice develops several propositions that are central to understanding corporate tax evasion and tests them econometrically using the 1980 corporate TCMP data set. This represents the first academic study of the corporate TCMP. Rice finds that two-thirds of corporations are noncompliant, with median unreported profits amounting to 12 percent of their reported median profits. The econometric analysis lends support to three main propositions. First, characteristics that assure public disclosure of information about a corporation also tend to encourage better tax compliance. Second, there are two opposing effects of firm profitability: managers of a corporation whose profit performance falls short of the industry norm may resort to noncompliance as a means of shaving costs, while high-profit companies may take advantage of their greater ability to underreport income without being audited. Finally, the marginal tax rate is positively associated with noncompliance, although the U.S. Treasury would forego far more revenue by cutting the marginal tax rate than it would raise via enhanced compliance. He also finds that noncompliance is positively associated with firm size.

The essay by Nourzad and Crane represents an innovative effort to learn about tax compliance from a different kind of cross-sectional data—information collected from state tax amnesties. They use data from the Michigan income tax amnesty program to investigate the determinants of federal and state tax evasion, taking into account the self-selection bias inherent in the data. They conclude that the federal tax rate has a statistically significant positive effect on federal tax evasion, but can find no demographic variables that are important. For Michigan state tax evasion, both true income and the state tax rate have significant positive effects on evasion. Also, state-level evasion appears to be complementary to federal evasion. This suggests that a careful matching of federal and state tax return data may be an effective compliance policy tactic.

Although the TCMP data are unequalled for their line-item information about detectable evasion, they have certain limitations. First of all, the data concern only noncompliance that is detected by IRS audits. Although the TCMP audits are notorious for their thoroughness, it is understood (even by the IRS) that their audits are more successful in detecting some kinds of noncompliance than others. For example, the IRS is not particularly effective at uncovering unreported income, but is much better at identifying overstated or undocumented deductions. Although some error in measuring evasion is unavoidable, repeated analysis of the same data set may reinforce the biases of the particular data collection method. Second, with TCMP data, it is generally impossible to distinguish between willful evasion and inadvertent misreporting or between an invented deduction and an actual but undocumentable deduction. By making certain assumptions, for example about the symmetry around zero of inadvertent mistakes, one can try to separately identify willful evasion, but these techniques are imperfect. Finally, any analysis of the TCMP data set is limited to the variables reported on the tax return, so that there is minimal demographic information and no information at all about taxpayer attitudes and other factors that may influence compliance behavior.

Because of these shortcomings, it is important that empirical researchers in this field look beyond the TCMP to learn about compliance. Several of the essays in this volume, including the Crane and Nourzad essay, do just that by relying on data from taxpayer surveys.

Steven M. Sheffrin and Robert K. Triest analyze the 1987 Taxpayer Opinion Survey to investigate the role of attitudes and perceptions in taxpayers' compliance decisions. Their estimation results suggest that attitudes are important determinants of compliance. They find that both having a negative attitude toward the tax system and perceiving other taxpayers as dishonest significantly increase the likelihood a person will evade taxes. Increases in the perceived probability of detection are found to decrease the likelihood of evasion. Surprisingly, personal knowledge of someone who has had difficulties with the IRS decreases the perceived probability of detection. Experimental results suggest that publicity concerning the overall extent of noncompliance may cause significant changes in taxpayers' perceptions of the probability of detection and the honesty of others.

Kent Smith also analyzes the 1987 Taxpayer Opinion Survey in order to study positive incentives for tax compliance. He finds that responsive service and procedural fairness are effective positive incentives that increase citizens' normative commitments to tax compliance. With an appropriate balance of enforcement and cooperative strategies, procedural fairness can also reinforce perceptions of effective enforcement. Normative commitment to compliance can, in turn, be positively reinforced by the effective detection and punishment of noncompliance, particularly for tax and other regulatory laws not rooted in values based on the relationships among individuals.

Karyl Kinsey next argues that enforcement techniques emphasizing detection and punishment have two opposing effects on tax compliance: (1) they force people to comply with the law, and (2) they negatively affect willingness to comply voluntarily. According to her analysis of survey evidence, respondents who have personally paid additional taxes as a consequence of an IRS enforcement contact perceive a greater certainty of detection for noncompliance and are more likely to intend to comply on future returns. However, previously noncompliant taxpayers who are not assessed additional taxes upon contact lower their perceptions of certainty and plan to continue past habits of noncompliance.

While the net effects of personal IRS contacts appear to be improved compliance, the results for vicarious contacts suggest little support for general deterrence effects. Instead, taxpayers appear to talk more about the fairness of their enforcement contacts than about IRS effectiveness in detecting noncompliance. Hearing vicarious reports of bad behavior by the IRS lowers both the perceived fairness of the tax laws and the personal willingness to comply.

The essay by Hessing, Elffers, Robben, and Webley is disquieting because it questions the consistency of data about tax compliance gathered from surveys with data from official studies of compliance. They discuss the results of a series of studies on tax evasion in the Netherlands, with special emphasis on the deterrent effect of tax law enforcement. One striking finding is a zero correlation between self-reported tax evasion and the officially measured tax evasion. Additional analyses indicated that although different sets of attitudes, norms (legal and social), and personality indicators correlated with admitted tax evasion, they were not related to the official measure of evasion.

The authors tentatively conclude that nonevaders do not need deterrence to keep them from evading or, alternatively, a small measure of deterrence is enough to keep them from doing so, and deterrence does not seem to have any effect on habitual evaders. If there is an effect of deterrence on evasion, it is in the wrong direction: there is a positive correlation between being punished for evasion in one year and willful evasion in the following year.

Social scientists are often envious of the physical scientist's ability to conduct controlled experiments. It is unlikely, however, that the IRS will ever be able to, in the interest of the advancement of knowledge and better policymaking, conduct five different enforcement policies in five different, but similar, states over an extended time. Social scientists can, however, conduct controlled experiments in a laboratory environment, and such work has yielded impressive results in fields such as strategic behavior and decision making under uncertainty.

Alm, Jackson, and McKee describe the results of laboratory simulations designed to investigate a variety of strategies that governments can pursue to increase tax compliance. They find that higher probabilities of detection and higher penalties increased compliance, although the effects were not large. Average compliance increased significantly when individuals found to be compliant were rewarded by a lottery, a fixed reward, or a reduction in future audit rates. The introduction of a public good financed by the taxes of all individuals also increased the average compliance rate.

The volume closes with a cautionary note. While data on noncompliance are difficult enough to find, the essay by Doreen McBarnet warns us that focusing on compliance or noncompliance with the rules as written may, for some purposes, be misleading. She argues that securing compliance may not be sufficient to achieve the goals of tax law enforcement. Compliance, far from being a solution to regulatory problems, can itself pose a major problem for tax policy and enforcement, and that compliance can be secured without control over tax policy—"compliance with rules" rather than "compliance with policy." McBarnet suggests that one answer is to regulate through laws that allow wide discretion to impose compliance with policy, perhaps by disallowing the lawfulness of activities that comply only in form but not in substance. Her interpretation of recent experience in the United Kingdom, however, suggests to her that there may be limits to this approach, limits imposed by the ideology of the rule of law.

If there is a persistent theme to the essays presented in this volume, it is a change in perspective away from deterring noncompliance toward positive encouragement for compliance—an emphasis on the "carrot" for compliance rather than the "stick" for noncompliance. Positive attitudes toward the tax system and pleasant, efficient contacts with the tax collection agency can increase compliance. This insight is especially important because, from the tax collection standpoint, it is extraordinarily expensive to arrange an enforcement regime so that, from a strict cost-benefit calculus, noncompliance does not appear attractive to many citizens. It follows that methods that reinforce and encourage taxpayer's devotion to their responsibilities as citizens play an important role in the tax collection process.

Furthermore, some of the research presented in this volume strengthens the notion that it is difficult to detect a quantitatively significant deterrent effect of sanctions. There are two extreme explanations of this difficulty. The first is that there is, in fact, no significant deterrent effect; the second is that our data and methods are too weak to detect a deterrent effect that is out there. My own view is that the latter explanation is closer to the truth, and that the present evidence is insufficient reason to abandon the "stick," properly applied, in conjunction with the "carrot." I eagerly await further research to confirm or deny this view.

Taxpayer Adaptation to the 1986 Tax Reform Act: Do New Tax Laws Affect the Way Taxpayers Think about Taxes?

Marco R. Steenbergen, Kathleen M. McGraw, and John T. Scholz

What changes take place in the citizen's beliefs, attitudes, and behavior when a new tax law is passed requiring some sacrifice on the part of the citizen? Does the impact of the law on the taxpayer's self-interest affect commitment to obey the law? Although compliance studies have identified a number of attitudes consistently related to compliance, little is known about how these attitudes are formed and what impact changing laws have on them. The purpose of this essay is to empirically investigate the impact of the 1986 Tax Reform Act (TRA) on tax attitudes and commitment to comply.

The TRA provides an unusual opportunity to study the dynamics of these relationships, because it imposed one of the most significant changes in tax laws in this century. These changes affected self-interest in very different ways for different taxpayers; Sharpe (1989) reported that after the TRA went into effect tax increases from the previous year averaged $1,700 for about 45 percent of all taxpayers, and tax decreases averaged $2,100 for another 45 percent. Thus the role of self-interest in changing beliefs and commitment to comply should be readily observable.

Furthermore, the TRA received broad political support as a reform to increase the fairness of tax burdens, although there was considerable skepticism among taxpayers about whether fairness increased or decreased. Thus, fairness evaluations should also vary among individuals in our study, and the impact of such evaluations on commitment can be analyzed and compared with the impact of evaluations based more exclusively on self-interest.

Our primary goal is to provide a cognitively informed account of how citizens respond to new tax laws. Although we are ultimately concerned with the impact of new laws on compliance, our focus here is on the commitment to comply rather than actual compliance. This focus permits us to emphasize the cognitive processes of adaptation, and should bring out most clearly those aspects of legal change that affect the way taxpayers think about taxes. Analyzing compliance behavior would require consideration of differential opportunities to follow through with behavioral intentions, and would involve the controversy arising from the use of self-reported compliance data. Analyzing commitment to comply reduces these problems, and provides a richer response to analyze than the dichotomous compliance variable.

We begin by outlining our hypotheses about the cognitive structure of tax beliefs and attitudes, which we will call a tax schema. The tax schema incorporates variables of the conventional compliance model, which assumes that personal, social, and legal inhibitors affect a taxpayer's commitment to comply, which in turn affects compliance. We then consider factors related to the TRA and the dynamics of how they influence the tax schema. We are particularly concerned with the process by which social discourse, individual evaluations of the TRA, and objective TRA changes affect the taxpayer's commitment to comply. Given the possible importance of subjective evaluations of the TRA in this process, we distinguish four different categories of evaluations potentially linked to compliance behavior: individual consequences, social consequences, individual fairness, and social fairness. The empirical study simultaneously analyzes the effect of objective TRA changes, subjective evaluations, and social discourse on the tax schema, focusing on the conventional compliance model in particular.

Continuity and Change in the Tax Schema

We begin by describing our assumptions about the cognitive structure of the taxpayer's tax schema, which provides a baseline for considering the dynamics of schematic change. Roth, Scholz, and Witte (1989, 149ff.) use the term *tax schema* to refer to "all understandings and value that an individual holds about the federal income tax system" (see also Sears and Citrin 1985 for a discussion of the tax schema). We will only outline the structure and cognitive organization among relationships established in survey-based compliance research, since the relationships themselves have been discussed in greater detail elsewhere (Kinsey 1987; Lewis 1982; Roth, Scholz, and Witte 1989). The nature of the relationships among the various cognitive elements of the schema, the degree of logical consistency, and the link between the cognitive elements and behavior, are not very well understood. Nevertheless, the literature on cognitive structure (Anderson 1983; Judd and Krosnick 1989) provides us with a number of clear guidelines for our analysis.

Continuity of the Tax Schema

First, we assume that the schema is organized hierarchically, as illustrated in figure 1. We will refer to beliefs and values at each level as nodes, each of

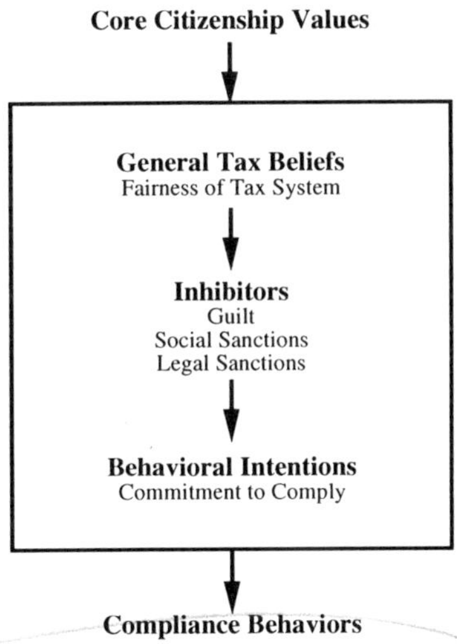

Fig. 1. Conventional view of the tax schema

which is linked with other nodes at higher and lower levels of the hierarchy. More abstract concepts or values at the top of the hierarchy constrain beliefs and attitudes at lower nodes, which become increasingly more concrete and oriented toward specific objects toward the base (Allport 1961; Rokeach 1973). The most abstract level includes core political values and ideologies (see also Conover and Feldman 1984; Hurwitz and Peffley 1987; Sears, Huddy, and Schaffer 1986 for hierarchical models of political reasoning). This level is common to schemas relevant to other policy domains as well.

The next level contains attitudes and beliefs specific to a taxpayer's tax schema. It includes domain-specific attitudes and values focused on the tax system, such as perceptions of the fairness of the tax system and policy preferences for tax policies. Although these beliefs have seldom been found to be directly related to commitment and compliance, they have been found to be related to lower nodes that, in turn, were related to commitment (Kinsey and Smith 1987), as illustrated in figure 1.

The lower, more concrete level includes specific attitudes and beliefs relating to behavioral intentions. The empirical literature on tax compliance focuses primarily on three "inhibitors" of noncompliance (see Grasmick and Bursick 1990; Roth, Scholz and Witte 1989): the perceived probabilities of legal sanctions, interpersonal sanctions (such as a loss of respect from family and friends), and personal sanctions (the experience of guilt that results from noncompliance). These tax-specific beliefs, in turn, influence the individual's behavioral intention (Ajzen and Fishbein 1977), in this case the level of commitment to comply with tax laws (Yankelovich, Skelly, and White 1984). It is this connection between inhibitors and commitment that we will emphasize.

Studies of similar hierarchical schemas in tax compliance and other domains typically have proceeded by examining the consistency between schema-relevant responses that are presumed to be structurally linked with each other. The structure of the schema has been inferred from the degree to which structurally linked responses are correlated (for a review, see Judd and Krosnick 1989). For example, strong correlations are expected between support for the political system and beliefs that the system is fair, that the taxpayer would feel guilty if he or she cheated, and that the taxpayer is committed to compliance. In other words, the good citizen is expected to be a good taxpayer. However, the empirical work within this tradition tends to view schematic structures as *static* phenomena, with little concern for such important dynamic issues as the processing and integration of new information or the nature and extent of attitude change (see Judd, Drake, Downing, and Krosnick 1991). Thus existing studies provide little guidance for our task of examining sources of *change* in the tax schema.

Change in the Tax Schema

Implicit in hierarchical schema models is the proposition that much reasoning is "top down" or "theory driven," such that specific beliefs are influenced by the more abstract concepts. This is particularly true under conditions of uncertainty, such as the introduction of a complex legal change: general concepts provide a framework for interpreting and evaluating ambiguous experiences (Taylor and Crocker 1981). Theory-driven processing does not preclude the possibility that changes take place at various levels of cognition in response to external changes, but implies that these changes then become transmitted to lower nodes in the schema.

Our working hypothesis is that the intermediate links between core values at the top of the hierarchy and behavioral intentions at the base are most susceptible to change. They appear most likely to provide the gateway by which the cognitive structure adapts to perceived changes in the environment. Core values are less susceptible to change from a given law (Rokeach 1973), particularly deeply held values that are linked with multiple domains. Research about the impact of mass media communications is consistent with this view: the mass media can influence specific message-relevant attitudes, but rarely change more basic values and orientations (Kinder and Sears 1985).

Specifically, we hypothesize that taxpayer evaluations of TRA changes will primarily influence general fairness measures and inhibitors, which will subsequently influence commitment. However, we expect that legal changes will make only marginal changes in the tax schema, compared with the basic continuity of beliefs and attitudes. We also test the extent to which legal changes have a direct impact on commitment that is not filtered through the hierarchical tax schema. The implications of these direct versus indirect effects will be discussed with the results.

TRA Impacts on the Tax Schema

We view the passage of a new law as a quasi-experimental intervention that allows us to test the extent to which the tax schema maintains continuity when the environment changes. We consider three factors by which this intervention may alter tax schema. The first factor measures the objective impact of the law on the individual's taxes. The obvious hypothesis is that when individuals discover (during the tax season) that the new law increases their taxes, they are more likely (by the end of the tax season) to perceive the laws as less fair. Thus they feel less guilt and social stigma associated with tax cheating and consequently reduce their commitment to comply. Conversely, decreased taxes should lead to more favorable judgments of fairness, more guilt and social stigma, and greater commitment to comply. To the extent that this logical sequence reflects actual cognitive processes, we would expect this hierarchical path of influence to be more important than the direct influences on commitment for self-interested objective changes imposed by the law.

The objective amount of tax increase or decrease imposed by the TRA on a taxpayer provides only one possible source of influence that a new law could have on the tax schema. Individuals must find out about the law to determine its impact on their tax bill, and the manner in which they obtain information may bias their resultant evaluations. An analysis that compared the impact of various information sources on taxpayers (McGraw, Scholz, and Steenbergen 1989) found that social influence (specifically, perceived attitudes toward noncompliance of the individuals with whom the taxpayer discussed taxes) had by far the strongest impact on the taxpayer's commitment and compliance. Again, individuals who discuss taxes primarily with those having little commitment are likely to change all attitudes in the direction consistent with lower commitment. Unlike the more hierarchical effects expected for objective changes, the attitudes of discussants toward compliance appear more likely to affect all levels independently. Any attitude could readily be activated and influenced during such conversations, because undirected conversations may touch on a range of topics relevant to different levels of attitudes. We include the attitudes of discussants in this analysis to represent the impact of the broad class of social influence affecting tax activities.

Finally, we analyze the impact on the tax schema of the taxpayer's subjective evaluations about the TRA. The objective TRA impact on the individual's taxes would presumably have little influence on the tax schema if it did not agree with the taxpayer's subjective assessment of this impact. Furthermore, the self-interested assessment of an actual change in tax provides only one dimension by which a law might be evaluated. A number of studies reviewed in Sears et al. (1980) found self-interest to be less related to policy preferences than other kinds of evaluations. Interpolating from these studies, the TRA impact on other social groups may be as relevant as impacts on the self in changing tax-related attitudes. In addition, evaluations of the fairness of impacts on self and society are also likely to be important. Since we wish to include all important dimensions of evaluation, we will test the impact of both the self-versus-social and the outcome-versus-fairness dimensions of TRA evaluation in our study. We include four measures.

The first measure, *individual outcomes,* has its roots in the classical utilitarianism of Bentham, Hobbes, and Smith. According to this view, people act to maximize their own utilities, secure pleasure, and avoid pain. The dominance of self-interest has been a particularly pervasive theme in public choice theories of economics (Downs 1957; Laver 1981; Mueller 1979), as well as motivational theories in psychology (Campbell 1975; Sears and Funk 1990; Wallach and Wallach 1983). Following Sears and Funk (1990, 148), we define self-interest as the (1) perceived short-to-medium-term impact of an issue on the (2) material well-being of (3) the individual's own personal life (or that of his or her immediate family). Personal outcomes associated with tax law changes include changes in personal tax liability due to TRA changes, the amount of time and effort needed to prepare and file taxes, and the probability of legal sanctions for noncompliance.

The second measure, *social outcomes,* reflects the utilitarian tradition of Mill, Sidgwick, and Edgeworth, which emphasized the maximization of social utility as indicated by such phrases as "the greatest good for the greatest number." This emphasis on social, as opposed to personal, outcomes is most evident in contemporary welfare economics (where "social utility" is frequently called the "social welfare function"; see Harsanyi 1977; Sen 1973), and is also evident in Campbell's (1975) psychological analysis of evolution and the collective welfare.

In the present context, social outcomes are the changes in tax liability associated with various groups in society. Social utility is usually defined (for example, in welfare economics) as either the sum or the mean of the utility levels of all individuals in a society. This kind of "greatest good" evaluation of the social outcomes associated with the TRA could be inferred—and is in this study—by summing across perceptions of the impact of the TRA on a variety of social groups: the more groups that benefit, the more positive the evaluation of the social outcomes.

The third measure, *individual fairness,* proposes that citizens evaluate new policies via normative criteria that differ from self-interest. Two broad classes of psychological theories have been concerned with the consequences of judgments of personal fairness: The first focuses on *distributive justice* (the fairness of outcomes, which include both rewards or resources and burdens or responsibilities; see Adams 1963 and 1965; Blau 1968; Homans 1961); the second focuses on *procedural fairness* (the fairness of the procedures used to allocate outcomes; see Lind and Tyler 1988; Tyler, Rasinski, and Griffin 1986). The analyses reported here are limited to the distributive dimension, because we are more concerned with the impact of legal changes rather than the administration of the law. The two questions in our scale report evaluations about the TRA's impact on the fairness of taxes owed by the respondent and by people at the respondent's income level.

The final measure, *social fairness,* refers to what Brickman et al. (1981) have labeled "macrojustice," or the aggregate fairness of an outcome distribution in a society. Taxpayers might use a number of different criteria to determine whether a societal-level distribution is fair. One is the social utilitarian principle noted previously, that the mean of the societal outcomes should be maximized. Rawls's (1971) principle ("Social and economic inequalities are to be arranged so that they are to the greatest benefit of the least advantaged") is also a principle of macrojustice, to maximize the outcomes at the lower end of the distribution. Numerous others exist, including a range or variance principle (minimize the discrepancy between the upper and lower ends of the distribution), equality (which many argue is properly conceived as a macro- rather than microjustice principle), and a normal distribution principle (Brickman et al. 1981; Sen 1973). Given the need to capture these complexities in some measure, we summed the individual's evaluation of the overall fairness of TRA and the fairness for several social classes. The data supported this simple approach, since all questions contributed to the reliability of the scale.

Each of the four measures is conceptually distinct, although it is not surprising that they are correlated. Elsewhere (Steenbergen, McGraw, and Scholz 1990) we argue that cognitive processing begins as objective changes are first perceived in terms of concrete individual and social outcomes attributed to the legal change. These outcome evaluations provide the basis for fairness judgments. We also suggest that individual outcomes generally influence the evaluation of societal-level outcomes. When evaluating a complex legal change such as the TRA, it is extremely difficult for citizens to assess changes in outcomes across multiple and diverse social groups. In contrast, the personal impact of the law is more readily apparent, salient, and easily accessible. When asked about personal fairness or the implications of the new law for others or society in general, the personal impact is likely to provide an anchor due to increased cognitive accessibility (Fazio 1989). In this study, we utilize appropriate tests that assume that the terms are related, but we do not attempt to analyze the complexities of the interrelationship.

There is substantial empirical evidence in various policy domains that the four evaluations have an impact on policy preferences and behavior, although we do not know of any previous work that has examined the four simultaneously. For example, Sears and Funk's (1990) review reveals strong and consistent self-interest (individual outcome) effects on support for tax policies (see also Sears and Citrin 1985), whereas the impact of self-interest is much weaker, particularly in comparison to symbolic attitudes, in other domains. Sears and Funk argue that the impact of self-interest is particularly robust in the tax domain because the individual stakes are clearer, and the magnitude of potential negative consequences greater, than in other political domains. We hypothesize that as the negative impact of the TRA increases, general tax beliefs, inhibitors, and behavioral intentions will become less supportive of compliance.

Tyler's (1990) analysis of legal compliance indicates that individual fairness evaluations (based on distributive fairness) associated with encounters with the police and court system have a significant impact on subsequent compliant behavior, controlling for previous behavior and legitimacy attitudes. The tax compliance literature has not analyzed impacts of new laws (Roth, Scholz, and Witte 1989), but evaluations of fairness of the tax system have been indirectly linked to compliance levels (Kinsey and Smith 1987). Hawthorne and Jackson (1987) determined that collective concerns (social outcomes) have a significant impact on tax policy preferences, and they concluded that collective considerations are at least as important as individual outcomes in structuring individual policy preferences. These studies suggest that the TRA evaluations should have a direct impact on tax-related attitudes and behavior. Although one could argue for even more dimensions of evaluations and could suggest alternative scales, we believe that the four measures we employ provide an appropriate test for the impact of the taxpayer's TRA evaluations on other tax beliefs and attitudes.

Study and Methods

The Study

In order to analyze the dynamics of tax compliance, our research design sought to detect changes in the tax schema and behavior resulting from the experience of filling out the first tax return most affected by the TRA. The data for these analyses come from a panel study of 471 New York taxpayers from Nassau and Suffolk counties on Long Island, New York. Taxpayers were interviewed in person around January, 1988, prior to working on the 1987 tax year return due in April, 1988. Respondents were reinterviewed by telephone in the summer of 1988. The second-wave respondents were screened to determine that they had filed their taxes by the time of the second interview, ensuring that they had all fully confronted the changes imposed by the TRA.

In order to increase analytic power, the sample was selected to include individuals most likely to be affected by the TRA. The IRS provided a list of all middle- and upper-income taxpayers within our selected geographic region who had filed federal income tax returns with itemized deductions (Schedule A) in each of the previous three tax filing seasons. We oversampled individuals filing more complex returns (25 percent of the sample filed Schedule C to report business income, and 10 percent filed Schedule E to report rents or royalty income). Moreover, in order to study carefully the cognitive processes of individuals who actually complete their own returns, we oversampled this group (two-thirds of the sample), relative to those who use professional preparers (one-third of this sample but 47 percent of taxpayers nationwide; see Wechsler 1989).

A total of 799 taxpayers were interviewed in the first wave of the panel between January and March, 1988. These in-person interviews averaged about sixty minutes and consisted of questions dealing with a wide variety of tax-related issues. The response rate for these preseason interviews was 62.2 percent, which compares favorably to other recent in-person tax interviews of less specialized samples of taxpayers (e.g., the 1980 Westat and 1984 Yankelovich, Skelly, and White studies reported 42 percent and 70 percent response rates, respectively). A total of 471 respondents completed the postseason, twenty-minute telephone interview in the summer of 1988, yielding an 82 percent response rate. The analyses reported here take this panel group of 471 cases as their basis.[1]

Given the relatively small size of the panel, we minimized the number of cases lost because of missing values for individual questions through mean imputation (see, e.g., Little and Rubin 1987): for each of the variables, the (relatively few) missing data points were replaced by the mean value obtained

1. Because of our selection criteria, the sample is older, better educated, and better off than the average taxpayer. The average age of the sample is 49, with a range from 24 to 89 years. Sixty-three percent are male (in the case of joint filing households, respondents were screened for the spouse who had primary responsibility for the filing of taxes), 86 percent are married, and 68 percent are employed full-time. The sample is well-educated, with 59 percent reporting some kind of college (two-year, four-year, or postgraduate), and politically conservative (68 percent of the sample). Finally, the modal reported income is between $25,000 and $50,000 (25 percent of the sample); approximately 35 percent reported a yearly income higher than $50,000, and a fairly large number refused to report their income (17 percent; more than 5 percent gave "don't know" or did not answer for other reasons).

from the valid cases. This method could not be applied to the critical variable measuring attitudes of discussants for those with no discussion, which reduced the number of cases to 359. Preliminary analyses indicate that the final sample and the larger, preseason sample do not differ significantly on attitudinal measures of concern in this study.[2]

Variables

Our study of the dynamic influences on the tax schema distinguishes between three sets of variables representing continuity of the tax schema and three sets representing sources of change accompanying the introduction of the TRA. These variables are used to explain each postseason tax node, as illustrated in figure 2. The impact of the preseason variables emphasizes the continuity over time in the tax schema and, as such, reflects stability. The links among the postseason variables, in keeping with the model shown in figure 1, reflect the hierarchical nature of the tax schema, so that general notions of tax system fairness guide the inhibitors that, in turn, predict commitment. Social context variables are also included to control for possible income and gender effects not directly related to TRA changes.

The variables representing continuity include pre- and postseason values and beliefs. The first, *tax system fairness,* is the response to the question, "Compared to other people like me, I pay more than my fair share in taxes." The three *inhibitors* were measured by asking the respondents to "imagine yourself in a hypothetical situation in which you deliberately and knowingly understated your income by $500." They then were asked to indicate "How likely is it that you would feel *guilty* if you did this?"; "How likely is it that people whose opinion you value would lose respect for you if they found out that you did this?" (*social sanctions*); and, "What is the probability that the IRS would find out?" (*legal sanctions*).[3] Responses to the guilt and social sanctions questions were provided on a scale with the response options of very likely, somewhat likely, somewhat unlikely, and very unlikely; responses to the legal sanctions questions were probability judgments ranging from 0 to 100 percent. Finally, *commitment* to comply is a multiple-item scale reflecting

2. There are some minor differences between the cases that have been left out of the analysis (respondents who did not discuss taxes) and those that have been included. The nondiscussants tend to be somewhat older, somewhat more conservative, and lower in income than the respondents who discussed taxes. Furthermore, the nondiscussants tend to make more use of professionals in preparing their taxes.

3. We followed each of these questions with the question "how important would this be for you?" as has been done in several other surveys. However, we have not included responses to the follow-up questions in our analysis, because they did not improve the explanatory power of the simple inhibitor questions.

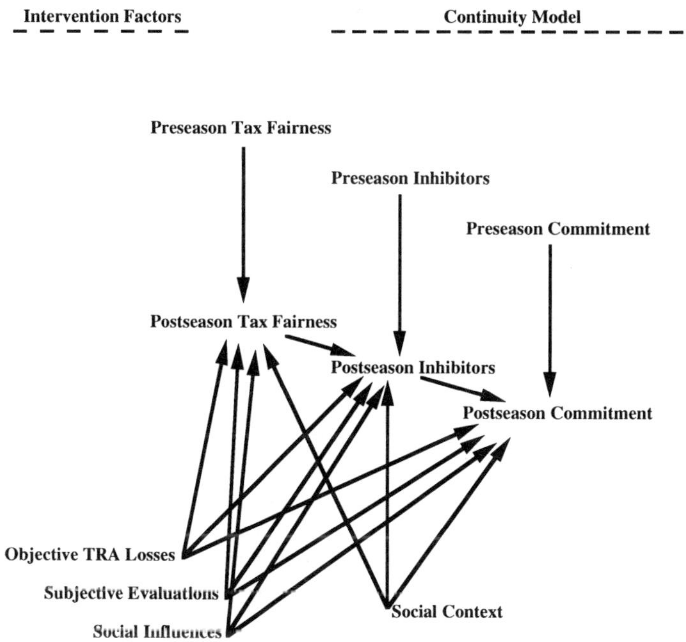

Fig. 2. Model of TRA effects on the tax schema

the respondent's judgment of the acceptability of engaging in illegal tax transactions, such as "earning $500 in cash from odd jobs and not reporting it" and "stretching medical deductions to include some expenses that are not really medical" (preseason scale comprised of six items, Cronbach's $\alpha = .84$; postseason scale comprised of three items, Cronbach's $\alpha = .66$).

Our primary concern focuses on the intervention effects relating to the TRA and taxpayer activities during the tax season. In a sense, these effects represent the discontinuity in the tax schema introduced by the legal intervention. In the model, they explain the residual (co)variance that is left after the preseason schema values, social context, and postseason schema structure have been taken into account. Direct effects of each intervention on each postseason node are included to test the degree to which these variables affect postseason commitment directly versus indirectly through the higher level nodes in the tax schema.

The variables representing the intervention effects include the objective loss of tax benefits, social influence during the tax season, and the four evaluative dimensions concerning the TRA that were discussed earlier. *Objective losses* were calculated by counting the number of tax items the individual reported having on the prior (1986) tax return that were adversely affected by the TRA. Specifically, these tax items were the personal exemption of a child's return, the tax on long-term capital gains, IRA deductions, the deduction for interest on consumer debt and credit cards, miscellaneous itemized deductions, tax losses from tax shelters, and the alternative minimum tax. It should be noted that the variable only counts the number of categories affected, not the amount of loss involved. Since these losses may have been offset by decreases in tax rates, they do not imply that the individual was worse off under the TRA than under the previous law. However, since the tax rates were decreased for everyone, this variable does provide a measure of the relative impact of the TRA—taxpayers who have lost more deductions and exclusions should be worse off relative to others. Furthermore, these losses might be cognitively more salient than the gains from decreased rates in any case, since each loss actually felt by the taxpayer is likely to weigh heavily in considerations of the fairness of the TRA. Consequently, those with greater values on this measure of objective loss should become more negative in their attitudes than those with lower values.

The *social influence* variable reflects the attitudes toward noncompliance among those with whom the taxpayer discussed taxes prior to the filing of the 1987 tax year return. In the postseason survey, the respondents were first asked to indicate whether they had discussed taxes with one of five social targets: spouse, family, friends, co-workers, or members of clubs and organizations. If discussions took place, the respondents were asked to indicate whether the discussant believes "it is acceptable or unacceptable for people to pay less tax than they legally owe." The *attitudes of discussants* variable is the average attitude of the discussant(s) with whom the respondent had talked about taxes.

To operationalize each of the four *TRA evaluations* (individual outcomes, individual fairness, social outcomes, and social fairness), multiple indicators from both waves of the study pertaining to specific evaluations of the TRA were assigned to the dimensions on theoretical grounds.[4] Items that detracted from the scale reliability were eliminated. The scaling procedure for each dimension entailed three steps: (1) recoding of the scale items so that high values reflect greater fairness and more positive outcomes; (2) standardization of the items; and (3) unweighted summation of the items to form a scale.

4. To assess the fit of the four-factor model for the evaluative dimensions, we conducted a confirmatory factor analysis in EQS (Bentler 1989), allowing the factors to be correlated. Although the four-factor solution does not fit the data, it clearly outperforms models that employ a smaller number of factors. Specifically, a model that only distinguishes outcomes from fairness performs worse, and a model with only the individual-versus-society distinction yields an improper solution.

Individual outcomes is a nine-item scale (Cronbach's α = .66), comprised of the following items (where the number in parentheses indicates that the measure was taken from either the first or second wave): expectation of a refund on the 1987 tax return (1); effect of TRA on respondent and family (1); anticipated difficulty in filling out tax returns due to TRA (1); effect of TRA on respondent and family (2); satisfaction with amount of taxes paid (2); amount of taxes owed in 1987 compared to 1986 (2); difficulty in filling out tax returns (2); expected versus actual refund (2); and negative surprises in taxes due to TRA (2). *Individual fairness* is a two-item scale (Cronbach's α = .78), the first the perceived fairness of the TRA for people of the respondent's income level (1), and the second the fairness of the respondent's taxes under the TRA (2).

Social outcomes is a six-item scale (Cronbach's α = .61), composed primarily of the perceived impact of the TRA on a number of social groups: effect on taxes paid by the poor (1); effect on taxes paid by the rich (1); effect on taxes paid by corporations (1); effect on business investments (1); effect on tax shelters (1); and the change in taxes owed by the rich as a result of the TRA (1). Finally, *social fairness* is a five-item scale (Cronbach's α = .62), including fairness of TRA for the rich (1); fairness for the poor (1); fairness for the elderly (1); fairness for the middle class (1); and the overall fairness of the TRA (2).

Method of Estimation

The full model portrayed in figure 2 uses the following system of equations to predict each node in the postseason tax schema (parameters for the variables are left out for the sake of brevity).

$$\text{Commitment}^{b} = \text{Commitment}^{a} + \text{Inhibitors}^{b} + \text{Interventions} + \text{Social Context} + \epsilon_1 \quad (1)$$

$$\text{Guilt}^{b} = \text{Guilt}^{a} + \text{Tax System Fairness}^{b} + \text{Interventions} + \text{Social Context} + \epsilon_2 \quad (2)$$

$$\text{Social Sanctions}^{b} = \text{Social Sanctions}^{a} + \text{Tax System Fairness}^{b} + \text{Interventions} + \text{Social Context} + \epsilon_3 \quad (3)$$

$$\text{Legal Sanctions}^{b} = \text{Legal Sanctions}^{a} + \text{Tax System Fairness}^{b} + \text{Interventions} + \text{Social Context} + \epsilon_4 \quad (4)$$

$$\text{Tax System Fairness}^{b} = \text{Tax System Fairness}^{a} + \text{Interventions} + \text{Social Context} + \epsilon_5 \quad (5)$$

The superscript *a* and *b* distinguish the preseason ([a]) from the postseason measure ([b]). The intervention variables include six measures: TRA tax increase, four subjective evaluations (individual outcomes, individual fairness, social outcomes, and social fairness), and social influence. The social context variables include the two measures of income and gender.

The system of equations is estimated simultaneously through full-information maximum-likelihood (FIML) estimation. This procedure has several advantages: (1) it produces more efficient estimates than alternative (limited-information) estimators that only consider one equation at a time (see, e.g., Judge et al. 1985);[5] (2) it provides a test of how well the model fits the data; and (3) it accounts for correlations among exogenous variables. Specifically, our estimation takes into account the assumption that all preseason schema values, intervention variables, and social context variables are correlated with each other and are not independent. This minimizes the possible bias in our estimations caused by interrelations among these variables not specified in our model. FIML estimation is easily implemented through standard statistical packages or special software for covariance structure analysis, of which LISREL is perhaps most commonly known. The results presented here were obtained using EQS (Bentler 1989), and details of the statistical procedure are presented in the appendix.

The availability of overall model tests allows us to compare the relative strength of alternative models that leave out different variables and links from the full model. We can, therefore, test the relative contribution of each set of intervention variables when the others are excluded from the equation. We can also test the importance of hierarchical versus direct influences on commitment (and by extension on compliance) by comparing direct and indirect models of intervention effects.

We utilize two tests of a model's goodness of fit. Full-information maximum-likelihood estimation produces a likelihood ratio test statistic indicating whether a model is fitting for a given significance level. It is frequently employed for sequential tests of nested models that are derived from one another by adding or restricting the effects of certain variables (see Bollen 1989b and the appendix). In addition, we use Bollen's incremental fit index (Bollen 1889a), which is derived from the likelihood ratio statistic.

The results of both tests for alternative models obtained by omitting variables from our five equations are shown in table 1. Of the baseline models, the independence model assumes that no relationship exists among

5. This is particularly relevant in the case of our model, since it includes correlations between the disturbance terms of several of our equations, namely those of equations 2–4. This feature of the model cannot be taken into consideration unless a full information estimation procedure is used.

the measures in our equations. The continuity model omits only intervention measures in all equations. By excluding the sources of change and including preseason measures, it provides a baseline emphasizing the critical links of past with present tax schema that account for the continuity of schema over time. The single intervention models include only the specified intervention measures. Of the models representing alternative structures of influence, the one with only direct effects includes intervention measures only in equation 1. The model with no direct effects includes them only in equations 2–5. The model with both effects reports estimates for the five equations, and the final model omits the tax increase variable from each equation.

The substantive issues arising from the comparisons shown in table 1 will be discussed later, but note here that the final two models do attain an acceptable level of significance well above the conventional standard of .05; higher probability statistics indicate stronger evidence that the hypothesized model is consistent with the observed sample (co)variances.

Table 2 reports the direct and indirect effects on postseason commitment based on the five equations. The direct effects reported in the first column are the standardized coefficients for equation 1. The indirect effects represent the influence of a variable that operates through any intermediate variables in the model, as illustrated in figure 2. For example, the intervention variables affect the inhibitors (equations 2–5), which, in turn, affect commitment (equation 1). The indirect effect reported in the second column is calculated by multiplying

TABLE 1. Comparison of Different Schema Structures and Variables Influencing Commitment

	Likelihood Ratio Test			Incremental Fit Index	
	Probability	Ratio	(*df*)	Independence Model	Continuity Model
Baseline models					
Independence model	.000	1254.4	(153)	—	—
Continuity model	.000	152.1	(51)	.916	—
Single intervention models					
Objective loss from TRA	.000	146.5	(46)	.917	.053
Subjective evaluations	.000	96.0	(31)	.947	.464
Attitudes of discussants	.000	82.5	(46)	.970	.656
Alternative structures of influence					
Only direct effects on commitment	.000	125.4	(45)	.934	.250
No direct effects on commitment	.004	50.5	(27)	.981	.812
Full model (both effects)	.305*	23.8	(21)	.998	.979
Full model without objective loss	.397*	27.2	(26)		

*$p > .05$

coefficients along a given path of influence, and then summing the indirect effects from all relevant paths for the given independent variable. The total effects reported in the third column provide the sum of the direct and indirect effects.

Table 3 reports the standardized coefficients for the remaining four equations, which estimate effects on the other nodes of the tax schema. To reduce the complexity of the table, the indirect effects on the inhibitors of intervention variables operating through tax fairness are not reported, since none are close to being significant. We will discuss these results by first looking at the continuity between pre- and postseason tax schema, then we will analyze each

TABLE 2. Effects of External Influences and Tax Schema on Postseason Commitment

	Direct Effects	Indirect Effects	Total Effects
I. Tax Schema			
General tax attitudes			
Tax system fairness (preseason)		−.003*	−.003
Tax system fairness (postseason)		−.010	−.010
Inhibitors (preseason)			
Guilt	—	.060***	.060
Social sanctions	—	.015	.015
Legal sanctions	—	−.004	−.004
Inhibitors (postseason)			
Guilt	.214***	—	.214
Social sanctions	.066	—	.066
Legal sanctions	−.023	—	−.023
Behavioral predisposition			
Commitment (preseason)	.268***	—	.268
II. Social Context			
Income	−.042	.005	.037
Female	.070	−.016	−.054
III. Intervention factors			
Objective change			
TRA tax loss	−.058	−.005	−.063
Evaluation of TRA changes			
Individual outcomes	.020	−.014	.005
Individual fairness	−.003	−.028*	−.031
Social outcomes	−.088*	−.006	−.094
Social fairness	−.013	−.007	−.020
Social influence			
Attitudes of discussants	.232***	.082***	.314

Notes: $N = 359$; unadjusted $R^2 = .320$. Entries are standardized maximum-likelihood regression coefficients estimated simultaneously with EQS. Mean values were substituted when values were missing for legal sanctions. All significance tests are two-tailed. No tests were included for total effects.

$*p < .10$. $**p < .05$. $***p < .01$.

intervention variable in turn, and finally consider the dynamics of the influence process.

Results

The Continuity Model and the Stability of Tax Schema

We begin by analyzing the continuity of tax schema over the tax season. As expected, the preseason attitudes representing continuity are critically important for explaining each attitude in the postseason tax schema. However, these factors by themselves are insufficient to provide a satisfactory model without including the intervention effects. Table 1 illustrates both the importance and insufficiency of the continuity model containing only preseason attitudes. This model provides a major improvement over the independence

TABLE 3. Effects on Postseason Schema Nodes

	Guilt	Social Sanctions	Legal Sanctions	Tax System Fairness
I. Tax Schema				
General tax attitudes				
Tax system fairness (preseason)	—	—	—	.286***
Tax system fairness (postseason)	−.044	−.037	−.091*	—
Inhibitors (preseason)				
Guilt	.278***	—	—	—
Social sanctions	—	.227***	—	—
Legal sanctions	—	—	.188***	—
II. Social Context				
Income	.019	−.009	−.061	.043
Female	−.042	−.029	.209***	.040
III. Intervention factors				
Objective change				
TRA tax loss	−.025	−.010	−.007	−.069
Evaluation of TRA changes				
Individual outcomes	−.057	−.005	−.010	.144***
Individual fairness	−.078	−.135**	.082	.047
Social outcomes	−.059	.093	−.036	.054
Social fairness	.001	−.105	−.047	.096
Social influence				
Attitudes of discussants	.297***	.219***	−.184***	.026
Unadjusted R^2	.251	.172	.174	.171

Notes: $N = 359$. Entries are standardized maximum-likelihood regression coefficients estimated simultaneously with EQS. Mean values were substituted when values were missing for legal sanctions. All significance tests are two-tailed.

*$p < .10$. **$p < .05$. ***$p < .01$.

model, accounting for most of the improvement in the incremental fit index. However, the intervention variables are required to achieve a satisfactory model in terms of a significant likelihood ratio statistic.

Tables 2 and 3 confirm that all preseason values of tax schema nodes are significant in predicting their postseason counterparts. It should be noted, however, that even with prior values as predictors, the explained variance in these equations only ranges between .17 and .32. Thus, as in most panel studies, we find that prior values of attitudes are, at best, imperfect predictors of current values. Part of the lack of continuity can be attributed to a form of measurement error endemic in panel studies using surveys; the judgment process individuals use when answering a question will vary even when the beliefs and attitudes on which the judgment is based do not change (Feldman 1990).[6]

The continuity in tax schema is also evident in the relationship between inhibitors and commitment, which does not change significantly from pre- to postseason. Since this direct comparison would add considerable complexity to our model, we summarize a separate regression test that focuses on only this critical link, as reported in Steenbergen, McGraw, and Scholz (1990). The three inhibitors were used to predict commitment separately for preseason and postseason responses, and the coefficients were tested to see if there were any significant changes.

This test clarified two important issues. First, there were no significant differences in the pre- and postseason coefficients, indicating that there was no change in the relationship between inhibitors and commitment. Second, the three inhibitors were all significant predictors of commitment and alone explained 18 percent of the variance for the combined surveys. As in most survey studies (see Roth, Scholz, and Witte 1989), guilt was the most clearly significant and legal sanctions the least, with the latter being significant only at the $p < .10$ level. The strength of the relationship between guilt and commitment was also evident in the results shown in table 2, since guilt was the only inhibitor significantly affecting postseason commitment. Both preseason and postseason guilt significantly affected commitment. The inclusion of preseason commitment to control for continuity rendered the other inhibitors shown in table 2 insignificant. In other words, guilt was the only inhibitor that exhibited significant dynamic influence over the *change* in compliance during the tax season, although social sanctions and (to a lesser extent) legal

6. We should note that the same kind of judgmental variance that affects survey responses is also likely to affect compliance decisions for which the same set of beliefs and attitudes are relevant. Such variance will inevitably attenuate the relationship between actions and attitudes and, therefore, limit the ability to predict compliance even with measures that minimize measurement errors.

sanctions were significant predictors of the *level* of commitment in both periods.[7]

In summary, the results provide only mild support for the basic image of the stable hierarchical tax schema portrayed in figure 1. Consistent with the hierarchical model, the simple analysis of the pre- and postseason surveys confirms the significant hierarchical relationships between inhibitors and commitment suggested in previous studies. Furthermore, the continuity model provides the lion's share of improvement in the fit index over the independence model in explaining postseason variables. On the other hand, changes in upper-level nodes (fairness, attitude, and inhibitors) are not clearly transmitted to behavioral intentions (commitment), since only postseason guilt has a clearly significant impact on postseason commitment. The continuity model itself is not significant without the intervention variables. We will now consider each set of intervention variables separately.

The Objective Loss from TRA Had No Detectable Effects on the Tax Schema

Although the TRA's changes in the tax code were large by historical standards, our study found that they had no detectable impact on the way taxpayers thought about taxes and on their commitment to comply. This conclusion was supported whether we look at the overall contribution of objective changes to the model or at the coefficients of influence on the different nodes of the tax schema.

Table 1 reports the explanatory power of models that included only one set of intervention variables. When only the objective loss variable was included, the incremental fit index for the continuity model increased by only .053, the smallest improvement of any of the intervention models tested. In fact, the model that omitted objective loss increased the probability associated with the χ^2 statistic for the model from .305 to a very respectable .397, indicating that objective loss contributed nothing to the model's explanatory power. Despite this poor performance, we included the variable in the model reported in tables 2 and 3 in order to explore the possibility of significant relationships with particular nodes of the tax schema. However, none of the coefficients for direct and indirect effects of objective loss shown in either table were significant even at the $p < .10$ level. The coefficients were not even

7. One reason for the relatively poor performance of legal sanctions in our data set may be the relatively large number of missing cases for this variable. This may indicate difficulties respondents had in answering the question in terms of probabilities, which would increase measurement error. Furthermore, the variable had relatively less variance since we substituted the mean value for all missing values to avoid the loss of these cases.

significant in an alternative (unreported) model in which objective loss was the only intervention variable, which would give the greatest likelihood of finding a significant relationship. We must conclude that, for our data set, objective changes in the taxpayer's own taxes induced by the TRA contributed little to changes in tax schema.

Three possible problems with our research design might mitigate this surprising result. First, we noted earlier that a measure more sensitive to the magnitude of tax loss might provide a better indicator. However, the poor performance of our simple count measure does not provide much hope that a more complex measure would do much better.

Second, changes in attitudes relating to taxes may have already taken place prior to our first survey, since the law was passed over a year before the survey. Some changes may already have taken place during coverage of the political debates prior to passage of the TRA, when preliminary evaluations of the TRA took place. But the TRA evaluation measures did have an impact on tax schema during the period of our study, as we shall see. Furthermore, respondents in the first survey did not exhibit much knowledge about specific provisions of the TRA. We suspect that knowledge about the individual impact of the TRA on a taxpayer's own tax return came primarily during the season. Even if there were some preliminary adjustments in tax schema, there should have been at least some evidence of changes as these adjustments were reinforced during the tax season.

Third, TRA changes may take longer than just one season to affect schema. We would agree that residual effects probably would continue over an extended time. However, we would expect that most adjustments to laws should have taken place during the period of our study, as taxpayers coped intensively with their first tax returns under the new law. Since we can find no evidence of primary adjustments during the first tax season, we would expect little further adjustment over a longer period of study.

Subjective Evaluations of TRA Had Moderate Effects on the Tax Schema

The subjective evaluations added considerable improvement to the model, confirming that evaluations of new laws do play a moderating role in changing policy-relevant attitudes and behavior. As indicated in the third column of table 1, subjective evaluations alone accounted for an increase of almost 50 percent in the incremental fit index for the continuity model. Despite this improvement, evaluations alone were not sufficient to provide a significant likelihood ratio test.

Evaluations had marginally significant impacts on commitment, as indicated in table 2. Social outcomes had a marginally significant direct impact, with taxpayers who believed that TRA lowered taxes for various social groups having greater commitment to comply than those who believed that TRA raised taxes. Individual fairness had a marginally significant indirect impact on commitment, with those who believed that TRA made their own taxes fairer having greater commitment. Judging by the size of the standardized coefficients, social outcomes had the greatest total effect on commitment of the four evaluations.

Evaluations generally had stronger effects on tax fairness and the inhibitors, as can be seen in table 3. Individual fairness significantly increased concern with social sanctions, with those perceiving the TRA to be fairer being more likely to have increased their belief that peers would disapprove of tax cheating. Individual fairness also had the greatest magnitude of influence in the expected direction on all the inhibitors. These multiple influences on inhibitors account for the significant indirect effect of individual fairness on commitment, as indicated in table 2.

Subjective perception of individual outcomes was the only other evaluation that affected the intermediate nodes of the schema, with a strong, significant effect on exchange equity. Those who perceived themselves to be hurt by the TRA tended to increase their belief that the amount of taxes they paid was too great, considering the benefits they received. The indirect effects through tax system fairness to the inhibitors were insignificant, and consequently were not reported in the table.

It should be noted that the lack of significant effects for individual evaluation measures may partially be due to the inclusion of four separate measures of evaluation. Since they are correlated, collinearity may result in a bias against finding significant relationships for each measure. However, since factor analysis and scale reliability measures both indicate that the four factors do not form a reliable single scale, and since each provides a distinctive theoretical category, the four evaluations were not combined into a single index. The likelihood test for models excluding evaluations falls below the significance level, confirming that the variables contribute more to the model as a block than is suggested by the significance levels of the individual coefficients.

Social Influence Had the Strongest Effects on Tax Schema

In contrast with objective losses and subjective evaluations of the TRA, the variable representing exposure to social influences during the tax season had strong, clear effects on the tax schema. The attitudes of discussants added substantially more to the continuity model's incremental fit index than did objective loss or subjective evaluations (see table 1), although it alone did not produce a fitting model. Furthermore, discussant attitudes had significant direct effects on all inhibitors (see table 3) and commitment (see table 2), and significant indirect effects on commitment through the inhibitors (table 2). Those who discussed taxes with individuals supporting compliance tended to increase their inhibitions against noncompliance and their commitment to comply. The magnitude of influence is also impressive, since discussant attitudes had about the same impact on postseason inhibitors and commitment as did the preseason measure of each variable.

One could argue that the TRA changes and evaluations might influence exposure to and perceptions of the discussants' attitudes and, therefore, indirectly account for the impact of social influence on the tax schema. For example, taxpayers most hurt by the TRA might have greater incentive to seek information from those who support cheating or may unconsciously attend more to discussants' negative views and attribute more negative attitudes to them. We tested this possibility by adding links from the four TRA evaluations to attitudes of the discussants, thus rendering the latter variable endogenous. This model resulted in strongly significant effects ($p < .01$) of individual fairness (operating through discussants' attitudes) on commitment, guilt, and social sanctions. Social fairness also had a weakly significant effect ($p < .10$) on legal sanctions.

However, this alternative model did not fit the data ($\chi^2 = 57.52$, $df = 29$, $p < .01$). Furthermore, even with this most favorable assumption about the causal relationship between evaluations and discussant attitudes, social influence still remained the most important influence on tax schema changes (as measured by the standardized estimates of total effects). For instance, the total effect of discussants' attitudes on commitment was approximately three times as large as the total effect of individual fairness.

Direct Effects versus Internal Processing within Tax Schema

The indirect effects shown in table 2 indicate that some of the influence of interventions occurs through internal processing; changes induced in higher nodes of the tax schema are transmitted down the hierarchy to lower nodes, ultimately changing behavioral intentions. Both the attitudes of discussants and evaluations of individual fairness had significant indirect effects on commitment. Discussant attitudes significantly affected all three inhibitors directly, while individual fairness had marginally significant direct effects on social sanctions. The indirect impact of discussant attitudes is understandably greater, given its consistent impact on all three inhibitors. The impact of individual outcomes on tax fairness did not translate into significant indirect effects on commitment, most likely because of the extra step in the pathway of influence and the relatively weak influence of tax fairness on the inhibitors.

However, the direct effects of the interventions on commitment appear to be more important than the indirect effects filtered through the schema's hierarchy. For all intervention variables except individual fairness, the direct effect coefficients are considerably larger than the indirect effect coefficient shown in table 2.[8] Particularly for the attitude of discussants, the only variable with significant coefficients for direct and indirect effects, the direct effects coefficient is almost three times greater than the indirect effects. In short, if we want to understand how interventions affect commitment, the direct impacts of interventions on commitment provide the greatest explanatory power.

On the other hand, if we wish to understand the impact of interventions on the full tax schema, the impact of interventions on other nodes must be included for the model to achieve an acceptable level of significance. Table 1 shows that the models in which interventions only affect commitment (the direct effects model) or only affect the other nodes but not commitment (the indirect effects model) produce insignificant likelihood ratio tests. The indirect effects model provides a more substantial improvement over the continuity model confirming that the interventions have substantial impacts on the other levels of the tax schema. But only the combined model achieves a significant likelihood ratio.

One implication of the greater impact of direct effects on each node is that tax schema nodes appear to be influenced more by external factors than by internal processes during the tax season. If we assume that the pressure for change occurs only when nodes are activated by some mental process, then direct effects of interventions occur on occasions when the intervention activates only one node in the schema. For example, discussions with co-workers unsupportive of compliance may activate the individual's feelings of guilt, causing a decrease in the degree of guilt associated with noncompliance. For this change to affect commitment as well, guilt and commitment would need to be activated either simultaneously or subsequently to this pairing of the intervention and guilt. The finding that indirect effects are weaker suggests that the pairings of each node with interventions occurs more frequently during the tax season than pairings of the nodes that would transmit such changes.

8. The smaller value of indirect effects may be due in part to the use of standardized coefficients. Since the absolute value of standardized coefficients is generally less than one, multiplying coefficients to obtain the indirect effect over a path will inevitably reduce the strength of relationships. However, the magnitude of the differences shown in table 2 suggests that the indirect effects are really of lesser importance.

Conclusion

Our results suggest that the TRA had only a modest impact on taxpayer attitudes and beliefs. Most surprisingly, our measure of the TRA's objective impact on the taxpayer's own tax situation had no noticeable effect on tax schemas. Only subjective evaluations of the TRA significantly altered attitudes and beliefs, mediating the impact of changes in the law on tax schemas. Even here, perceptions of individual outcomes played less of a role than perceptions of individual fairness and social outcomes associated with the TRA.

Taxpayers systematically changed their attitudes and beliefs during the tax season, but the biggest impact in our study came from the social influence of discussions about taxes during the season, not from evaluations related to the TRA. The perceived attitudes of individuals with whom our respondents discussed taxes had consistently strong impacts on inhibitors and commitment related to compliance. Furthermore, discussants' attitudes had as much influence on postseason beliefs as the taxpayers' preseason beliefs! It may be that the major changes introduced by the TRA made taxpayers more susceptible to social influence during the 1988 tax season, although our analysis of informational activities during that season does not suggest many differences from prior years among our respondents (see McGraw, Scholz, and Steenbergen 1989).

From a broader perspective, our results suggest that tax attitudes and, ultimately, compliance behavior are only weakly affected by changes in laws, even laws with a considerable impact on individual self-interest. The social processes through which individuals find out about the contents of new laws appear to have considerably more impact on tax schema than subjective evaluations of the laws and objective measures of their impact (see McGraw, Scholz, and Steenbergen 1989).

APPENDIX: STATISTICAL PROCEDURES

This appendix describes some details of the statistical procedures that were used in our analysis. First, details are provided on full-information maximum-likelihood estimation. Second, the test procedures are described.

Estimation

Full-information maximum-likelihood estimation seeks estimates of the parameters in a model to maximize the likelihood of the data given the estimates. In essence, this means that the estimates are chosen in such a way that they generate a covariance structure among the variables that is as close as possible to the observed sample (co)variances. In doing this, all equations of the model are considered simultaneously and relationships and constraints between equations are taken into consideration (see Bollen 1989b; Judge et al. 1985).

In order for full-information maximum-likelihood estimates to produce correct standard errors and a correct test statistic, the distribution of the endogenous variables conditional on the exogenous variables should be multivariate normal (see Browne 1984). Mardia (1970) describes several procedures to test for violations of this assumption, including a test for multivariate kurtosis. (As Browne [1984] has demonstrated, it is, in particular, multivariate kurtosis that creates problems for full-information maximum-likelihood estimation.) Application of this test to our sample, fortunately, indicates that our analyses were not plagued by serious aberrations from multivariate normality: Mardia's normalized test statistic is $-.2138$, approximate $p = .415$.

Testing Models

Maximum-likelihood estimation produces a likelihood ratio test statistic, T, that is given by $(N - 1)$ times the minimum of the loss function that is evaluated to generate the parameter estimates (N is the sample size). This minimum corresponds to the function value that is obtained upon convergence of the algorithm. When the model has been correctly specified (and a number of other conditions have been fulfilled), T is asymptotically χ^2 distributed, with degrees of freedom equal to the number of nonredundant elements in the sample covariance matrix minus the number of parameters that have been estimated. The smaller T is when compared to the degrees of freedom, the more support for the model exists. The likelihood that the data have actually been produced by the model is given in the p-value that is derived from the χ^2 distribution; large p-values mean that the model fits the data well. As a cut-off point for accepting or rejecting any given model, we have taken a p-value of .05.

The likelihood ratio test can also be used to compare models that are nested in one another. Nested models are models that can be obtained from one another by constraining certain parameters or by relaxing restrictions on parameters. Let M_0 and M_1 denote two models and let M_1 be nested in M_0 so that M_0 has a larger number of unrestricted parameters. The corresponding likelihood ratio test statistics for these models are T_0 and T_1. Now, if T_0 fits the data well, $T_1 - T_0$ is asymptotically χ^2 distributed, with degrees of freedom equal to the number of restricted parameters in M_1. Hence, it becomes possible to test the restrictions in M_1; if the quantity $T_1 - T_0$ is small compared to the degrees of freedoms, there is reason to accept the restrictions; otherwise, the restrictions do not seem to be reasonable.

The use of differences between likelihood ratio test statistics for nested models comes close to using incremental or comparative fit indices. The latter have been introduced, in part, because the likelihood ratio test cannot always be fruitfully employed (see Bentler 1990; Bentler and Bonett 1980 for extensive discussions of the logic of incremental fit indices). The logic of model comparison, however, is worked out in more detail for incremental fit indices than for differences in likelihood ratio tests. That is, incremental fit indices compare models to some baseline model, M_i, which may be any theoretically compelling model (see Sobel and Bohrnstedt 1985), but is usually an independence model that postulates that there are no mutual effects among the variables. Different standards of comparison have been discussed in the literature, but for the present purposes, Bollen's (1989a) *incremental fit index* (IFI) is used, since this statistic has less sampling variance than other statistics that are available. Let M_k be a model in which M_i is nested, and let T_i and T_k refer to the respective likelihood ratio test statistics. Then, IFI is given by

$$\mathrm{IFI} = (T_i - T_k)/(T_i - df_k) ,$$

where df_k is the degrees of freedom of model M_k. The incremental fit index is a so-called normed index, which means that its range is restricted from 0 to 1. Low values of IFI indicate that a model M_k hardly adds to the model fit in comparison to the baseline. Alternatively, high values of IFI imply a large contribution to model fit in going from model M_i to model M_k. In essence, this means that giving up the restrictions on some of the parameters of M_i improves the fit substantively, even though M_k still need not be a fitting model.

An advantage of such incremental fit indices as IFI is that they are additive. That is, as long as a series of k models are nested in each other, any of the models can be compared to any other model by comparing their incremental fit indices. For example, assume that M_1 is another model in the sequence and that M_1 is less restrictive than M_k; hence, M_k is nested in M_1. Then M_1 can be compared to M_i and an incremental fit index, say IFI_1, is obtained. However, M_1 can also be directly compared to M_k to yield insight in the effects for model-fit of the restrictions that differentiate these two models. This is easily done, however, by subtracting IFI_1, from IFI_k, where IFI_k is the index obtained from comparing M_k to M_i.

REFERENCES

Adams, J. S. 1963. "Toward an Understanding of Inequity." *Journal of Abnormal and Social Psychology* 67:422–36.

Adams, J. S. 1965. "Inequity in Social Exchange." In *Advances in Experimental Social Psychology,* ed. L. Berkowitz, 2:266–300. New York: Academic Press.

Ajzen, I., and M. Fishbein. 1977. "Attitude-Behavior Relations: A Theoretical Analysis and Review of Empirical Literature." *Psychological Bulletin* 84:888–918.

Allport, G. W. 1961. *Pattern and Growth in Personality.* New York: Holt, Rinehart and Winston.

Anderson, J. R. 1983. *The Architecture of Cognition.* Cambridge, Mass.: Harvard University Press.

Bentler, P. M. 1989. *EQS Structural Equations Program Manual.* Los Angeles: BMDP Statistical Software.

Bentler, P. M. 1990. "Comparative Fit Indexes in Structural Models." *Psychological Bulletin* 107:238–46.

Bentler, P. M., and D. G. Bonett. 1980. "Significance Tests and Goodness of Fit in the Analysis of Covariance Structures." *Psychological Bulletin* 88:588–606.

Blau, P. M. 1968. "Social Exchange." In *International Encyclopedia of the Social Sciences,* ed. D. L. Sills, vol. 7. New York: Macmillan.

Bollen, K. A. 1989a. "A New Incremental Fit Index for General Structural Equation Models." *Sociological Methods & Research* 17:303–16.

Bollen, K. A. 1989b. *Structural Equations with Latent Variables.* New York: Wiley.

Brickman, P., R. Folger, E. Goode, and Y. Schul. 1981. "Microjustice and Macrojustice." In *The Justice Motive in Social Behavior: Adapting to Times of Scarcity and Change,* ed. M. J. Lerner and S. C. Lerner, 173–204. New York: Plenum.

Browne, M. W. 1984. "Asymptotically Distribution-Free Methods for the Analysis of Covariance Structures." *British Journal of Mathematical and Statistical Psychology* 37:62–83.

Campbell, D. T. 1975. "On the Conflicts between Biological and Social Evolution and between Psychology and the Moral Tradition." *American Psychologist* 30:1103–26.

Conover, P. J., and S. Feldman. 1984. "How People Organize the Political World: A Schematic Model." *American Journal of Political Science* 28:95–126.

Downs, A. 1957. *An Economic Theory of Democracy.* New York: Harper and Row.

Fazio, R. H. 1989. "On the Power and Functionality of Attitudes: The Role of Attitude Accessibility." In *Attitude Structure and Function,* ed. A. R. Pratkanis, S. J. Breckler, and A. G. Greenwald, 153–80. Hillsdale, N.J.: Erlbaum.

Feldman, S. 1990. "Theory, Measurement, and the Survey Response." Paper presented at the annual meeting of the American Political Science Association, San Francisco.

Grasmick, H. G., and R. J. Bursick. 1990. "Conscience, Significant Others, and Rational Choice: Extending the Deterrence Model." *Law and Society Review* 24:837–62.

Harsanyi, J. C. 1977. "Morality and the Theory of Rational Behavior." *Social Research* 44:623–56.

Hawthorne, M. R., and J. E. Jackson. 1987. "The Individual Political Economy of Federal Tax Policy." *American Political Science Review* 81:757–74.

Homans, G. C. 1961. *Social Behaviour: Its Elementary Forms.* London: Routledge and Kegan Paul.

Hurwitz, J., and M. Peffley. 1987. "How Are Foreign Policy Attitudes Structured: A Hierarchical Model." *American Political Science Review* 81:1099–1120.

Judd, C. M., R. A. Drake, J. W. Downing, and J. A. Krosnick. 1991. "Some Dynamic Properties of Attitude Structures: Context-Induced Response Facilitation and Polarization." *Journal of Personality and Social Psychology* 60:193–202.

Judd, C. M., and J. A. Krosnick. 1989. "The Structural Bases of Consistency among Political Attitudes: Effects of Political Expertise and Attitude Importance." In *Attitude Structure and Function,* ed. A. R. Pratkanis, S. J. Breckler, and A. G. Greenwald, 99–128. Hillsdale, N.J.: Erlbaum.

Judge, G. G., W. E. Griffiths, R. C. Hill, H. Lütkepohl, and T. Lee. 1985. *The Theory and Practice of Econometrics.* New York: Wiley.

Kinder, D. R., and D. O. Sears. 1985. "Public Opinion and Political Action." In *Handbook of Social Psychology,* ed. G. Lindzey and E. Aronson, 3:657–741. New York: Random House.

Kinsey, K. A. 1987. "Survey Data on Tax Compliance: A Compendium and Review." American Bar Foundation Working Paper 8716. Chicago: American Bar Foundation.

Kinsey, K. A., and K. W. Smith. 1987. "Income Tax Cheating: Opportunities and Preferences." American Bar Foundation Tax Compliance Working Paper 87-1. Chicago: American Bar Foundation.

Laver, M. 1981. *The Politics of Private Desire*. New York: Penguin.

Lewis, A. 1982. *The Psychology of Taxation*. New York: St. Martin's Press.

Lind, E. A., and T. R. Tyler. 1988. *The Social Psychology of Procedural Justice*. New York: Plenum.

Little, R. J. A., and D. B. Rubin. 1987. *Statistical Analysis with Missing Data*. New York: Wiley.

McGraw, K. M. 1989. "The Influence of Fairness and Outcomes on Evaluations of Tax Experiences." Paper presented at the annual meeting of the Law and Society Association, Madison, Wis.

McGraw, K. M., J. T. Scholz, and M. Steenbergen. 1989. "The Impact of Discussion on Taxpayer Responses to the 1986 Tax Reform Act." Paper presented at the 1989 IRS research conference, The Impact of the Tax Reform Act of 1986, Washington, D.C.

Mardia, K. V. 1970. "Measures of Multivariate Skewness and Kurtosis with Applications." *Biometrika* 57:519–30.

Mueller, D. C. 1979. *Public Choice*. Cambridge: Cambridge University Press.

Rawls, J. 1971. *A Theory of Justice*. Cambridge, Mass.: Harvard University Press.

Rokeach, M. 1973. *The Nature of Human Values*. New York: Free Press.

Roth, J. A., J. T. Scholz, and A. D. Witte. 1989. *Taxpayer Compliance: An Agenda for Research*. Philadelphia: University of Pennsylvania Press.

Sears, D. O., and J. Citrin. 1985. *Tax Revolt: Something for Nothing in California*. Cambridge, Mass.: Harvard University Press.

Sears, D. O., and C. Funk. 1990. "Self-interest in Americans' Political Opinions." In *Beyond Self-Interest,* ed. J. Mansbridge, 147–70. Chicago: University of Chicago Press.

Sears, D. O., L. Huddy, and L. G. Schaffer. 1986. "A Schematic Variant of Symbolic Politics Theory, as Applied to Racial and Gender Equality." In *Political Cognition,* ed. R. R. Lau and D. O. Sears, 159–202. Hillsdale, N.J.: Erlbaum.

Sears, D. O., R. R. Lau, T. R. Tyler, and H. M. Allen. 1980. "Self-Interest versus Symbolic Politics in Policy Attitudes and Presidential Voting." *American Political Science Review* 74:670–84.

Sen, A. 1973. *On Economic Inequality.* Cambridge: Oxford University Press.

Sharpe, K. 1989. "Taxpayer Perceptions and Misperceptions." In *The Impact of the Tax Reform Act of 1986: Did it Improve Fairness and Simplicity?* Internal Revenue Service Document 7302. Washington, D.C.: Department of Treasury.

Sobel, M. E., and G. W. Bohrnstedt. 1985. "Use of Null Models in Evaluating the Fit of Covariance Structure Models." In *Sociological Methodology 1985,* ed. N. B. Tuma, 152–76. San Francisco: Jossey-Bass.

Steenbergen, M., K. McGraw, and J. Scholz. 1990. "Citizenship and the Cognitive Structure of Tax Compliance." Paper presented at the annual meeting of the American Political Science Association, San Francisco.

Taylor, S., and J. Crocker. 1981. "Schematic Bases of Social Information Processing." In *Social Cognition: The Ontario Symposium,* ed. E. T. Higgins, C. P. Herman, and M. P. Zanna, 89–134. Hillsdale, N.J.: Erlbaum.

Tyler, T. R. 1990. *Why People Obey the Law.* New Haven: Yale University Press.

Tyler, T. R., K. Rasinksi, and E. Griffin. 1986. "Alternative Images of the Citizen: Implications for Public Policy." *American Psychologist* 41:970–78.

Wallach, M. A., and L. Wallach. 1983. *Psychology's Sanction for Selfishness: The Error of Egoism in Theory and Therapy.* San Francisco: W. H. Freedman.

Weschsler, P. 1989. "1986 Tax Revision Breaks Its Promise." *Newsday,* March 15.

Westat. 1980. "Executive Summary: Individual Income Tax Compliance Factors Study." Study for the Internal Revenue Service. Rockville, Md.: Westat, Inc.

Yankelovich, Skelly, and White. 1984. *Taxpayer Attitudes Study: Final Report.* Prepared for the Internal Revenue Service. New York: Yankelovich, Skelly, and White, Inc.

Commentary

Eugene Steuerle

The authors of this study are largely responsible for the development of a valuable data set for studying compliance and its relationship to attitudes and economic variables. In this particular study, they especially emphasize the impact of the Tax Reform Act of 1986 on attitudes and, through those attitudes, on the commitment of taxpayers to comply with the law. The principal conclusion of this study—only one of several to be produced with this data set—is that tax reform had little impact on the willingness of taxpayers to comply.

The outcome is not surprising, as will be detailed in these remarks. In general, the reasons are twofold. First, the type of survey data used here is necessarily limited in its ability to show precise relationships among variables in detailed models. Second, tax reform made only modest changes in the after-tax income of individuals. Tax reform was not large enough to have a dramatic impact on individuals relative to both their habitual way of thinking and the more dramatic, but common, changes in income and life-style that likely occurred over the same period.

Some Limitations

The authors themselves mention a number of the limitations of their data or analysis. Some simply could not be avoided by the time that this study was undertaken, as they were inherent in the data. Nonetheless, it may prove useful to provide a listing here.

First, the interviews took place just before and after the 1987 filing season. The study would capture changes in attitude only over a brief filing period, but not changes due to the publicity that took place during the period leading up to enactment of tax reform nor to later considerations of the effects of tax reform after several filing seasons had transpired. For example, those engaged in tax shelters and finding their returns more complicated would face the largest transition cost in 1987. In later years, both the learning process and the elimination of shelters from one's portfolio would have reduced the complications of filling out returns under the new, but now more familiar, set of rules.

Second, selection bias is always present in these types of surveys. In many estimated equations, the sample was composed of 359 respondents out of 799 original contacts.

Third, some variables are quite similar to each other and hard to distinguish. For instance, tax system fairness ("compared to other people like me, I pay more than my fair share of taxes") and individual fairness ("fairness of taxes owed under TRA for people of respondents' income level") seem to measure the same attitude.

Fourth, it would have been nice to have had available more socioeconomic variables, a desire that I know the authors share. (The authors should explain how income is converted into an independent variable in the study.)

Fifth, there is little likelihood that one can identify well the functional form of the relationship among the variables. Accordingly, it should not be surprising that some results are weak. The estimated impact of indirect effects on compliance attitudes might be weaker than direct effects, for instance, simply because the former relationship is removed one additional step and, therefore, suffers from functional form misspecification at two stages.

Sixth, although the influence of the attitudes of others is an important finding, the inclusion of one's spouse in the group of discussants makes it more likely that at least some respondents simply identified the dependent variable (their own attitude) with the independent variable (the attitude of their spouses).

Special Problems with the Measurements of Change Due to Tax Reform

Some special problems exist with the variable used to measure tax reform effects. The variable called "tax loss" is defined as the sum of eight tax items the respondent identified as relevant to his or her own tax return which were adversely affected by the TRA (e.g., IRA deductions that were restricted).

Take tax reform, however, in its purest context: the elimination of a variety of tax breaks in exchange for a rate reduction. In this simple example, one would expect all taxpayers who, say, report eight changes to identify up to seven increases in taxes and only one source of decrease. For those with fewer sources of increase, the rate reduction often was correspondingly less. In sum, the number of tax increases listed by individuals may help explain the mental process through which they developed their attitude toward tax reform, but it does not define tax loss (or gain) per se.

One measure of "individual outcomes" from tax reform is also bothersome. This measure was stated as "the amount of taxes owed in 1987 as compared to 1986." Correctly specified to identify actual outcomes (but not necessarily perceived outcomes), the taxpayer should be asked whether taxes in 1987 were higher than they would have been if the taxpayer had filled out the alternative return that would have applied in 1987.

Few taxpayers can make this type of comparison. Even if they can, they probably would not take the trouble. (I served as the original organizer and coordinator of the Treasury Department's tax reform project, and I never did it, which may say as much about me as about the difficulty of the task.) A second-best solution for purposes of the survey might have been to ask the taxpayer whether or not taxes as a percentage of income went up or down before and after tax reform, although this, too, would have confused changes in income with changes in the tax laws.

As actually phrased, the question leads the respondent to think that one measure of the outcome of tax reform was whether or not nominal taxes went up. This is misleading if the goal is to measure actual outcomes. On the other hand, the authors may have taken the type of variable actually used by the taxpayer to assess whether or not tax reform helped them or not. That is, the variable they used may be more related to perceived outcome than actual outcome. To the extent one is dealing with the impact of perceptions on attitudes toward compliance, the perceived outcome variable may still be appropriate.

A Perception Problem

Clearly the problem of perception affects the way in which taxpayers reacted to tax reform. It provides, perhaps, the best explanation of why so many of the results reported in this study were not significant. Ask yourself why there was a perception problem throughout tax reform. Almost no taxpayer had a counterfactual set of circumstances by which to make comparisons. The press often played on the impact of tax changes one at a time, so that few persons understood how the whole package came together. Even those with intimate knowledge of the process were often misled. At a National Tax Association meeting, one of the authors of a major study on tax reform noted that insurance companies had really taken a beating because they had won back little or nothing in their battle to try to retain certain preferences. Yet, in fact, insurance companies were big winners in tax reform because rate reductions were substantially in excess of the base broadening that they suffered.

If tax reform had a major impact on after-tax incomes of most individuals, the errors of perception might have been smaller relative to actual outcomes. Tax reform, however, did not change after-tax incomes very much (nor in a revenue-neutral bill was it meant to make much of a change). The vast majority of taxpayers saw their own direct tax liabilities change by less than 0.5 percent or 1.0 percent of income.

Now for a typical taxpayer, tax liability is about 10.0 percent of income, so that a change in tax of even 5.0 percent of tax liability is still only 0.5 percent of income. Follow through, if you will, the other changes faced by this taxpayer. Again, assuming that he or she is typical, the income fluctuation in a single year is likely to be on the order of at least 7.0 percent of income. Suppose income goes up by 7.0 percent. Absent tax reform, the taxpayer's tax liability (even in a proportional tax system) probably goes up by about 7.0 percent over the previous year's tax liability, which translates to another 0.7 percent of income. Now make some comparisons. This taxpayer sees income go up by 7.0 percent, offset by a 0.7 percent increase in tax liability because of the additional income subject to tax, followed by a decrease in tax liability of 0.5 percent of income due to tax reform. The net change in income equals +6.8 percent with tax reform, versus +6.3 percent of income without tax reform. Obviously, the net change in income due to tax reform is going to be understood by few taxpayers. In effect, the effect of tax reform was often exaggerated. Yes, tax reform reduced the value of tax expenditures by close to $200 billion per year—a major political achievement. But its net impact on the after-tax income of the typical taxpayer was quite small.

Summary

In sum, the study performed by the authors represents an important attempt to measure changes in taxpayers' attitudes, but we should not find it surprising that they concluded that tax reform had, at best, a small effect on taxpayer attitudes and beliefs. Relative to total taxes and total income, the real impact of reform was only modest, and, hence, it should have affected attitudes and beliefs only modestly. The authors are right to stress the variables they do find significant—the feeling of guilt and the attitudes of others—as more dominant and important influences on commitment to comply. I hope they will continue to enlighten us on these relationships and maintain their efforts to reveal the information contained in the valuable data set they have been instrumental in developing.

How Taxpayers Think about Their Taxes: Frames and Values

John S. Carroll

How often have we heard that "nothing is so certain as death and taxes"? Taxpaying is one of the most ubiquitous activities of modern life, and a major opportunity for most citizens to relate to government. Personal income taxes are a considerable burden, in terms of money, time, and aggravation. Taxation is a major political issue: presidents try to avoid the public's wrath yet reduce the deficit by advocating "users' fees" and "revenue sources" rather than more taxes.

The tax laws regarding personal income specify that there is a legal obligation to file a timely return, report tax liabilities, and pay taxes owed (Internal Revenue Code, U.S.C. Title 26). Unlike sales taxes that are merely added to our bills, compliance with the income tax system requires affirmative actions from each taxpayer. Unlike most of the criminal code that establishes proper behavior for all citizens with few exceptions, the tax codes are highly individualized, depending on the particular circumstances of the taxpayer (e.g., amount of income, types of income, kinds of expenses, or family structure). This complexity is the result of both the complexity of modern life and the use of the tax code as an instrument of public policy to distribute the costs of government, encourage particular behaviors, and please particular interest groups.

The net result of such complex regulations is that there are many ways to fall short of legal obligations, accidentally or deliberately. A taxpayer could fail to file a return, underreport legal or illegal income, report deductions as the wrong type (e.g., mixing personal and business), overstate deductions, or simply refuse to pay what is owed. This could happen because the taxpayer is ignorant, lazy, careless, deliberately cheating, following common practices in occupational groups or workplaces, heeding incorrect advice from the IRS,

This study was supported by National Science Foundation grant SES-8719659, with assistance and indirect funding provided by the Internal Revenue Service.

making a symbolic protest against the tax system or the uses of tax money, reacting to a personal sense of injustice, taking the advice of a tax professional who recommends strategies that shade into illegality (see Kidder and McEwen 1989), or many other reasons.

As a psycholegal problem, the question for researchers is: "Why do people pay, or fail to pay, taxes?" The tax laws exist to alter people's behavior, based on presumptions of how people will react to the law. Through incentives and threats and public statements of what the community considers proper and improper, the law is used as an instrument to shape and maintain behavior.

Personal Income Tax as a Decision Problem

In this essay, I view taxpaying from a decision-making viewpoint. Because of the ubiquitousness of the tax laws, at least one adult per family must take some action each year to fulfill their tax obligations. Because of the complexity of the tax laws, taxpayers in different situations will have different possible ways of fulfilling these obligations. Taxpaying is somewhat like risky decision making in that the taxpayer has various legal and illegal alternatives, and the consequences of these choices are not fully known.

It is evident that taxpaying is quite different from the types of decision problems typically studied in behavioral decision research. In laboratory or field settings, most previous psychological research has relied upon more controlled and bounded decision problems. Typically, the decisions are easily separable, repetitive, standardized, or controlled in some ways; made during a short time frame by an individual or a small group; and have identifiable consequences that (usually, but not always) are of modest magnitude and accrue soon after the decisions are made. Isenberg (1984) has criticized decision research for missing the complexities of ill-structured packages of decisions, such as those faced by high-level managers.

In taxpaying, however, there is a web of interconnected decisions that extend over long periods of time, have potentially grave consequences, and occur in an extended social context. By a web of decisions, I mean that taxpaying involves decisions about many issues, including tax planning and investments, record keeping, the use of tax preparers, sources of information and assistance, strategies for itemizing and setting up personal businesses, dealing with "gray areas" in the tax codes, and tactics for willing noncompliance. These decisions may occur throughout the year and across years: decisions about investments have long-term consequences, and routines for record keeping and tax preparation tend to persist for years. Taxpaying is also a *social* process: information, experiences, and strategies are passed around occupational and friendship networks. Cheating on taxes may be an expression of individual morality, but it may also be a "social disease" transmitted and legitimated in social groups.

For these reasons, this essay represents an initial exploration of the ways a decision-making perspective can be brought to the study of taxpaying and also how the study of taxpaying can broaden and further develop the decision-making perspective that emerged from the study of simpler decision situations. In the next section, I will describe how the decision-making perspective adds to the existing paradigms of research within economics and sociology. The focus will be on key theoretical concepts, particularly the concept of framing, and on the research methods appropriate to the study of decision making. I will then describe an exploratory study of taxpayers focused around these key concepts.

Research Paradigms for the Study of Taxpaying

Taxpaying has been studied by researchers from many social science disciplines, most typically economics and sociology. Economists presume that tax behavior is produced by underlying self-interest through the analysis of the consequences of behavior. Sociologists tend to focus on individually or socially constructed interpretations, values, and norms. The difference is similar to asking "what will make me better off" or asking "what ought I to do" (see Scholz 1985).

The Study of Self-Interest

Tax cheating can be seen as a rational act (see Allingham and Sandmo 1972; Becker 1968) that is responsive to the expected risks and benefits of compliance and noncompliance. Within this framework, compliance is based on the value of the marginal tax dollar and the risks incurred by noncompliance. Individuals have more or less opportunity to cheat, the economy creates more or fewer incentives for differently situated people, and the IRS has various methods of surveillance, audit, and legal penalties. Economic analyses have focused on the impact of changes in the audit rate, marginal tax rate, and so forth (see Witte and Woodbury 1985).

There is ample research evidence that taxpayers are responsive to risks and opportunities. Kagan (1989) pointed out that compliance is nearly perfect on those items that are reported to both the IRS and to taxpayers, such as salary subject to withholding and interest income. Compliance is poor on items that have little or no "paper trail," such as cash transactions, some types of business expenses, or charitable contributions. Klepper and Nagin (1989) suggest that taxpayers behave as if they believed that cheating on one particular line item would influence the likelihood of being caught on other line items. As a result, taxpayers choose to cheat on only their best personal opportunities and only to the extent that seems safe. Safety in this sense could have multiple meanings, including safe from being audited, safe from being detected if audited, and safe from being treated as a criminal if detected (i.e., the discrepancy could be an error, a misinterpretation, or otherwise excusable from serious penalties).

However, such monetary and legal consequences are not the whole story. For example, a very careful study of reactions to the risk of floods (Kunreuther et al. 1978) is informative on this point. According to utility principles, federally subsidized flood insurance was offered at highly favorable rates, assuming that residents had accurate risk and cost data and combined them to maximize utility. Yet a national survey of flood prone areas revealed that residents assessed their risks and costs differently than experts did, and, even considering residents' *own* assessments, those who bought insurance and those who did not exhibited similar distributions of expected utility. Instead, it appeared that residents' purchasing decisions depended on considerations such as whether neighbors and relatives bought insurance, what their relationship was to their insurance agent, and whether they could tolerate another thing to worry about.

The economic model can be expanded to include nonmonetary consequences of compliance and noncompliance. The process of being audited itself is unpleasant, including the invasion of privacy, the time to gather up every bit of financial records, the anxiety about the outcome, and having to answer to a lowly government auditor. Further, being caught carries various social risks, such as loss of reputation, job, family, and so forth. Of course, this depends on the nature of a taxpayer's social environment: some people may commonly discuss cheating among colleagues and family, others may feel that they would gain a certain distinction or respect if their cheating were known. For example, the wages of domestics are determined by concepts of fair compensation that include "normal" income underreporting understood both by upper-class employers and domestics (Rollins 1985). Similarly, restaurant employees may get meals as an untaxed fringe benefit, and college professors may go on a winter ocean cruise that qualifies as a "professional conference" even if no one attends the educational sessions (Kidder and McEwen 1989). Interpersonal networks can therefore reduce the fear of legal sanctions or the likelihood of social sanctions (see Ekland-Olsen, Lieb, and Zurcher 1984; Mason 1987).

Norms and Values

Although the economic model can be extended to include social consequences, at some point it stops resembling the economic model. On the one hand, the components of the consequence calculation become subjective and socially constructed rather than objective aspects of marginal tax rates and audit rates. These subjective factors include the overprediction of the likelihood of audit (Yankelovich, Skelly, and White 1984), leading to the curious notion that providing taxpayers with an accurate perception of risks (which is less than they currently fear) could actually increase cheating. Similarly, the particular outcomes that are envisioned are highly subjective and person or group specific. Although these perceptions should come to equilibrium as taxpayers experience the tax process, repeated changes in the tax laws and conflicting information in the media as well as more local networks may make it quite difficult for many people to reach an accurate assessment of outcomes.

On the other hand, even granting the subjective nature of risky consequences, taxpayers may not use consequence information in the way that is presumed by the rational economic model. Theories of bounded rationality suggest that taxpayers may have unstable preferences (see Fischhoff, Slovic, and Lichtenstein 1980), highly simplified decision strategies (see Montgomery 1983; Simon 1955), and misunderstanding of uncertainty or probability (see Einhorn and Hogarth 1985; Tversky and Kahneman 1974).

Diverging even more directly from the model of economic rationality, sociologists and political scientists suggest that taxpayers may not be processing personal consequences, but, rather, are focused on doing the "right thing," where "right" may be determined from legal, moral, social, and utilitarian, as well as a personal consequences viewpoints. This is a "norm-processing" rather than an "outcome-processing" model of decision behavior (see Scholz 1985). One of the most consistent findings in survey research about taxpayer attitudes and behaviors is that those who report compliance believe that their friends (and taxpayers in general) comply, whereas those who report cheating believe that others cheat (see Cahalan and Ekstrand 1980; Yankelovich, Skelly, and White 1984).

The sense of fairness is very important for maintaining the legitimacy of taxpaying. When people think taxes are unfair, they spend less time reporting carefully and may be motivated to produce what they perceive to be a fair outcome even when this does not conform to the law. Public opinion polls show, during the 1970s, an increasing sense of unfairness and failure to get value from tax dollars (see ICF 1985). In short, people may be motivated to work hard to report accurately and pay what they owe by their sense that the laws and their application are fair in terms of the distribution of tax payments, the ways taxes are spent, the process of tax reporting and paying, and the way they are treated by the IRS (see Kinder and Sears 1985; Tyler 1990).

Decision Making

An analysis of taxpaying actions based on behavioral theories and limited rationality would suggest that people adopt a standard set of procedures or rules to carry out taxpaying and do not reevaluate the rules unless something captures their attention. This is the concept of "standard operating procedures" (see Cyert and March 1963) or "standing decisions" (see Cook 1981). However, these decision rules are likely to differ across individuals. Clarke and Cornish (1985) and Weaver and Carroll (1985) have both noted that experience makes a difference in the kinds of information monitored, opportunities investigated, and risks assessed when considering illegal behaviors. Taxpayers will also differ in the routines they employ and the way they react to such major shifts in the tax environment as the Tax Reform Act of 1986.

Indeed, studies of criminal decision making show that potential criminals fail to gather appropriate information about alternatives, such information often coming *after* they commit crimes and possibly are caught (see California, Assembly Committee on Criminal Procedure 1975; Paternoster et al. 1982), and have considerable difficulty combining multiple pieces of relevant information into a single judgment, using simplified strategies rather than the expected utility rule (see Carroll 1978 and 1982). Research on taxpayers also shows various misconceptions, including overestimates of the likelihood of audit and misunderstanding the role of the IRS in tax law creation (see Aitken and Bonneville 1980; ICF 1985).

The assessments we make about taxpaying, including what is considered appropriate, legitimate, fair, expensive, or cheap, depend on the way comparisons are made. Comparisons are made to expectations and referent others and through analogies that give meaning to our actions.

As examples of the use of analogies, taxpayers who view the tax process as "compliance with the law" would have a very different view than those who use the analogy of "payment for services," and these would, in turn, differ from those who see taxpaying as "giving to the common good." All of these analogies are correct but *partial* understandings of the tax process. The first person would pay taxes if they believe the law is just or if they fear the consequences of breaking the law or if they are the kind of person whose self-image is law-abiding. The second person would pay taxes if they believe that government services justify their payment; if they do not like the way government spends (their) money, they will be less motivated to pay their share. The Reagan administration tendency to frame taxes as an indication of government waste and a drag on the economy may have increased the sense of unfairness. The third person would pay taxes if they felt part of the country—if their citizenship or their empathy for the needy was salient. Research has shown that people treat "insiders" with fairness, but feel free to rip off "outsiders" (see Barley 1991). Continuing from motivation to behavior, Scholz (1985) suggested that taxpayers who frame taxpaying as "compliance" would have strategies for identifying legal obligations and fulfilling them, whereas those who frame taxpaying as "avoidance" would have strategies for identifying loopholes and scams.

In regard to smaller scale comparisons or reference points, research on taxpayer decision making clearly suggests that the refund line on April 15 is very salient, and may matter more than the total taxes paid during the year (see Loftus 1985). Those who have to pay on April 15 delay their tax work and spend more time looking for ways to reduce taxes. In the study I will describe, one taxpayer set the goal of getting the payment under $2,000 and redid his taxes six times until that goal was reached. Still another wrote, "I would need $3,000 in deductions to owe nothing." Those who get money back do their tax work early and are much happier about the process. This suggests that most people have assimilated their withholding to their income and think primarily in terms of the out-of-pocket gains and losses on April 15.

However, some of my taxpayer participants recognized that getting a refund was actually a *loss*. After all, an interest-free loan to the government has been made. In a rational-economic sense, it is better to come up owing money (without penalties) than to come up getting money back, despite the natural pleasure of getting a check rather than writing one. Yet, as one taxpayer wrote in a diary, "in spite of having more money during the year, I still rather miss the large tax refund checks . . . Still *feels* like a loss." This suggests that withholding is important in cutting the pain of paying. If the withholding system were to be expanded, it might be sensible to consider paying interest to taxpayers who overwithhold, both to encourage a sense of fairness and to encourage people to guess about withholding in a direction that favors the government.

Research Methods

The research methods employed have been those most common in their respective fields. Economists have relied most heavily on indices of costs and benefits of taxpaying embodied in income levels, marginal tax rates, audit rates, and other quantitative measures of compliance arising from detailed data bases developed through intensive audit procedures by the IRS. Sociologists tend to rely on taxpayer surveys that address tax behavior through retrospective self-reports, as related to various attitudinal and demographic measures.

Both methods are rather distant from taxpayer *behavior*. Audit procedures can identify many types of errors, yet are less effective at identifying some other types of errors or deliberate efforts to conceal income or fabricate deductions. Rarely do we have a sense of *why* the taxpayer acted in a particular way (economists do not need this information because the theory attributes all actions to rational calculations). Surveys offer the opportunity to listen to taxpayers' opinions, yet this method relies on the ability and willingness of respondents to answer accurately months after the behavior of interest. All too often, respondents give their own *theories* of tax behavior, or *rationalized justifications* for their behaviors (see Nisbett and Wilson 1977).

It would be ideal if we could follow taxpayers over time, through the web of decisions in a tax year (or more) and, during that time, obtain a close understanding of their thoughts and behaviors. Decision researchers have used a set of research techniques known as "process-tracing methods" that include concurrent verbal protocols (asking people to think aloud while they decide), records of information acquisition, tests of short-term memory, and response time recording (see Carroll and Johnson 1990). These methods are well adapted for use in controlled, short-term decision situations; process-tracing methods could not be used for months at a time. In the next section, I describe an exploratory study that sought to achieve a reasonable balance between the need for detailed longitudinal data and the practical limitations placed upon researchers.

A Study of Taxpayer Decisions in Response to the 1986 Tax Reform Act

During the 1988 tax season, 100 taxpayers in the Boston area were interviewed at the beginning and end of the tax season, kept daily diaries of tax-related thoughts and behaviors, and did their major tax preparation work in the presence of a research assistant who instructed them to "think aloud" and tape-recorded their thoughts. These taxpayers were volunteers selected to have a range of middle to upper income, moderately complex tax forms, and to be 75 percent self-filers (25 percent use a tax preparer). They were offered $100 in cash or as a charitable donation.

The respondents are a heterogeneous sample along several important dimensions, including income, occupation, gender, marital status, and age. However, they are unusual in at least two respects: 95 percent of the sample are white and 86 percent have completed college (45 percent have some postgraduate education). This suggests that the kind of people who would volunteer for an MIT study of taxpaying have some appreciation for the importance of research and some sense of trust in how their data would be used. Their self-reported noncompliance was substantial: 49 percent reported they had understated income in the last three years and 17 percent reported they had overstated deductions (57 percent reported one and/or the other). Most surveys find understating of income by about 30 percent of the respondents, although Hite (1988) found some types of respondents whose income understating in the past five years was as high as 67 percent.

The study partially addressed the likelihood that taxpayers would revise their strategies and habits after the Tax Reform Act of 1986 and, therefore, reveal usually tacit behavior. We are in the process of analyzing these data, but I will provide some preliminary results organized around the themes of framing and fairness. In particular, I will focus on indexes of framing and fairness in the diary data in relation to more typical items from the interviews. Unfortunately, only eighty-two respondents gave one or more codable statements in their diaries, and only sixty of these used a codable frame in their diaries. The analysis proceeds in three parts: first, I examine the frames that were used, and relate the complexity or sophistication of these frames to background information about the respondents; second, I examine satisfaction with the "final figures" as a function of frame use and background factors; and third, I look at noncompliance and its determinants.

Framing

Our initial analyses have focused on framing in terms of reference points or comparisons. Identifiable statements in the diary refer to several kinds of comparisons: (1) whether the respondent will receive a refund or have to pay, a REFUND frame; (2) a comparison of the refund, taxes, or deductions to last year's amounts, a LASTYEAR frame; (3) the TOTALTAX paid; (4) the PERCENT of income paid as taxes; (5) a comparison of refund or amount to pay against EXPECTED amounts; (6) a comparison of amounts against OTHER people; (7) a comparison of amount to pay against CASH on hand; and (8) an ECONOMIC assessment of the value of withholding, such as a recognition that overwithholding is an interest-free loan to the government, taxes owed indicates having use of the money during the year, and setting a target of paying 90 percent of the tax liability in order to use the money and not incur penalties.

For example, one respondent made the following statement.

> I made $1,500 more in 1987 than in 1986 and in 1987 I will only be paying about $6 more in taxes. . . . It appears the new tax laws have been working in my benefit. In spite of actually having more money during the year, I still rather miss the large tax refund check. . . . Still *feels* like a loss. (#273, 2/7)

This expresses four frames: a TOTALTAX frame, a LASTYEAR frame comparing tax payments, satisfaction within the ECONOMIC frame by recognizing that less withholding has some value, and dissatisfaction in the REFUND frame.

Of all framing statements in the diaries, nearly 60 percent were REFUND statements. This is the frame that Loftus (1985) suggested is important for the understanding and control of taxpaying behavior. Indeed, many of the other frames imply that the refund or payment is examined first, and then compared to last year, expectations, cash on hand, other people, and so forth. Because of the small number of diary references to some of the above frames, the PERCENT frame was combined with TOTALTAX, and the OTHER and CASH frames were combined.

It is possible to assess these frames in a rough ordinal scale of SOPHISTICATION. This reflects two concerns: the amount of knowledge or insight into the economics of taxpaying, and the amount of information processing necessary to utilize the frame. It is evident that the REFUND frame is the least sophisticated, both in the sense of ignoring the real "costs" of taxes and in the sense that it pays attention only to the concrete dollars that are paid or received at one point in time. Similarly, the ECONOMIC frame is the most sophisticated, in that it involves abstract concepts, assembles information from several different sources, and demonstrates more insight into the underlying structure of tax economics. Frames that compare the refund to another simple reference point such as LASTYEAR's refund, the EXPECTED refund, or some other amount such as CASH on hand, appear to be one level up from the REFUND frame due to their focus on the concrete refund and the addition of a benchmark or target figure. Finally, those frames based on TOTALTAX seem to be moderately sophisticated because they rely on the aggregated payments (a taxpayer does not directly experience total tax paid in the way that they experience a refund or final payment), but not as complex in reasoning as the ECONOMIC frame. Of course, should this rough scale of SOPHISTICATION prove interesting, refinements would be desirable.

The SOPHISTICATION scale gave each respondent who had provided at least one framing statement in the diary a score between 1 and 4. This score represents the highest level of the frame that was used in the diary. A score of 1 was given if they used only the REFUND frame; a 2 was given for LASTYEAR, EXPECTED, and OTHER; a 3 was given if they used TOTALTAX; and a 4 was reserved for anyone who used the ECONOMIC frame at least once. In the example cited previously, all four frames were coded for the respondent, but the SOPHISTICATION score reflects the presence of the ECONOMIC frame with a coding of 4.

Informal hypotheses were readily induced that frame sophistication should be related to age, education, occupation, tax form complexity, tax knowledge, use of various sources of information, and use of a tax preparer. Correlations with these and other likely candidates showed that greater sophistication was significantly associated with reporting the IRS as a useful source of information (for TY1986), higher level of education, itemizing on Schedule A, and *not* reporting friends and relatives as useful sources of information (for TY1986). Nonsignificant relationships with correlations about .20 were found with greater tax knowledge measured by ten questions about changes in the tax laws, higher occupational status, and reporting the media as useful sources of information for the previous year's taxes. Although it cannot be a predictor of frame sophistication, tax knowledge at the end of the tax season was even more strongly associated with frame sophistication than tax knowledge at the beginning of the tax season. Table 1 presents these relationships. A multiple regression analysis to predict sophistication from these variables indicated that the most important variable was education level. No other variable added significantly to the predictive power of education level.

Satisfaction

Respondents were asked, "How pleased or displeased were you with the final figures and the amount you had to pay or the refund you will receive: would you say you were very pleased, somewhat pleased, neither pleased nor displeased, somewhat displeased, or very displeased?" This five-point satisfaction scale was compared against various demographic, framing, and fairness

TABLE 1. Predictors of Frame Sophistication

	Frame Sophistication			
Predictor	1	2	3	4
Age	35.2	39.8	42.4	39.3
Education[a]	3.2	3.2	3.5	3.8**
Occupational status[b]	1.8	2.0	1.5	1.3
Use of accountant[c]	7	32	25	17
Schedule A[c]	73	96	100	100**
IRS helpful[c]	0	8	9	50**
Media helpful[c]	33	40	55	67
Friends/relatives helpful[c]	47	44	0	33*
Tax knowledge (1/88)[d]	3.5	3.5	4.9	4.0
Tax knowledge (postfiling)[d]	4.7	4.3	5.2	6.5**
Refund or payment[e]	1.2	0.8	0.5	−0.6
Refund-guess[e]	1.3	1.6	−0.5	1.2
N	15	25	12	6

[a] 1 = high school, 2 = some college; 3 = four-year college; 4 = postgraduate.

[b] 1 = highest (doctors, professors, vice presidents); 3 = medium (grade school teacher, grocery owner, bank teller); 5 = low (lower level sales; medium-skilled workers).

[c] Table entries are percentages of respondents answering affirmatively.

[d] Number of correct responses to ten questions on changes in the tax laws.

[e] For $\$ > 0$, $\log(\$ + 1)$; for $\$ < 0$, $-\log(-\$ + 1)$.

$*p < .10$. $**p < .05$.

indicators. Since satisfaction should be related to dollars paid, we used the actual payment or refund (transformed on a log scale), and payment or refund adjusted by subtracting the respondents' best guesses of their payments or refunds obtained in the initial interview (again, transformed). We used both frame sophistication and separate indicators of other framing statements.

Because of the high variability in the number of frame statements among respondents, we chose the simplest possible index of frame use that captured the content of frame-based judgments. Each category of frame statement was coded with a positive, negative, or neutral code, indicating whether the respondent seemed satisfied or dissatisfied in terms of that frame. For each respondent, these codes were summed within the category and truncated to −1, 0, and +1, in order to avoid basing too much of the analysis on those respondents who expressed frames more frequently.

Satisfaction showed no relationship with any demographic variables, including income, satisfaction with income, age, education, occupation, or use of a tax professional. As expected, satisfaction was significantly related to tax liability or refund, including both the amount paid or refunded and the difference between the amount paid and expectations from the January interview (see table 2). Satisfaction was also significantly related to diary coding of several frames: REFUND, LASTYEAR, EXPECTED, and ECONOMIC. Nonsignificant correlations above .20 were found with lower levels of frame sophistication and diary comments about the unfairness of tax procedures.

Multiple regression analyses with these significant variables showed that the strongest predictors were the comparison of the refund or payment against previous predictions, and the content of the EXPECTED frame. Both of these variables suggest that these taxpayers are not simply responding to their

TABLE 2. Correlation of Satisfaction with Refund and Frames

	r
Refund or payment[a]	.34**
Refund-guess[a]	.34**
SOPHISTICATION	−.26*
REFUND frame	.32**
LASTYEAR frame	.21*
TOTALTAX frame	.08
EXPECTED frame	.30**
COMPARE frame	.06
ECONOMIC frame	.25**

[a]For $\$ > 0$, $\log(\$ + 1)$; for $\$ < 0$, $-\log(-\$ + 1)$
*$p < .10$. **$p < .05$.

refund or payment, but have set up important expectations about this result, against which the actual figures are evaluated. For example, one respondent reported a phone conversation with an accountant in which the accountant said, "his ruff [sic] memory guess was that I would be getting about $50 back from the state and $500 from federal. I was a little disappointed I was hoping for more of a refund" (#75, 4/12).

Respondents with more sophisticated frames tend to be less happy with what they had to pay, or what they will get refunded. This may be due to the fact that these respondents have had less withheld during the year so they would not get a refund, and are expressing their reaction to the current payment. As shown in table 1, the highest sophistication respondents are the only group who did not receive a refund on average.

Noncompliance

Respondents were asked, "How likely is it that you (or your spouse) left any income—even a small amount—off your federal tax return. Would you say that you definitely have, you probably have, you probably have not, or you definitely have not?" and "Do you think that the amount of the deductions that you claimed this year was definitely more than what you were entitled, probably more, exactly the right amount, probably less, or definitely less?" Among all respondents, 38 percent reported definitely or probably leaving off income and 8 percent reported definitely or probably overdeducting. We also asked respondents, "For this year's tax return, do you think that the overall amount of tax you paid was definitely greater than the amount that you legally owed, probably greater than the amount you owed, exactly what you owed, probably less than the amount you owed, or definitely less than the amount you owed?" Among all respondents, 15 percent reported paying probably or definitely less than they owed.

Interestingly, these measures of noncompliance appear inconsistent at first look. As shown in table 3, many respondents underreport income or overdeduct, yet assert that they have paid at least what they legally owe. Apparently, we must divide respondents into at least three groups: (1) "honest" taxpayers who report doing what the law requests, including those who do not take advantage of all tax-reducing provisions; (2) "pseudocheaters" who misreport income and/or deductions but believe they have "done no harm" in the sense that the outcome is no less than they owed; and (3) the "classic cheaters" who misreport income and/or deductions and admit they have paid less than they legally owe. It should be interesting to look more deeply into whether the pseudocheaters distort the concept of "legally owe," ignore small amounts of money, or are misreporting in one area in order to make up for something else, such as an overly complex way to save money that they have avoided, or deductions they have ignored because they have not kept receipts. The one respondent who denies underreporting income or overdeducting, yet reports paying less than legally required, must be confused, nervous, or guilty about something (unless he or she has invented a new way to cheat).

Honest Taxpayers, Pseudocheaters, and Classic Cheaters

We compared the three-category noncompliance variable against various demographic variables, framing, and satisfaction. From the diaries, we also derived measures of fear, morality, norms, saving money, and saving time or effort. The noncompliance category was significantly related to income, age, percentage of income subject to withholding, refund or payment, satisfaction, reporting the media as useful, and diary comments about cheating intentions, fear of getting caught, saving money, saving time, morality, and norms.

Discriminant analysis revealed two discriminant functions, the first of which was the degree of noncompliance, with classic cheaters highest, honest taxpayers lowest, and pseudocheaters in the middle. This cheating measure was predicted by lower income, cheating intentions in the diary, and fewer diary comments about fear (or comments about lack of fear). The second discriminant function differentiated the pseudocheaters from the other groups and was predicted by diary comments about saving time in the tax process.

These data support the idea that respondents may cheat under the justification that they are coping with an overly complex procedure. For example, one respondent had to fill out the lengthy Form 8598 that deals with home mortgage deductions, due to a home equity loan. The respondent had to choose between the "short, quick way" to fill out the form and the

> *exact* way—in which you can deduct more interest (because of medical or educational expenses) but is *extremely complicated* because of the need to document home improvements and other expenses related to any of the mortgages which I held on the property. I opted, when I figured my

TABLE 3. Measures of Noncompliance for Tax Year 1987

	Pay More Than or Correct Amount	Pay Less Than Correct Amount	Total
Report all income and deduct less than or correct legal amount	50	1	51
Underreport income or deduct more than legal amount	29	13	42
Total	79	14	93

> taxes, not to use this route because of the extreme difficulty in putting all this information together. (#116, 2/26)

After several weeks, including various comments about the complexity of taxes in general and Form 8598 in particular, the respondent finished the tax work. After rechecking the calculations,

> I made some additional calculations: (1) total interest paid on mortgage and home equity loan, (2) total of mortgage interest plus 65 percent of home equity loan interest, (3) I took the average of these, subtracted it from the actual interest deduction I was entitled to on Form #8598 and buried the difference (about $400–450) as a "contribution" deduction. I felt somewhat guilty but also somewhat smug and justified since I perceived I wasn't even getting my 65 percent interest deduction on the home equity loan interest and that I was probably penalizing myself because I could not (or did not want to bother) with filling out the incredibly complicated (record-wise) Part III of Form 8598. (#116, 3/19)

Underreporting Income and Overdeducting

Noncompliance on the income side was significantly related to lower income, more income not subject to withholding, reporting a tax professional as a useful source of information about this year's taxes, diary statements about an intention to cheat, diary statements about saving time in the tax process, and statements about a relative lack of fear. These relationships are presented in table 4. Discriminant analysis showed that underreporting was most strongly predicted by lower income and diary comments about saving time and less fear. Use of a tax professional was associated with underreporting.

Noncompliance on the deduction side was significantly related to postseason tax knowledge, reliance on a friend or relative as a source of information in the prior year, and receiving a better-than-expected refund. Nonsignificant relationships near $r = .20$ were found with satisfaction and occupational status. Discriminant analysis showed that overdeducting was significantly predicted by usefulness of friends/relatives as information sources (for tax year 1986) and higher tax knowledge.

An interesting example of the social nature of noncompliance is provided by one respondent whose diary reports,

> Had dinner with some friends, discussed tax writeoffs. Specifically—day care expenditures, they hike it up to what they feel is an acceptable rate. (#92, 1/23)

Later in tax season, this theme of overdeduction and social support appears again.

> . . . get $2000 back [refund]. I was satisfied with the number, but looked at my 1986 tax and found out I took quite a bit higher number on charitable contributions so I went back and added more on. On certain categories like charitable contributions it isn't good to vary too greatly from year to year. Now I get even more back. One thing I will always do is try to get money back. My friends and I talk about this and all agree. We can't see what the govt. is doing for us and we have no control over how the money is spent. (#92, 2/19)

Discussion

Diaries as Data

The diaries seem to have provided useful and provocative data; however, there are several limitations and cautions to their use. First, not everyone was diligent enough to provide a diary; some provided only the most factual statements about receiving W-2s and 1099s and doing paperwork. Others spoke at length and in great detail about their mental processes, values, concerns, discussions with others, and so forth. Thus, the diaries are not representative, in any simple way, of our respondents.

TABLE 4. Predictors of Noncompliance

	Underreport Income		Overdeduct	
Predictor	No	Yes	No	Yes
Income[a]	3.8	3.2**	3.6	3.5
Withholding coverage	86.3	73.2**	82.4	76.5
Refund-guess[b]	1.2	0.7	0.8	3.2*
Satisfaction	2.5	2.5	2.7	1.6*
Use of accountant[c]	21	39**	29	25
Friends/relatives helpful[c]	32	27	24	68**
Knowledge (post)	4.8	4.9	4.7	6.5**
Diary fair procedure[d]	−.15	−.17	−.19	.40**
Diary fear[d]	.18	−.10**	.10	−.20
Diary save time[d]	.04	.31**	.14	.20
Diary cheat intent[d]	.10	.31**	.15	.40

[a]1 = 0–$14,999; 2 = $15,000–$24,999; 3 = $25,000–$49,999; 4 = $50,000–$74,999; 5 = $75,000–$99,999; 6 = $100,000–$249,000; 7 = $250,000 or more.

[b]For $\$ > 0$, $\log(\$ + 1)$; for $\$ < 0$, $-\log(-\$ + 1)$.

[c]Table entries are percentages of respondents answering affirmatively.

[d]Mean on the −1/0/+1 scale.

$*p < .10$. $**p < .05$.

Second, the diaries are not the equivalent of concurrent verbal protocols. Our desire was to obtain measures of decision processes as close to the actual events as possible, rather than waiting for the end of the tax season (or longer) to get retrospective reports. Although the diaries are *closer* to these events of interest, they still represent an end-of-the-day reconstruction of events (or worse, since some respondents may have filled in several days at once after a lapse of diligence). Thus, the events in a daily diary report are not necessarily in temporal order. A reasonable temporal unit is the person-day (i.e., what a respondent wrote on one day occurred after the previous day and before the next). An analysis of the corelationships of statements on the same day, using person-days as the unit, showed very little of interest about frame statements (e.g., a large proportion of most types of frame statements are found on the same days as statements in the REFUND frame).

Third, differences between people in their diary reports may reflect differences in the ability to *articulate* their thoughts or write them down, rather than differences in their decision processes. For example, respondents who have accountants may have readier access to certain "economic" words that they put into their diaries, whereas respondents who are thinking in sophisticated terms write down vague statements about their "refund" or "payment" or "expectations." Further, of course, many people are unwilling to write down their inner thoughts. If this reasoning is correct, then the best use of the diaries may be as rich examples of particular lines of thought, rather than as a data base for quantitative analysis.

Fourth, the diaries were very difficult to code reliably. Coders need to be both diligent and well-versed in the tax process and in the concepts of fairness and frames. Given the small numbers of diary statements in some domains and the difficulties in finding adequate coders, all results from the diaries must be considered preliminary.

Frames

Our analyses, however, do suggest some interesting conclusions. Among a very educated set of respondents, using a very liberal coding rule, the frequency of sophisticated economic frames was quite low. From the diaries, we could code only six of sixty (10 percent) respondents in the highest category.

Frame sophistication seems to be related to direct tax experience and to general educational characteristics. Thus, exposure to itemizing and IRS advice is associated with sophistication. It seems that the more sophisticated people use the mass media and the IRS, but not their friends and relatives, to gather information. Higher education is the single best predictor of a more sophisticated tax frame. The higher status occupational groups tend to be more sophisticated, but this seems primarily due to their higher education. It is interesting that the use of a tax professional is unrelated to sophistication: perhaps there are counteracting effects, whereby sophisticated people have reasons to approach and to avoid accountants.

We attempted to draw some connections between frames and satisfaction with taxpaying. Satisfaction was most strongly related to what people had to pay, but the relationships between payments, expectations, and diary comments were difficult to tease out, given so few respondents. The best predictors seemed to be the amount respondents paid compared to what they had guessed they would have to pay (or receive as a refund) in January interviews and diary comments about their payment or refund relative to expectations. Thus, for many of these respondents, there is some evidence that the REFUND frame is *not* the major determining factor, but rather the EXPECTATION frame. They are more pleased if they pay *less* or get a *larger* refund than expected, not simply whether or not they get a refund.

Noncompliance

Some interesting results appeared in our analysis of noncompliance. There appears to be an ambiguous group of respondents who are not following the tax rules (they underreport income and/or overdeduct), yet report that they are not cheating the government out of any money. This group is most strongly predicted by diary comments regarding saving time. One interpretation is that these respondents are taking shortcuts that seem fair to them, and benefit by saving time rather than deliberately lowering their tax liability. It is also possible that these respondents are deliberately avoiding knowledge of their true tax liability and are, therefore, able to justify lazy tax practices and a little cheating.

A somewhat different pattern of significant relationships occurred between noncompliance on the income side and noncompliance on the deductions side. Underreporting income was associated with lower income, a lower proportion of income subject to withholding, reliance on a tax professional, and diary comments about saving time and lack of fear. It may be that people with more complex returns, more sources of income, and less of it subject to withholding neglect to report income, in part, because the reporting process is so tedious and the income is nearly untraceable. This is certainly consistent with consequence processing. It is not clear what role, if any, the tax professional plays in this. None of our diaries directly suggest that tax professionals are aware of nonreported income. Overdeduction was associated with the use of friends and relatives for information and greater tax knowledge. It is interesting that many of the respondents say they have inflated deductions, but also report that the amount of taxes they paid was close to what they legally owed. This suggests that many consider their overdeductions to be either trivial or a small entitlement, or they believe they are redressing other overpayments.

REFERENCES

Aitken, S. S., and L. Bonneville. 1980. *A General Taxpayer Opinion Survey.* Washington, D.C.: CSR Inc.

Allingham, M. G., and A. Sandmo. 1972. "Income Tax Evasion: A Theoretical Analysis." *Journal of Public Economics* 1:323–38.

Barley, S. R. 1991. "Contextualizing Conflict: Notes on the Anthropology of Disputes and Negotiations." In *Research on Negotiation in Organizations,* ed. M. Bazerman, B. Sheppard, and R. Lewicki, 3:165–99. Greenwich, Conn.: JAI Press.

Becker, G. 1968. "Crime and Punishment: An Economic Approach." *Journal of Political Economy* 76:169–217.

Cahalan, M., and L. E. Ekstrand. 1980. *Who are the Tax Cheaters and Why Do They Cheat?* Rockville, Md.: Westat, Inc.

California. Assembly Committee on Criminal Procedure. 1975. "Public Knowledge of Criminal Penalties." In *Perception in Criminology,* ed. R. L. Henshel and R. A. Silverman, 74–90. New York: Columbia University Press.

Carroll, J. S. 1978. "A Psychological Approach to Deterrence: The Evaluation of Crime Opportunities." *Journal of Personality and Social Psychology* 36:1512–20.

Carroll, J. S. 1982. "Committing a Crime: The Offender's Decision." In *The Criminal Justice System: A Social-Psychological Analysis,* ed. V. J. Konecni and E. B. Ebbeson, 49–67. San Francisco: Freeman.

Carroll, J. S. 1989. "A Cognitive-Process Analysis of Taxpayer Compliance." In *Taxpayer Compliance,* vol. 2: *Social Science Perspectives,* ed. J. Roth and J. Scholz, 228–72. Philadelphia: University of Pennsylvania Press.

Carroll, J. S., and E. J. Johnson. 1990. *Decision Research: A Field Guide.* Newbury Park, Calif.: Sage.

Clarke, R. V., and D. B. Cornish. 1985. "Modelling Offenders' Decisions: A Framework for Research and Policy." In *Crime and Justice: An Annual Review of Research,* ed. M. Tonry and N. Norris, 6:147–85. Chicago: University of Chicago Press.

Cook, P. J. 1981. "Research in Criminal Deterrence: Laying the Groundwork for the Second Decade." In *Crime and Justice: An Annual Review of Research,* ed. N. Morris and M. Tonry, 2:211–68. Chicago: University of Chicago Press.

Cyert, R. M., and J. G. March. 1963. *A Behavioral Theory of the Firm.* Englewood Cliffs, N.J.: Prentice-Hall.

Einhorn, H. J., and R. M. Hogarth. 1985. "Ambiguity and Uncertainty in Probabilistic Inference." *Psychological Review* 92:433–61.

Ekland-Olson, S., J. Lieb, and L. Zurcher. 1984. "The Paradoxical Impact of Criminal Sanctions: Some Microstructural Findings." *Law and Society Review* 18:159–79.

Fischhoff, B., P. Slovic, and S. Lichtenstein. 1980. "Knowing What You Want: Measuring Labile Values." In *Cognitive Processes in Choice and Decision Behavior,* ed. T. Wallsten, 117–41. Hillsdale, N.J.: Erlbaum.

Hite, P. A. 1988. "An Examination of the Impact of Subject Selection on Hypothetical and Self-Reported Taxpayer Noncompliance." *Journal of Economic Psychology* 9:445–66.

ICF. 1985. *Summary of Public Attitudes Survey Findings.* Report to the IRS. Washington, D.C.: ICF, Inc.

Isenberg, D. J. 1984. "How Senior Managers Think." *Harvard Business Review* 62(6):81–90.

Kagan, R. A. 1989. "On the Visibility of Income Tax Law Violations." In *Taxpayer Compliance,* vol. 2: *Social Science Perspectives,* ed. J. Roth and J. Scholz, 76–125. Philadelphia: University of Pennsylvania Press.

Kidder, R., and C. McEwen. 1989. "Taxpaying Behavior in Social Context: A Tentative Typology of Tax Compliance and Noncompliance." In *Taxpayer Compliance,* vol. 2: *Social Science Perspectives,* ed. J. Roth and J. Scholz, 47–75. Philadelphia: University of Pennsylvania Press.

Kinder, D. R., and D. O. Sears. 1985. "Public Opinion and Political Action." *The Handbook of Social Psychology,* 3d ed., ed. G. Lindzay and E. Aronson. New York: Random House.

Klepper, S., and D. Nagin. 1989. "The Anatomy of Tax Evasion." *Journal of Law, Economics, and Organization* 5:1–24.

Kunreuther, H., R. Ginsberg, L. Miller, P. Sagi, P. Slovic, B. Borkan, and N. Katz. 1978. *Disaster Insurance Protection: Public Policy Lessons.* New York: Wiley.

Loftus, E. F. 1985. "To File, Perchance to Cheat." *Psychology Today,* April, 34–39.

Mason, R. 1987. "A Communications Model of Taxpayer Honesty." *Law and Policy* 9:246–58.

Montgomery, H. 1983. "Decision Rules and the Search for a Dominance Structure: Towards a Process Model of Decision Making." In *Analysing and Aiding Decision Processes,* ed. P. Humphreys, O. Svenson, and A. Vari, 343–69. New York: North-Holland.

Nisbett, R. E., and T. D. Wilson. 1977. "Telling More Than We Can Know: Verbal Reports on Mental Processes." *Psychological Review* 84:231–59.

Rollins, J. 1985. *Between Women: Domestics and Their Employers.* Philadelphia: Temple University Press.

Scholz, J. T. 1985. "Coping with Complexity: A Bounded Rationality Perspective on Taxpayer Compliance." *Proceedings of the Seventy-Eighth Annual Conference on Taxation.* Denver: NTA-TIA.

Simon, H. A. 1955. "A Behavioral Model of Rational Choice." *Quarterly Journal of Economics* 59:99–118.

Tversky, A., and D. Kahneman. 1974. "Judgment under Uncertainty: Heuristics and Biases." *Science* 185:1124–31.

Tyler, T. R. 1990. *Why People Obey the Law.* New Haven: Yale University Press.

Tyler, T. R., and R. J. Bies. 1990. "Beyond Formal Procedures: The Interpersonal Context of Procedural Justice." In *Applied Social Psychology and Organizational Settings,* ed. J. S. Carroll, 77–98. Hillsdale, N.J.: Erlbaum.

Weaver, F. M., and J. S. Carroll. 1985. "Crime Perceptions in a Natural Setting by Expert and Novice Shoplifters." *Social Psychology Quarterly* 48:349–59.

Witte, A. D., and D. F. Woodbury. 1985. "The Effect of Tax Laws and Tax Administration on Tax Compliance: The Case of the U.S. Individual Income Tax." *National Tax Journal* 38:1–14.

Yankelovich, Skelly, and White. 1984. *Taxpayer Attitudes Survey: Final Report.* Washington, D.C.: Internal Revenue Service.

Commentary

Silvia A. Madeo

John Carroll has undertaken the very ambitious task of trying to learn more about why people pay, or fail to pay, taxes by analyzing data from diaries. That analysis is not yet complete, and thus the essay presented here must be evaluated as a work in progress. Many of the questions I will raise will no doubt be addressed once the analysis is complete and the essay is in final form.

The introduction leads the reader to expect some insight into taxpaying as a "web of interconnected decisions" such as tax planning, record keeping, the use of a paid preparer, developing tactics for tax compliance, and so forth. Unfortunately, we learn little about these decisions from the analysis performed, even though the type of data collected should allow the researcher to address these issues. For example, respondents could be partitioned by whether or not they employed a paid preparer. Differences between the two groups could be analyzed to try to understand why some taxpayers use preparers and others do not.

Another interesting discussion in the introduction concerns the possibility that taxpayers develop a standard set of procedures for paying their taxes, and this "SOP" will continue until there is a major shift in the tax environment, such as the Tax Reform Act of 1986. The data were collected during "the 1988 tax season," apparently in an effort to capture how different taxpayers responded to this shift in the tax environment. However, the analysis presented does not attempt to measure that response even though it appears that prior and current noncompliance was reported by respondents. Was the TRA enough of a shift in the tax environment to encourage different behavior and what factors were related to whether or not a taxpayer's behavior changed?

As the title suggests, the analysis focuses on issues of framing and fairness as revealed in the diaries of 100 respondents kept during the "1988 tax season." Although the essay is not specific, it appears that this period is defined as January 1 through April 15, 1988. The purpose of the analysis is to discover whether the respondents used particular reference points or frames when referring to taxes, whether the frames used were "sophisticated," and whether the frames were related to satisfaction with the amount of tax paid. Some specific comments and questions related to the analysis follow.

1. The essay should clearly indicate the period of time over which diaries were kept. If the period is January 1 through April 15, then the data cannot capture all of the "web of interconnected decisions" related to taxpaying. For example, adjustments to withholding or undertaking tax planning strategies might occur at any time during the year.
2. It is not clear whether the analysis is by respondent or by frame. The author states that 60 of the 100 respondents gave one or more codable statements that could be interpreted as a frame. One respondent who mentioned obtaining a refund six times could have a significant effect on the analysis.
3. Respondents made eight different identifiable types of framing statements, four of which were combined into two frames. One of these combinations (tax paid related to cash on hand combined with tax paid relative to tax paid by others) is not intuitively appealing. One factor appears to address equity concerns, whereas the other addresses the respondent's short-term liquidity concerns.
4. The next step in the analysis was to assign a sophistication score to each respondent based on which framing statements were made. The measures of sophistication and their ordering are problematic and an explicit definition of sophistication would be helpful. It *appears* that the definition being used is that the taxpayer has some understanding of the time value of money, with the sophisticated respondent being one who recognizes that overwithholding is an interest-free loan to the government. One might argue that a taxpayer who recognizes the time value of money and yet fails to adjust withholding to avoid a large refund is not very sophisticated. Likewise, why is mentioning total tax paid more sophisticated than mentioning the fact that a refund is expected? Or, why is a respondent who compares the amount of tax paid with that paid by someone else more sophisticated than one who does not make this comparison. A more sophisticated taxpayer might realize that he does not know enough about the other taxpayer's situation to make a fair comparison. As the author states, "some refinements are certainly possible."
5. Informal hypotheses are developed about what factors are related to frame sophistication. At the very least, these hypotheses should indicate whether positive or negative correlations are expected. Concerns with the frame sophistication measures and with their ordering are not lessened when the analysis reveals that one of the two variables asso-

ciated with greater sophistication is "reporting the IRS as a useful source of information" whereas the use of a tax preparer is not associated with greater sophistication. Perhaps a different result would be obtained if the respondents were stratified by income level.

6. Respondents also were asked how likely it was that they had left any income, even a small amount, off their tax return and whether they had overstated deductions. The most surprising result of this analysis was that income level appears to be a somewhat stronger predictor of noncompliance than does income not subject to withholding. In controlled experiments and in empirical studies based on IRS data, source of income (opportunity) has been found to be a much more salient factor than level of income.

In summary, diaries undoubtedly provide a richer set of data than do controlled experiments; however, the preliminary results presented here make the disadvantages of working with these data all too clear. In addition to the limitations of diaries as data that are discussed by the author, it is apparent that an analysis of the data in a way that will provide meaningful insights is very difficult.

The Effect of Audits and Socioeconomic Variables on Compliance

Kurt J. Beron, Helen V. Tauchen, and Ann Dryden Witte

The study of tax compliance promises important scientific and policy insights. From a scientific point of view, the reporting of tax liabilities provides an arena in which we can observe the compliance behavior of most of the adult population. This contrasts markedly with economists' studies of most criminal behavior (e.g., murder or property offenses) where a small, and possibly aberrant, portion of the population is at risk. At this time of large budget deficits, understanding compliance behavior also offers the possibility of "painlessly" reducing the deficit. The potential richness of the tax arena has not escaped the research community and studies of tax compliance behavior have burgeoned. Yet progress has been somewhat disappointing. Researchers report seemingly contradictory results and empirical research on tax compliance has only recently moved beyond approaches used to study the deterrence of general criminal offenses. We believe that at this juncture, it is useful to assess the currently published research findings and try approaches consistent with some recent theoretical developments in compliance research. A critical approach seems particularly valuable at this time because of the extensive research that is underway on this topic. In this essay, we begin by synthesizing the currently published econometric literature on tax compliance. This task is important because existing studies report quite different estimates of the effects of audits and socioeconomic variables on compliance. We also estimate a three-equation model for taxpayers' reported income and tax liability and for the probability of an audit. This work reflects the insights of recent game-theoretic models of compliance. It also provides new results and suggests explanations for some of the seemingly contradictory findings that appear in the literature.

The work reported in this essay was made possible by a grant from the National Science Foundation and the financial support of the University of North Carolina's Research Council. Their support of our work in no way indicates support for our approach or conclusions. We thank Dennis Cox and Bill Lefbom of the U.S. Internal Revenue Service for helping us obtain the data.

Our empirical work differs from previous studies seeking to estimate the deterrent effect of audits in two ways: (1) our dependent variables in the compliance equations are taxpayer reports rather than a variable related to auditor estimates of noncompliance, and (2) we estimate a structural equation for audits. Previous empirical work uses estimates of compliance based on IRS auditors' findings. Given the difficulty of IRS auditors in detecting unreported income, such dependent variables provide results that can be very difficult to interpret. Examining the reporting decisions of taxpayers avoids much of this problem. In addition, we specify a structural model that allows us to infer the factors affecting taxpayers' income reports and reports of subtractions (i.e., adjustments, exemptions, deductions, and credits) on the tax return. Other compliance research considers only a single compliance decision, for example, an overall compliance rate.[1] We know, however, that the probability of detection is much higher for subtractions than income reports, and we suspect that taxpayer behavior differs for these two different types of compliance activities. Noncompliance from underreports of income is often an act of omission, while noncompliance from overstatement of subtractions requires actual misstatements. In addition, we specify and estimate an equation for audits. The endogeneity of audits has been recognized in theory but has only recently been reflected in empirical models. Finally, we focus attention on sociodemographic factors that have appeared in the literature and emphasize their importance in controlling for the tastes and preferences of taxpayers.

Our essay is organized as follows. In the next section, we present our conceptual framework; the third and fourth sections describe the data and the empirical model; the fifth and sixth sections contain a discussion of the empirical results for our structural and reduced-form models, respectively; and the final section contains our conclusions.

Conceptual Framework

Our model of tax compliance and enforcement is a simultaneous equation model with equations for taxpayers' reports and for the odds of an audit. To reflect the reporting behavior of taxpayers, we include equations for reported adjusted gross income (AGI) per return and the reported total tax liability per return. We use separate equations for reported AGI and tax liability because of the differences in the magnitude and possible causes of income underreporting and the overstatement of subtractions. The results for the reported AGI equation allow us to determine the factors affecting income reporting, while a

1. Klepper and Nagin (1987) use the 1982 TCMP data to examine how factors related to individual line items on the return affect compliance.

comparison of the results for the reported AGI and tax liability equations allow us to infer the factors associated with the overstatement of subtractions.[2]

The literature suggests reported AGI and total tax liability depend on the enforcement policies of the tax authorities, income, tax rates, and tastes and preferences (for a recent survey of the literature see Roth, Scholz, and Witte 1989, particularly chap. 2). Although not explicitly mentioned in the literature, the theoretical models of tax compliance also imply that taxpayers' reports depend on provisions of the tax code regarding income exclusions and subtractions. We chose audits as the measure of enforcement policy because this is the enforcement action that has been of most interest in the literature and the IRS believes that audits are its most effective instrument for stimulating accurate taxpayer reports (Comptroller General 1976, 1). The specification of the audit equation derives from the IRS audit selection process, discussed in the fourth section (for descriptions of this process, see Comptroller General 1976; Weddick 1983; Wilt 1986).

The IRS selects the largest proportion of returns for audit using computerized formulas, known as the DIF formulas. The parameters of the DIF formulas are estimated using data from the IRS's Tax Compliance Measurement Program (TCMP). Under this program, every three or four years the IRS selects approximately 50,000 returns to be examined by its best auditors. Taxpayers are asked to substantiate every line item on their return, and auditors record both what the taxpayers filed and what they believe to be the correct report. These data are used to estimate equations that relate the extent of underpayment to the characteristics of the filed return. In subsequent years, the IRS uses the parameter estimates from these equations to score each return filed in regard to its audit potential. The returns with the highest scores are targeted for audit. The actual number of returns audited through the DIF program depends on the reporting behavior of taxpayers, the type and number of audit personnel available, and the amount of audit resources involved in special audit programs.[3] To reflect this audit selection process, we model the odds of an audit as determined by taxpayers' reports that are endogenous, by taxpayer characteristics that the IRS both observes and may legally use for audit selections, and by the level of IRS resources.

2. Adjustments have, of course, been subtracted from income to obtain AGI. Thus, when considering results for our AGI equation, some subtractions will be included. However, adjustments to income in 1969 were very small (less than $700,000, or less than 0.1 percent of reported AGI) and, thus, our results should not be affected much by adjustments. Reported AGI reflects mainly the income-reporting decision. Our data contain no measures of income before adjustments.

3. For additional details regarding the audit selection process see Tauchen and Witte 1986b.

The Data

Tax return data are for 1969 returns filed in 1970, and audit data relate to audits performed in 1969. The information on audits is from the IRS's Project 778 data base (see Roth, Scholz, and Witte 1989 for a description). This data set contains the first publicly available information based on IRS audited returns and the data is aggregated by the IRS to the three-digit zip code level. More recent, individual-level IRS audit data has recently become available on a limited basis to researchers who work closely with the IRS (for an example of work using these data, see Tauchen, Witte, and Beron 1989). However most published research has used the older and more aggregated 1969 data set, and we wish to build on the structure that earlier research has established. Using the same data and level of aggregation eases comparisons of our model and findings with existing research.

We obtain our data on reported AGI and total tax liability and on the number of returns filed from the Statistics of Income (SOI) files. Our measures of income and of tastes and preferences come from the 1970 Census of Population and Housing. A few of the variables existed as part of the Project 778 data set and the rest are obtained directly from census tapes. Information on IRS audit resources is obtained from an internal IRS document (Internal Revenue Service 1969).

All data except that on IRS work load (returns per full-time-equivalent employee) are aggregated to the three-digit zip code level to match the data available on audits. Information on IRS work load is aggregated to the IRS District Office level because this is the administrative unit responsible for conducting audits. IRS Districts are coterminous with state boundaries except in the most populous states (e.g., California) where multiple districts are established.

TABLE 1. Definitions of the IRS Audit Classes

Acronym	Definitions of Audit Class
LI-SD	Low-income tax returns taking the standard deduction (AGI < \$10,000 with no Schedule C or F)
LI-ID	Low-income tax returns taking itemized deductions (AGI < \$10,000 with no Schedule C or F)
LI-C&F	Low-income proprietor tax returns (AGI below \$10,000 with Schedule C or F)
MI-W&S	Middle-income wage and salary workers (AGI between \$10,000 and \$50,000 with no Schedule C or F)
MI-C&F	Middle income proprietor tax returns (AGI between \$10,000 and \$30,000 with Schedule C or F)

Information on audits is available for seven groups (called audit classes) defined on the basis of AGI and income source (e.g., whether some income is received from a business or farm). The definitions of the audit classes used in the analysis are given in table 1. The IRS separates the returns into these audit classes because it believes that compliance behavior varies across groups and develops separate audit selection formulas for each group.

Both the IRS and academic researchers (Dubin and Wilde 1988; Witte and Woodbury 1985) have tested for the homogeneity of taxpayer behavior across the audit classes and concluded aggregation is not appropriate. Therefore, we estimate separate models for the different audit classes. Since we are able to obtain income estimates for only the five low (incomes below $10,000 in 1969 dollars) and middle (incomes between $10,000 and $30,000 for proprietors and between $10,000 and $50,000 for wage and salary workers in 1969 dollars) income audit classes, we present results for only these audit classes. There are no good estimates of income for the two high-income groups from the census or other sources.[4] These high-income returns account for less than 1 percent of the returns filed in 1969.

The Empirical Model

Our model is a three-equation model for reported AGI per return (AGI^r), reported total tax liability per return (T^r), and the log odds of an audit for each IRS audit class (A). We discuss our specification for the two reporting equations first, and then turn our attention to the specification of the audit equation.

We see reported AGI and total tax liability as determined by the log odds of an audit (our measure of enforcement actions that is endogenous),[5] the degree to which noncompliance can be detected (D) in an audit (our measure of the penalties), the level of income (I), a vector of variables that reflect important aspects of the tax code regarding filing requirements, income exclusions, and subtractions from income (TC),[6] and a vector of sociodemographic

4. For example, census data contain only open-ended income categories for high-income individuals.

5. Note that if the taxpayer report affects the odds of an audit, it is the parameters on these variables, not the simple odds of an audit, that will affect taxpayer compliance. We consider the approach taken in this essay a first approximation to properly modeling compliance behavior when the taxpayer's reports affect the odds of an audit. For a discussion of a way to model compliance when the audit rule depends on taxpayer behavior, see Tauchen and Witte (1986a, 1986b).

6. It would also be desirable to control for aspects of the tax code related to avoidance behavior. Our data do not allow us to do this. Fortunately, our data were for a year prior to the large-scale avoidance associated with limited partnerships. Our results, however, may reflect avoidance as well as evasion behavior in some instances.

variables that control for differences in tastes and preferences (S^r). Formally, our two equations for taxpayer reports are

$$\mathrm{AGI}^r = a_0 + a_1 A + a_2 D + a_3 I + a_4 TC + a_5 S^r + e_g ,$$

and

$$T^r = b_0 + b_1 A + b_2 D + b_3 I + b_4 TC + b_5 S^r + e_t ,$$

where the e's are random error terms and the a's and b's are the parameters to be estimated.

Our measure of the log odds of an audit is based on the audit coverage in the geographic area and is discussed below. We cannot measure penalties directly due to data limitations and so we seek to measure them indirectly through our measures of detectability. The vast majority of audits result in some change, usually an increase, in tax liability, but the taxpayer generally receives no formal penalty and is only assessed the taxes due plus interest for the period of nonpayment.[7] Thus, for most taxpayers it is what the auditor uncovers that is the important factor in determining the costs of noncompliance.

We seek to control for the degree of detectability in two ways. First, we estimate separate equations for reported AGI and tax liability. As the IRS readily acknowledges (see, e.g., Internal Revenue Service 1983), it is far more able to uncover overstatements of subtractions from income than understatements of income. Thus, we expect audits to have a stronger effect on reported tax liability, where overstatements of subtractions as well as underreporting of income are reflected, than on reported AGI.

Second, we include two variables related to information reported to the IRS and other types of record keeping. In 1969, the major paper trails used by the IRS were the W-2 forms.[8] To reflect the relative availability of W-2s, we include the percentage of employment in manufacturing and in the service industries. Income from manufacturing firms is generally covered by W-2 reporting and any underreporting of income is likely to be detected by an audit. In contrast, income earned in the service industries is more likely to be

7. In 1969, 70 percent of all returns audited resulted in auditors' findings that adjustments were necessary. Yet, of the 2.5 million returns audited, only 25,110 were received by the appellate division and 2,293 were received for full-scale criminal investigation (see Commissioner of Internal Revenue 1970).

8. There was information reporting on dividend and interest income in 1969, but the IRS had not perfected its matching programs and, therefore, did not make very effective use of this type of information.

in a form (e.g., cash or commissions) less subject to detection. Even the proprietor audit classes in areas where much employment is in manufacturing are likely to have "paper trails" for receipts because of the record keeping of large manufacturing enterprises and because a significant portion of the income for individuals in the proprietor audit classes is from wages and salaries. Therefore, we include these two variables for all audit classes.

Our measure of income is from the census and is constructed by calculating the average income in each three-digit zip code that corresponds to each audit class. For example, the average income used with low-income tax returns taking the standard deduction is the average conditional on income being below $10,000. This is comparable to the requirement for AGI being below $10,000 in the audit class. We chose census income as our measure of "true" income rather than an estimate of income from TCMP audit results because even the thorough TCMP audits fail to uncover a substantial fraction of unreported income.[9] We have not explicitly introduced a measure of the marginal tax rate as an explanatory variable because, for our data set, the tax rate lacks variation that is independent of income.[10] The coefficient on our income variable should, therefore, be interpreted as measuring the effect of changes in income on compliance when the tax rates change with income according to the tax code.

To reflect relevant features of the tax code, we include variables for the proportion of the population over sixty-five, average family size, the proportion of the population owning their home, and the proportion unemployed. Each of these is measured using census data aggregated to the three-digit zip code level to correspond to the IRS-released data. These variables control for legitimate nonfilings by very low income individuals (i.e., in 1969, generally those with incomes below $600), the special allowances for senior citizens, the exemptions for dependents, the tax deductibility of mortgage interest and property taxes, and the exclusion of unemployment benefits from income. Some of these variables also may be related to tastes and preference regarding tax compliance. For instance, in areas with high unemployment, there might be more resentment of the government and less willingness to pay the mandated taxes. The two variables measuring employment structure (the propor-

---

9. The IRS estimates that auditors can uncover only $1 in every $3 that is reported on 1099 documents (Internal Revenue Service 1983). Until 1979, the TCMP auditors were not provided with 1099 forms.

10. It is worth noting that the census measure of income has a coefficient of variation across audit classes of .07 or higher, suggesting sufficient variation for estimation. To determine if some independent marginal tax effect could be uncovered, we developed a marginal tax rate variable reflecting differences in state tax codes and differences in subtractions related to variations in costs of living and other factors. The marginal tax variable performed essentially as an income proxy, perhaps due to the aggregate nature of our data.

tion of the population employed in manufacturing and in services) may serve to control for the most important adjustment to income, the adjustment for employee business expenses, as well as detectability.

The theoretical work on tax compliance provides relatively little direction in selecting the variables that reflect tastes and preferences. The limited empirical work on tax compliance and the survey research do, however, provide some valuable guidance (see Jackson and Milliron 1986; Kinsey 1984a; Witte and Woodbury 1983b for surveys of these literatures). The variables consistently related to tax compliance behavior include sex, race, education, age, and place of birth. We included three-digit zip code census measures of each in our models.

Our specification of the taxpayer compliance equations differs from the literature in that our dependent variables are reported AGI and tax liability, rather than measures derived from tax auditor estimates of noncompliance. The use of reported AGI and tax liability in the equations for the taxpayers' behavior is implied by much of the theoretical literature and recommended by the National Academy of Sciences' Panel on Research on Taxpayer Compliance (Roth, Scholz, and Witte 1989). We believe using variables related to the taxpayers' reports offers an important advantage. With reported AGI and total tax liability as dependent variables, the error term can be interpreted as arising from the stochastic nature of taxpayers' behavior or from omitted variables (e.g., knowledge of the tax code). When the dependent variable is affected by tax auditors' estimates of unreported income, these assumptions and interpretations are not valid. In this case, the error term reflects any elements of the auditors' and taxpayers' behaviors not captured by the model.[11]

Interpretation of the estimated coefficients is simplified when reported income is the dependent variable. With this specification, the effects of explanatory variables can arise either from taxpayers' reporting behavior or from specific provisions of the tax code. In the alternate specification with a dependent variable influenced by tax auditors' findings, the effects of explanatory variables also might reflect the auditors' behavior. Sorting out even the separate effects of the tax code and compliance behavior may not be easy, but at least the tax code is known, and, thus, one can make a reasonable interpreta-

11. An additional advantage is that, with our formulation, it is reasonable to assume a normal distribution for the equation error terms and to use standard estimation techniques. With auditor estimates, however, the error term is not continuously distributed because taxpayers' reports and auditors' findings often coincide. In addition, the distribution of the error term may be asymmetric because underreports of taxable income are far more common than overreports. While there has been recent progress on methods to handle these difficulties (see Schmidt 1989), the issue is not resolved, particularly within a simultaneous equation framework.

tion of the coefficients for the reported AGI and tax liability. In contrast, little is known about tax auditors' behavior except that they miss a substantial amount of underreporting and that they are far better at catching overstatements of deductions and exemptions than at uncovering underreports of income. This lack of information compounds the task of interpreting the coefficients in an equation for unreported income (or for percentage of noncompliance) considerably and is a primary reason that we use taxpayer reports as the dependent variables in the compliance equations.

The third equation in our model is the equation for the log odds of an audit. We see the log odds as determined by reported AGI and reported total tax liability that are endogenous to the model, by a vector of variables observed by the IRS and that may be legally used to select returns for audit (S^a) and by the level of IRS resources (R). Formally,

$$A = c_0 + c_1 \text{AGI}^r + c_2 T^r + c_3 S^a + c_4 R + e^a$$

where e^a is the random error and the c's are the parameters to be estimated. We choose the log odds of an audit as the dependent variable for the audit equation for two reasons. First, this functional form ensures that the probability of an audit is between zero and one. Second, the specification nests the random audit strategy, assumed in much theoretical work, as a special case (see Reinganum and Wilde 1985; Tauchen and Witte 1986a). A random audit strategy would be implied if only measures of IRS resources were significantly related to the log odds of an audit.

The variables related to information available from the filed tax returns and that the IRS may potentially use for audit selection are the measures of employment structure, the unemployment rate, the proportion of the population over sixty-five, average family size, and the proportion of the population who own their homes. Our measure of IRS resources is the number of returns per full-time-equivalent district employee.[12]

Although all federal tax returns in any audit class are scored by the same DIF formula for audit potential, the chances of a tax return being audited, ceteris paribus, differ considerably across IRS Districts. The primary reason is related to resource availability. Based on the DIF scores, the IRS develops an annual master plan for the number of return examinations to be conducted by audit class in each district. However, the IRS has not been able to locate its staff in a fashion to carry out its plan. In some regions, it has audited substantially fewer returns than indicated by the optimal base plan, whereas it has

12. Our count of the number of IRS full-time-equivalent employees excludes those at the regional service centers, because they do not conduct audits, and the district employees who handle alcohol, tobacco, and firearms enforcement.

audited substantially more in other regions. Since much of the reason for the differences in the probability that tax returns are selected for audit, ceteris paribus, is related to resource constraints, we use a measure of IRS audit resources to control for differences in the audit rules across taxpayers.

Note that it is the variation in the completion of the optimal plan across districts that is important in this respect rather than just the difference in resources across regions. A difference in resources relative to the number of returns is not necessarily evidence (by itself) that the audit selection rule varies across taxpayers. If the IRS targets its resources toward areas believed to be particularly noncompliant, then higher than average resources might simply reflect a higher concentration of noncompliant taxpayers. There is considerable evidence in government reports (see Comptroller General 1976; Wilt 1986), however, that the IRS has not been able to distribute its resources among districts in a way to maximally achieve its revenue and compliance goals, given its total budget (see also Long 1985).

The model is identified by use of exclusion restrictions that are justified based on institutional, legal, and informational constraints. Specifically, we identify the two reporting equations by excluding our measure of IRS resources from these equations. The level of IRS resources affects reporting behavior only indirectly, through its effect on the likelihood that a taxpayer is audited. This is similar to the approach taken by Dublin, Graetz, and Wilde (1987). Identification of the audit equation is obtained by the exclusion of economic and sociodemographic variables not available to the IRS on the tax return or information documents (e.g., whether an individual was foreign born) or, if available, cannot legally be used to select returns for audit (e.g., sex).

The model is estimated by two-stage least squares. We use a single-equation method rather than a systems method of estimation because we believe that some of our equations (e.g., the equation for reported AGI) are more completely specified than others (e.g., the audit equation) and so are concerned about spreading any omitted variable bias across equations (see Intriligator 1978 for a discussion of this issue).

Empirical Results for the Structural Model

Tables 2 through 4 contain the results of the two-stage least squares estimation for the reported AGI and tax liability and for the log odds of an audit equation. Note first that the model explains much of the variation in reported AGI and tax liability and in the log odds of an audit for each of the five audit classes. As we had anticipated, we model reporting behavior more successfully than auditing behavior. For reported AGI, the R^2s range from .14 for low-income wage and salary workers with itemized deductions to .79 for low-income proprietors; for tax liability, the range of the R^2s is from .13 for middle-income wage and salary workers to .78 for low-income proprietors. Our model explains between 7 percent (for low-income wage and salary workers with itemized deductions) and 31 percent (for low-income proprietors) of the variation in the log odds of an audit.

TABLE 2. Empirical Results for Reported Adjusted Gross Income: 2SLS (t-values in parentheses)

	Audit Class				
Variable	LI-SD	LI-ID	LI-C&F	MI-W&S	MI-C&F
Log odds of an audit—endogenous	648.13	1693.37	450.75	2491.81	1072.27
	(2.87)	(1.05)	(3.20)	(0.72)	(1.07)
Income	.27	.43	.60	.97	.90
	(6.47)	(4.96)	(14.46)	(8.72)	(15.78)
Detectability:					
% Employed in manufacturing	8.77	−.34	2.67	15.18	4.00
	(3.52)	(−0.10)	(2.21)	(0.67)	(0.74)
% Employed in services	6.30	20.37	−8.23	−8.87	11.42
	(1.55)	(−1.40)	(−2.84)	(−0.26)	(0.65)
Sociodemographics:					
% High school education	3.52	2.91	−8.38	−15.89	−22.23
	(.90)	(0.42)	(−5.05)	(−2.71)	(−3.11)
% Nonwhite	.11	−.97	.42	5.13	1.71
	(.11)	(−0.40)	(0.49)	(0.45)	(0.35)
% Female-headed households	−29.52	−20.83	25.98	60.09	52.45
	(−1.90)	(−1.05)	(4.76)	(2.12)	(2.17)
% Foreign born	11.87	10.52	−7.24	−52.80	−49.04
	(2.70)	(0.55)	(−2.48)	(−1.79)	(−2.67)
Average age	−6.80	−70.51	−6.68	23.20	26.12
	(−.50)	(−0.88)	(−0.78)	(0.53)	(0.70)
Tax code variables:					
% Over 65 years	14.63	65.70	−13.58	35.69	56.51
	(1.24)	(0.93)	(−2.46)	(1.29)	(2.51)
Average family size	39.95	278.49	−70.99	−274.90	−389.80
	(.44)	(0.96)	(−1.40)	(−1.05)	(−1.58)
% Housing owner occupied	1.55	.30	2.44	−3.51	1.61
	(.76)	(0.08)	(1.55)	(−0.37)	(0.23)
% Unemployed	39.04	67.97	13.55	−36.47	18.00
	(3.37)	(3.10)	(1.41)	(−0.77)	(0.39)
Constant	4442.44	12238.68	3958.82	7785.44	3319.67
	(4.25)	(1.59)	(3.72)	(0.58)	(0.72)
R^2	.42	.14	.79	.52	.58
F	47.30	10.26	248.66	66.96	83.74
N	858	852	858	827	801

As might be expected, the coefficients on income are by far the most significant of the estimated coefficients in the reported AGI and tax liability equations. The coefficients on income in the reported AGI equations range from .27 for low-income taxpayers taking standard deductions to .97 for middle-income wage and salary workers. Taxpayers in all audit classes re-

TABLE 3. Empirical Results for Reported Total Tax Liability: 2SLS (t-values in parentheses)

	Audit Class				
Variable	LI-SD	LI-ID	LI-C&F	MI-W&S	MI-C&F
Log odds of an audit—endogenous	109.60	290.17	71.50	2035.37	648.83
	(2.66)	(1.04)	(3.21)	(0.89)	(1.72)
Income	0.07	0.10	0.09	0.27	0.22
	(9.17)	(6.38)	(14.42)	(3.68)	(10.01)
Detectability:					
% Employed in manufacturing	1.42	0.65	0.32	12.77	0.49
	(3.14)	(0.11)	(1.66)	(0.86)	(0.24)
% Employed in services	.46	−4.15	−2.03	−16.77	−3.90
	(0.62)	(−1.65)	(−4.43)	(−0.76)	(−0.59)
Sociodemographics:					
% High school education	0.61	0.23	−1.45	−7.87	−10.15
	(0.85)	(0.19)	(−5.53)	(−2.04)	(−3.78)
% Nonwhite	−0.31	−0.53	−0.36	2.43	−1.59
	(−1.66)	(−1.27)	(−2.61)	(0.33)	(−0.88)
% Female-headed households	−4.81	−3.66	2.49	16.33	14.22
	(−1.69)	(−1.06)	(2.89)	(0.88)	(1.57)
% Foreign born	1.75	1.92	−1.48	−30.73	−24.65
	(2.19)	(0.58)	(−3.20)	(−1.59)	(−3.58)
Average age	2.89	−4.79	3.96	20.96	24.95
	(1.16)	(−0.35)	(2.94)	(0.73)	(1.78)
Tax code variables:					
% Over 65 years	1.78	10.74	−2.35	4.26	14.21
	(0.82)	(0.88)	(−2.68)	(0.24)	(1.68)
Average family size	−11.02	5.07	−35.74	−256.13	−280.03
	(−0.67)	(0.10)	(−4.44)	(−1.49)	(−3.02)
% Housing owner occupied	−.32	−1.06	−.32	−5.82	−.63
	(−0.85)	(−1.67)	(−1.26)	(−0.94)	(−0.24)
% Unemployed	−0.12	−1.78	−5.38	−46.40	−16.92
	(−0.05)	(−0.47)	(−3.54)	(−1.49)	(−0.99)
Constant	381.16	1449.62	257.94	5966.08	1270.73
	(1.99)	(1.09)	(1.53)	(0.68)	(0.73)
R^2	.56	.22	.78	.13	.35
F	81.77	18.50	231.84	9.34	33.03
N	858	852	858	827	801

ported significantly less than an additional dollar of AGI for each extra dollar of income.

The low coefficients for our low-income taxpayers appear to result largely from failures to fully report income to the IRS. Consider alternative explanations. Legal exclusions of certain types of income from taxation and legal adjustments to income account for some differences between income and reported AGI. Further, in 1969, some individuals (i.e., those with incomes below $600 unless they had net earnings from self-employment above $400) in the low-income groups (i.e., AGIs below $10,000) were not required to file. Still, recall that we include variables to control for the major income exclusions (the proportions over sixty-five to control for the exclusion of Social Security benefits and the unemployment rate to control for the exclu-

TABLE 4. Empirical Results for the Log Odds of an Audit (× 1000): 2SLS (t-values in parentheses)

	Audit Class				
Variable	LI-SD	LI-ID	LI-C&F	MI-W&S	MI-C&F
Reported AGI ($1000s)—	6.16	−0.82	0.48	−0.03	0.10
endogenous	(7.79)	(−2.02)	(1.68)	(−0.50)	(1.34)
Reported tax liability ($100s)—	−23.91	1.88	0.06	−0.02	−0.60
endogenous	(−8.39)	(1.25)	(0.04)	(−0.07)	(−1.72)
IRS resources:					
Returns per FTE	32.68	−31.75	−95.62	−40.35	−104.16
	(0.62)	(−1.27)	(−3.12)	(−1.49)	(−2.90)
Detectability:					
% Employed in manufacturing	−15.35	−0.03	−3.44	−4.17	7.41
	(−3.51)	(−0.02)	(−1.57)	(−3.03)	(3.81)
% Employed in services	−22.72	3.94	20.79	13.31	23.28
	(−4.60)	(1.72)	(5.54)	(4.47)	(5.67)
Tax code variables:					
% Over 65 years	25.06	−26.29	0.13	10.74	13.23
	(2.80)	(−3.43)	(0.02)	(1.77)	(1.63)
Average family size	−69.83	81.90	121.76	38.70	100.36
	(−0.70)	(1.50)	(2.01)	(0.79)	(1.47)
% Housing owner occupied	−16.95	2.31	−1.87	1.65	−4.63
	(−5.46)	(0.84)	(−1.03)	(0.97)	(−2.06)
% Unemployed	−210.55	4.25	30.48	12.49	−26.51
	(−6.43)	(1.51)	(1.62)	(0.79)	(−1.23)
Constant	−14509	−121	−6998	−3721	−4445
	(−8.53)	(−0.79)	(−10.50)	(−10.63)	(−9.45)
R^2	.16	.07	.31	.13	.09
F	17.71	6.51	42.26	13.65	8.52
N	858	852	858	827	801

sion of unemployment compensation), adjustments (the two employment structure variables to control for employee business expenses, the largest adjustment to income in 1969), and some major causes of extremely low income (the unemployment rate and the proportion of the population over sixty-five).[13]

The coefficients on income in the tax liability equations provide an estimate of the marginal tax rate on total income (income before exclusions and adjustments by the tax code). The marginal tax rates implied by these coefficients do not seem unreasonable. For the low-income groups, the estimated marginal rate is between 7 and 10 percent. As expected, middle-income groups had higher marginal rates (22 percent for middle-income proprietors and 27 percent for middle-income wage and salary workers).

We find that increasing the odds of an audit significantly increases reported AGI for two groups and tax liability for three groups. The magnitudes of the effects of audits on tax compliance are modest with the elasticities for reported tax liability with respect to the audit variable being between .19 and .31 when significant. These elasticities imply that a 1.00 percent increase in audit coverage would lead to approximately a $1.4 billion increase in tax revenue in current dollars for the five audit classes considered. This is an increase in 1969 tax revenue from these groups of approximately 0.69 percent.

As expected, high audit rates appear more effective in eliciting accurate reporting of subtractions from income than accurate reporting of income. The elasticity of reported AGI with respect to the audit variable is smaller than the elasticity for reported tax liability for all five audit classes, and the difference in elasticities is more pronounced for the middle- than the low-income audit classes. These findings support the IRS's belief that its auditors are better able to find overreported subtractions than underreported income. The findings are also consistent with survey findings (Westat 1980) that relatively more of the noncompliance for blue-collar communities is from underreported income, whereas, for white-collar communities, relatively more is from overstated subtractions from income.

Recall that we have no direct measure of penalties, but estimate separate equations for reported AGI and tax liability and include two measures of detectability (the proportion of employment in manufacturing and in services)

13. We do not control for some exclusions (e.g., income on municipal bonds), adjustments (e.g., contributions to retirement plans by the self-employed), and causes of incomes below the filing level (e.g., dependent teenagers). Still, it seems unlikely that such exclusions, adjustments (total adjustments were less than 0.1 percent of AGI in 1969), and legitimate nonfilings could explain the low rate at which income appears in reported AGI.

as admittedly crude proxies for penalties. Our results provide some limited support for greater detectability being associated with compliance. Specifically, the finding that reported tax liability is more responsive to audit rates than is reported AGI supports the hypothesis that the effectiveness of high audit rates in eliciting honest reporting on the tax return is related to the detectability of noncompliance. It appears that much of the effect of audits operates through subtractions from income that must be substantiated by the taxpayer rather than through income reporting.

For two of the low-income groups we find higher levels of employment in manufacturing (where most income may be reported to the IRS by the employer) to be associated with higher levels of reported tax liabilities. Also, for these low-income groups, we find higher levels of employment in services (where a substantial portion of all income may not be covered by W-2 or other reports) to be associated with lower levels of reported tax liability.[14]

Socioeconomic Results

Results for sociodemographic variables are interesting and help to explain some seemingly incongruous findings in the literature. As in other studies that include measures of both income and education (e.g., Dubin, Graetz, and Wilde 1987), we find that, if anything, taxpayers in areas with a more educated population report lower AGI and tax liability. In their summary of the factors related to tax compliance, Jackson and Milliron (1986) suggest that the more educated may be less compliant because they better understand the opportunities for evasion and are more willing to play the audit lottery than are the less educated. Studies that omit income from the specification (e.g., Dubin and Wilde 1988) find that the educated are, if anything, more compliant with the tax laws. Indeed, if we omit income from our specification, the coefficients on the education variable become positive. Income and education are, however, highly correlated. With income omitted from the specification, the education variable serves partially as an income proxy and the estimated coefficients on education must be interpreted accordingly.

The proportion of the population that is nonwhite is not significantly related to income reporting behavior for any of the groups we consider,

14. Remember that these employment structure variables are also included to control for legal subtractions from income. We would expect individuals in the service industries to have higher levels of employee business expenses and contributions to self-employment pension plans. Such adjustments would lead to negative coefficients on the proportion employed in services in the reported AGI equation. However, the effect should not be very large, because total adjustments were only 0.1 percent of AGI in 1969.

although reported tax liability is significantly lower for nonwhites than for whites in two of the low-income audit classes. The findings for race in other studies are mixed. The results obtained depend, to some extent, on the dependent variable used and on whether income is included as an explanatory variable. When income is excluded and an estimate of the compliance rate that is indirectly related to auditors' findings is used as the dependent variable (see Dubin and Wilde 1988; Witte and Woodbury 1985), the results, when significant, show that whites are more compliant than other racial groups for most, but not all, audit classes. In contrast, our results that control for income and use taxpayers' reports as dependent variables show no evidence that whites are significantly more accurate in their income reports and only weak evidence that whites are significantly more accurate in their reports of subtractions from income. Clearly, economists' understanding of the relationship between race and compliance is not very strong. This mirrors the results in the general crime literature.[15] The results for the proportion foreign born and the proportion of households headed by females generally support previous work. Except for low-income wage and salary workers, we find, as do previous studies, that areas with a relatively large proportion of families headed by females and a relatively small proportion of the population foreign born tend to report higher AGI and tax liability. The better compliance for areas with a larger percentage of families headed by women appears to result predominantly from higher income reports.

The variables related to the taxpayers' ages are the percentage of the population older than sixty-five and the average age of the population between eighteen and sixty-five. The coefficients on these variables may reflect any age or cohort effects related to compliance. In addition, the variable for the percentage of the population over sixty-five is used to control for the exclusion of Social Security benefits from taxable income and the extra exemption allowed individuals over sixty-five. The coefficients on this variable will be related to both age and tax code effects and would be negative if being over sixty-five affected reporting only through the special provisions of the tax code for older taxpayers.

As in other studies using information related to 1969 returns (Clotfelter 1983; Dubin and Wilde 1988; Witte and Woodbury 1985), our results provide some, but not overwhelming, support for the common perception that older taxpayers are more compliant than younger ones. For two audit classes (low- and middle-income proprietors) we find a significant and positive relationship between reported tax liability and average age. For middle-income proprietors we also find significantly higher reported income and tax liability in areas with

15. For a discussion, see Blumstein et al. (1988); Schmidt and Witte (1984); Wilson and Herrnstein (1985).

a relatively higher proportion of the population over sixty-five. For low-income proprietors, the relationship is reversed. We believe the finding for the low-income audit class is a result of the regressive structure of the tax code benefits afforded individuals over sixty-five. At low-income levels the tax code effects outweigh any additional compliance behavior of older individuals, whereas the compliance effect is predominant at higher income levels.

The remaining three variables were included to control for the subtractions from income allowed by the tax code. When significant, the results for average family size and proportion of owner-occupied housing are as anticipated: negative and significant in the tax liability equation, reflecting the exemptions for children and the deductions for mortgage interest payments and property taxes.

The findings for the unemployment variable do not seem to reflect the exclusions of unemployment compensation from reported AGI. Indeed, the coefficient on the unemployment rate in the reported AGI equation is significantly positive for two of the low-income groups. It may be that income reporting increases with the unemployment rate because of increased filings associated with attempts to secure tax refunds.

The coefficient on the unemployment rate is significantly negative in the tax liability equation only for low-income proprietors. Our results suggest that unemployment has only a very weak association with compliance and any tendency for areas with high rates of unemployment to have lower levels of compliance stems from overstatements of subtractions, not understatements of income. Thus, it does not appear that the effect of unemployment can be explained by operation in the underground economy. The effects may be due to antigovernment attitudes or to a simple attempt to overcome financial stress by obtaining a bigger tax refund. Studies that use an estimated compliance rate based on auditor findings as the dependent variable for compliance equations (Dubin and Wilde 1988; Witte and Woodbury 1985) generally find increased unemployment to be associated with decreased compliance. We suspect that these results may largely reflect the auditors' ability to detect overstated deductions.

As noted earlier, our results for the audit equation, reported in table 4, although significant are not very strong. We find the log odds of an audit to be significantly associated with information available on taxpayers' returns for all audit classes. That is, we find no support for the IRS pursuing a random audit strategy for any audit class. For four of the five audit classes we consider, auditing is significantly associated with the endogenous taxpayers' reports (i.e., by reported AGI and total tax liability). For the remaining audit class (middle-income wage and salary workers), the odds of an audit are not significantly affected by the endogenous taxpayer reports but are significantly affected by variables related to information available on taxpayers' returns.

Specifically, for middle-income wage and salary workers, we find that the odds of an audit are higher in areas where a larger percentage of individuals is employed in services and other nonmanufacturing jobs and where there is a higher percentage of the population over sixty-five. We suspect that these variables are proxying specific aspects of taxpayers' reports that we do not observe, although they might be mirroring IRS targeting of specific professions or income sources.

Reduced-Form Results

Economic studies of taxpayer compliance have focused on audits as the enforcement activity of the IRS. This is perhaps a natural choice, given the theoretical and empirical models for participation in other illegal activities and the IRS's emphasis on the importance of audits. Yet, as reported in the previous section, both our work and the previous literature find relatively weak deterrent effects from audits. Admittedly, this empirical work is based on aggregate data, and, given the relatively low audit coverage, this is a potential problem. In addition, the emphasis on audits may be misplaced. The IRS undertakes many other enforcement and service activities, such as matching the income claims on the return against 1099 and W-2 documents, checking math errors, providing information and education programs, pursuing delinquent accounts, instituting detailed investigations, and recommending civil and criminal cases against tax evaders. The reduced-form estimates for reported AGI and tax liability reveal that these other activities also may have significant compliance effects.

While estimates of the structural equations suggest that compliance behavior varies markedly across taxpayer groups and that audits have limited deterrence effects, the reduced-form equations reveal a consistent pattern of compliance behavior and show significant effects of IRS activities. Consider the reduced-form results for reported tax liability given in table 5. These results indicate that increases in IRS work load (returns per full-time-equivalent employee) consistently and significantly decrease reported tax liability.[16] When coupled with our weaker structural findings regarding the effects of audits, this result suggests that IRS activities other than audits may have significant effects on compliance.

The reduced-form results for the sociodemographic- and tax code–related variables also are far more significant and consistent than in the

16. The reduced-form results for the reported AGI equation are also available upon request. As with the structural equations, the reduced-form results show that the IRS activities have a greater effect upon reported subtractions than on reported income.

TABLE 5. Empirical Results for Reported Total Tax Liability: Reduced Form (t-values in parentheses)

	Audit Class				
Variable	LI-SD	LI-ID	LI-C&F	MI-W&S	MI-C&F
Returns per FTE (1000s)	−9.16	−7.13	−8.24	−47.37	−45.83
	(−4.74)	(−3.07)	(−4.58)	(−2.71)	(−2.53)
Income	0.08	0.09	0.11	0.21	0.19
	(26.31)	(22.37)	(37.67)	(19.26)	(16.64)
Detectability:					
% Employed in manufacturing	0.50	−0.19	0.27	0.33	2.25
	(3.51)	(−1.08)	(2.08)	(0.28)	(1.78)
% Employed in services	−1.14	−1.70	−.99	2.06	5.53
	(−4.65)	(−5.60)	(−4.33)	(0.90)	(2.26)
Sociodemographics:					
% High school education	−1.19	−0.92	−0.88	−6.38	−6.61
	(−8.23)	(−5.31)	(−6.60)	(−5.48)	(−5.37)
% Nonwhite	−0.21	−0.32	−0.31	−3.47	−2.73
	(−2.08)	(−2.54)	(−3.29)	(−3.42)	(−2.42)
% Female-headed households	2.43	−0.60	4.10	26.35	22.19
	(4.42)	(−0.89)	(8.00)	(5.20)	(4.04)
% Foreign born	0.15	−1.40	−2.07	−16.25	−16.72
	(0.45)	(−3.50)	(−6.68)	(−5.18)	(−5.08)
Average age	7.11	8.70	4.96	30.57	31.02
	(7.45)	(7.59)	(5.58)	(3.64)	(3.45)
Tax code variables:					
% Over 65 years	−2.81	−1.48	−2.88	12.83	13.55
	(−4.44)	(−1.95)	(−4.88)	(2.40)	(2.37)
Average family size	−46.46	−43.22	−21.96	−169.48	−183.14
	(−8.89)	(−6.87)	(−4.51)	(−3.59)	(−3.62)
% Housing owner occupied	−0.76	−0.86	−0.53	−1.86	−1.93
	(−4.29)	(−4.05)	(−3.21)	(−1.18)	(−1.16)
% Unemployed	−3.04	−2.64	−3.53	−37.28	−34.08
	(−2.90)	(−2.09)	(−3.61)	(−3.93)	(−3.45)
Constant	−80.23	85.03	−243.22	−1655.81	−1477.21
	(2.84)	(2.49)	(9.24)	(−6.10)	(−5.25)
R^2	.80	.71	.88	.57	.53
F	259.74	160.68	470.63	85.97	71.46
N	857	851	857	826	800

structural model.[17] The variability of the structural results across taxpayer classes may be due, at least in part, to IRS activities other than audits affecting compliance and perhaps to academic researchers not being very successful in modeling the audit process.

Conclusions

What can be concluded regarding compliance behavior from previous work that has used data related to 1969 tax returns (e.g., Clotfelter 1983; Dubin and Wilde 1988; Witte and Woodbury 1985) and the results reported here? This question is important for at least two reasons. First, there are now a number of studies that use data related to 1969 returns and there is some controversy surrounding the reported results. Second, the 1969 data sets contain information only available through the IRS and the recent work represents the first time personnel outside the IRS have been allowed to analyze such data and publish results. It is important that we learn as much as possible from the 1969 results, because the IRS is now making more recent data available and several researchers are working with these new data sets.

All authors who consider the issue conclude that, for most audit classes, audits have positive effects on compliance but that the magnitudes of the effects are small. Further, different models suggest that audits deter noncompliance for different groups. Witte and Woodbury find deterrent effects (mainly lagged effects) for all audit classes except the low-income class that takes standard deductions. Dubin and Wilde find a significant deterrent effect for low-income wage and salary workers who take standard and itemized deductions. (For high-income wage and salary workers, they find that a higher probability of an audit is associated with less compliance.) We find a significant deterrent effect of audits for low-income returns with standard deductions, and for both low- and middle-income proprietors. Obviously, the results critically depend on model specification. This suggests that economists' understanding of the effects of audits is not very thorough. For some audit classes, part of the problem may be that there is very little noncompliance. None of the empirical studies have found a significant deterrent effect of audits for middle-income wage and salary workers, who were the most compliant audit class in 1969. Interestingly, the audit class for which our model provides the best description of compliance behavior is also the least compliant audit class,

17. As in the structural model, we believe that the significant and negative coefficients on the variables of the proportion of the population over sixty-five for the low-income classes result from the nature of the income exclusions and exemptions allowance given to older taxpayers. At low-income levels, these tax code effects swamp the compliance effects associated with age.

namely low-income proprietors. Given the attention focused on how audit coverage affects tax compliance, it is disappointing that empirical research has not made more progress. We believe that the major reasons for the lack of progress relate to the data and the secrecy surrounding the IRS's audit selection formulas. Most studies that have considered the effect of audits on compliance have used data that is aggregated to at least the three-digit zip code level. The use of such data to estimate the audit selection rule is potentially a severe problem. With audit coverage in the range of 1 to 5 percent, the audit selection system is primarily an outliers process. To be more specific, the DIF audit selection formulas are primarily selecting returns that are outliers in terms of reporting behavior. The averaging implicit in aggregate data washes out most information on outliers and, therefore, may only very poorly reflect the audit selection rule. An additional reason empirical studies may not have found consistently significant deterrent effects is that the economic research has concentrated on the effects of only one IRS enforcement activity, audits. Other enforcement and service activities of the IRS (e.g., taxpayer services and document matching for W-2 and 1099 forms) also may have significant compliance effects. Part of the reason the reduced-form models show a more consistent deterrent effect than do the structural models may be related to how other IRS activities affect compliance. While little is known about the effects of other IRS enforcement efforts or service activities, some work has been done on how programs directed at return preparers affect reporting behavior (see, e.g., Scotchmer 1989).

While results from the 1969 data sets allow no definite conclusions regarding the effects of audits on compliance, they provide guidance regarding the type of sociodemographic variables to include as controls for "tastes and preferences." Specifically, the results from the study of the 1969 data base suggest that the age, sex, and race of the taxpayer and the taxpayer's education and country of birth affect compliance. The results of work with the 1969 data base also suggest that it is important to consider the provisions of the tax code when constructing and interpreting the coefficients on sociodemographic variables. Variables such as the age of the taxpayer may be related both to specific provisions of the tax code and to attitudes toward compliance.

Careful comparison of existing work also indicates that, when interpreting the coefficients of compliance models, it is important to consider the model specification carefully. The results appear sensitive to the dependent variable used and to the vector of explanatory variables included. All previous research that has used 1969 data bases has estimated a single compliance equation with a dependent variable that is either directly (Clotfelter 1983) or indirectly (Dubin and Wilde 1988; Witte and Woodbury 1985) linked to auditors' findings.[18] The results of this research need to be interpreted with care, because coefficients reflect auditors' as well as taxpayers' behavior. For example, our results suggest that previous findings (Dubin and Wilde 1988; Witte and Woodbury 1985) that increased unemployment is generally associated with decreased compliance may be due to tax auditors' abilities to uncover overstated deductions.

REFERENCES

Blumstein, A., J. Cohen, J. A. Roth, and C. A. Visher, eds. 1986. *Criminal Careers and "Career Criminals."* Washington, D.C.: National Academy Press.

Clotfelter, C. T. 1983. "Tax Evasion and Tax Rates: An Analysis of Individual Returns." *Review of Economics and Statistics* 47:363–74.

Commissioner of Internal Revenue. 1970. *1970 Annual Report.* Washington, D.C.: Department of the Treasury.

Comptroller General. 1976. *How the IRS Selects Individual Income Tax Returns for Audit.* Washington, D.C.: General Accounting Office.

Comptroller General. 1979. *Who's Not Filing Income Tax Returns?* Washington D.C.: General Accounting Office.

Dubin, J. A., M. J. Graetz, and L. L. Wilde. 1987. "Are We a Nation of Tax Cheaters? New Econometric Evidence on Tax Compliance." *American Economic Review* 77:240–45.

Dubin, J. A., and L. L. Wilde. 1988. "An Empirical Analysis of Federal Income Tax Auditing and Compliance." *National Tax Journal* 16:61–74.

Internal Revenue Service. 1969. *IRS Office Location.* Washington, D.C.: IRS.

Internal Revenue Service. 1983. *Income Tax Compliance Research: Estimates for 1973–1981.* Washington, D.C.: IRS.

Intriligator, M. D. 1978. *Econometric Models and Applications.* Englewood Cliffs, N.J.: Prentice-Hall.

Jackson, B. R., and V. C. Milliron. 1986. "Tax Compliance Research, Findings, Problems and Prospects." *Journal of Accounting Literature* 5:125–65.

Kinsey, K. A. 1984a. "Survey Data on Tax Compliance: A Compendium and Review." Working Paper 84-1. Chicago: American Bar Foundation.

Kinsey, K. A. 1984b. "Theories and Models of Tax Evasion." Working Paper 84-2. Chicago: American Bar Foundation.

Klepper, S., and D. Nagin. 1989. "The Anatomy of Tax Evasion." *Journal of Law, Economics, and Organization* 5:1–24.

Long, S. 1985. "The Impact of Information on Law Enforcement." Working Paper, School of Business Administration, Syracuse University. Photocopy.

---

18. The dependent variable used by Witte and Woodbury (1985) and Dubin and Wilde (1988) is particularly troublesome. The measure of compliance is created from the DIF scores, and results using this dependent variable will reflect the DIF formulas as well as taxpayer and auditor behavior.

Poterba, J. A. 1987. "Tax Evasion and Capital Gain Taxation." *American Economic Review* 77:234–39.

Reinganum, J. F., and L. L. Wilde. 1985. "Income Tax Compliance in a Principal-Agent Framework." *Journal of Public Economics* 26:1–34.

Roth, J., J. Scholz, and A. D. Witte, eds. 1989. *Tax Compliance: An Agenda for Research.* Philadelphia: University of Pennsylvania Press.

Schmidt, P. 1989. "Statistical Issues in Modeling Taxpayer Compliance." In *Taxpayer Compliance: An Agenda for Research,* ed. J. Roth, J. Scholz, and A. D. Witte. Philadelphia: University of Pennsylvania Press.

Schmidt, P., and A. D. Witte. 1984. *An Economic Analysis of Crime and Justice.* Orlando, Fla.: Academic Press.

Scotchmer, S. 1989. "The Effect of Tax Advisors on Tax Compliance." In *Tax Compliance: Social Science Perspectives,* ed. J. Roth and J. Scholz, 182–99. Philadelphia: University of Pennsylvania Press.

Tauchen, H. V., and A. D. Witte. 1986a. "Economic Models of How Audit Policies Affect Voluntary Tax Compliance." In *Proceedings of the Annual Conference of the NTA-TIA,* 39–45. Columbus, Ohio: National Tax Association.

Tauchen, H. V., and A. D. Witte. 1986b. "The Impact of Law and Administrative Rules and Compliance." Proposal to the National Science Foundation. Available from the National Bureau of Economic Research.

Tauchen, H. V., A. D. Witte, and K. J. Beron. 1989. "Tax Compliance: An Investigation Using Individual TCMP Data." NBER Working Paper no. 3078. Cambridge, Mass.: National Bureau of Economic Research.

Weddick, J. L., Jr. 1983. "Looking for a Needle in a Haystack—How the IRS Selects Returns for Audit." *The Tax Advisor,* November.

Wilson, J. Q., and R. J. Herrnstein. 1985. *Crime and Human Nature.* New York: Simon and Schuster.

Wilt, D. E. 1986. "Trends in DIF and DIF-Related Source Examinations." In *Trend Analysis and Related Statistics,* 47–56. Washington D.C.: IRS.

Witte, A. D., and D. F. Woodbury. 1983a. "The Effect of Tax Laws and Tax Administration on Tax Compliance." Working Paper 83-1, Department of Economics, University of North Carolina, Chapel Hill. Photocopy.

Witte, A. D., and D. F. Woodbury. 1983b. "What We Know About Factors Affecting Compliance with the Tax Laws." In *Income Tax Compliance Research: A Report of the ABA Section on Taxation,* ed. P. Sawicki, 133–48. Washington, D.C.: American Bar Association.

Witte, A. D., and D. F. Woodbury. 1985 "The Effect of Tax Laws and Tax Administration on Tax Compliance." *National Tax Journal* 38:1–13.

Commentary

Jonathan S. Feinstein

In their essay, Beron, Tauchen, and Witte present a valuable analysis of tax compliance, both contributing a number of new empirical findings and synthesizing some of the earlier work in this area. The authors are experienced researchers with a thorough grasp of the relevant issues, and they present a balanced and clear account of their work. I found their discussion helpful in making sense of the myriad results cited in this literature. I also found a number of their new results (or new emphases) provocative. However, I perceive a number of problems with their analysis, both in terms of specification and interpretation. In the following, I will address both the strengths and weaknesses of the essay, taking up in turn questions of specification, data, and results.

Specification

The authors posit a linear regression system with three equations: the first refers to income reported by filers, the second to tax liability claimed, and the third to the probability of audit. Two aspects of this model stand out as useful extensions of the standard approach. First, the separation of income reporting from liability: noncompliance in the first category occurs when a filer understates adjusted gross income, whereas noncompliance in the second category also includes overstated deductions. As the authors point out, these two categories of noncompliance are conceptually distinct and may respond differently to the risk of audit or to specifics of the tax code. I believe this point was first made by Klepper and Nagin (1989), but it is not yet widely accepted. Secondly, the authors emphasize that the probability of audit should enter into the income reporting and liability equations (since a greater chance of audit should deter evasion) and, most interestingly, is endogenous. The authors have been pioneers in introducing this specification, and it is an important step forward.

Unfortunately, other aspects of the specification are quite troubling. The authors emphasize that they are using reported income and reported tax liability rather than direct measures of noncompliance. They are correct in noting that measures of noncompliance are typically poorly measured, because IRS auditors do not catch all evasion on a return (invalidating even TCMP noncompliance data); however, this problem can be dealt with using detection-controlled models of the kind discussed in Alexander and Feinstein (1987) and Feinstein (1990). I find their measure even more worrisome. Of course, at a certain theoretical level, the use of income reported would be fully equivalent to use of noncompliance data. At a practical level, however, noncompliance is only a very small fraction of income (for most, if not all, of the filer groups considered in the essay). As their true measure of income, the authors use a census measure, which is included as an independent variable in the two reporting equations. Since evasion is rarely more than a few percent of income, I would expect such a measure to be very close to a perfect fit. The specification then relies on the difference between these two income measures to pick up the link to the audit probability and all other socioeconomic variables, and interprets these links as measures of propensity to evade. This is surely a problem of the tail wagging the dog. There is bound to be enormous noise (relative to the evasion "signal") in this difference for at least two reasons. First, the census measure is itself imperfect. Second, the specification is a simple linear regression, whereas numerous exemptions and deductions will make the relationship between income and tax return data highly complex and nonlinear.

These observations lead to a number of additional worrisome implications. First, the R^2 measures for the regressions are simply not relevant to the issue of compliance: almost all of the explanatory power of the regressions undoubtedly derives from the regression of one income measure on another; from this viewpoint, I find the reported R^2s surprisingly low. Further, most of the coefficients must simply be interpreted as proxies for tax return nuances that are correlated with socioeconomic characteristics (such as family size, retirement status, or homeownership).

I have a few constructive suggestions about how this specification might be improved. On the one hand, I would recommend moving from a simple linear specification to a richer specification, such as a translog kind of model. This would at least help control for some of the nonlinearities. On the other hand, it would be even better to use some sort of tax simulation program to account directly for the tax code effects of various filer characteristics.

My final set of comments about the specification relates to the audit variable. At a number of places in the text, the authors refer to the game-theoretic model in which the audit probability on any given return is neither zero nor one, but instead is between zero and one, reflecting a mixed strategy (see Reinganum and Wilde [1986] for the original contribution). I believe the authors misapply this result in interpreting their model. Although the audit probability is random for any given return, it is assuredly not random for an entire zip code region. An audit value between zero and one for aggregate data should be interpreted as a simple fraction—that is, that fraction of the district's returns will be audited. Jumping ahead a little bit, I believe the authors use a confusing terminology in their discussion of results. They seem to imply that an increased probability of audit increases reported income and tax liability and claim that this result contradicts the "random audit" hypothesis. If random audit refers to an audit policy that is completely unrelated to income reporting and filer characteristics, this is correct. But in modern game-theoretic parlance, "random strategy" refers to a mixed strategy in which the probability of audit lies strictly between zero and one. In the game-theoretic context, a higher chance of audit (say one-half instead of one-quarter) will, indeed, discourage noncompliance; hence, "random audit" is consistent with their results. Also, it must be remembered that randomness in each district does not imply equal probability across districts. Finally, although the audit variable is allowed to be endogenous, the model is not a structural econometric model of the underlying game; Erard and Feinstein (1990) present such a model.

Data

The authors fit their model using 1969 tax return data aggregated to the three-digit zip code level. As a way of relating their work to certain previously published studies, this is a fine choice of data. However, I see two problems with this choice. First and foremost, tax compliance is an individual household decision that should be studied with individual-level data. Given that such data is available from the IRS (witness Alexander and Feinstein 1987; Clotfelter 1983; Erard 1990; Feinstein 1990; Klepper and Nagin 1989), I feel it would be preferable to use it. The only advantage the aggregate data has is that a measure of audit probability is included, but even this may be able to be obtained at the microlevel. A second problem is that the data is very old. Though some of the earlier studies of tax compliance worked with this data, most recent studies have moved on to the 1982 or 1985 TCMP data. Third, I have a question that unfortunately may also be a concern: it appears that the audit data refer to audits performed in 1969, which would then not cover returns filed in 1969, but earlier returns. If this is so, it implies that the audit data are mismatched to the remaining data.

Overall, the authors have put together a quite comprehensive data set. One variable that does not appear is any measure of occupation (other than the crude breakdown into manufacturing and service employment). In some other work, I have found that certain occupational groups (such as lawyers and doctors) have different compliance patterns than the general population, and it would be nice to study those questions in this context. I bring this up, in part, because I believe such data would be available from the Bureau of the Census.

Results

In general, the authors present a rich and thorough battery of results. I found this the most valuable part of the essay. In some cases, new results are presented and interpreted, while the authors make a clear and conscientious effort to link their work to earlier studies in other cases. I will simply comment here on the results that I found especially provocative.

The authors find that higher levels of education typically reduce compliance, and, using a number of supplementary regressions, point out that this effect can be compounded with income effects if both variables are not included in the model. I found this result plausible; my one concern would be that better educated people are better at finding legal loopholes as well as being more willing to gamble on noncompliance (it's not clear these two can be distinguished in the model). I would hope that this result will be explored further in the future.

The authors also find that increased unemployment decreases tax liability, but has little impact on income reported (after controlling for true income using the census measure). Again, this is interesting and worthy of further investigation. I was not convinced by the authors' claim that this result indicates that "underground" economy activities are not more evasion prone. I believe such activities are probably missing on both tax returns and the census data and thus are entirely invisible to the model.

Finally, the authors run a number of auxiliary regressions that indicate that the IRS deters evasion through a number of activities that are separate from the audit process. Judging from the IRS's own view on this topic, this seems likely. In conversations with IRS officials, it has become clear that they believe compliance can be increased by being more "friendly" to filers and by advertising or otherwise broadcasting the compliance message. Again, I think this topic deserves further research.

REFERENCES

Alexander, Craig, and Jonathan S. Feinstein. 1987. "A Microeconometric Analysis of Individual Income Tax Evasion." Massachusetts Institute of Technology. Mimeo.

Clotfelter, Charles. 1983. "Tax Evasion and Tax Rates: An Analysis of Individual Returns." *Review of Economics and Statistics* 65.

Erard, Brian. 1990. "Tax Practitioners and Tax Compliance: A Microeconometric Analysis of the Decision to Engage a Tax Preparer and its Consequences." Ph.D. diss., University of Michigan.

Erard, Brian, and Jonathan S. Feinstein. 1990. "An Econometric Model of the Tax Compliance Game." Stanford University Graduate School of Business. Mimeo.

Feinstein, Jonathan S. 1991. "An Econometric Analysis of Income Tax Evasion and Its Detection." *RAND Journal of Economics* 22.

Klepper, Steven, and Daniel Nagin. 1989. "The Anatomy of Tax Evasion." *Journal of Law, Economics, and Organization* 5.

Reinganum, Jennifer, and Louis L. Wilde. 1986. "Equilibrium Verification and Reporting Policies in a Model of Tax Compliance." *International Economic Review* 27.

The Influence of Tax Audits on Reporting Behavior

Brian Erard

The Internal Revenue Service estimates that the gap between income taxes owed and income taxes voluntarily paid amounted to $95 billion in 1986—a figure representing nearly one-half of the federal budget deficit for that year. This revelation prompted Congressman Byron L. Dorgan to launch a bipartisan task force investigation of ways to reduce the tax gap. One of the recommendations of the task force was to raise the audit rate from its 1986 level of 1.14 percent to 2.50 percent by 1992. If this recommendation were to be enacted, the increased examinations, in principle, could have both direct and indirect revenue consequences. A higher audit rate would translate directly into increased tax revenues through the collection of greater amounts of unpaid taxes and penalties. In addition, there would be two potential sources of indirect revenue gains. First, if audited taxpayers respond to the examination experience by improving their compliance in subsequent years, then a higher frequency of tax audits should promote additional future tax revenues. Second, if taxpayers who are not audited nevertheless perceive a greater threat of examination, they also may improve their compliance behavior. Although researchers have had some success in quantifying the direct impact of tax examinations on tax revenue, relatively little is known about the indirect effects of tax audits on tax compliance. In this essay, the influence of tax audits on subsequent year reporting behavior is investigated using IRS data sources on taxpayers who were the targets of an audit in one year and, purely by chance, were the subjects of a second audit two years later.

This essay is based on research that I performed while I was an employee of the Internal Revenue Service. I am grateful to Charles Bennett, Alan Plumley, Joel Slemrod, and Aileen Thompson for their helpful comments and suggestions; to Mary Helen Risler for her valuable assistance; and to the Internal Revenue Service, particularly Dennis Cox, for providing me with the support necessary to perform this analysis. The opinions expressed in this essay are my own, and they should not be attributed to the Internal Revenue Service.

Conceptual Issues

In the early economic models of tax evasion (e.g., Allingham and Sandmo 1972), tax audits do not provide any information that would influence future reporting behavior. In these models, taxpayers are already aware of the (exogenous) probability of audit and detection; they know their true taxable incomes; and they are familiar with the penalties for noncompliance. Based on this information, they choose an amount to report to maximize expected utility. An audit is simply an instance of a taxpayer losing the "tax lottery"; no information is gained that would be useful in future reporting decisions. In more recent models, researchers allow for the possibility that taxpayers may not be fully aware of their tax circumstances. For example, in Alm (1988), Beck and Jung (1989), Scotchmer (1989), and Scotchmer and Slemrod (1989), taxpayers are uncertain of their true levels of taxable income. Under conditions of uncertainty, it is feasible that an audit might play a valuable informational role that would influence future taxpayer reporting activities. Taxpayers who want to comply with the tax laws may gain a better understanding of how the laws apply to their particular circumstances from an audit. This would make it possible for them to file more accurate returns in the future. In contrast, strategic tax evaders may use the information they obtain from audits to develop more effective noncompliance strategies. In addition to gaining a better understanding of their true tax liabilities, these individuals may learn about such enforcement issues as the detectability of noncompliance, opportunities for the appeal of tax judgments, and criteria for the imposition of penalties that would be of use to them in forming future reporting strategies.

An important issue ignored in most models of tax compliance is the repeated nature of tax reporting activities. Greenberg (1984) examines the issue of auditing within a multiperiod framework. His results indicate that making audit probabilities contingent on the results of previous audits can be effective in reducing the overall level of tax evasion. Tax evasion is discouraged in his model by a policy of auditing all future returns of persistent tax offenders. If audit probabilities are conditioned on prior audit experience, it is plausible that taxpayers will take this information into account when forming noncompliance strategies, as they do in Greenberg's model.

The quality of a taxpayer's audit experience also may influence his or her subsequent reporting decisions. Tittle (1980) summarizes evidence indicating an important relationship between perceptions of fairness and compliance with societal rules and regulations. A positive audit experience may encourage future tax compliance; a negative audit experience may discourage it.

Prior Empirical Research

Although a fair amount of empirical research has been performed on the general deterrent effect of an audit (e.g., Beron, Tauchen, and Witte 1988; Dubin and Wilde 1988; Tauchen, Witte, and Beron 1989; Witte and Woodbury 1985) there have been relatively few studies of the specific deterrent effect of an audit on subsequent year reporting behavior. Spicer and Lundstedt (1976) examine the relationship between prior audit experience and tax compliance using survey data on 130 Ohio households. The authors find a positive relationship between an index of reported tax evasion and prior audit experience based on a multiple regression; however, the authors do not state how the evasion index was created. If the index was based on reported prior tax evasion, then the results simply may be an indication that returns that understate income are relatively more likely to be audited.

Spicer and Hero (1985) perform an experimental study of factors influencing taxpayer compliance decisions. This study involves a game played by thirty-six University of Colorado undergraduates in which the participants were asked to make tax reports based on their true income, a random audit probability, and a preannounced penalty rate. The game was played for ten rounds.[1] The results indicate a significant positive relationship between tax compliance on the final round and the number of prior audit experiences. This finding is rather curious, given the random nature of the audit selection process used in the experiment. The authors do not state whether participants were able to observe the frequency of audits taking place in each round. If the frequency of audits could not be observed, it is plausible that taxpayers relied on personal audit experience to gauge the random audit probability. An alternative explanation is that those participants who experienced a number of audits began to doubt that the audit selection process was, in fact, random. A second finding from this study is that the level of evasion on the final round of play is positively correlated with the level of evasion on the first round, indicating the persistence of noncompliance over time.

Long and Schwartz (1987) investigate the impact of tax audits on subsequent year reporting behavior using audit data from an IRS Taxpayer Compliance Measurement Program (TCMP) panel study. This data source contains information on 2,171 taxpayers who were subjected to audits of their 1969 tax returns and, subsequently (without prior warning), of their 1971 returns.[2] The

---

1. The participants were informed of the length of the game prior to beginning play.

2. The data used in this study consist of a stratified random sample from the population of filers of nonbusiness returns with adjusted gross incomes of less than $50,000 and filers of business and farm returns with less than $10,000 income.

TCMP audits experienced by these taxpayers differed from ordinary operational IRS audits in two important ways. First, the returns were randomly chosen for audit. IRS ordinarily targets returns for audit that are expected to result in substantial tax changes. The random nature of the audit selection process for this experiment makes it possible to compare the audit results for 1969 returns in the sample with those for 1971 returns without the need to control for the possible confounding influences of a nonrandom audit selection criterion. Second, the audits were unusually thorough in that every line item on the return was examined. In contrast, ordinary IRS audits typically concern only a small number of issues relating to a tax return. The thoroughness of the TCMP audits allows relatively accurate measurement of tax noncompliance. The authors perform a statistical comparison of audit results for the 1969 and 1971 tax returns in the sample. Differences in both the frequency and magnitude of tax adjustments across years are examined. The results indicate that the 1969 TCMP audit was marginally effective in reducing the overall frequency of 1971 tax noncompliance by taxpayers in the sample, but not its average size. In addition, the frequency of large tax adjustments (adjustments of more than $1,000) was not significantly different between the samples of 1969 and 1971 tax returns. Unfortunately, the very features that facilitated an analysis of the data—random selection and audit thoroughness—limit the generalizability of the results from this study to the responses of taxpayers experiencing ordinary operational audits. Because taxpayers were notified that TCMP audit selection was random, they may not have formed the same perceptions as they would have had they been selected for audit under an ordinary program. Moreover, as the authors point out, the unusual thoroughness of the audits may have resulted in atypical taxpayer experiences.

Data Sources

The current study is based on two IRS data sources. The first is the 1982 IRS TCMP Survey. This data source contains the results of thorough, line-by-line audits of a large stratified random sample of 1982 federal individual income tax returns. In addition to information about the 1982 tax return audits, the data file includes limited information about the prior year return characteristics of all taxpayers in the TCMP sample, including whether their previous two tax returns were audited. In contrast to the 1982 TCMP examination, any audits of 1980 or 1981 tax returns would have been ordinary operational audits. Thus, the data set contains information about two groups of individuals: (1) taxpayers who were targeted for an ordinary audit in one year who, purely by chance, were selected for a thorough TCMP audit in a subsequent year; and (2) taxpayers who were selected for a thorough TCMP audit who had not been audited in the recent past. In addition to indicators for whether either of a taxpayer's previous two tax returns were audited, the data file contains information concerning the results of these prior audits. The file contains the net amount of recommended tax and penalty assessments for those taxpayers who agreed with the auditor's finding. In those cases where the recommended tax and penalty assessments from a prior audit were appealed, the data file contains the actual amount of tax and penalty assessments that were imposed if the case was settled by the time the 1982 TCMP data set was created. Unfortunately, the tax and penalty assessment field for prior audits that were not settled by this time contains the same code used to indicate that the prior audit resulted in no recommended tax change, thus rendering these two cases indistinguishable. Another potential limitation of this data source is that, in a small number of cases, the audit of a prior year tax return may have been a direct result of the 1982 TCMP audit.[3]

The second data source is based primarily on the 1985 TCMP Survey. Although the TCMP survey for that year does not include the prior audit history of taxpayers, this information was obtained through a social security number match with IRS records on audits of 1983 and 1984 tax returns that were closed by the end of the 1988 processing year. These records include nearly all 1983 audits and the vast majority of 1984 audits that were performed. Information from the 1985 TCMP Survey was used to identify those 1983 and 1984 tax return audits that were initiated in response to the 1985 TCMP examination. The data obtained through this match includes the examiner-recommended tax and penalty assessments resulting from the prior audits. Also available is information concerning the disposition of prior audit cases. From this information, it is possible to determine whether the taxpayer agreed with the examiner-recommended tax and penalty assessments or if these assessments were protested. Unfortunately, this data source contains no information about the prior year return characteristics of taxpayers in the 1985 TCMP Survey who did not experience a prior audit.

Clearly these two data sources have different relative merits and flaws. The first data source contains some information about prior year return characteristics both for taxpayers who experienced prior audits and for those who did not. However, the data on prior audit assessments is incomplete, and no information is available concerning the disposition of prior audit cases. The second data source contains no information about the prior year return characteristics of taxpayers who were not audited, but it contains complete

3. According to IRS sources, it is possible that the recording of prior year audit histories may have taken place after some of the 1982 TCMP cases were completed and posted to the master file. As a result, a small number of the prior year return audit cases identified may actually have been initiated in response to findings from the 1982 TCMP examination.

information on prior audit assessments as well as the disposition of prior audit cases.

In the next section, a methodology is developed for taking advantage of the relative merits of these data sources to investigate the influence of tax audits on subsequent year reporting behavior.

Methodology

Both of the data sources for this study contain the audit history of the returns taxpayers filed for the two years preceding the filing of the TCMP tax year return. Tax returns normally are selected for audit over a period of approximately one year, beginning in October of the year the returns are filed. For example, 1990 tax year returns are due in April 1991. Audit selection for these returns will most likely take place between October, 1991, and September, 1992. As a result of the timing of the audit selection process, many audits of returns filed for the tax year immediately preceding the TCMP tax year would not have taken place prior to the filing of TCMP tax year returns. Consequently, I focus on the impact of audits of returns filed two years prior to the filing of the TCMP tax year return on TCMP tax year compliance.

Two approaches are used to examine the influence of a tax audit on subsequent year reporting behavior. The first approach involves an examination of whether taxpayers who experienced tax changes from a prior year audit experienced lower tax changes from their subsequent year TCMP audits. Such a finding would be consistent with the notion that audits have a positive influence on subsequent year tax compliance. However, because factors other than prior audit experience are not controlled for, the results of this analysis will be subject to alternative explanations. If other aspects of the taxpayers' compliance decisions were changing over the periods under investigation, then they, rather than the audit, may be responsible for the observed changes in reporting behavior. For measurement reasons, only taxpayers who experienced substantial tax changes as a result of their prior year audits are used in the comparison. Because ordinary operational audits generally involve only a small number of line items on a return, nondetection of tax noncompliance is a relatively more serious problem for these audits than it is for TCMP audits. A small audit change resulting from an ordinary examination might indicate either a relatively compliant return or a return with large amounts of undetected noncompliance. By focusing only on cases in which the prior year return audit uncovered substantial noncompliance, nondetection of tax noncompliance poses a less serious problem. If a prior year return shows a great deal of noncompliance and a subsequent year return subjected to a more thorough audit shows little noncompliance, this is relatively strong evidence of a movement toward more compliant reporting. As pointed out by Susan B. Long, however, it is expected that a group of taxpayers with large prior audit assessments, even in the absence of a positive audit effect, would show some reduction in overall tax noncompliance simply because of regression toward the mean. Thus, an improvement in compliance by taxpayers with substantial prior year audit assessments would not provide conclusive evidence of a positive influence of tax audits on subsequent year tax compliance.

The second approach to examining the influence of tax audits on subsequent year tax compliance involves an analysis of whether, after controlling for factors that influence the compliance decision, taxpayers who have experienced recent prior audits differ in their compliance behavior from those who have not experienced recent prior audits. A difficulty in performing this analysis is that the selection of returns for ordinary operational audits is not random. Rather, selection is based on IRS perceptions of the likelihood that an audit will uncover substantial reporting errors. If compliance behavior is correlated over time, it is important to control for the role of the audit selection process in subsequent year compliance outcomes. It is possible to control for this process in a limited way using the 1982 TCMP data set. This set contains the prior year levels of reported income as well as indicators for presence of Schedule C (business) and Schedule F (farm) returns for all taxpayers in the sample. When the IRS selects returns for audit, it classifies returns into audit classes on the basis of these variables.[4] Audit coverage tends to be greater within the business and farm return classes than the nonbusiness classes. Moreover, within a return category, audit coverage tends to be higher among the upper reported-income classes.[5] Within an audit class, the IRS selects returns for audit based on tax return characteristics and other available information that are judged to be significantly related to tax noncompliance.

To analyze the influence of an audit on subsequent year reporting behavior, a two-equation sample selection model is estimated. The first equation is a probit specification of the IRS decision to audit a taxpayer's 1980 tax return. This decision is modeled as a function of the limited information available on the prior year return characteristics of the taxpayer. The second equation specifies noncompliance on the TCMP year tax return as a function of taxpayer characteristics, including prior audit experience. To account for the mass of taxpayers in the sample who apparently file perfectly compliant returns, a tobit specification for TCMP tax year noncompliance is employed.[6] The model is specified as follows.

---

4. Actually, the income concepts used for classification (total positive income and total gross receipts) are somewhat different than the measure that is available (adjusted gross income).

5. This information is detailed in the 1982 Annual Report, Commissioner and Chief Counsel, IRS, 50.

6. Taxpayers who either correctly report or overreport taxable income are treated as compliant taxpayers in this model.

$$A_i^* = \beta_1' X_{1i} + \epsilon_{1i} ,$$

and

$$N_i^* = \beta_2' X_{2i} + \gamma A_i + \epsilon_{2i} ,$$

where A_i^* is a latent variable for the propensity of IRS to audit the ith taxpayer's prior year return; A_i is a dummy variable for whether or not the ith taxpayer's prior return actually was audited; N_i^* is a latent variable for the propensity of the ith taxpayer to underreport taxable income on his or her 1982 tax return; and X_{1i} and X_{2i} are vectors of explanatory variables for the ith taxpayer. The prior audit indicator is included to capture the influence of an audit on subsequent year reporting behavior.

To control for possible sample selection bias resulting from the prior year audit selection procedure, a correlation, ρ, is allowed between the disturbances ϵ_{1i} and ϵ_{2i}. It is assumed that these disturbances are jointly normally distributed with variances of one and σ^2, respectively. If ρ were equal to zero, this would imply the absence of sample selection bias from the prior year audit selection process. In this case, the prior year audit equation would be independent of the subsequent year noncompliance equation in the model, and single equation tobit estimation could be employed to consistently estimate the impact of a prior audit on TCMP year tax noncompliance. A zero correlation would exist if taxpayer compliance decisions were independent across tax years. In this case, unobservable factors that influenced the IRS's decision to audit a return in one year would be uncorrelated with subsequent year tax noncompliance. In their experimental study, Spicer and Hero (1985) find that taxpayer compliance decisions are positively correlated over time. A positive value for ρ would imply that unobserved factors that positively influenced the chances of an audit in one year (other factors held constant) would be associated with greater subsequent year tax noncompliance.

The following example illustrates the importance of accounting for the role of the audit selection process in subsequent year compliance outcomes. Suppose that the same taxpayers were responsible for deliberate noncompliance each tax season and that audits had no impact on their reporting behavior. One tax season, the tax authority learns of the reporting strategy being used by these willful evaders and audits all returns consistent with the known evasion strategy. In the subsequent year, a random sample of tax returns is subjected to audit. The results indicate that taxpayers who experienced a recent prior audit tend to have greater levels of noncompliance than those who did not experience a recent prior audit. Unless the prior year audit selection procedure were taken into account, a researcher would incorrectly conclude from this finding that audits have a detrimental impact on subsequent year tax compliance. The failure to appreciate the difference between the role of audit experience and the role of audit selection in subsequent year compliance outcomes can result in biased inferences.

Although the IRS, perhaps, does not have such accurate knowledge of the identities of tax evaders as the tax authority in the above example, it is capable of identifying factors that are correlated with noncompliance on tax returns. If unobserved factors that influence the IRS's decision to audit a return (e.g., suspicious-looking deductions) represent manifestations of persistent behavioral factors influencing taxpayer compliance decisions (e.g., an enduring desire to "beat the system"), it is important to control for the role of the audit selection process in subsequent year compliance outcomes. In my model, the role of audit selection in subsequent year tax noncompliance is captured by the correlation term; the role of audit experience in subsequent year tax noncompliance is captured by the audit dummy.

Because audit rates tend to be low, the vast majority of observations in the data set are for taxpayers who did not experience a recent prior audit. To reduce the computational burden involved in the estimation of the model, only a one-in-eight randomly chosen subsample of taxpayers with no recent prior audit experience is used in the estimation. The entire subsample of taxpayers with a prior audit experience is used. To correct for the bias introduced by this choice-based sampling approach, a method developed by Manski and Lerman (1977) involving the maximization of a pseudolikelihood function is employed. This procedure involves weighting the contribution of each observation to the likelihood function by the reciprocal of its probability of being kept in the sample.[7] This procedure generates consistent and asymptotically normally distributed estimators.

Results

In this section, the results of the two approaches for analyzing the influence of tax audits on subsequent year reporting behavior are presented and discussed.

Results of the First Approach

The first approach to analyzing the influence of an audit on subsequent year reporting behavior is to examine whether taxpayers who experienced large audit adjustments on their prior year tax returns tended to experience smaller audit adjustments on their TCMP year tax returns. Table 1 presents information on the real (1982 dollars) tax and penalty assessments for taxpayers who

7. For example, since the probability that the return of a taxpayer with no recent prior audit experience is kept in the sample is 1/8, observations from this category are given a weight of 8

TABLE 1. Frequency of TCMP Tax and Penalty Assessments by Prior Year Audit Assessment Range for Taxpayers with Large Prior Year Audit Assessments (in percentages)

TCMP Assessment	Prior Year Audit Assessment Range		
	$501 to $1,000	$1,001 to $5,000	More than $5,000
		Tax Year 1982[a]	
Less than −$500	6.83	7.97	2.70
−$500– −101	0.12	3.80	1.61
−$100– −1	5.56	0.90	0.18
$0	28.61	10.78	21.16
$1–100	16.29	5.67	8.99
$101–500	21.82	31.41	2.17
$501–1,000	8.97	15.64	20.25
$1,001–5,000	10.00	19.82	16.99
More than $5,000	1.81	4.00	25.95
Unweighted *N*	663	255	68
		Tax Year 1985[b]	
Less than −$500	1.19	4.92	3.84
−$500– −101	0.79	12.64	3.42
−$100– −1	5.24	4.89	2.49
$0	24.09	11.39	16.28
$1–100	9.42	6.31	10.03
$101–500	32.59	27.86	11.37
$501–1,000	14.06	12.25	3.67
$1,001–5,000	11.53	16.27	32.86
More than $5,000	1.10	3.49	16.05
Unweighted *N*	204	356	176

[a]Prior year is 1980.
[b]Prior year is 1983.

experienced audits of their TCMP year returns in a period subsequent to their being audited for the returns they filed two years earlier.[8] Only taxpayers experiencing a real assessment of more than $500 on their prior year returns are included in the table. The statistics are weighted to make the results representative of the general filing population. Both the 1982 and 1985 TCMP data sources indicate a strong tendency for improvement in compliance by taxpayers with substantial prior year audit assessments. For the 1982 TCMP

8. In the case of the 1982 TCMP data source, no taxpayers were included who experienced audits of their 1981 tax returns. The purpose of this measure was to minimize the possibility that the 1980 tax return was audited as a result of the 1982 TCMP examination.

data source, only 21 percent of taxpayers experiencing a prior audit assessment in the $501 to $1,000 range experienced a TCMP audit assessment of this much or more, while 29 percent of these individuals had no audit assessment at all from their TCMP examinations. For the 1985 TCMP data source, the corresponding figures are 27 percent and 24 percent, respectively. For the 1982 TCMP data source, only 24 percent of all taxpayers experiencing a prior audit assessment in the $1,001 to $5,000 range received a TCMP audit of this amount or more, while 11 percent had no audit assessment at all from their TCMP examinations. For the 1985 TCMP data source, the corresponding figures are 20 percent and 11 percent, respectively. For the 1982 TCMP data source, only 26 percent of taxpayers experiencing a prior year assessment in the greater than $5,000 range experienced a TCMP audit adjustment that was also in this range, and 21 percent actually had no audit assessment at all from their TCMP examinations. The corresponding figures from the 1985 TCMP data source are 16 percent and 16 percent, respectively. The unweighted statistics (not presented) show less dramatic, but still substantial, improvements in reporting behavior by these taxpayers. In contrast to the Long and Schwartz (1987) finding for taxpayers with large prior year audit assessments, the results presented here are encouraging, particularly when one considers that TCMP audits are relatively more likely than operational audits to detect any noncompliance that is present. Although a fair proportion of taxpayers experience substantial audit assessments in both years, a much larger proportion show improved tax compliance from the prior audit year to the TCMP tax year; in fact, perfect TCMP year tax compliance is observed for a substantial proportion of these individuals. Although this result is consistent with a positive influence of audits on subsequent year tax compliance, the evidence is not conclusive. As mentioned previously, some improvement in compliance is expected among taxpayers with large prior audit assessments simply as a result of regression toward the mean.

Explanatory Variables for the Second Approach

The second approach to analyzing the influence of tax audits on subsequent year tax reporting behavior is to estimate a two-equation sample selection model of prior year audit selection and current year tax noncompliance. This model involves the joint estimation of a probit specification for whether a taxpayer's 1980 income tax return was audited and a tobit specification for the level of noncompliance on the taxpayer's 1982 tax return. The explanatory variables included in the probit equation are:

- CON80—a unit vector for estimating the constant term;
- INC80—the maximum of the taxpayer's reported adjusted gross in-

come or \$5,000, divided by \$100,000 as a normalization;
- SCHC80—a dummy for whether the taxpayer completed a Schedule C (business) return for tax year 1980; and
- SCHF80—a dummy for whether the taxpayer completed a Schedule F (farm) return for tax year 1980.

As discussed in the previous section, these variables are related to the classification scheme used in determining audit coverage rates.

The dependent variable in the tobit equation for noncompliance is the difference between the examiner-determined and taxpayer-reported levels of taxable income, divided by \$1,000 as a normalization. This is a rather broad measure of noncompliance that accounts for inaccurate reporting of both income and deduction items. The explanatory variables for the compliance equation were selected after considering the variables used in previous TCMP studies of tax compliance by Clotfelter (1983), Alexander and Feinstein (1987), and Erard (1990). The variables used in the current study include:

- CON—a unit vector for estimating the constant term;
- IMAR—a dummy for married return;
- TOTDEP—the total number of dependents;
- I65—a dummy for the taxpayer claiming age exemption;
- INCOME—the maximum of adjusted gross income or \$5,000, divided by \$100,000 as a normalization;
- EASY—a dummy for a return with wages, salaries, and interest as the only income source, with interest income less than \$400;
- SCHC—a dummy for Schedule C return;
- SCHF—a dummy for Schedule F return;
- SCHD—a dummy for Schedule D return;
- MTAX—the statutory marginal tax rate; and
- AUD80—a dummy for audit of 1980 tax return.

Wherever possible, the explanatory variables are based on examiner-determined values. This is desirable in that examiner-determined values should represent a better approximation of true taxpayer characteristics. To distinguish clearly between the subpopulation of taxpayers who experienced a prior audit of their 1980 tax returns and the subpopulation of taxpayers who did not, taxpayers experiencing audits of their 1981 tax returns are excluded from the analysis. In addition, taxpayers whose second prior year return was not a 1980 tax return also are excluded from the study.[9]

9. These two exclusion criteria resulted in the elimination of 262 observations.

Results of the Second Approach

Table 2 presents (weighted) summary statistics for selected variables from the 1982 and 1985 data files.[10] Separate statistics are presented for taxpayers with and without prior audit experiences. Notice that taxpayers who have experienced prior audits tend to have much higher levels of income, are relatively more likely to file Schedules C, D, or F, and are relatively unlikely to have "easy" returns. For the subsample of taxpayers in the 1985 data file who experienced a prior audit, the table also provides the proportions of taxpayers who experienced no audit assessment, agreed with a recommended audit assessment, protested a recommended audit assessment, or failed to acknowledge a recommended audit assessment.

The audit-induced changes in taxable income and tax amount tend to be substantially larger for taxpayers with prior audit experience than for taxpayers with no prior audit experience. Although this finding would be consistent with a negative influence of audits on subsequent year reporting behavior, it also may be attributable to other factors that differ among the two groups of taxpayers. This issue is investigated using the sample selection model described in the previous section. The results of the analysis indicate a small and statistically insignificant value for the correlation ρ between the disturbances of the two equations in the model. This result is somewhat surprising, because it implies that there is no correlation between unobserved factors that influenced the IRS decision to audit a taxpayer's 1980 return and unobserved factors that influenced the taxpayer's 1982 tax report. As mentioned previously, such a finding is consistent with the notion that, in the absence of an audit, taxpayer compliance decisions are independent across tax years; however, this assumption seems implausible. One would expect that a taxpayer who has a relatively high propensity toward noncompliance in one tax year, in the absence of any substantial changes in his or her circumstances, will have a relatively high propensity toward noncompliance in subsequent years as well.[11]

Table 3 presents the results of estimating the single equation tobit model that applies under the zero disturbance correlation restriction that cannot be rejected by the data. The coefficient of the prior audit experience dummy is positive but not statistically significant. A significant positive coefficient would imply that tax audits have a detrimental impact on subsequent year tax

10. The weighting procedure accounts both for the original stratification of the data sample and the one in eight sampling rule for taxpayers with no prior audit experience.

11. Even if the noncompliance is unintentional, it seems likely that a taxpayer who is prone to making reporting errors in one year, in the absence of any substantial changes in his or her circumstances, will be likely to make reporting errors in subsequent years as well.

TABLE 2. Summary Statistics

Characteristic	Prior Audit	No Prior Audit
	1982 Data Set	
Married	66.7%	51.0%
Age over 65	13.9%	11.6%
Easy filer[a]	9.3%	31.8%
Schedule C filer	29.3%	10.8%
Schedule F filer	4.5%	3.5%
Schedule D filer	29.4%	9.6%
Total dependents	0.89	0.68
Adjusted gross income	$41,390	$19,996
1982 income change	$ 2,600	$ 887
1982 tax change	$ 842	$ 226
Unweighted *N*	1,489	5,744
	1985 Data Set	
Married	67.4%	51.5%
Age over 65	10.1%	11.1%
Easy filer[a]	7.1%	30.8%
Schedule C filer	28.4%	12.1%
Schedule F filer	5.7%	2.3%
Schedule D filer	28.8%	11.9%
No change	24.3%	—
Agreed	50.1%	—
Protest	2.5%	—
Other	23.1%	—
Total dependents	1.08	0.69
Adjusted gross income	$43,497	$23,415
1985 income change	$ 2,686	$ 975
1985 tax change	$ 815	$ 279
Unweighted *N*	1,837	5,631

[a]Only wage and interest income, with interest income less than $400.

compliance. The second column of the table presents the results of an extended analysis in which two additional variables are included in the compliance equation.[12] The first additional variable is equal to 100 times the ratio of 1980 tax and penalty assessments to total 1980 tax liability (including penalties) for taxpayers who experienced a positive 1980 audit assessment.[13]

12. The full sample selection model was estimated for this specification. Since the estimated correlation again was both small and insignificant, the tobit model results are presented.

13. Recall that a zero value is recorded in the assessment field for taxpayers whose cases were unsettled by the time the 1982 TCMP audit was performed. This introduces some unavoidable specification error in the extended analysis.

For all other taxpayers, this variable has a value of zero. The second additional variable is equal to 100 times the ratio of the absolute value of the audit assessment to total reported tax liabilities for taxpayers who experienced a negative 1980 tax assessment. For all other taxpayers, this variable has a value of zero. These variables are included to examine whether there is a relationship between the size of 1980 tax assessments as a percentage of tax liability and 1982 tax noncompliance, after controlling for other factors. The results indicate that 1982 tax noncompliance tends to be larger for taxpayers with large positive 1980 tax assessments as a proportion of tax liability than for taxpayers with similar characteristics whose 1980 tax returns were not

TABLE 3. Results for 1982 Data

Variable	Basic Analysis	Extended Analysis
Constant	−3.787	−3.805
	(−12.94)	(−12.99)
Married	0.157	0.157
	(.62)	(.61)
Total dependents	0.192	0.193
	(2.33)	(2.34)
Age over 65	−0.766	−0.759
	(−2.49)	(−2.46)
Easy filer	−1.143	−1.184
	(−2.28)	(−2.36)
Schedule C filer	4.128	4.125
	(20.16)	(20.12)
Schedule F filer	3.896	3.891
	(17.96)	(17.87)
Schedule D filer	0.578	0.579
	(2.82)	(2.82)
Income	0.204	0.206
	(6.42)	(6.53)
Marginal tax rate	8.992	9.075
	(15.41)	(15.55)
Prior audit	0.371	−0.227
	(.89)	(−.47)
Positive percent change	—	0.042
		(3.16)
Negative percent change		0.025
		(.84)
σ	7.30	7.30
	(179.3)	(179.5)
Likelihood function	−20,332.6	−20,330.3
Unweighted N	7,233	7,233

Note: T-statistics are in parentheses. The dependent variable is the change in taxable income (in thousands of dollars).

audited. In this extended model, the coefficient on prior audit experience becomes negative, but it remains statistically insignificant.

Table 4 presents the results of applying the same basic tobit model of noncompliance to the 1985 TCMP data. Because a substantial number of 1983 tax return audit cases were not closed by the time taxpayers filed their 1985 tax returns, the results are presented both for the entire sample of returns and for a restricted sample that includes only those taxpayers whose audits

TABLE 4. Results for 1985 Data

	Basic Analysis		Extended Analysis	
Variable	Full Sample	Restricted Sample	Full Sample	Restricted Sample
Constant	−6.366	−6.250	−6.375	−6.260
	(−17.90)	(−16.50)	(−17.95)	(−16.50)
Married	−0.298	−0.290	−0.297	−0.292
	(−1.12)	(−1.02)	(−1.11)	(−1.02)
Total dependents	0.012	0.019	0.012	0.018
	(0.15)	(.21)	(.15)	(.26)
Age over 65	−0.911	−0.888	−0.914	−0.887
	(−2.92)	(−2.68)	(−2.93)	(−2.67)
Easy filer	0.561	0.558	0.537	0.532
	(1.03)	(.97)	(.99)	(0.93)
Schedule C filer	4.651	4.670	4.660	4.670
	(22.00)	(20.60)	(21.98)	(20.60)
Schedule F filer	1.526	1.500	1.530	1.500
	(5.45)	(4.96)	(5.46)	(4.95)
Schedule D filer	−0.174	−0.119	−0.168	−0.117
	(−.81)	(−.52)	(−.78)	(−.50)
Income	0.013	0.058	0.013	0.057
	(.316)	(1.44)	(.32)	(1.41)
Marginal tax rate	20.86	20.34	20.88	20.36
	(22.90)	(20.80)	(22.80)	(20.81)
Prior audit	1.395	0.790	0.405	−0.324
	(3.70)	(1.33)	(.56)	(−.28)
Agreed	—	—	0.920	1.290
			(1.03)	(.93)
Protest	—	—	0.046	−0.634
			(.27)	(−0.11)
Other	—	—	2.580	3.653
			(2.44)	(1.81)
σ	7.70	7.61	7.70	7.61
	(167.8)	(155.9)	(167.0)	(155.0)
Likelihood function	−19,627	−16,693	−19,265	−16,692
Unweighted *N*	7,468	6,414	7,468	6,414

Note: T-statistics are in parentheses. The dependent variable is change in taxable income (in thousands of dollars).

were closed by the time they filed their 1985 returns. The results for the basic analysis are quite similar for the full and restricted data sets. They both imply a positive relationship between prior audit experience and tax noncompliance, although the result is statistically significant only for the full data sample. The statistically significant result for the full data sample is driven by those taxpayers whose 1983 audit cases were not settled by the time they filed their 1985 returns. Perhaps these taxpayers did not wish to alter their reporting behavior prior to learning the final outcome of their prior audit cases. An extended analysis was performed in which additional explanatory variables for the disposition of the 1983 audit were included. These variables concern whether the examiner-recommended audit assessment was agreed to, protested, or not acknowledged by the taxpayer. The base case, captured by the prior audit dummy in this specification, is that of a taxpayer experiencing no audit change as a result of his or her 1983 tax return examination. The estimated coefficient of the prior audit dummy in this specification is negative, indicating an improvement in compliance for taxpayers experiencing a prior audit with no additional tax assessment, but its value is not statistically significant. The dummy variable for the "other" disposition category is the only disposition variable to have a significant coefficient. The positive value of this coefficient indicates that noncompliance by taxpayers in the "other" disposition category increased following their prior year audit experience. This category consists of certain problem cases, including taxpayers who refused to acknowledge the examiner-recommended 1983 tax assessments and those who could not be reached regarding the examiner-recommended 1983 tax assessments.

Sensitivity Analysis

As discussed previously, it is somewhat troubling that the hypothesis of sample selection bias (a nonzero value for ρ) is rejected by the data. It has been argued that if unobserved factors influencing compliance behavior are positively correlated across tax years, the value of ρ also should be positive. To examine the sensitivity of the results to the value of the correlation coefficient, the sample selection model was reestimated restricting the value of ρ to take on the values of .1, .2, and .4, respectively. Table 5 presents the results of this experiment.[14] Notice that even with $\rho = .1$, a prior audit experience is estimated to have a negative and significant influence on subsequent year tax noncompliance, after controlling for other factors. The impact of a prior audit

14. The prior audit equation is not of primary interest in this essay. To protect IRS interests, the estimated coefficients for this equation are not presented.

TABLE 5. Results for the Constrained Selection Model

Variable	$\rho = .1$	$\rho = .2$	$\rho = .4$
Constant	−3.752	−3.723	−3.679
	(−12.78)	(−12.69)	(−12.63)
Married	0.160	0.160	0.195
	(.62)	(.63)	(.77)
Total dependents	0.193	0.193	0.198
	(2.34)	(2.35)	(2.46)
Age over 65	−0.768	−0.769	−0.746
	(−2.47)	(−2.48)	(−2.45)
Easy filer	−1.143	−1.152	−1.140
	(−2.29)	(−2.30)	(−2.29)
Schedule C filer	4.167	4.200	4.210
	(20.32)	(20.47)	(20.60)
Schedule F filer	3.903	3.916	3.929
	(17.86)	(17.87)	(17.77)
Schedule D filer	0.580	0.578	0.633
	(2.80)	(2.80)	(3.11)
Income	0.208	0.224	0.245
	(4.37)	(4.80)	(5.14)
Marginal tax rate	9.000	8.989	8.858
	(15.10)	(15.10)	(15.03)
Prior audit	−1.423	−3.103	−6.544
	(−3.26)	(−7.21)	(−16.10)
σ	7.29	7.32	7.37
	(178.1)	(178.6)	(177.4)
Likelihood function	−21,284.5	−21,290.5	−21,333.0
Unweighted *N*	7,233	7,233	7,233

Note: T-statistics are in parentheses. The dependent variable is change in taxable income (in thousands of dollars).

becomes quite important as the value of ρ increases. Restricting ρ to take on a positive value imposes the assumption that taxpayers who were selected for audits of their 1980 returns, in the absence of the audit experience, would have been more noncompliant than taxpayers with similar observable characteristics who were not selected for audits of their 1980 returns.

The econometric results presented here are based on the unweighted sample of returns.[15] Similar results are obtained when a weighted analysis is performed. In addition, comparable results are obtained when the examiner-recommended change in taxes is substituted as the dependent variable in the tobit compliance equation. Finally, a bivariate probit model of prior year audit

15. However, weighting in the sense of controlling for choice-based sampling is employed.

selection and subsequent year tax noncompliance was estimated. The implications of the results of that analysis are comparable to the tobit results presented here.

Summary

Two approaches to investigating the impact of tax audits on subsequent year reporting behavior were employed. The first approach involved an examination of whether taxpayers who experienced a large audit change in one year showed improved tax compliance in a subsequent year. The results of investigating two separate data sources indicate that a substantial proportion of taxpayers demonstrate improvements in compliance following a large audit assessment. Although this result is consistent with a positive influence of audits on subsequent year tax compliance, the evidence is not conclusive. At least a portion of the improvement in tax compliance is attributable to regression toward the mean. Moreover, this approach does not control for other aspects of the taxpayer's compliance decision that may have been changing over the period between the initial audit and the subsequent year TCMP audit.

In the second approach, a sample selection model was estimated to examine whether taxpayers who experienced a prior audit differed in their subsequent year reporting behavior from taxpayers who did not experience a prior audit, controlling for taxpayer characteristics and the prior year audit selection process. The results do not indicate a positive relationship between taxpayer compliance and prior audit experience after controlling for these factors. However, the correctness of this finding hinges on the restriction, accepted by the data, that the unobserved factors influencing prior year audit selection are uncorrelated with the unobserved factors influencing subsequent year tax noncompliance. It is plausible that those taxpayers who are targeted for an audit in one year would be relatively more likely, in the absence of the audit, to file noncompliant returns in future years than taxpayers with similar observable characteristics who are not targeted for an audit. If this assumption is imposed in the form of a restriction on the correlation term in the sample selection model, then a significant deterrent effect of tax audits on subsequent year reporting behavior is obtained.

REFERENCES

Alexander, Craig, and Jonathan S. Feinstein. 1987. "A Microeconometric Analysis of Income Tax Evasion." Massachussetts Institute of Technology. Mimeo.

Allingham, Michael G., and Agnar Sandmo. 1972. "Income Tax Evasion: A Theoretical Analysis." *Journal of Public Economics* 1:323–38.

Alm, Jim. 1988. "Uncertain Tax Policies, Individual Behavior, and Welfare." *American Economic Review* 78:237–45.

Beck, Paul J., and Woon-Oh Jung. 1989. "Taxpayers' Reporting Decisions and Auditing Under Information Asymmetry." *Accounting Review* 64:468–87.

Beron, Kurt J., Helen V. Tauchen, and Ann Dryden Witte. 1988. "A Structural Equation Model for Tax Compliance and Auditing." NBER Working Paper no. 2556. National Bureau of Economic Research.

Clotfelter, Charles T. 1983. "Tax Evasion and Tax Rates: An Analysis of Individual Returns." *Review of Economics and Statistics* 65:363–73.

Dubin, Jeffrey A., and Lois L. Wilde. 1988. "An Empirical Analysis of Federal Income Tax Auditing and Compliance." *National Tax Journal* 41:61–74.

Erard, Brian. 1990. "Tax Practitioners and Tax Compliance: A Microeconometric Analysis of the Decision to Engage a Tax Practitioner and its Consequences." Ph.D. diss., University of Michigan.

Greenberg, J. 1984. "Avoiding Tax Avoidance: A (Repeated) Game-Theoretic Approach." *Journal of Economic Theory* 32:1–13.

Long, Susan B., and Richard D. Schwartz. 1987 "The Impact of IRS Audits on Taxpayer Compliance: A Field Experiment in Specific Deterrence." Paper presented at the annual meeting of the Law and Society Association, Washington, D.C.

Manski, Charles F., and Steven R. Lerman. 1977. "The Estimation of Choice Probabilities from Choice Based Samples." *Econometrica* 45:1977–89.

Scotchmer, Suzanne. 1989. "Who Profits from Taxpayer Confusion?" *Economics Letters* 29:49–55.

Scotchmer, Suzanne, and Joel Slemrod. 1989. "Randomness in Tax Enforcement." *Journal of Public Economics* 38:17–32.

Spicer, Michael W., and Rodney E. Hero. 1985. "Tax Evasion and Heuristics: A Research Note." *Journal of Public Economics* 26:263–67.

Spicer, Michael W., and S. B. Lundstedt. 1976. "Understanding Tax Evasion." *Public Finance* 31:295–305.

Tauchen, Helen V., Ann Dryden Witte, and Kurt J. Beron. 1989. "Tax Compliance: An Investigation Using Individual TCMP Data." NBER Working Paper no. 3078. National Bureau of Economic Research.

Tittle, Charles R. 1980. *Sanctions and Social Deviance*. New York: Praeger.

Witte, Ann Dryden, and Diane F. Woodbury. 1985. "The Effect of Tax Laws and Tax Administration on Tax Compliance: The Case of the U.S. Individual Income Tax." *National Tax Journal* 38:1–13.

Commentary

Susan B. Long

A great deal of research and attention have been focused upon taxpayer compliance with U.S. federal income tax statutes over the past decade or more. While almost everyone working in the area has acknowledged limitations in the data on taxpayer compliance, the full implications of these deficiencies for the development of sound theoretical knowledge, or practical policy guidance, have yet to be squarely faced.

The Wrong Paradigm?

A threshold issue is: "What paradigm is most appropriate for studying taxpayer compliance?" Or, stated even more pointedly, "Is taxpayer compliance a matter of choice or a random event?" I will argue that if you use official government statistics to measure taxpayer noncompliance, traditional choice behavior models are largely inappropriate.

The framework used by most researchers, including Brian Erard in this volume, has been based upon a paradigm that assumes—explicitly or implicitly—that taxpayer compliance is choice behavior. Such a paradigm may, indeed, be appropriate when the focus of a study is tax evasion where intent is a defining element of the behavior. But tax evasion is only one source—perhaps even a minor source at that—of taxpayer noncompliance. At best, choice models can only inform us about certain restricted types of taxpayer noncompliance. However, even these models will tell us very little about this restricted subclass of tax behaviors if we use inappropriate data.

I have come to believe that using official government statistics—whether these be tax gap estimates or data from regular or research tax audits such as from the Internal Revenue Service's Taxpayer Compliance Measurement Program (TCMP)—to test traditional choice behavior models is largely inappropriate. Yet TCMP data and similarly based government measures are perhaps the most common tax compliance data used to analyze such choice models, at least in nonexperimental settings. I hasten to add that I am not immune from my own criticism since perhaps the first compliance study using

TCMP data outside the IRS was one I conducted employing an econometric-based deterrence model over a decade ago (Long 1980b).[1]

Why are TCMP data and other similarly based government compliance measures largely inappropriate for modeling taxpayer compliance as choice behavior? I believe that they are largely unsuitable because these official government data sources are dominated by actions that do not arise out of any conscious choice by the taxpayer to disobey the law.[2]

What evidence do I have to support such an assertion? First, little of what is picked up by TCMP is classified by the IRS's own auditors as fraud or even as negligence. For example, in the latest available TCMP survey covering federal income tax returns filed by individuals, less than 5 percent (4.9 percent) were found to warrant negligence penalties and on only 2 out of every 1,000 returns were civil fraud penalties imposed.[3] This means that even if every individual return in the country were given a thorough audit by the IRS, at most 0.2 percent of the returns—a mere 166,000 returns nationwide according to TCMP—would be found to warrant civil fraud penalties. This tax fraud rate of roughly 2 per 1,000 returns filed has been essentially unchanged in TCMP surveys over the past twenty years (see Long 1980a and 1981; Long and Burnham 1990). Thus, much of what TCMP measures is not willful tax fraud or even negligence, but misreporting that arises from other sources—including inadvertence, misunderstanding of what are often complicated tax provisions, or ambiguity and uncertainties in tax requirements.[4]

1. Indeed, much of my work over the past decade has utilized TCMP data. I have also sought to make TCMP data more accessible to researchers through the development of documented data sets, and it was through a 1975 lawsuit I brought under the public disclosure law (5 U.S.C. 552) that required the IRS to give individuals outside the government access to TCMP data for the first time (see Long vs. Internal Revenue Service, C75 228S (WD Wash), 596 F.2d 362 [9th Cir. 1979], *cert. denied,* 446 U.S. 917 [1980]).

2. While a discussion of other sources of data is outside the scope of these remarks, the two other major sources of data on taxpayer noncompliance—self-reports from surveys and observational data from experiments—are not immune to this same limitation. Self-reports are often based upon questions that do not ask the subject to differentiate between intended versus unintended misreporting. On the other hand, experimental data, particularly when realism in the reporting task is simulated, can give rise to a substantial number of inadvertent errors because of the very complexity of the reporting task (see, for example, Robben et al. 1990).

3. This figure is based on auditor recommendations, not actual civil penalty assessments, which may not be upheld on appeal. Further, because these are civil penalties, they are imposed under less stringent standards than would be applied in bringing a criminal fraud prosecution.

4. I would be the first to agree, as I have argued elsewhere (Long 1980a and 1981) that the actual rate of tax fraud is considerably higher than that reflected in TCMP data. Even the more thorough TCMP audits may not do a very good job of detecting misreporting arising from fraud, while the fraudulent motive behind some misreporting that is discovered may not be unearthed by the IRS. Hence, when one uses TCMP-based measures, it would be inappropriate to assume one is examining choice behavior—that is, willful noncompliance.

Second, the temporal pattern of noncompliance behaviors Richard Schwartz and I found when we followed a random sample of taxpayers over time (see Long and Schwartz 1987) using TCMP panel data also suggests that traditional choice behavior models are largely inappropriate. To a surprising extent, whether taxpayers were compliant on one return had very little association with what TCMP found they had done on a subsequent return.

Indeed, which of three tax compliance categories (underreporting, correct reporting, or overreporting) TCMP classified taxpayers by was surprisingly random over time. Further, to the extent there was persistence in behavior from one return to the next, it was the case that misreporting detected by TCMP increased the odds of the taxpayer misreporting in their subsequent return *without regard to the direction of these errors*. That is, the fact that taxpayers underreported their tax on the first return was as likely to be associated with them *over*reporting as it was with them *under*reporting tax on a subsequent return (and vice versa). This is hardly behavior consistent with traditional choice models.

The pattern we found is, of course, congruent with choice behavior at a societal, rather than individual, level. In the panel, it appeared that those with more complex returns ran a greater risk of committing underreporting as well as overreporting errors. Research by others, as well as by my colleague Judyth Swingen and myself, also shows a very strong association with the complexity of reporting requirements and TCMP-based error rates.[5]

Clearly, as a society, whether we pass complex or simple tax provisions is a matter of choice. To this extent then, TCMP-based measures of noncompliance can be viewed as the outcome of choice behavior at the societal level, because we are often implicitly legislating more or less noncompliance through the specific types of tax provisions enacted. But my original point that TCMP-based measures appear largely unsuitable for testing traditional choice models about an individual's tax compliance decisions still remains.

Limits of TCMP-Based Research on the Impact of Tax Audits

I want to turn next to a consideration of what we can learn from TCMP-based research on the impact of tax audits in general and, more particularly, on the essay on this topic by Brian Erard. Here again we will see that strengths and weaknesses of taxpayer compliance data limit the conclusions we can reach.

Two separate TCMP-based studies of the impact of tax audits are reported by Erard. In both, an individual-level choice model is analyzed using

5. See, for example, Clotfelter (1983), Klepper and Nagin (1987 and 1989), Long and Swingen (1986, 1988a, 1988b). See also Swingen and Long (1988a and 1988b).

two different research designs—designs, Erard is frank to admit, which are dictated by the "different relative merits and flaws" (p. 99) of the two data bases.

Classic Regression Effects

In the first investigation, taxpayers were selected for the study because audit-based compliance data were available for them at two points in time *and* the first audit had found substantial tax underreporting (at least $500). Erard then contrasts the results from this initial audit with compliance on a subsequent year return that had coincidentally been examined by the IRS as part of a TCMP survey. Because, for this group of taxpayers, compliance was on average higher on the second return than on the first, he concludes (p. 100) that this provides "relatively strong evidence" of the positive influence of audits on compliance.

The problem with such a conclusion is that these results may simply be a statistical artifact—an example of the classic "regression effect" that occurs when groups are selected because they evidence some extreme characteristic (see Campbell and Stanley 1963, 10–12). Taxpayers included in the study were atypical ("extreme") in two respects. First, the IRS had selected their returns for the first audit presumably because IRS auditors thought these taxpayers were likely to have underreported their tax. Second, of those singled out for this first audit, only taxpayers found the most noncompliant within this already select group were retained in the study.

As was originally observed by Francis Galton (1877) in examining the size of peas, whenever characteristics or behaviors are less than perfectly correlated over time, groups selected *because they evidence extreme characteristics* will show, on average, a reduction in such characteristics over time (absent other forces). Galton (1886a, 62; 1886b, 258) coined the term *regression* for this effect and demonstrated its occurrence in a wide variety of contexts (see, particularly, Galton 1889 and 1894). As others following Galton have shown, whether examining heights of fathers and sons, educational test scores, attitudes, or socioeconomic indicators (see, for example, Campbell and Stanley 1963; Pearson 1896; Pearson and Lee 1903; Thorndike 1942), this regression toward the mean follows as a pure mathematical necessity of the selection criteria used. The more "extreme" the basis of selection, the larger the expected regression toward the mean—just as Erard found.[6]

6. The regression effect will also be larger to the extent that population characteristics are less strongly correlated across time. Since audit-based compliance levels for individual taxpayers appear only weakly correlated over time, regression toward the mean may be particularly pronounced.

Had Erard selected taxpayers whose initial audit results were "extreme" in the opposite direction (taxpayers initially highly compliant), he would have doubtless found a similar regression toward the mean with these taxpayers becoming less compliant after their initial audit. Indeed, such results were noted by the IRS in an in-house study (1975) that took an approach similar to Erard's but focused on taxpayers who were located at both ends of the spectrum—either extremely compliant or extremely noncompliant. Those initially extremely noncompliant became more compliant after their audit experience, while those extremely compliant became less compliant. Later reanalysis (see Long and Schwartz 1987) showed these findings to be entirely an artifact of the research design, due to the bias caused by selecting cases because of their initial "extreme" compliance or noncompliance levels.

The Limits of Statistical Controls in Correcting for Selection Bias

The second study reported by Erard assesses the impact of audits on subsequent compliance by comparing two groups of taxpayers—one previously audited, one unaudited. Unfortunately, the makeup of the two groups was not equivalent. Only the recently audited group had been singled out for examination by the IRS, presumably on "the likelihood that an audit [would] . . . uncover substantial reporting errors" (Erard, p. 101). In an attempt to correct for this selectivity bias in the makeup of the two groups, Erard introduces a variety of statistical controls to substitute for the absence of experimental controls. Depending upon the a priori assumptions imposed and statistical controls introduced, Erard is able to generate estimates of audit impact that vary anywhere from a conclusion that audits foster subsequent noncompliance, to one that audits have no significant effects at all, to one that they do indeed deter subsequent misreporting. (To produce any estimated deterrent effect, however, Erard finds that a constraint that is inconsistent with the observed data must be imposed on the nature of the selectivity bias.)

Thus, within an individual choice paradigm, the nature of these data does not allow reliable conclusions to be drawn about the impact of tax audits on the subsequent behavior of taxpayers. Given the sensitivity of the findings to small changes in model specifications, it appears unlikely that this indeterminacy can be solved using these data simply by imposing ever more elaborate assumptions or sophisticated statistical estimation procedures. Something more is needed.

Erard's work does illustrate the value of a thorough examination of the potential sensitivity of empirical results to the assumptions and/or estimation procedures used. Researchers would be well advised to follow his example and carefully scrutinize the robustness of their own results to variations in the specifications or assumptions imposed.

Just as important, as Erard did, one must honestly report the outcome of these examinations—not simply select out for recounting that particular combination of model specifications and assumptions that produce the desired result. Readers (including reviewers of manuscripts) need to insist that such a sensitivity analysis be carried out and reported before findings from research can be adequately weighed.

But, at the same time, readers must be realistic in their expectations. Sensitivity of results using nonexperimental designs and government, audit-based data will no doubt be the rule, not the exception. Thus, the more thorough the exploration for potential flaws, the more weaknesses that are likely to turn up. Until researchers are rewarded for carrying out a thorough sensitivity analysis, we are unlikely to see such practices widely adopted and reported. The very thoroughness Erard used in examining the robustness of his findings is much to be commended.

The Importance of Counterintuitive Results

Finally, Erard's second study turns up some interesting counterintuitive results. Erard found, contrary to his expectations, that TCMP data rejected his proposed controls for sample selection bias. He notes (p. 107) that this could occur "[if] taxpayer compliance decisions [were] independent across tax years," but rejects this possibility as "implausible" (p. 107). However, as I have noted, the assumption that officially measured compliance is the end result of a taxpayer "decision" may be too simplistic (see also Kinsey 1988). As a result, an independence condition may not be as unreasonable as previously assumed.

There is a second possible explanation for these counterintuitive results that Erard does not examine. This concerns the issue of how well the IRS targets returns for audit. Erard notes (p. 107) that he found "no correlation between unobserved factors that influenced the IRS decision to audit a taxpayer's 1980 return and unobserved factors that influenced the taxpayer's 1982 tax report." While this could occur if taxpayer compliance levels on 1980 and 1982 returns were largely independent, it could also arise if, in the aggregate, the factors that influenced the IRS decision to audit a return were not closely related to a taxpayer's officially measured compliance level.

In a recent study cited by Erard (Long and Burnham 1990), David Burnham and I found that while TCMP estimates that slightly less than 1 percent (0.8 percent) of all returns underreport tax liability by $5,000 or more, these rates are much higher on business than on nonbusiness returns and rise sharply with increases in income level (see table 1). While the rate of audits is also higher for business and higher income returns, these rates do not rise as rapidly as the number of returns in business and higher income classes with significant reporting errors. Thus, as shown in table 1, for those underreporting tax by $5,000 or more, the odds of audit are the reverse of what is commonly thought. The IRS audits eleven times the number of low-income, nonbusiness returns making significant tax errors, but only examines one-fourth the number of high income business returns making equivalent underreporting errors. Thus, Erard's counterintuitive finding should cause us to look more closely at some widely held assumptions, including those concerning how the IRS targets returns for examination.

Conclusion

The nature of officially measured taxpayer noncompliance, including the inherent limitations of such measures, makes research based on such data particularly sensitive to model specifications and assumptions. Too often, the correctness of basic assumptions that taxpayer compliance is choice behavior, that such decisions persist over time, or that the IRS effectively targets returns for audit is simply presumed even though these may not be appropriate in all contexts. All assumptions, including choices in model specification, should be made explicit and their reasonableness continually reassessed in view of the observed structure of the data.

While facing up to these issues can prove helpful, it is unlikely to be a panacea. In the end, no amount of sophisticated analysis can substitute for better data. At some point, the limits of current compliance data must be faced

TABLE 1. IRS Targeting of Audits by Income Level

Income Level	Returns Underreporting by $5,000 or More	Relative Number of Audits[a]
All Returns	0.8%	
Nonbusiness		
$25,000 or less	0.1	11 times
$25,000 to $50,000	0.5	2½ times
$50,000 or more	2.9	⅚ times
Business (Schedule C)		
$25,000 or less	1.6	about right
$25,000 to $100,000	7.5	⅓ times
$100,000 or more	16.0	¼ times

[a]The relative number of audits represents the number of returns audited in each income level compared to the number of returns with underreporting errors of $5,000 or more in that income class.

and improved compliance measures developed before our knowledge can progress.

REFERENCES

Campbell, Donald T., and Julian C. Stanley. 1963. *Experimental and Quasi-Experimental Designs for Research.* Chicago: Rand McNally.

Clotfelter, Charles T. 1983. "Tax Evasion and Tax Rates: An Analysis of Individual Returns." *Review of Economics and Statistics* 65:363–73.

Galton, Francis. 1877. "Typical Laws of Heredity." *Proceedings of the Meetings of the Members of the Royal Institution of Great Britain,* vol. 8, pp. 282–301; reprinted in *Nature* 15:492–95, 512–14, 532–33.

Galton, Francis. 1886a. "Family Likeness in Stature." *Proceedings of the Royal Society of London* 40:42–73.

Galton, Francis. 1886b. "Regression Towards Mediocrity in Hereditary Stature." *Journal of the Anthropological Institute of Great Britain and Ireland* 15:246–63.

Galton, Francis. 1889. *Natural Inheritance.* London: Macmillan.

Galton, Francis. 1894. "Discontinuity in Evolution." *Mind* 19:362–72.

IRS. 1975. "Effect of a Prior Year TCMP Audit." Internal Revenue Service internal memorandum.

Kinsey, Karyl A. 1988. "Measurement Bias or Honest Disagreement? Problems of Validating Measures of Tax Evasion." American Bar Foundation Working Paper 88-11. Chicago: American Bar Foundation.

Klepper, Steven, and Daniel S. Nagin. 1987. "The Role of Tax Practitioners in Tax Compliance." Working Paper, Carnegie Mellon University. Photocopy.

Klepper, Steven, and Daniel S. Nagin. 1989. "The Anatomy of Tax Evasion." *Journal of Law, Economics, and Organizations* 5:1–24.

Long, Susan B. 1980a. *The Internal Revenue Service: Measuring Tax Offenses and Enforcement Response.* U.S. Department of Justice, National Institute of Justice. Washington, D.C.: U.S. Government Printing Office.

Long, Susan B. 1980b. "Measuring Deterrence: Imperfect Data and Estimation Bias." Ph.D. diss. University of Washington.

Long, Susan B. 1981. "Estimating Criminal Tax Violations." *Tax Notes* 12, no. 23:1325–26.

Long, Susan B., and David Burnham. 1990. "Solving the Nation's Budget Deficit with a Bigger, Tougher IRS: What Are the Realities?" *Tax Notes* 48, no. 6:741–57.

Long, Susan B., and Richard Schwartz. 1987. "The Impact of IRS Audits on Taxpayer Compliance: A Field Experiment in Specific Deterrence." Paper presented at the annual meeting of the Law and Society Association, Washington, D.C.

Long, Susan B., and Judyth A. Swingen. 1988a. "Complexity, Opportunity, and Compliance." Paper presented at the annual meeting of the Law and Society Association, Vail, Colo.

Long, Susan B., and Judyth A. Swingen. 1988b. "The Role of Legal Complexity in Shaping Taxpayer Compliance." In *Lawyers on Psychology and Psychologists on*

Law, ed. Peter J. Van Koppen, Dick J. Hessing, and Grat van den Heuvel, 127–46. Amsterdam: Swets and Seitlinger.

Long, Susan B., and Judyth A. Swingen. 1986. "The Impact of Complexity on Tax Compliance: An Exploratory Assessment." Paper presented at the annual meeting of the Law and Society Association, Chicago.

Pearson, Karl. 1896. "Mathematical Contributions to the Theory of Evolution.—III. Regression, Heredity, and Panmixia," reprinted in K. Pearson (1948), *Early Statistical Papers,* 113–78. Cambridge: Cambridge University Press.

Pearson, Karl, and Alice Lee. 1903. *Biometrika,* 2:357.

Robben, Henry S. J., Paul Webley, Russell H. Weigel, Karl-Erik Warneryd, Karyl A. Kinsey, Dick J. Hessing, Francisco Alvira Martin, Henk Elffers, Richard Wahlund, Luk van Langenhove, Susan B. Long, and John T. Scholz. 1990. "Decision Frame and Opportunity as Determinants of Tax Cheating: An International Experimental Study." *Journal of Economic Psychology* 11:341–64.

Swingen, Judyth A., and Susan B. Long. 1988a. "A Look Back at the 1988 Filing Season." *Tax Notes* 41, no. 2:1343–48.

Swingen, Judyth A., and Susan B. Long. 1988b. "Mathematical and Clerical Errors During the 1987 Filing Season." *Tax Notes* 39, no. 6:759–65.

Thorndike, R. L. 1942. "Regression Fallacies in the Matched Groups Experiment." *Psychometrika* 7:85–102.

The Corporate Tax Gap: Evidence on Tax Compliance by Small Corporations

Eric M. Rice

I tell you, the average American cheats every way they can on the government. That's the truth. But they do it the honest cheating way.
—from group interviews (Westat 1980a, 42)

There is a popular perception of widespread corporate tax evasion involving substantial sums,[1] a perception that is supported by the IRS's Tax Compliance Measurement Program (TCMP) and its operational corporate audits. According to the latest IRS estimates and projections (IRS 1988),[2] the U.S. corporate tax gap—the difference between tax receipts based on voluntary reporting and what the IRS views as the correct amount of tax due—increased 60 percent between 1982 and 1988, from $14.2 billion to $22.8 billion. By 1992, this shortfall is projected to have risen to $31.1 billion (equal to 22.7 percent of the projected corporate tax receipts of $137.2 billion).

While the IRS credits the 1986 income tax reform with slowing the growth of *individual* income tax evasion, its estimates for the corporate income tax demonstrate no such tendency. Instead, the estimated ratio of the

I am grateful for direction received from Martin Feldstein, Lawrence Katz, Lawrence Summers, and Anne Witte, and thank Alan Auerbach, Richard Caves, Daniel Feenberg, James Hines, Louis Kaplow, James Poterba, Henry Reiling, Ana Revenga, Joel Slemrod, and Mark Wolfson for comments. Thanks also to Dennis Cox, Frederick Judd, and Brian Erard of the IRS Tax Compliance Analysis Group for access to the data and their assistance. I am responsible for all remaining errors and omissions.

1. For example, Tighe (1985) claims that many businesses maintain two sets of accounts in order to evade taxes.

2. See the third section for a brief critique of the reliability of the TCMP data on which IRS estimates and projections are made.

corporate tax gap to the gap for individual filers jumped from little more than 20 percent throughout the early 1980s, to about 40 percent currently. (This occurred even though the ratio of corporate income tax receipts to individual income tax receipts only increased from about 19 percent to about 23 percent during the same period.) The IRS's measure of the corporate tax gap amounts to nearly a quarter of the Treasury's annual corporate tax receipts, and, as corporate earnings rise, this tax gap measure rises about proportionally.

Yet despite its real-world importance, corporate income tax evasion has attracted essentially no scholarly analysis.[3] One reason is that existing theoretical models of tax evasion have focused only on the individual income tax. A second reason is that, in contrast to the individual income tax, no corporate income tax compliance microdata have previously been made available to the research community for analysis. A further reason has to do with the fundamental dilemma about empirical research on tax compliance: how much faith to place in the ability of financial audits to uncover and to measure accurately illicit corporate activity. Since corporations have strong incentives to avoid disclosing their misconduct, any tax compliance data set will invariably suffer from substantial measurement error. In fact, this last problem should concern all empirical researchers of tax compliance.

During a part of 1988, the IRS Compliance Analysis Group graciously made available its corporate tax compliance microdata for my research. This data set is a stratified random sample of approximately 30,000 small corporations.[4] Aside from the IRS's own tabulations, this is the first analysis ever made using corporate tax compliance data. Accordingly, the initial objective of my study is to describe this publicly unknown data set.[5] The TCMP data I use reveal pervasive noncompliance—two-thirds of the sample corporations are noncompliant—that involves a substantial share of profits. Noncompliance divides almost evenly between unreported revenue and overstated expenses.

I also develop an econometric model to test several propositions about the determinants of corporate tax compliance. Because the value of unre-

---

3. There are only a few exceptions of which I am aware. In one section of Marrelli (1984), a theoretical study of value-added tax evasion, the author compares the relative incentive to evade a value-added tax to that for a profits tax; this exercise demonstrates that any results can be reversed by changing assumptions about risk aversion. And in three notes in the *National Tax Journal,* Kreutzer and Lee (1986 and 1988) and Wang and Conant (1988) debate whether the opportunity to evade a profits tax can theoretically alter a monopolist's optimal production plan.

4. I.e., corporations with assets of less than $10 million, of which I consider only those with assets of $1 million to $10 million.

5. To protect the secrecy of its audit formulas, the IRS allows academic researchers only very limited access to its compliance microdata.

ported income equals exactly zero for a large fraction of corporations, I argue that there may be a sample selection bias problem. I suggest that the variable of behavioral interest, the corporation's propensity to underreport, is censored, and, therefore, I use a tobit maximum likelihood specification to account for selection bias. Another complication arises because some taxpayers actually report *more* than their full tax obligation. In response, I put forward alternative interpretations of the observed "overreporting," and consider their econometric implications.

The econometric results lend support to three main propositions. First, characteristics that assure public disclosure of information about a corporation's operations also tend to encourage better tax compliance. This conclusion is based on findings that compliance is positively associated with being publicly traded and with belonging to a highly regulated industry, and that corporations whose operations are shielded from view through their dealings with a tax haven country demonstrate very poor compliance. Second, firm profitability exerts two opposing compliance effects. Managers of a corporation whose profit performance falls short of its industry norm may resort to noncompliance as a means of shaving costs. In contrast, high-profit companies may take advantage of their greater ability to underreport income without being audited. These related implications derive from findings that deviations from the sample's median industry profit rate correspond positively with tax compliance, while deviations from the samplewide median profit rate correspond negatively. And third, the marginal tax rate is associated negatively with compliance, although a reduction in the marginal tax rate would cost the government one dollar in revenue for every 5.3 cents it could raise via enhanced compliance. Poor compliance is also associated with firm size and with being located in IRS-identified poor compliance regions. I find no clear association of compliance and service industries or the use of an outside CPA for tax preparation.

Explaining Corporate Tax Evasion

The basic premise of the theoretical model is that a company decides how much of its taxable income to report to the tax authorities based on its tax obligation, the penalty for detection of unreported income, and its probability of audit.[6] Formally, a risk-neutral corporation maximizes expected net profits, $E(N)$, by choosing R, the part of taxable income it reports, as shown in equation 1.

6. This theoretical model has roots in the Srinivasan model of individual income tax evasion (1973).

$$\max_{R} E(N) = G - tR - \{[(f \cdot t \cdot U) + FC] \cdot P(U,S,\gamma)\} \tag{1}$$

where

N = Net (after-tax) profits,
G = Gross (true) taxable income,
R = Reported taxable income,
t = Proportional rate of corporate tax,
f = Fine for detected evasion > 1,
U = Unreported income $\equiv G - R$,
FC = Fixed cost of an audit,
P = Probability of an audit,
S = Susceptibility to detection, and
γ = 0 for privately held corporations and = 1 for publicly traded corporations.

The first two components on the right-hand side comprise the certain part of the firm's receipts and costs, given its choice of R. For simplicity, t is assumed to be proportional. The bracketed component is the penalty function faced by the firm if it gets audited, weighted by the probability of audit. The less the firm reports, the lower is its tax burden. At the same time, reporting less profit raises the probability of audit. This framework implicitly assumes that a firm's true profits are revealed in the event of a tax audit.[7]

The cost of an audit has two components: any fixed costs of being audited, plus the total penalty to be paid on any evaded income. Fixed costs are conventionally thought of as (net-of-tax-deductions) business costs, such as accounting and legal expenses; but they may also be thought of as damage to reputational capital or the personal and moral cost of violating a social rule.[8] The penalty for tax evasion in the United States is typically payment of the tax due, multiplied by one plus a fractional fine.[9]

In the model, corporations are motivated by an endogenous probability

7. This strong assumption is convenient but not essential. One can substitute the "probability of detection" for the "probability of audit." Then, the fixed costs become those incurred only when an audit uncovers some amount of evasion, such as a fraud penalty or criminal sanctions.

8. An additional cost of being audited is that detection of current or past noncompliance is likely to increase the probability of future audits (and, in a multiperiod model, one would want to incorporate this cost explicitly).

9. Until 1982, which includes the tax year of these data, the fine for negligent noncompliance equaled 25 percent of the unpaid taxes. The fine in cases involving fraud was 50 percent.

of audit, defined here as $P = P(U, S, \gamma)$. Empirical evidence from the individual income tax tends to support the suggestion that different detection risks across individuals—perceived and actual—have a significant, positive compliance effect.[10]

Since a greater amount of evasion is likely to draw the attention of the tax authorities, $P(\cdot)$ is assumed to be increasing and concave in U (i.e., $P_U > 0$, $P_{UU} < 0$).[11] Variable S measures a corporation's inherent susceptibility to audit, so that $P_s > 0$. Susceptibility depends in two ways on firm attributes, such as size, location, or lines of business. On the one hand, some business attributes make a firm's operations inherently less transparent to the tax authorities. These include importing and exporting (which may allow transfer pricing), operating foreign affiliates (see Hines and Hubbard 1990), activities commonly conducted in cash, activities whose inputs or outputs can be diverted to personal consumption, businesses with substantial intangible assets, and services. On the other hand, to the extent that the IRS uses these same attributes to choose who to audit, susceptibility to audit *increases* for firms whose operations are relatively *less* transparent.

Finally, companies whose shares trade publicly have a greater inherent probability of audit. Unlike privately held firms, publicly traded corporations are subject to important public disclosure requirements and independent financial auditing, which tend to expose to the authorities any underreporting they might do. Thus, I assume that the firm characteristic $\gamma = 1$ shifts $P(\cdot)$ upward for every level of underreported earnings.

The firm's first-order condition for the optimal reporting of taxable income is

$$U = [(1/f + P(\cdot))\cdot P_U^{-1}] - (FC/ft) \,. \qquad (2)$$

Note that a sufficiently large fixed cost of audit may induce an optimizing management to protect itself by *overreporting*.[12]

---

10. See Beron, Tauchen, and Witte (1988); Dubin and Wilde (1986); Mason and Calvin (1984); Tauchen and Witte (1985); Witte and Woodbury (1985). If detection risk does not in fact affect compliance, then the effect of $P(\cdot)$ might instead be modeled as a constant.

11. One might also imagine that the tax authorities would be alerted by a low reporting *ratio* (i.e., R/G). However, the many negative and near-zero values for taxable corporate income render this measure meaningless.

12. If U has a large effect on the probability of audit, and fixed costs are not too big (i.e., $1/P_U > FC/t$), the model gives predictable signs for the relationship of unreported income to the fixed costs of audit, the fine, and the marginal tax rate (i.e., $\partial U/\partial FC < 0$, $\partial U/\partial f > 0$, and $\partial U/\partial t > 0$). Unsurprisingly, the model gives indeterminate signs for $\partial U/\partial S$ and $\partial U/\partial$; in the case of susceptibility to audit, this reflects that it triggers more auditing, which in turn induces greater compliance; and being publicly traded induces both better compliance and a greater probability of audit.

The top issue of empirical controversy in the personal income tax compliance literature concerns the relationship between the marginal tax rate and compliance, both because of inconclusive research results and its importance for policy.[13] Although theoretical and policy analyses tend to assume an inverse relationship, Graetz and Wilde (1985) accurately sum up the literature as follows:

> The myth that high marginal tax rates cause non-compliance is the most pervasive of all. In fact, that lowering tax rates will induce greater compliance is a claim supported neither by the theory of tax compliance nor by the empirical evidence.

For this reason, it is useful to single out one special case of the present model in which the marginal tax rate does *not* affect income tax compliance. As the fixed cost of audit goes to zero, the cost of noncompliance becomes proportional to the tax rate (i.e., just $f \cdot t$). Accordingly, the last term disappears from the firm's first-order condition:

$$U = [P(\cdot) + (1/f)] \cdot P_{\bar{U}}^{-1} \ . \tag{2a}$$

Since the tax rate falls out of the first-order condition (i.e., $\partial U / \partial t = 0$), unreported income may then be characterized as $U\ (f,\ \gamma,\ S)$.

An Overview of the Corporate TCMP

The corporate TCMP intensively scrutinizes the tax and financial records of a stratified random sample numbering approximately 30,000 corporations out of the population of 1.5 million corporations with assets of less than \$10 million. The IRS assigns some of its most experienced auditors to pore over records much more thoroughly than in a standard operational audit.

Before proceeding, I want to discuss the fundamental dilemma of empirical research into such illegal activities as tax evasion. While the IRS naturally bases its estimates of the aggregate tax gap on the TCMP, one cannot help wondering how much actual evasion can be found, even by this intensive auditing procedure. The empirical part of this study relies on the TCMP being able to reveal at least the *relative* magnitudes of tax evasion between taxpayers.

Yet it is possible that the TCMP picks up little more than differences

---

13. See Clotfelter (1983); Cox (1984); Friedland, Maital, and Rutenberg (1978); Poterba (1987); Slemrod (1985).

across corporations in their likelihood of being found out once they are chosen at random for TCMP audits. It may also be capturing variability in audit quality. In addition, there are important timing issues that distort the TCMP statistics. As a relatively simple example, consider the improper expensing of an investment that should be depreciated. The TCMP registers as noncompliance the entire disallowed amount, even though the deduction has not been permanently disallowed, but only *deferred* across subsequent tax years. Thus, the true amount of noncompliance is just the interest the government forgoes as a result of the premature realization of a legitimate expense.

More damaging is the concern that the TCMP monitors something entirely other than tax evasion. Perhaps the TCMP succeeds only at revealing instances where a corporation takes an aggressive tax stance or honest differences of legal opinion between the business community and the IRS.[14] One bit of evidence for this alternative interpretation of the data is the IRS's estimation that the tax gap would be reduced by as much as 30 percent after all appeals.[15] Perhaps little of what people commonly think of as evasion shows up in these audits. Actual tax evasion may simply be untraceable, because it is either too far outside the law or completely "off the books."

Although one should keep this philosophical dilemma in mind, it cannot be resolved here and I know of no better way to get at the issue of evasion. In what follows, I proceed (on the whole) under the assumption that noncompliance according to the TCMP corresponds to true noncompliance. Accordingly, where I use the convention of calling the difference between reported and audited magnitudes "evasion," the more skeptical reader is invited to substitute the more neutral terms *tax gap* or *noncompliance*.

The IRS uses the TCMP primarily to estimate compliance levels and to improve auditing and enforcement. Its decision to perform an operational audit depends on a corporation's relative Discriminant Index Function (DIF) score. The closely guarded DIF formulas depend on a vector of taxpayer return characteristics, and have only been partly inferred for individual taxpayers by researchers who study detection probabilities. For part of 1988, the IRS allowed direct access to TCMP data for a small number of outside

14. The use of auditing outcomes to measure evasion is sometimes also criticized because auditors are believed to have an anticipated or target dollar yield for each operational audit. A target yield might be expected to cause the audit outcome to converge to the auditor's prior belief. To some extent, TCMP audits avoid this bias, since taxpayers are randomly chosen and the auditors are not under pressure to achieve a specified dollar yield.

15. However, these appellate statistics are only suggestive. For one thing, considerations such as the cost of litigation may lead the IRS or the appellant to settle for an amount other than true income. In addition, appeals are filed only by taxpayers who believe that their income was overestimated. Those for whom the IRS underestimates income are less likely to appeal

researchers; more recently out of concern for the security of the DIF formulas, they have again curtailed much of this access.

The 1980 TCMP data divide broadly into small corporations (assets less than $1 million) and medium-sized corporations ($1–10 million).[16] However, the vast majority of the so-called small corporations differ from the popular concept of corporate businesses: they are primarily professional practices and small businesses that incorporate for tax reasons and whose fictitious corporate entity cannot be distinguished from the persons of its officers. Accordingly, I restrict the analysis to the TCMP's 6,735 medium-sized corporations. These medium-sized corporations' shares of total reported corporate taxable income and tax collections amount to 7.2 percent and 13.8 percent, respectively. They are also responsible for 16.2 percent of the corporate tax gap.

Medium-sized corporations are further subdivided into two strata: asset class A (over $5 million) and asset class B (under $5 million). Table 1 sets forth the populations and sample sizes of the two groups, as well as illustrating the aggregate level of corporate evasion for each corporate population.[17] The ratio of unreported to reported income is 31 percent in asset class A and 42 percent in asset class B.[18]

In comparison, the IRS estimates this ratio to be only 23 percent for all asset classes of small and medium-sized corporations, which would appear to attribute worse compliance to asset class A and B corporations. However, about a third of this difference can readily be explained: extrapolating from my sample, nearly one-tenth results from uncorrected data errors in the IRS's Reported Taxable Income series and an additional one-quarter from the fact that the IRS subtracts overreporting from its estimate of unreported income. Part of the remaining two-thirds of the differential may, indeed, point to worse compliance among corporations in the large asset classes. In addition, part probably reflects the fact that larger corporations keep more formalized records, which would offer IRS auditors a clearer paper trail.[19]

16. The TCMP does not examine the records of larger corporations. The IRS's relationship with larger corporations is quite different from that with small and medium-sized corporations. First, they face an audit rate of nearly 100 percent. Second, their tax bill is *negotiated* with the IRS, rather than arising from a system in which the firm reports its profits and the IRS follows up by evaluating that report.

17. The population estimates are extrapolations from the TCMP samples, using IRS weightings for each observation.

18. To avoid exaggerating this ratio, I define reported taxable income for these purposes as the sum of the positive income reports. With respect to overreporters, I use their audited income in lieu of reported income, and eliminate their overreporting from the unreported income aggregate variable. My treatment of taxes paid and unreported is analogous.

19. As a further point of comparison, the IRS estimates this fraction to be 18 percent for 1980 *individual* income. Again, this difference may reflect true differences in the tendency of

TABLE 1. Corporate Income and Compliance

	Asset Class A	Asset Class B
Corporate population[a]	16,648	118,591
TCMP sample	2,690	4,045
Sampling rate	16.2%	3.4%
Corporate taxable income[b]		
Reported	$7,466	$16,801
Unreported[c]	$2,347	$6,979
Proportion of reported	31.4%	41.5%
Corporate income tax[b]		
Reported	$2,951	$5,955
Unreported[c]	$532	$1,747
Proportion of reported	18.0%	29.3%

[a]Based on IRS estimates.
[b]In millions of dollars.
[c]Figures for unreported income are calculated by multiplying TCMP estimates by an "expansion factor" of 2.39, which is used by the IRS to capture the TCMP's relative inability to detect certain kinds of unreported income (see IRS 1988); includes overreporting.

The aggregate amount of taxes paid by asset class A and B corporations equals 40 and 35 percent of their income, respectively. However, the ratio of taxes paid to the tax gap is a good deal smaller than the share of income that goes unreported: 18 percent and 29 percent for asset classes A and B, respectively. These compare with IRS estimates for 1980 of 37 percent for all small and medium-sized corporations and 25 percent for large corporation income taxes, as well as 22 percent for individual income taxes.

There are two reasons unreported income is relatively larger than unpaid taxes for asset classes A and B: (1) corporations with current-year operating losses (i.e., negative taxable income) may exaggerate their losses, despite the absence of any current-year tax *advantage,* in order to carry the loss backward or forward to other tax years; and (2) similarly, many corporations that underreport positive taxable income in the current year have *prior-year* losses *to carry forward* so that their noncompliance induces no change in the current-year tax due.[20]

individuals versus corporations to comply with tax laws. However, I suspect that, in large measure, it has to do with the differential opportunity for noncompliance; third-party reporting may be a relatively strong enforcer of individuals' tax compliance; furthermore, corporate compliance is relatively high when measured against taxpayers' *opportunities* to evade (i.e., in terms of *income* for individuals, but *value added* or *total revenue* for corporations). And to the extent that the TCMP compliance measures aggressive tax stances and differences of legal opinion, corporate taxpayers would likely appear less compliant.

20. I would speculate that smaller corporations, like individuals, are much less likely than

TABLE 2. Median Statistics for Sample Firms

	Asset Class A	Asset Class B
Median total revenue[a]	$2,598,168	$920,608
Median total expenses[a]	$2,150,124	$799,041
Median taxable income[a]	$205,441	$82,252
Median corporate income tax due[a]	$55,767	$17,450
Median labor force[b]	125	NA
Percentage of corporations found underreporting	68.0%	67.7%
Percentage underreporting $1000 or more	93.1%	91.0%
Median amount of unreported income	$20,000	$9,875
Proportion of reported median income	11.6%	13.6%
Median amount amount of tax gap	$3,913	$2,020
Proportion of reported median income tax	6.4%	12.1%

Note: NA = not available.
[a]Per TCMP audit.
[b]Among 1,207 firms for which Labor Force figures were obtained.

Table 2 shows a profile of a typical corporation, using TCMP data to describe median statistics for each asset class.[21] To get some idea of the size of these corporations, note that the median 1981 work force of corporations in asset class A was 125.[22] More than two-thirds of all corporations fail to report part of their current-year income. Only 25 percent of all corporations report exactly the audited amount of income, although a small fraction of non-compliant corporations underreports by only $1,000 or less.[23] The median amount of unreported income in both asset classes is large both absolutely and relative to median income. In comparison, the median amount of tax gap is also substantial, but somewhat smaller relative to the median tax due. Table 3 reports the industry distribution of the TCMP sample (asset class A) and Table 4 contains miscellaneous information about the sample corporations that is relevant to the econometric study.

large corporations to employ tax losses strategically. This is consistent with the observation that the unreported income and unpaid taxes ratios are nearly the same for smaller corporations and individuals.

21. Since the distributions of taxable income, income tax, underreported income, and tax gap are highly skewed, their means exaggerate the extent of evasion. For instance, the mean of unreported income for those that underreport is $86,742, while the median is only $20,000. Accordingly, I report median values, whose magnitude is nonetheless impressive.

22. This figure only applies to the 1,207 firms for which I was able to identify the labor force variable.

23. Compare these figures with individual tax returns, of which 48 percent of individual income tax returns agree with the audited amount and 70 percent report within $50 of audited income.

The comparison of unreported income to taxable income is just one metric of the share of revenues that the government forgoes. However, one might instead wish to consider noncompliance relative to corporations' opportunity to evade. To some extent, this can be inferred from their level of business activity, for which two indicators are total revenue and total expenses.

Total revenue consists of receipts from all sources, less the calculated cost of goods sold. The revenue categories that involve the largest dollar amounts of tax gap are gross profit, the cost of goods sold, ordinary and capital gains, interest and dividends, and rents received. Total expenses are all operating costs and tax deductions. The largest expense categories are salaries and wages, bad debts, officers' compensation, interest paid, repairs, rents

TABLE 3. Industry Representation in the TCMP Sample of Asset Class A Corporations

Type	SIC Codes	Industry Name	Percentage Representation
Highly Regulated Industries			
	60, 61	Banking, savings	12.6
	65	Real estate	8.6
	67	Investment holding	2.1
	48	Communications	1.2
	63, 64	Insurance	0.9
	62	Securities brokerage	0.8
	49	Utilities	0.4
Subtotal			26.6
Other Services			
	52–57, 59	Retail	7.2
	40–47	Transportation	2.9
	70–76	Services	2.8
	80–89	Professional services	1.9
	27	Printing and publishing	1.8
	58, 78, 79	Entertainment	1.8
Subtotal			18.4
All Other Industries			
	34–39	Manufacturing	13.0
	15–17	Construction	8.8
	50	Wholesale—durables	9.3
	51	Wholesale—nondurables	6.8
	01, 06, 20, 21	Agriculture and food processing	5.7
	28–33	Primary materials production	4.1
	10–14	Mining	2.9
	22, 23	Textiles	2.5
	24–26	Lumber, wood, paper, and furniture	2.0
Subtotal			55.1

TABLE 4. Additional TCMP Tabulations

	Asset Class A	Asset Class B
Percentage of returns prepared in-house	9.2	5.9
Percentage of corporations having dealings with a tax haven country	2.7	1.5
Median number of hours invested by IRS in each TCMP audit	80	56
Percentage of audits conducted by an agent with high civil service grade (GS-12 or GS-13)	80.7	61.7
Percentage of corporations with zero current-year tax due		
per Tax Return	30.4	28.8
per TCMP Audit	28.0	26.8

paid, and taxes paid.[24] Looking again at table 2, the comparison of unreported income to these alternative measures makes noncompliance seem much smaller.

Figure 1 shows how similarly corporate tax compliance is distributed among firms in the two asset classes. In both groups, a quarter of the corporations reported the correct amount of taxable income. In both groups, more than two-thirds of the corporations failed to report their full income. And in both groups, there is a small fraction of the corporations in both asset classes that *overreported* their taxable income.

A similar pattern emerges when compliance is disaggregated into the percentage of corporations with unreported revenue and the percentage with overstated expenses (figs. 2 and 3). Yet in both asset classes, a large majority of firms are found to be compliant with respect to revenue. Thus, relatively more of the cases of noncompliance revealed through the TCMP audits involve disallowed expenses.

The obvious question to ask is whether the observed compliance difference between income and expenses is real or just a result of systematic measurement error. Specifically, one might be inclined to attribute the compliance difference to the different burdens of proof for the two types of items: corporations must document any expense items, whereas the IRS must prove that the corporation earned unreported revenue. However, total revenue also

24. To better see the fundamental dilemma about whether or not the TCMP measures only evasion or also honest mistakes and disagreements over tax laws, consider just a couple of line items: Is "bad debts" noncompliance an attempt to cheat or a difference of opinion about the correct timing of a legitimate deduction? Does "repairs" noncompliance constitute only evasion or also disputes over expensing of capital expenditures?

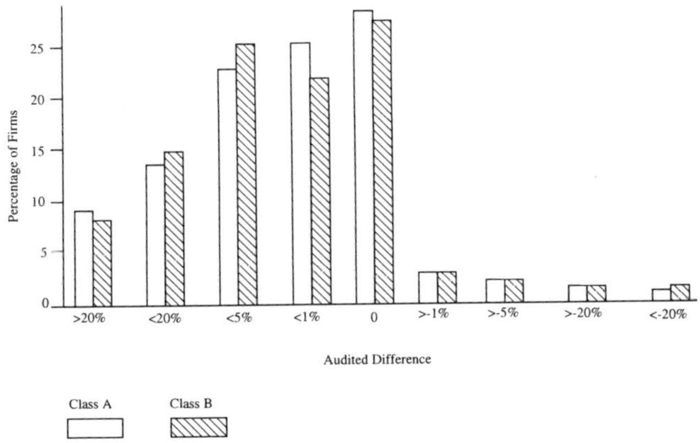

Fig. 1. Noncompliance as a percentage of value added

includes a large expense component—the cost of goods sold—that the corporation must document. So the "burden of proof" argument does not fully resolve why total expenses account for so much more noncompliance than does total revenue.

Table 5 draws a picture of the corporations that overreport taxable income. Fewer than seven percent of corporations fall into this category, in contrast to 14 percent of individual income taxpayers (Roth, Scholz and Witte 1989). This presumably reflects the fact that the average corporation is more informed than the average individual about the tax codes.[25] Compared to underreporters, overreporters comprise less than a tenth as many corporations, and twice as many overreporters are off by only a small amount. Their median audited income difference is also much less, and their current-year tax difference is tiny.[26] Econometric issues concerning overreporting are taken up in the next section.

---

25. I initially suspected that the widespread use of sophisticated outside tax preparers could explain why fewer corporations than individuals overreport. And, indeed, fewer than 10 percent of tax returns are prepared by an employee of the corporation (see table 4), while just over half of individual returns are prepared by taxpayers themselves (Internal Revenue Service 1980). Yet although one typically thinks of outside preparers as *less,* not more, error prone, returns prepared by CPAs and attorneys overreport 50 percent *more* on average than do in-house preparers. Perhaps in-house corporate preparers are also highly qualified, but are better informed about the business, or perhaps it reflects *risk aversion* on the part of small-scale, independent tax professionals.

26. This last fact reflects that 36 percent of corporations that overreport (representing 75 percent of overreported income) have current- or prior-year operating losses and so their current-year tax due is zero in either case (versus 28 percent and 23 percent, respectively, for underreporters and their unreported income).

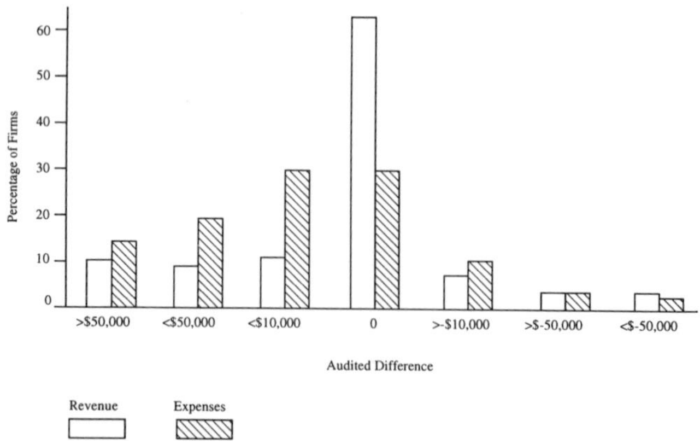

Fig. 2. Noncompliance through underreported revenue or over-reported expenses in asset class A firms

TCMP data are widely acknowledged to be the best available measure of tax compliance. Still, the TCMP's main failing is its inability to pick up all noncompliance. The IRS estimates that the TCMP for individuals uncovers only one-third of unreported income. Perhaps because compliance is better for line items for which a paper trail exists, the IRS calculates that the TCMP catches approximately half of the aggregate corporate noncompliance. Thus, the TCMP likely represents only a lower (and probably somewhat distorted) bound on true noncompliance.

Propositions Concerning Corporate Tax Evasion

One set of questions I explore econometrically concerns whether the characteristics that insure public disclosure of information about corporations' operations also tend to encourage better tax compliance. The first of these is the hypothesis, developed in Rice (1990), that a publicly traded firm will report

TABLE 5. Corporations that Overreport

	Asset Class A	Asset Class B
Percentage of corporations found overreporting	6.0	6.7
Percentage overreporting more than $1,000	81.7	80.6
Median amount of overreported income	$9,422	$6,485
Median amount of overpaid tax	$894	$466

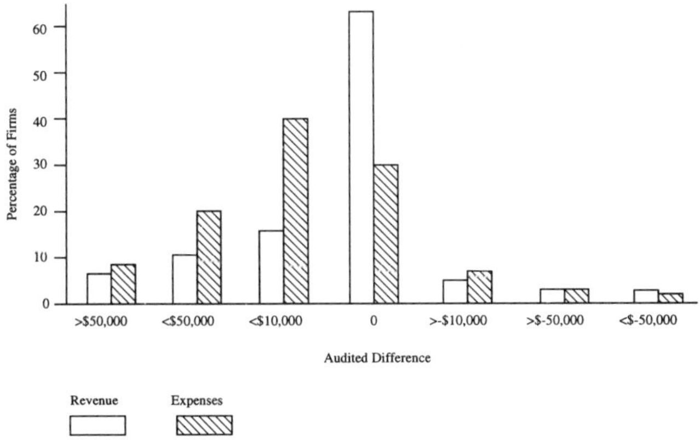

Fig. 3. Noncompliance through underreported revenue or over-reported expenses in asset class B firms

more of its taxable income than will an identical, privately held firm. The reasoning is that (1) SEC disclosure requirements compel publicly traded corporations to reveal their earnings more fully; (2) in a publicly traded corporation, any benefits of evasion accrue primarily to principals (shareholders)—who might be unaware of the risks taken for their benefit by their agents (managers)—while the punishment in the event of detection (e.g., dismissal) devolves on their agents;[27] (3) public shareholders may induce corporations to report their earnings more fully, since the value of their shares depends on reported profits (and the IRS requires a corporation to reconcile differences between its annual report and its tax return); and (4) managers of publicly traded corporations have an incentive to report earnings fully, since they typically receive a large part of their compensation in the form of stock options (see Benston 1985; Murphy 1989), and since their compensation is usually tied to the share price of their employer (see Coughlan and Schmidt 1989; Murphy 1989).

The empirical analysis controls for other corporate characteristics to determine whether being publicly traded has this hypothesized procompliance effect. If, instead, this effect either fails to materialize or is negative, how might one explain it? It has been suggested that the IRS is lax in reconciling annual reports with tax returns, thereby weakening the link between trading

27. Note that the agency issue could theoretically work in the opposite direction, as in the case where agents are rewarded for using any means of enhancing earnings—including evasion—but only the firm is subject to any penalty.

publicly and the probability of audit. Alternatively, corporations that file with the SEC may evidence a relatively larger tax gap, despite their relatively good tax compliance, because their clear paper trail enhances IRS auditors' ability to uncover such discrepancies as do exist.[28]

A second question regarding information disclosure considers industries that might be expected a priori to deviate from the median level of compliance. For instance, one might anticipate better compliance among highly regulated industries, most of which provide services. Conversely, practitioners' literature on corporate tax evasion tends to point to services in general as a locus of noncompliance (presumably because of the difficulty of measuring the costs of production and the quantity and value of output). Therefore, it seems useful to distinguish between services generally thought of as highly regulated and all other services, and compare these against all other industries.

A third information disclosure question seeks to quantify the role of tax haven countries in corporate tax evasion. While tax havens exist to facilitate tax avoidance, they also are sometimes implicated in cases of tax evasion. Thus, an intuitive hypothesis holds that a relationship with a tax haven country will correspond to lower tax compliance, in large part because this relationship is shielded from the IRS. In an attempt to capture any such relationship, I include a dummy variable for corporations that make use of a tax haven country (i.e., those that admit it to the IRS or that are discovered to do so).

However, I warn against overinterpreting the resulting coefficient, for two reasons. First, although it may be possible to observe correctly whether a corporation maintains a tax haven relationship, it may also be that many corporations have such a relationship, but the IRS discovers only relatively few.[29] If this problem is empirically important, the bias introduced will render the tax haven coefficient smaller in magnitude.

The second reason is that having a tax haven relationship represents an endogenous choice for a firm. Thus, the direction of causation between a tax haven relationship and noncompliance is uncertain. For example, it is plausible that noncompliance is simply easier to achieve or conceal for firms that have a tax haven relationship. Yet it is equally logical that firms that intend not

---

28. These ideas could be incorporated in the model (as could be done for some analogous issues) by modifying TCMP unreported income to be a function of "true" unreported income along with other firm and auditor characteristics.

29. Suppose, for example, that an examiner's ability to elicit information about a tax haven relationship from a company is correlated with his or her ability to uncover evasion by that company. Then any observed lower compliance among corporations with tax haven relationships might be spurious. Conversely, if a corporation's tax haven relationship is relatively observable, its probability of detection is greater, thereby inducing higher compliance.

to comply with the tax laws will establish a tax haven relationship to facilitate their doing so. For this reason, the correct interpretation of a significant tax haven coefficient in the empirical equations would be merely that it signals that these two variables are associated, rather than that the former causes the latter. The inherent limitations of this approach to understanding foreign tax havens gave impetus to a subsequent, more detailed study by Hines and Rice (1990).

Another set of hypotheses examines whether compliance is negatively or positively related to corporate profitability. The rationale for a negative relationship is that a corporation with below average true profitability will be more suspicious in the eyes of the IRS (and so raise the probability of an audit) if it reports even lower earnings than will a company with above average true profits that reports average earnings.[30] Alternatively, compliance and profitability may be positively correlated if, for example, managers in each industry are pressed to achieve some minimum profit performance (measured, say, as the deviation from median industry profitability). In this case, managers of low-profit corporations may resort to noncompliance to enhance actual net profits.[31] The net impact of these opposing profitability effects must be resolved empirically.

One complication in analyzing this question is inherent in using imperfect audits to measure "true income." Suppose that two corporations earn and underreport the same amount, but only one gets caught. Both the measures of profitability and of unreported income depend on this audit, and so one would observe worse compliance among more profitable corporations. This sort of measurement error biases the analysis in favor of finding a positive coefficient on profitability.

The third main question to be addressed in the econometric analysis is the effect of marginal tax rates on tax compliance. That high marginal tax rates encourage tax evasion was common currency in the recent debate on tax reform. Yet, as I have discussed, the theoretical and empirical debate remains unresolved. The theoretical model I presented previously generally indicates an inverse relationship (although it also studies a special case in which no relationship exists). The econometric analysis in the next section tests whether the marginal tax rate (as defined in appendix A) is a determinant of com-

30. Scotchmer (1987) makes the analogous point for the individual income tax. Conversely, a less profitable corporation may be liquidity constrained, and so might resort to underreporting as a means of enhancing cash flow.

31. This hypothesis has analogies in research concerning the impact of a profit squeeze on airline safety, on a company's willingness to fight unionization, and on charitable giving. In the theoretical model, this would suggest a more complicated specification of nonpecuniary fixed costs of an audit.

pliance. Of policy interest is the question: "If tax rates and compliance are inversely related, is there a Laffer-type effect?" (i.e., is the revenue loss arising from a cut in marginal tax rates more than offset by the revenue enhancement induced by improved tax compliance at that lower level of tax rates?).

In addition, I try to assess the view that taxpayers in certain geographic regions are inherently less compliant. In talking with IRS compliance officials, I found consensus that (roughly) six locales have reputations for poor tax compliance, both in individual and corporate tax returns and across all audit classes. These are California, Southern Florida, New York City, Chicago, Anchorage, and Las Vegas. IRS officials presume that these differences primarily reflect different social attitudes that tend to be found in more open and transient places. However, these compliance differences may disappear in the multivariate regression analysis after controlling for differences in other taxpayer characteristics.

Unfortunately, the level of aggregation of my geographic variable prevents me from considering all six of these locations. However, one of my regional groupings is California and another is Florida (in which most of the corporations sampled are located in southern Florida). Accordingly, I include a dummy variable for each of these two regions.[32]

Another hypothesis that this analysis permits us to test is that small businesses are less compliant than large ones. Tax professionals frequently express this view, reflecting, in part, their common belief that tax authorities are less likely to "go after a small fish."[33] It also seems to derive from the idea that evasion in a larger corporation necessarily requires the complicity of more employees (some of whom do not stand to gain directly) and tends to violate procedures that are more formalized.

On the other hand, the higher level of business activity in larger companies offers them more scope for noncompliance, and recent accounting literature argues that larger firms have a political incentive to lower their reported earnings.[34] Moreover, if the fixed costs of noncompliance are im-

32. According to IRS compliance officials, IRS auditors are distributed geographically to assure that taxpayers with an identical DIF score have an identical probability of audit. If, in fact, the IRS has not been able to assign its desired number of auditors to the two low compliance regions used in the study (California and Florida), this would lower the probability of audit in those regions and would artificially increase the magnitude of these coefficients (i.e., make them more negative).

33. See, for example, Donaldson (1973); Lynch (1973). Of course, this effect is largely eliminated by controlling for firm audit class, which is exactly what the econometric study does by using only one audit class.

34. Watts and Zimmerman's "size hypothesis" (1986) claims that larger firms use accounting strategies more aggressively to defer their reported earnings. The authors attribute this to the

portant, firm size should be correlated positively with noncompliance, because noncompliance will offer increasing returns to scale.

In addition, there may be a statistical bias resulting from errors in measuring the value-added variable (composed of taxable income plus salaries, wages, and officers' remuneration), used as a proxy for firm size. A large firm requires better records to monitor the performance of its agents than does a small firm. If these better records allow the TCMP to conduct a more successful audit, the audit will be relatively more successful in fully revealing true taxable income, as well as in diminishing overstated expenses for salaries, wages, and officers' remuneration. The sign of the net bias from these effects is, therefore, ambiguous.[35]

Finally, a recent theoretical proposition and empirical result to arise from the individual income tax literature concerns the ambiguous effect that professional tax preparers have on compliance.[36] Preparers allegedly induce higher compliance on tax items where the correct value is unambiguous, but they reduce compliance by exploiting tax code ambiguities. Accordingly, one cannot say, a priori, whether outside tax preparers induce relatively more or less evasion. Perhaps it depends also on the type of preparer. One striking observation from the data in table 3 is that a huge proportion of corporations in both asset classes hire outside tax preparers. Moreover, an overwhelming share of these seek a CPA rather than an attorney, a certified agent, or any other type of outside preparer. Therefore, it seems reasonable to include a dummy variable to control for a possible difference between corporations that use CPAs and those that do not.

Note, however, several reasons why the use of this variable might produce a biased or imprecise coefficient. First, noncompliance by a professional tax preparer will presumably escape TCMP detection with relative ease; this biases the results in favor of a finding that tax preparers induce compliance. Conversely, the results may be biased in the other direction to the extent that tax preparers inhibit tax evasion but encourage aggressive tax stances, and the TCMP financial audits observe aggressive stances but not true evasion. Furthermore, the choice of a tax preparer is an endogenous firm decision. Finally, the variable "Return Prepared by a CPA" may be noisy, inasmuch as reputable accounting firms may serve to signal their clients' compliance, while other

---

political costs for a large (and therefore visible) firm that is perceived to have earned excessive profits or demonstrated excessive profits growth. Support for this hypothesis might also be inferred from Zmijewski and Hagerman's probit finding (1981) that the use of accounting strategies to defer earnings is a positive function of firm size.

35. I will subsequently discuss how the bias can be bounded to some extent.

36. See Klepper, Mazur, and Nagin (1988); Klepper and Nagin (1989); Mazur and Nagin (1987); Westat (1980b).

CPAs serve to assist their clients to evade tax. As with the tax haven dummy, a finding that the dummy for preparation by a CPA has a significant coefficient should at most be interpreted as a signal of correlation, not one of causation.

A final consideration is the bias introduced due to the fact that, in a TCMP survey year, the number of corporate TCMP audits is a large share of all corporate tax audits. Specifically, in 1980 (as in other years) the IRS conducted its typical 40,000 operational audits, with audit selection based on each corporation's IRS audit selection formula score (or DIF score). But unlike other years, TCMP conducted an additional approximately 30,000 *random* audits in 1980. This factor significantly changes the usual relationship between the DIF score and the probability of being audited.

For example, if a variable enters positively into the DIF formula, then corporations with that positively correlated characteristic will be audited relatively less frequently in a TCMP year, compared to corporations without it, than would be the case in a non-TCMP year. Consequently, in a TCMP year, the fact of possessing the positively correlated characteristic is less strongly correlated with the probability of audit than is the case in an ordinary tax year. Conversely, the likelihood of audit for corporations without the characteristic is increased in TCMP years. Therefore, there will be an upward bias in the absolute size of the coefficient on any variable that is used to calculate the DIF score.

The difficulty in using this information is that one cannot know which variables enter the DIF formula and how. Among the variables used here, only two—tax havens and low-compliance region dummies—can be presumed to enter the DIF formula in a particular direction. If, as I presume, these variables are positively correlated with the DIF formula, then their coefficients will be biased upward. The biases would be analogous if certain industry-group variables also enter the DIF formula, however it is less certain whether they do and, if so, with what sign.

The Econometrics of U.S. Corporate Tax Compliance

In this section, I assess econometrically the propositions I have set forth. I begin by assuming the following linear specification for equation 3.

$$U = a_0 + a_1 \text{ Marginal Tax Rate} + a_2 \text{ Public Dummy} + a_3 \text{ Susceptibility} + \epsilon, \qquad (3)$$

where U is unreported income. Coefficient a_0 captures the effects of the fine and of the fixed cost of audit, which are presumed fixed across firms, in addition to the true constant.

Although a firm's true susceptibility to detection, S, is unobservable, I posit that it can be summarized by a linear function $S = S$(firm size, profitability, industry). As described in the previous section, firm size can be expected to increase the susceptibility to detection. In the empirical specification, the primary measure of firm size is total audited value added by a corporation. In addition, I was able to collect the labor force variable for 1,207 of the corporations, and to use this as an alternative measure in tests run on this subsample.

The previous section also discusses the effect of profitability (measured by the profit rate) on susceptibility, as well as the direct effect of relative profitability (the deviation from the industry median) on compliance. Industry enters $S(\cdot)$ because corporations in each industry will tend to engage in activities that are similarly susceptible to detection. In this regard, I single out corporations in highly regulated service industries, whose operations are thus relatively transparent to the IRS, versus those in all other service industries.

Three final elements of the estimating equation are controls for low-compliance geographic regions, for tax preparation by a CPA, and for the IRS examiner's civil service grade. The first of these shifts the slope of the equation for corporations from Florida or California, while the second does the same for returns prepared by a nonemployee CPA. The third indirectly captures some of the IRS's auditing error in measuring the audited taxable income variable (used for true taxable income). It assumes that an examiner's ability to detect evasion grows with job experience, and uses civil service grade as its measure.[37]

Tentatively, I wish to estimate:

$$\begin{aligned} U = \beta X + u = \; & \beta_1 . \gamma + \beta_2 \rho + \beta_3 \eta + \\ & \beta_4 \pi + \beta_5 \tau + \beta_6 \sigma + \beta_7 \nu + \\ & \beta_8 \theta + \beta_9 \phi + \beta_{10} \psi + u \; , \end{aligned}$$

where γ = dummy for publicly traded, ρ = dummy for regulated service industry, η = dummy for tax haven affiliation, π = profit rate, τ = marginal tax rate, σ = firm size, ν = dummy for other, unregulated services, θ =

37. The directors of the audit program of TCMP themselves believe that more senior auditors are relatively more successful at uncovering noncompliance. In addition, they advised me that, *within each audit class*, auditors are assigned to cases randomly (rather than difficult cases being matched to more experienced auditors). If this IRS assertion is correct, it lessens the likelihood that this variable is endogenously determined. If not, the direction of the bias cannot be determined: if senior auditors are given cases involving large dollar amounts of underreporting, there would be a negative bias (i.e., the observed coefficient would be of greater [negative] magnitude); if instead they are given cases that are difficult to crack, there would be a positive bias.

dummy for geographic region, ϕ = dummy for tax return prepared by external professional, and ψ = Civil Service grade.

The main econometric complication arises because corporations will generally not intentionally report to the IRS more than their true taxable income.[38] As a result, the unreported income variable is censored from below at the point of zero evasion: one observes an atom of fully compliant corporations, each of which has a different propensity for tax compliance. This censoring biases the OLS coefficients on the independent variables downward.

The problem actually involves two concepts of noncompliance. The first measures agents' underlying propensity to underreport (*PU*), based on that agents' characteristics, *X*. Thus, *PU* may be interpreted as the unobservable shadow price for full compliance (i.e., the transfer that would be necessary to make corporate managers indifferent between full compliance and $1 of noncompliance), for which the dollar value may range from negative to positive infinity. The second concept is observed actual underreporting (*AU*), such that

$$AU = PU \quad \text{if } PU \geq 0,$$
$$AU = 0 \quad \text{if } PU < 0.^{39} \tag{4a}$$

Although *AU* is useful for estimating aggregate compliance, *PU* is more interesting for the purposes of this study, since it measures the behavioral relationship between the characteristics of a corporation and its compliance tendencies. For corporations that underreport ($PU \geq 0$), one can observe

$$PU = \beta X + u \, . \tag{4b}$$

This sort of selectivity model may be estimated using a tobit maximum likelihood specification.

One shortcoming of the tobit model, as I will discuss, is its inability to differentiate between corporations that are exactly compliant and the small percentage of corporations that actually overreport their true taxable income. For the present, I follow Clotfelter (1983) in setting unreported income to zero for overreporters.

38. A fraction of corporations actually do overreport, the implications of which are dealt with subsequently.

39. Alternatively, it may be seen as reflecting the fixed cost of noncompliance that must be surpassed before the potential gains of underreporting actually induce observed noncompliance. In this second interpretation: $AU = PU$ if $PU \leq B_i$ and $AU = 0$ if $PU < B_j$, where B_j represents the flyed barrier against noncompliance for the ith corporation. This model can be estimated in the same way as the first, although the coefficients would be unidentified since they include the unobservable B_j.

TABLE 6. Tobit Model Estimates of Determinants of Tax Evasion for Sample Selection

			Overreporting as Full Compliance (with interactions)		Model Corrected for Taxpayer Mistakes	
Variable	Mean	SD	Estimate	SE	Estimate	SE
Constant (in thousands of dollars)	—	—	−56	101	−269*	132
Publicly traded	0.036	0.186	−61.000*	29,800	−75,800*	38,900
Highly regulated services	0.27	0.44	−44,600*	14,900	−86,600*	19,600
Dealings with a tax haven country	0.027	0.163	132,400*	32,900	132,000*	42,700
Profitability (in hundred thousand dollars)[a]	3.92	8.66	5,800*	1,200	6,400*	1,600
Deviation from median industry profit	−0.6%	22.7%	−1,768*	363	−2,028*	451
Marginal tax rate	38.7%	13.3%	700	600	1,500*	800
Firm size (in millions of dollars)[b]	1.35	1.57	14,843*	4,996	22,489*	6,286
Other services	0.18	0.39	12,400	14,900	13,300	19,000
Florida	0.04	0.20	57,800*	26,300	106,400*	32,700
California	0.11	0.31	27,200	17,000	42,900*	21,700
Return prepared by CPA	0.88	0.32	−20,300	16,600	−24,200	21,500
Auditor's Civil Service grade	12.1	0.7	8,100	7,100	19,900*	9,300
Log likelihood		—	−25,948		−19,301	

Notes: The dependent variable is the dollar difference between audited and reported income; calculated point estimates are rounded to the nearest hundred dollars. Taxable income is interacted with marginal tax rate, publicly traded, tax haven, highly regulated services, other services, Florida, California, return prepared by a CPA, and auditor's Civil Service grade; these interaction term coefficients are reported in appendix table A, and are factored into the appropriate coefficients here using the mean level of the variable interacted with.

[a]Taxable income, controlling for capital assets. The capital assets control variable is included in the regressions, but not reported; its coefficient does not significantly differ from zero.

[b]Value added.

*$p = .05$.

Table 6 sets out the tobit model point estimates.[40] Since the impact of a dummy variable (or the other discrete variables) on the dollar amount of noncompliance is surely magnified for larger and more profitable corporations, any statistically significant coefficients on such dollar-denominated independent variables as profitability and value added might simply reflect this misspecification. For this reason, I add interactions of each discrete variable with the taxable income variable. The coefficients on the discrete variables are evaluated at the mean income for asset class A.[41]

40. Appendix table A1 reports all of the tobit coefficients separately, including interaction terms.

41. I also report tobit results without these interactions in the first column of appendix table A1. The specification with interactions seems clearly superior to that without, since five of the nine interaction terms are highly significant and its log likelihood is somewhat increased. Further-

The coefficients on the publicly traded corporations, highly regulated services, and tax haven dummies are as predicted—with statistically significant point estimates of −$61,000 and −$44,000, and $132,400, respectively.[42] I also find that more profitable corporations are relatively less compliant, with a reporting gap point estimate of $5,800 per $100,000 of earnings; conversely, a 1 percentage point deviation from the median industry profit rate of a firm is associated with moderately enhanced income reporting of $1,768. As explained previously, one expects profitability to have an ambiguous compliance effect and its coefficient to be biased upward, because the same auditing error in measuring profitability also affects overall unreported income in the same direction. If one knew the boundaries of any such bias, one could evaluate its magnitude. The logical measure of the approximate lower bound on the true value of profitability is its *reported* value. Using this measure, the potential bias would be negative. And, indeed, the same tobit test using *reported* firm and industry profitability decreases the size of the profitability coefficient somewhat and renders it statistically insignificant at the 5 percent level. It also causes the industry profitability deviation variable to disappear entirely. These suggest that the true relationships are nonnegative, but smaller than the reported coefficient. As a result, conclusions about the relationship between profitability and tax compliance should be considered tentative.

The marginal tax rate coefficient is positive and of moderate size, but not significant at the 5 percent level (although appendix A explains why my coefficient may be smaller than the true coefficient). Firm size, as measured by total value added, demonstrates a positive and statistically significant compliance effect ($14,843 per million dollars),[43] which corresponds to an elasticity of one-third.[44] The geographic dummy effects do not disappear in

---

more, the results of the two specifications are similar in almost all respects; the only notable differences are that, in the specification with interactions, the coefficient on publicly traded becomes statistically significant and that on California becomes smaller and loses its significance.

42. Although as I have explained previously, the tax haven variable is endogenous and may be especially difficult to measure.

43. Recall that coefficient estimates all pertain to PU, the *propensity* to underreport, rather than AU (for fully compliant corporations, $PU \geq AU = 0$). I also tried to test the effect of firm size by substituting the labor force variable for value added, using the 1,207 corporation subsample for which I obtained this variable. I again found a large positive coefficient, but it was not statistically significant.

44. This coefficient may be subject to a statistical bias, the direction of which is uncertain. Yet the bias should be reversed if one measures value added using *reported* taxable income, but *audited* wages, salaries, and officers' remuneration. I used this modified firm size variable in an identical regression in order to put a bound on the effect of the bias, and found that the coefficient actually increases in size by almost half, and remains strongly significant and positive. This suggests that, if anything, the reported coefficient underestimates the relationship of firm size with tax compliance.

the tobit test. Instead, the coefficient on Florida, one of the two poor compliance regions, is large, negative, and statistically significant, with a point estimate of $57,800. And while the California coefficient is not significant at the 5 percent level, it cannot be ignored either: its point estimate is a large and positive $27,200, with a *t*-statistic of 1.60. Finally, the coefficients for other service industries, tax preparation by an outside CPA, and auditor's Civil Service grade are of moderate size but not statistically significant.

Overreporting

A second econometric consideration concerns corporations that overreport their taxable income. Figure 1 demonstrates that about 6 percent of all corporations in each asset class overstate taxable income to some extent. Previous analyses explain overreporting in two ways. First, the use of certain tax provisions is likely to trigger a costly tax audit, even when the provisions are applied legitimately and no fine will ultimately be imposed; in such a case, honest taxpayers may forgo using such provisions to reduce the probability of being audited. Second, overreporting signals that taxpayers misinterpret the tax laws.[45]

If the first explanation predominates, it is correct to interpret overreporters as fully compliant taxpayers, as I have so far. However, if taxpayer mistakes are also important, the analysis should correct for them. By definition, honest mistakes should be symmetrically distributed about a mean of zero. The upper quadrants of figure 4 show the observable compliance distribution; the lower quadrants reflect this presumptive distribution of taxpayer mistakes. Obviously, if overreporting consists of mistakes, it is wrong to treat negative mistakes as evasion while considering corporations that make positive mistakes as full compliance.

Feinstein and Alexander (1986) attempt to account for individual taxpayer mistakes by asserting that a taxpayer's propensity to make mistakes is a function that can be inferred from available taxpayer characteristics. They then posit a distribution of this function and use maximum likelihood methods to identify it. While econometrically clever, the model is identified only by its distributional assumptions. It is, therefore, difficult to interpret the correction, which in any case yields little difference in the estimated coefficients or their significance.

Given the informational limitations, a more reasonable approach is to assume that low-magnitude corporate noncompliance always represents a mis-

45. In fact, overreporting can actually signal noncompliance—as in the case of a corporation whose net operating loss carry forward will expire unless it illegitimately disguises future earnings as current taxable income. However, with only one year of tax audit data available, there is no way to identify overreporting that constitutes noncompliance.

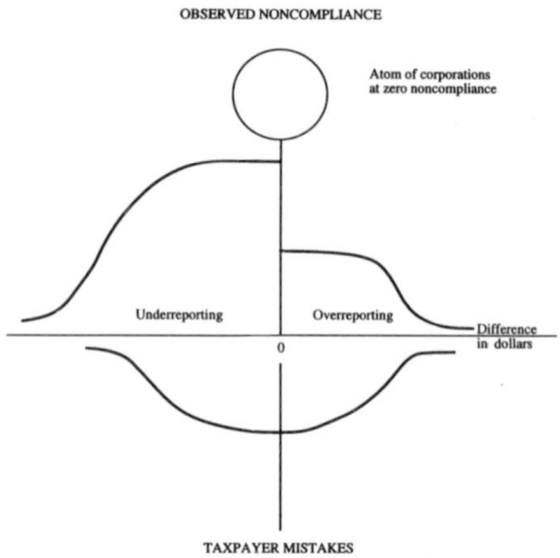

Fig. 4. Apparent compliance versus taxpayer mistakes

take, and so treat only large amounts of noncompliance as tax evasion. I ran the earlier tobit model setting underreporting that was relatively small (as well as all overreporting) equal to zero. I defined "relatively small" arbitrarily, as no more than one-tenth of 1 percent of a corporation's capital assets.[46] With this 0.001 band, 49.1 percent of all corporations are deliberately noncompliant, 47.5 percent are fully compliant, and only 3.3 percent overreport.

By this means, I attempt to treat the symmetrical mistakes more similarly, since now only about half of the presumed accidental underreporting is counted as evasion. At the same time, I try to focus primarily on the relevant observations for the purposes of both researchers and the TCMP: nontrivial cases of evasion that do not result from inadvertence.[47] My main objective in using this "correction" is to verify whether accounting for overreporting substantially changes the tobit results.

Table 6 also reports the results after correcting for taxpayer mistakes,

46. One may think of this precise value of 0.001 as simply representative, since the tobit results are strikingly similar for a wide range of alternative bands, and also since all nontrivial coefficient changes move monotonically as this band is enlarged from zero to substantially greater than 0.001. I use the 0.001 band for convenience, in that it is a round number that nearly halves the number of overreporters. I was reluctant to use a much larger band because even the 0.001 band begins to substantially challenge the spirit of the TCMP survey by reclassifying almost 20 percent of the sample from "noncompliant" to "compliant."

47. One might argue that a shortcoming of this simple approach is its failure to explain an important asymmetry: that a majority of the presumed "mistakes" inside the band are made in favor of the taxpayer. Yet it is not clear that the distribution of taxpayer mistakes in terms of dollar amounts will be symmetrically distributed.

with most coefficients remaining similar in sign and significance to the earlier tests. The correction causes several of the point estimates to increase in magnitude, but only the increase for highly regulated services is statistically significant. It also causes the positive coefficients on California and on auditor's Civil Service grade to grow in size and to attain statistical significance.

More important, the relationship between the marginal tax rate and compliance, which in the uncorrected tobit is positive and of moderate size but not statistically significant, doubles in size with the correction and becomes statistically significant. As has been alluded to previously, appendix A explains why the marginal tax rate coefficient may be understated. In addition, appendix B reports the results of probit tests of noncompliance—informal tests of the correctness of the tobit specification and its coefficients—which find significant and positive marginal tax rate coefficients (both with and without the correction). These two observations favor the corrected specification over the initial one. The marginal tax rate effect may imply that the fixed costs of an audit are important, so that, as the marginal tax rate increases, the benefits of noncompliance increasingly outweigh the higher risks of audit or detection. However, the relationship of tax compliance and the marginal tax rate falls far short of demonstrating a Laffer-type curve—a cut in marginal corporate tax rates costs nineteen dollars in forgone revenue for every dollar raised via the channel of a smaller tax gap.[48]

Conclusions and Policy Implications

This study is the first public, statistical analysis of the corporate TCMP. As such, it makes special efforts to describe the data. However, my primary focus is to examine several propositions about the nature of corporations that evade income tax.

The study lends strong support to three main propositions. First, characteristics that assure public disclosure of information about a corporation's operations also tend to encourage better tax compliance. This conclusion is based on findings that compliance is positively associated with being publicly traded and with belonging to a highly regulated industry, and that corporations whose operations are shielded from view through their dealings with a tax haven country demonstrate very poor compliance. Second, high-profit companies may take advantage of their greater ability to underreport income without being audited, whereas managers of a corporation whose profit per-

48. More precisely, decreasing the marginal tax rate (i.e., for income subject to the top bracket only) faced by each corporation in asset class A would cost $66.7 million per year in forgone revenue, but would shrink the tax gap by only $3.5 million per year.

formance falls short of its industry norm may resort to noncompliance as a means of shaving costs. These conclusions derive from findings that higher profits seem to coincide with worse compliance, while deviations from the sample's median industry profit rate correspond positively with tax compliance (although these findings may be exaggerated because of measurement error). And third, the marginal tax rate is associated negatively with compliance, although a cut in the marginal tax rate would cost the U.S. Treasury a dollar in revenue for every 5.3 cents it could raise via enhanced compliance.

The study rejects the common presumption of a positive relationship between firm size and tax compliance, finding, instead, that the reporting gap grows with the amount of a firm's value added (with an estimated elasticity of one-third to one-half).[49] However, I am unable to reject the IRS's view that there exist certain high-evasion geographic regions; rather, I find that, even after controlling for many other likely explanatory variables, a large reporting gap remains for corporations located in the two presumed poor compliance regions for which data were available. I fail to find an unambiguous relationship of compliance with service industries or with the use of an outside CPA for tax preparation.

I account to some extent for the econometric problem of overreporting by establishing a band within which I consider over- or underreporting as a taxpayer mistake. The corrected tobit model produces results that are similar to the uncorrected test, but finds significant effects for the marginal tax rate, for the second presumed poor compliance region, and for auditor quality.

Without commenting on the welfare implications of either tax evasion or of its reduction, the study offers a few implications for tax administration. In particular, public information disclosure is strongly associated with high tax compliance. For this reason, the IRS could require corporations to report whether they are publicly traded, or it could ascertain whether a corporation is among the 25 percent of corporations in highly regulated industries, and use this information in audit selection. Moreover, disclosure requirements such as those faced by publicly traded corporations may also be efficaciously applied to all corporations.

In addition, the positive association of tax noncompliance with having a tax haven relationship might give reason for the U.S. government to redouble its efforts to forge tax treaties that grant exchange of information with tax haven countries. It also suggests that more routine collection of information regarding tax haven relationships might enhance audit selection.

The study's findings suggest a more intensive auditing use (and perhaps

49. These trade-offs are calculated using the uncorrected and corrected tobits, respectively.

verification) of the industry variable by the IRS. In particular, auditors might consider industry standards of profitability. Finally, the study indicates that there does not appear to be a Laffer-type effect via the channel of the marginal tax rate; accordingly, the greater tax compliance resulting from lower corporate income taxes cannot be expected to offset substantially the concomitant revenue loss.

APPENDIX A: DATA AND VARIABLES

The IRS conducts its corporate TCMP irregularly every 3 to 7 years, and each audit focuses on a single tax year. The "TCMP IV-4" used here is the latest completed survey, which uses returns for the 1980 tax year. It selects firms from its Business Master File, with sampling ratios varying according to asset class. Asset class A (corporations with assets of $5,000,000 to $9,999,999) is a sample of 2,696 from an estimated population of 16,648. Asset class B (corporations with assets of $1,000,000 to $4,999,999) is a sample of 4,050 corporations from an estimated population of 118,445. This means that the IRS sampled asset class A nearly five times as heavily as it did asset class B.

Out of the 2,696 corporations in asset class A, 3 were eliminated because it was not possible to determine whether or not they were publicly traded (discussed below), and 3 others were rejected because their "sample code" indicated that they had been wrongly classified as belonging to asset class A. Wrong sample codes also eliminated 5 observations in asset class B.

The extent of corporate TCMP data errors is extraordinarily high. About 7 percent of the observations in both asset classes contain at least one entry of the "per tax return" or "per TCMP audit" value of total revenue, taxable income, or income tax that is wrongly signed as positive. These errors are easily detectable with simple consistency checks.

Of particular concern are the more than 5 percent of negative taxable income observations in asset class A that are wrongly classified as positive (in either or both of the "reported" or "audited" categories). For the asset class A corporate population, the errors do not greatly distort the aggregate *amount* of unreported income, since error correction reveals $218 million of underreporting that is almost precisely offset by $226 million of misclassified overreporting. However, the mistakes cause a substantial misclassification of corporations as overreporters when they are actually underreporters.

Data correction reveals that 21 percent of the seeming overreporters were incorrectly classified as underreporters. Yet because the overwhelming proportion of corporations are actually underreporters, the error correction among underreporters reduces the *amount* of their seeming noncompliance, but causes only 0.1 percent of them to be reclassified into the overreporters' camp.

Another two-fifths of the taxable income data errors involve corporations that exactly report their correct taxable income, but where both reported and audited entries had been misidentified as positive. In such cases, the only problem is that the errors distort the taxable income variable for research purposes. As an example, by correcting all errors in the audited taxable income variable, the aggregate value of the series rises by 10.3 percent.

This widespread measurement error is likely to undermine studies made without access to the TCMP microdata and without efforts to correct these data. While data correction does not greatly change the dollar amount of evaded income, it does increase the IRS's estimates of the prevalence of corporate tax evasion and alters the compliance status of numerous corporations. The IRS would do well to make these corrections itself to improve its DIF calculations and aggregate compliance estimates.

The econometric analysis required certain information not contained in TCMP records. In order to determine whether a corporation was publicly traded at or near the 1980 TCMP tax year, I first referred to the Standard and Poor's *Register of Corporations* and the Dun and Bradstreet *Million Dollar Directory,* using for identification each corporation name, SIC code, and zip code from the TCMP sample. I then used Disclosure's *SEC Filing Companies* microfilm to verify the date the corporations went public and, if it was taken private, when that occurred. For three of the corporations, there was a publicly traded corporation by the same or a similar name, but I was unable to assure myself that my listing was or was not the publicly traded one. In these cases, I eliminated the corporation from the sample.[50]

I also used the *Register of Corporations* and the *Million Dollar Directory* to obtain the labor force variable where possible (for 1,207 of the observations). Since few corporations in asset class B are listed in these outside references, I used only asset class A for the econometric analysis.

With respect to the marginal tax rate, Poterba (1987) discusses two problems in this variable as generally used. First is its high correlation with income; second is that cross-sectional studies purport to identify changes in the marginal tax schedule, but generally confuse them with what is more easily observed: differences in taxpayers' marginal tax brackets. This latter difficulty leads Clotfelter (1983) to try for identification by using average state marginal tax rates.

Unfortunately, it is not possible to use state income tax rates to determine the marginal tax rate faced by corporations—even with microdata. One reason is that for corporations, more than for individuals, (corporate headquarters) location is a choice variable. Even more problematically, many corporations in the sample operate across state lines. Accordingly, jurisdiction for state income tax purposes is apportioned across states by formulas involving sales and locations of operations and of labor force. Therefore, it is neither possible to determine nor meaningful to think of a specific marginal state income tax rate.

I instead calculate a measure that more accurately reflects the true marginal federal income tax schedules that corporations face, and is consistent with recent accounting theory (see Scholes and Wolfson 1991). My approach conceives of nega-

---

50. I include as "publicly traded" four corporations that filed disclosure statements only through 1979 or beginning in 1981 (i.e., in the year prior or subsequent to the observation year).

tive taxable income or of an operating loss carryover (OLC) as an option that may be exercised to lessen future tax liabilities or an asset to be applied against past tax liabilities. Conveniently, it is also much less correlated with income than are standard tax rate tables. Moreover, it provides variation in the tax schedule each corporation faces, depending on its past accumulation of net operating losses and its probable future profits or losses.

Given corporations' heavy reliance on OLCs, it would be inaccurate simply to apply the statutory rates to current-year taxable income. The procedure I use to estimate the marginal tax schedules produces a single schedule for the 73 percent of corporations with positive current-year taxable income and no prior-year OLC, seven schedules for corporations with an OLC, and eight schedules for corporations with negative current income but no OLC.

In each case, I use a simple weighted least squares regression to calculate expected future income, to determine any possible future operating loss *carrybacks* and the year in which any current-year loss would be extinguished. Corporations with positive current income and no OLC are subject to the statutory tax rate schedule, applied to their income less any expected carryback from future years.

A second group consists of corporations with OLCs. These corporations may carry the OLC forward, applying it against current income and up to six additional years of future income until it is completely offset. For these corporations, the marginal benefit of underreporting depends on the present value of taxes for the year in which the OLC is expected to be extinguished. Depending on the size of the OLC, current income, and expected future income, the corporation would be subject to one of seven marginal tax schedules.

The third class of corporations has negative current income but no OLC. Such a firm may immediately apply the current loss against its income in the past three years. I estimate the marginal tax rate on this past-year's income, less the operating loss carryback. If the current loss more than offsets past income, it will be carried forward; in this case, the calculation is similar to the case of corporations with OLCs.

This marginal tax rate formulation implicitly assumes that corporations passively apply their OLCs to offset their earnings. Thus, the present value of the OLC falls, as does the marginal tax rate, for each year a corporation must carry a loss forward for lack of sufficient current income to exploit the OLC fully. However, to the extent that corporations can act strategically to exploit OLCs—for example, by merging with profitable firms or by altering their taxable income through investment, production, financing, or accounting decisions—the present value of the OLC will not decline as rapidly as I have assumed. Therefore, my marginal tax rate variable overstates the true variation in rates. The corollary of having overstated the range of the marginal tax rate is that the coefficient on my measure of marginal tax rate will be smaller than the true relationship.

I have asserted above that the return to equity capital may be a determinant of susceptibility. However, in medium-sized corporations, there is no measure of "equity capital" that is consistent across corporations. For example, corporate bonds may be held by large shareholders and, if so, should probably be considered equity capital. Therefore, capital assets serves, instead, as a proxy for equity capital in the statistical analysis. Note that, although the two measures are different, IRS auditing decisions

TABLE A1. Tobit Model Estimates

	Overreporting as Full Compliance				Model Corrected for Taxpayer Mistakes	
	No Interactions		With Interactions			
Variable	Estimate	SE	Estimate	SE	Estimate	SE
Constant (in thousands of dollars)	−175	97	−56	101	−269*	132
Publicly traded	49,884	31,435	−22,583	30,957	−42,355	40,647
Highly regulated services	45,264*	14,506	−34,912*	14,809	−83,325*	19,852
Dealings with a tax haven country	123,719*	34,143	64,837	33,513	50,327	44,585
Profitability (in millions of dollars)[a]	7,817*	1,096	−22,537*	11,210	−25,438	14,309
Deviation from median industry profit	−2,177*	336	−1,768*	363	−2,028*	451
Marginal tax rate	−346	506	223	504	758	668
Assets (in millions of dollars)	262	405	−578	378	−6,214	4,917
Value added (in millions of dollars)	−18,859*	5,274	14,843*	4,996	22,489*	6,286
Other services	−5,915	15,662	934	16,734	2,330	21,349
Florida	58,488*	27,726	43,098	29,167	95,675*	36,348

California	55,656*	17,625	−47,596*	19,113	−33,108	24,569
Return prepared by CPA	−13,284	17,524	67,725*	17,969	−74,571*	23,470
Auditor's Civil Service grade	10,101	7,558	4,457	7,903	16,301	10,371
Interactions of taxable income (in thousands of dollars) with						
Publicly traded			−99*	26	−86*	33
Highly regulated services			−25	25	−8	32
Dealings with a tax haven country			173*	28	210*	36
Marginal tax rate			1.3*	0.5	2.0*	0.6
Other services			30	17	28	21
Florida			38	28	28	34
California			192*	18	195*	22
Return prepared by CPA			119*	18	129*	23
Auditor's Civil Service grade			9	9	9	12
Log likelihood	−26,060		−25,948		−19,301	

Notes: The dependent variable is the dollar difference between audited and reported income.

[a]Taxable income, controlling for capital assets. The capital assets control variable is included in the regressions, but not reported.

$*p = .05$.

also must depend on a similar proxy measure, since the IRS suffers from the same lack of more detailed information.

The "return" is also a difficult concept, since the fungible economic return may be distributed otherwise, for instance as officers' remuneration or some other expense item. I simply use taxable income, excluding operating loss carryovers, as a measure of the return. Since the capital assets variable is kept constant in the regression as the return varies, the coefficient on taxable income measures the compliance effect of changing corporate profitability.

The unreported income variable is the difference between taxable income "per Tax Return" and "per TCMP audit." I discuss in the text the questionable reliability of this "per TCMP audit" measure. And finally, note that the measure I obtained from the IRS for the cost of goods sold is imperfect in that it also includes that part of wages attributed to creating the inventory of goods.

Table A1 presents my complete regression results, including each interaction term.

TABLE B1. Probit Model Estimates of Determinants of Tax Compliance

	Overreporting as Full Compliance (with interactions)		Model Corrected for Taxpayer Mistakes	
Variable	Estimate	SE	Estimate	SE
Constant (in thousands of dollars)	−0.37	0.48	−1.32*	0.47
Profitability (in hundred thousand dollars)[a]	0.005	0.007	0.004	0.006
Firm size (in millions of dollars)[b]	0.039	0.026	0.070*	0.020
Effective marginal tax rate	0.009*	0.003	0.011*	0.003
Publicly traded	−0.45*	0.13	−0.40*	0.14
Dealings with a tax haven country	−0.02	0.16	−0.05	0.16
Deviation from median industry profit	0.29	0.17	0.09	0.17
Highly regulated services	−0.34*	0.07	−0.43*	0.07
Other services	−0.11	0.07	−0.08	0.07
Florida	0.24	0.14	0.49*	0.13
California	0.05	0.08	0.13	0.08
Return prepared by CPA	−0.020	0.080	−0.005	0.079
Auditor's Civil Service grade	0.09*	0.03	0.12*	0.03
Log likelihood	−1,614		−1,743	

Notes: The dependent variable is the noncompliance decision; calculated point estimates are rounded to the nearest hundred dollars. Interaction term coefficients are factored into the coefficient of interest using the mean level of the variable interacted with.

[a]Taxable income, controlling for capital assets. The capital assets control variable is included in the regressions, but not reported.

[b]Value added.

$*p = .05$.

APPENDIX B: PROBIT VERIFICATION

As an informal text of the tobit results, I consider the analogous probit regression for the "Noncompliance Decision" as a means of comparing the signs and relative size of the coefficients. Of course, the coefficient magnitudes are not comparable across the two methods. Table B1 reports the probit point estimates, which are generally consistent with the tobit findings.

In particular, the probit test is consistent with the corrected tobit's marginal tax rate finding, since both the uncorrected and corrected probits find this coefficient to be positive, significant, and of moderate size. Similarly, the lack of statistical significance of the coefficient on profitability is consistent with my conclusion that the relationship is ambiguous.

The probit and tobit coefficients differ with respect to the dummy for firms that have dealings with a tax haven country, in that the probit tests fail to replicate the large, significant, and positive coefficients, finding instead no relationship. In addition, while significant in the uncorrected probit, the coefficient on deviation from industry profit rate lacks statistical significance in the corrected probit. This suggests that the tobit model is not literally correct—and of course one expects that the model will suffer some degree of specification error—in its statistical assumption that this single coefficient can capture both the effect of an explanatory variable on the noncompliance decision and, conditional on noncompliance, the amount of noncompliance.

REFERENCES

Allingham, M., and A. Sandmo. 1972. "Income Tax Evasion: A Theoretical Analysis." *Journal of Public Economics* 1:323–38.

Benston, G. 1985. "The Self-Serving Management Hypothesis: Some Evidence." *Journal of Accounting and Economics* 7:67–84.

Beron, K., H. Tauchen, and A. Witte. 1988. "A Structural Equation Model for Tax Compliance and Auditing." NBER Working Paper no. 2556. Washington, D.C.: National Bureau for Economic Research.

Clotfelter, C. 1983. "Tax Evasion and Tax Rates: An Analysis of Individual Returns." *Review of Economics and Statistics* 65:363–73.

Coughlan, A., and R. Schmidt. 1989. "Executive Compensation, Management Turnover and Firm Performance: An Empirical Investigation." *Journal of Accounting and Economics* 7:43–66.

Cox, D. 1984. "Raising Revenue in the Underground Economy." *National Tax Journal* 37, no. 3: 283–88.

Disclosure Incorporated. 1981. *SEC Filing Companies*. Bethesda, Md.: Disclosure Inc.

Donaldson, J. 1973. "The Commissioner's Enforcement Policies." In *Tax Fraud*, ed. G. Holmes and J. Cox. Ann Arbor, Mich.: Institute of Continuing Legal Education.

Dubin, J., and L. Wilde. 1986. "An Empirical Analysis of Federal Income Tax Auditing and Compliance." *National Tax Journal* 41, no. 1: 61–73.

Dun's Marketing Services. 1981. *Million Dollar Directory: America's Leading Public and Private Companies.* Parsippany, N.J.: Dun's Marketing Services.

Feinstein, J., and C. Alexander. 1986. "A Microeconometric Analysis of Income Tax Evasion." Massachusetts Institute of Technology. Mimeo.

Friedland, N., S. Maital, and A. Rutenberg. 1978. "A Simulation Study of Income Tax Evasion." *Journal of Public Economics* 13:107–16.

Graetz, M., and L. Wilde. 1985. "The Economics of Tax Compliance: Fact and Fantasy." *National Tax Journal* 38:355–63.

Heckman, J. 1979. "Sample Selection Bias as a Specification Error." *Econometrica* 47:153–161.

Hines, J., and R. Hubbard. 1990. "Coming Home to America: Dividend Repatriations by U.S. Multinationals." In *Taxation in the Global Economy,* ed. A. Razin and J. Slemrod, 161–207. Chicago: University of Chicago Press.

Hines, J., and E. Rice. "Fiscal Paradise: Foreign Tax Havens and American Business." NBER Working Paper no. 3477. Washington, D.C.: National Bureau of Economic Research.

Internal Revenue Service. 1980. *A General Taxpayer Opinion Survey.* Washington, D.C.: Internal Revenue Service.

Internal Revenue Service. 1988. *Income Tax Compliance Research: Gross Tax Gap Estimates and Projections for 1973–1992.* Washington, D.C.: Internal Revenue Service.

Kinsey, K. 1984. *Survey Data on Tax Compliance: A Compendium and Review.* Chicago: American Bar Association.

Klepper, S., M. Mazur, and D. Nagin. 1988. "Expert Intermediaries and Legal Compliance: The Case of Tax Preparers." Carnegie Mellon University. Mimeo.

Klepper, S., and D. Nagin. 1989. "The Anatomy of Tax Evasion." *Journal of Law, Economics, and Organization* 5, no. 1: 1–24.

Kreutzer, D., and D. Lee. 1986. "On Taxation and Understated Monopoly Profits." *National Tax Journal* 39, no. 2: 241–43.

Kreutzer, D., and D. Lee. 1988. "Tax Evasion and Monopoly Output Decisions: A Reply." *National Tax Journal* 41, no. 4: 583–84.

Lynch, J. "Basic Criminal Penalties." In *Tax Fraud,* ed. G. Holmes and J. Cox. Ann Arbor, Mich.: Institute of Continuing Legal Education.

Marrelli, Massimo. 1984. "On Indirect Tax Evasion." *Journal of Public Economics* 25:181–96.

Mason, R., and L. Calvin. 1984. "Public Confidence and Admitted Tax Evasion." *National Tax Journal* 37:489–96.

Mazur, M., and D. Nagin. 1987. "Tax Preparers and Tax Compliance: A Theoretical and Empirical Analysis." Carnegie Mellon University. Mimeo.

Murphy, K. 1989. "Corporate Performance and Managerial Remuneration: An Empirical Analysis." *Journal of Accounting and Economics* 7:11–42.

Poterba, J. 1987. "Tax Evasion and Capital Gains Taxation." *American Economic Association Papers and Proceedings* 77:234–39.

Rice, E. 1990. "Firms' Reluctance to Go Public: The Deterrent Effect of Financial Disclosure Requirements." Ph.D. diss., Harvard University.

Roth, J., J. Scholz, and A. Witte, eds. 1989. *Taxpayer Compliance: An Agenda for Research.* Philadelphia: University of Pennsylvania Press.

Scholes, M., and M. Wolfson. 1991. *Taxes and Business Strategy: A Planning Approach.* Englewood Cliffs, N.J.: Prentice-Hall.

Scotchmer, S. 1987. "Audit Classes and Tax Enforcement Policy." *American Economic Association Papers and Proceedings* 77:229–33.

Slemrod, J. 1985. "An Empirical Test for Tax Evasion." *Review of Economics and Statistics* 67:232–38.

Srinivasan, T. N. 1973. "Tax Evasion: A Model." *Journal of Public Economics* 2:339–46.

Standard and Poor's. 1981. *Register of Corporations, Directors, and Executives.* New York: McGraw-Hill.

Tauchen, H., and A. Witte. 1985. "Economic Models of How Audit Policies Affect Voluntary Tax Compliance." In *Proceedings of the Seventy-eighth Annual Conference,* 39–45. Columbus, Ohio: National Tax Association.

Tighe, C. 1985. "The Underground Economy." *Illinois Business Review* 42:10–11.

Wang, L., and J. Conant. 1988. "Corporate Tax Evasion and Output Decisions of the Uncertain Monopolist." *National Tax Journal* 41, no. 4: 579–81.

Watts, R., and J. Zimmerman. 1986. *Positive Accounting Theory.* Englewood Cliffs, N.J.: Prentice-Hall.

Westat. 1980a. *Individual Income Tax Compliance Factors Study: Qualitative Research Results.* Rockville, Md.: Westat, Inc.

Westat. 1980b. *Self-Reported Tax Compliance: A Pilot Survey Report.* Rockville, Md.: Westat, Inc.

Witte, A., and D. Woodbury. 1985. "The Effect of Tax Laws and Tax Administration on Tax Compliance: The Case of the U.S. Individual Income Tax." *National Tax Journal* 38:499–513.

Yitzhaki, S. 1974. "A Note on Income Tax Evasion: A Theoretical Analysis." *Journal of Public Economics* 3:201–2.

Zmijewski, M., and R. Hagerman. 1981. "An Income Strategy Approach to the Positive Theory of Accounting Standard Setting/Choice." *Journal of Accounting and Economics* 3, no. 2: 129–49.

Commentary

Jeffrey K. MacKie-Mason

Rice has written what seems to be the first careful empirical study of corporate tax evasion at the level of the individual firm. His effort extends the work of Alexander and Feinstein (1986), Erard (1990a and 1990b), Dubin and Wilde (1988), and Beron, Tauchen, and Witte (1988) on individual tax compliance. I commend Rice for working carefully with a large data set rife with coding errors, and for presenting substantial descriptive information for the reader since the data set is unfamiliar.

There are two results that are especially interesting because they are specific to corporations, with no direct personal tax analogue. First, circumstances that increase the firm's "transparency" to the IRS are correlated with lower evasion; second, having low profits relative to the industry median is correlated with higher evasion.

However, I am careful to say these results indicate only *correlations*. There are too many important data and modeling problems at this stage of the research to be convinced that the results are robust, or that they have a clear structural interpretation.

Rice discusses several data problems. I think the most important one may be measurement error, and that it does not receive enough attention. In fact, nearly every result in the essay may be the result of uncontrolled measurement errors. Rather than a model of the determinants of corporate tax evasion, the results may be estimates of a model of IRS failures to detect evasion. The problem is endemic to the research in this area that relies on IRS data: the econometrician's ability to explain evasion depends heavily on the extent to which the IRS has correctly measured the amount of each firm's evasion (conditional on performing an audit). Unfortunately, most of the explanatory variables are plausibly related to both the amount of evasion and to the IRS's detection success. Thus, there is a fundamental identification problem that Rice has not solved, ignoring it by assuming that the IRS's detection of evasion is perfect.

Some examples illustrate the problem. One of Rice's major conclusions is that public disclosure requirements encourage compliance. Yet his estimated coefficient on the "publicly traded" dummy is insignificantly different from zero; only the coefficient on "traded" times "value added" is significant. But if IRS detection is imperfect, then we might expect larger, more sophisticated firms with more complex structures (i.e., those that are publicly traded and have large value added) are better at hiding their noncompliance, and thus appear in the data to be more compliant.

Rice also finds a positive correlation between evasion and the use of tax havens. But he only knows if the firm uses a tax haven if the IRS discovers that fact (or the firm honestly reports), and thus this correlation may simply be affirming a near tautology that the more successful the IRS is at detection, the more it detects.

Another conclusion Rice reaches is that high-profit firms evade more. However, he measures profits as the amount detected by the IRS. The more noncompliance the IRS finds, the higher profits will be. Thus, this result may also be measuring detection success rather than a behavioral relation between profitability and evasion incentives. Likewise, Rice finds that the firm's marginal tax rate is positively correlated with evasion, but his measure of the marginal tax rate will be higher for firms with higher detected income (because of the effect of loss carryforwards on the marginal tax rate calculation). The more evasion detected by the IRS, the higher is measured income and the tax rate, and thus the correlation may again be due to detection success, not evasion incentives.

No one, including IRS agents, believes that detection of corporate evasion is perfect even with a thorough audit. Thus, without controlling for detection measurement errors, we cannot give Rice's results his preferred structural interpretation; he could equally well be measuring detection success. I will now turn to modeling issues, and begin by pointing out that the detection success issue has been treated with statistical methods in papers by Alexander and Feinstein (1986), Erard (1990b), and Feinstein (1989 and 1990). Rice could follow these authors in their attempt to model evasion and detection as a simultaneous system.

My major criticism of the modeling also applies to most of the related papers that I have cited here. I have come to believe that the tobit specification that most of these papers employ is clearly incorrect for the evasion behavior under study, and that the misspecification may lead to severe problems.

The standard model of evasion in this literature, and also explained by Rice, predicts a continuous distribution over both positive and negative noncompliance propensities. This seems sensible: taxpayers facing high fixed costs of an audit or with high degrees of risk aversion will rationally over-report tax liability to reduce the probability of an audit. In particular, nothing in the model predicts a large cluster of perfectly complying taxpayers, yet that is a glaring stylized fact in both the corporate and individual data sets.

Rice and his predecessors treat the large mass of returns with exactly zero evasion by assuming that a tobit specification holds. The tobit model is appropriate when we observe the value of a latent variable only above some truncation point, while for the rest of the observations we know that the latent variable falls below the truncation but not its value. For the tobit estimator to be consistent, the truncation point must be exogenous, say as the result of a measurement problem (e.g., the thermometer did not take readings below the freezing point) or external market constraints (e.g., institutional rules against short sales). There are no such measurement problems or market constraints in the tax evasion setting.

The issue concerns a fundamental flaw in our understanding of evasion preferences. The tobit approach assumes that some taxpayers would prefer to overpay their taxes, but that they are not allowed to, or we are not allowed to see how much they overpaid. In fact, if taxpayers want to overpay, there is nothing stopping them from doing so, and there is nothing about the TCMP audit process that would prevent us from observing their overpayment. Thus, we must conclude that there is something about taxpayer preferences that makes a large number cluster at perfect compliance, but estimating the tobit specification is based on assuming a very different type of preferences.

Figure 1 illustrates the problem. The theoretical model in Rice's essay and the tobit specification both assume that true mean preferences lie along a line, as in the figure. However, the observed data look something like the scatter of points shown. The tobit specification assumes that, for all the zero observations on evasion, people would like to be overcomplying (with observations centered around the preference line) but we cannot observe their true preferences. The method then estimates the parameters of the assumed true line, as drawn on the figure.

In fact, there is nothing preventing taxpayers from overpaying, and so we should presume that the true preferences generate the data below x^* as well as above. Clearly, the tobit method is estimating the wrong preferences. The problem is quantitatively very important: about 30 percent of Rice's data is clustered at zero evasion. The tobit approach is not much better than throwing out 30 percent of the data and saying that we have no idea why those taxpayers exhibit perfect compliance. Since we cannot explain one of the most crucial features of evasion preferences with the tobit specification, we should be suspicious about the rest of the results.

As a separate remark on method, I do not find Rice's approach to modeling taxpayer mistakes to be compelling. His method of calling "small" deviations from zero "mistakes" and recoding them is ad hoc and likely to bias the results. Rice chooses not to use the method of Alexander and Feinstein (1986) for taxpayer mistakes because they rely on a specific distributional assumption. But Rice's method does too: he assumes a uniform distribution. If the

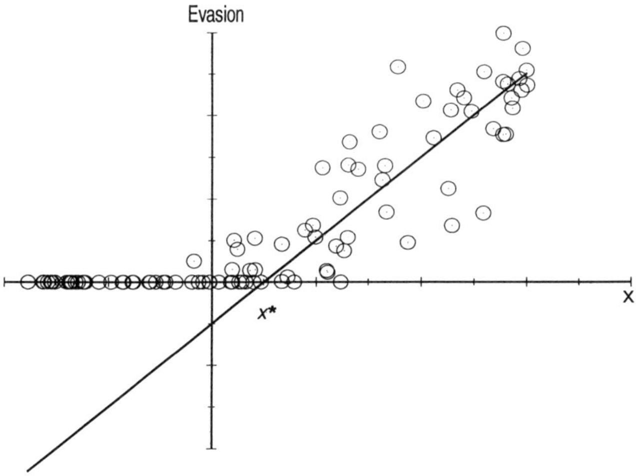

Fig. 1. Tobit versus reality

tails of the mistake distribution are, in truth, decreasing, then Rice's uniform distribution correction miscodes some of the propensity to evade. Further, since some taxpayers should rationally choose to overcomply, treating their behavior as mistakes further biases the estimation of evasion preferences.

Clearly, I do not think that this essay is the last word on corporate tax evasion. However,it is a very good first investigation. The detailed descriptive information is informative, and the statistical results point out some interesting features of the data. The methods have too many problems to support a compelling structural analysis, but they are, for the most part, consistent with the state of the art in this area. It is time for the art to move forward if we are to learn anything more from the rich but problematic IRS audit data used in so many recent studies.

REFERENCES

Alexander, C., and J. Feinstein. 1986. "A Microeconometric Analysis of Income Tax Evasion." Massachusetts Institute of Technology. Typescript.

Beron, K., H. Tauchen, and A. Witte. 1988. "A Structural Equation Model for Tax Compliance and Auditing." NBER Working Paper no. 2556. Cambridge, Mass.: National Bureau for Economic Research.

Dubin, J., and L. Wilde. 1988. "An Empirical Analysis of Federal Income Tax Auditing and Compliance." *National Tax Journal* 41:61–74.

Erard, B. E. 1990a. "The Influence of Tax Audits on Reporting Behavior." University of Toronto. Typescript.

Erard, B. E. 1990b. "Tax Practitioners and Tax Compliance: A Microeconometric Analysis of the Decision to Engage a Tax Preparer and its Consequences." Ph.D. diss., University of Michigan.

Feinstein, J. 1989. "An Econometric Analysis of Income Tax Evasion and Its Detection." Stanford Graduate School of Business. Typescript.

Feinstein, J. 1990. "Detection Controlled Estimation." *Journal of Law and Economics*. Forthcoming.

Analyzing Income Tax Evasion Using Amnesty Data with Self-Selection Correction: The Case of the Michigan Tax Amnesty Program

Steven E. Crane and Farrokh Nourzad

The issue of income tax evasion has been subjected to a great deal of scrutiny by economists. Since the pioneering work by Allingham and Sandmo (1972), the standard approach to analyzing the individual's evasion decision has been to employ a portfolio-choice framework in which the optimal level of evasion is obtained from maximizing the expected utility of income after taxes and penalties.

Using this approach, four factors have been commonly found to affect the decision to evade. These are the individual's true income, the tax rate, the probability that the evader will be detected, and the penalty rate to which detected evaders are subjected. In most cases, a positive relationship between the level of evasion and the individual's true income, and negative relationships with both of the compliance policy tools are obtained. With respect to the tax rate, however, most models have been unable to determine an unambiguous relationship due to potentially opposing income and substitution effects.[1]

We wish to thank James Alm, Cyrus Chu, Brian Erard, Susan Martin, Matthew Murray, Joel Slemrod, Michael Udell, and our colleagues at Marquette University. We also acknowledge financial support from Marquette University College of Business Administration Miles Fund.

1. A tax rate increase produces a substitution effect that leads to greater evasion because it increases the marginal return to successful evasion. On the other hand, by reducing disposable income, a higher tax rate generates an income effect that may lead to more or less evasion depending on the individual's attitude toward risk. As long as risk aversion is a decreasing function of income, the income effect is negative. Therefore, unless risk aversion increases with income, or the substitution effect is strong enough to dominate the income effect, one obtains the counterintuitive result that higher tax rates lead to reduced evasion, or that the effect is indeterminate. A qualification to this was pointed out by Yitzhaki (1974), who showed that if taxes are proportional and fines are levied on evaded taxes rather than evaded income, there would be no substitution effect.

Considerable additional work has been done within this basic analytical framework. Perhaps most important have been attempts to endogenize various critical parameters, such as the penalty rate and the probability of detection (e.g., Koskela 1983). The model has also been made more complicated by introducing an endogenous labor supply decision (e.g., Pencavel 1979; Sandmo 1981) and by adding richness to various aspects of the tax system, such as its degree of progressivity (e.g., Marchon 1979; Pencavel 1979). The consequences of these extensions typically have been that few, if any, unambiguous predictions can be extracted from the model.

Recently, a number of authors have approached the tax evasion question from a different perspective, using the tools of game theory (e.g., Graetz, Reinganum, and Wilde 1986; Reinganum and Wilde 1986 and 1988). In principle, this approach holds much promise, because it is perhaps the most effective way to truly endogenize the compliance policy variables in such a way as to adequately address the strategic aspects of the interaction between the taxpayer and the tax authority. However, it is a bit too soon to tell how successful this emerging literature will be in generating usable general conclusions regarding the evasion decision.[2]

Empirically, a fairly extensive literature has emerged. Most of this empirical work has its roots in the traditional portfolio-choice approach to modeling the decision to evade. What distinguishes these studies is how they cope with the obvious measurement difficulties associated with analyzing an illegal activity such as tax evasion. Indeed, a variety of innovative approaches to measuring evasion have been employed.

Some researchers (e.g., Friedland, Maital, and Rutenberg 1978; Geeroms and Wilmots 1985; Spicer and Becker 1980) have designed experiments or conducted surveys in order to generate relevant data. Others (e.g., Crane and Nourzad 1986; Tanzi 1983) have approached the problem from a macroeconomic perspective. An attempt has even been made to develop an evasion index from the distribution of tax returns within tax brackets (Slemrod 1985). Only a few authors (e.g., Clotfelter 1983; Dubin and Wilde 1988; Klepper and Nagin 1989; Witte and Woodbury 1985) have been able to develop direct measures that are representative of evasion behavior under actual tax systems. Of these, only Clotfelter has been able to examine the issue at the individual level.

This essay presents an empirical investigation that is based on the tradi-

2. One interesting finding thus far is that a tax rate change generates an additional effect through its impact on the marginal return to auditing. It has been shown that, under some simplifying assumptions and for certain audit classes, this effect dominates the conventional tax rate effect leading to a negative overall impact (see Graetz, Reinganum, and Wilde 1986). This result holds independently of the taxpayer's attitude toward risk.

tional theoretical framework but uses a new approach to measuring and analyzing income tax evasion. It explains how data from state income tax amnesty programs can be used to construct direct measures of income tax evasion at the individual level. We then demonstrate how these measures can be examined empirically, despite complications due to both the self-selected nature of the data and the possible interaction between the decisions to evade at the federal and state levels.

The rest of our essay is organized as follows. The next section makes the case for using amnesty data to analyze evasion and discusses the methodological procedures needed to address the complications that arise due to self-selection bias and the presence of multiple taxing jurisdictions. The third section provides a brief overview of the income tax structure and the tax amnesty program in the state of Michigan, the source of the data used in this study. In the fourth section we present our empirical model of Michigan state income tax evasion and our estimation results. This is followed by some concluding comments in the fifth section.

Using Amnesty Data to Study Evasion

Amnesty Data as Evidence of Evasion

State income tax amnesty programs represent what we believe is a new source of microdata that allows the construction of direct measures of tax evasion. Participants in these programs are effectively admitting that they cheated and are indicating the magnitude of their noncompliance. Thus, the variable most difficult to quantify in an empirical evasion study, the level of noncompliance, is readily available. This is especially true if one focuses on amnesty filers who amended a return that was previously filed, rather than individuals who filed for the first time under amnesty.[3] Assuming information from these amended filers' original returns is available, construction of an evasion measure is straightforward. One simply assumes that the amended returns represent the "truth" and compares the figures on these returns with their counterparts on the original returns.[4]

In many cases, amnesty returns provide considerable information useful

3. It is not clear what to do with the nonfilers, either theoretically or empirically. This is explained in n. 15, relating to our discussion of the data used here.

4. This seems to be a plausible assumption because it is unlikely that one who has voluntarily admitted to evading on a particular tax return would file a false amended return. This is especially true if it is announced that the amnesty returns may be audited as well. However, it may be argued that an individual might admit only a portion of his or her evasion in the hope of reducing the chances of additional auditing, which could find the remaining evasion.

for constructing independent variables as well. Given the assumption that the taxpayer is truthful when filing under amnesty, the information on the amended return will reveal such important taxpayer attributes as true income, and perhaps a usable marginal tax rate or certain demographic characteristics.

What will most likely be lacking, however, are compliance policy variables. Because amnesty data are primarily cross-sectional and penalty provisions are usually uniform across individuals,[5] no measure of the monetary cost of evasion is likely to be available. By the same token, reliable measures of either a subjective probability of detection or an objective audit rate proxy are not likely to be readily available at the state level. Thus, at best, some indirect control for detection probability is all that is likely to be possible.

The Issue of Selectivity Bias

A major drawback of using amnesty data for the purpose of analyzing evasion behavior is the probable self-selection bias due to the fact that amnesty filers themselves determined whether or not they would participate in the program. Clearly, those evaders who voluntarily chose to participate in a particular state's amnesty program may not be representative of the population of income tax evaders as a whole in that state, much less evaders in general. Fortunately, while complicated, it is possible to deal with this type of self-selection bias econometrically. This involves using a maximum likelihood technique that incorporates not only the variables influencing the evasion decision, but also those influencing the subsequent decision to participate in the amnesty program.

The procedure can be described as follows. We wish to estimate an evasion function such as

$$y_i = X_i\beta + u_i, \quad i = 1, 2, \ldots, n, \tag{1}$$

where y_i is a measure of evasion, X_i is a vector of the determinants of evasion, β is a vector of unknown parameters, and u_i is a random error term with mean zero and variance σ^2. But because evaders who are also amnesty participants are a self-selected group, estimating equation 1 using ordinary least squares (OLS) would result in biased estimates. This is because the distribution from which the sample comes is truncated in that it does not include nonparticipating evaders.[6]

5. Usually many years are open for filing. However, given bad memory and the expiration of the statute of limitations, one suspects most returns are for the most recent years.

6. For a survey of the literature on the selectivity bias that arises from different types of self-selected samples along with remedial procedures, see Maddala 1983, chap. 9. Also see

Correcting the selectivity bias in amnesty data requires one to incorporate knowledge of factors that influenced the decision of amnesty-taking evaders to participate in the amnesty program. If such factors can be identified, one can obtain unbiased maximum likelihood (ML) estimates of the parameters of equation 1 using the following likelihood function (Maddala 1983, 266–67).

$$\prod_i \left[\frac{\Phi\{[Z_i\delta - (\zeta/\sigma)(y_i - X_i\beta)]/(1 - \zeta^2)^{1/2}\}}{\Phi(Z_i\delta)} \right]$$

$$(2\pi\sigma^2)^{-1/2} \exp\left[-\frac{1}{2\sigma^2}(y_i - X_i\beta)^2 \right] \tag{2}$$

where Z_i is a vector of factors influencing the participation decision, δ is a vector of unknown parameters, $\Phi(\cdot)$ is the distribution function of the standard normal, ζ is the correlation coefficient between u_i and the error term of the participation function, and all other notations are as defined previously.[7]

The term in the large bracket is the ratio of the conditional probability of participation in the amnesty program, given $(y_i - X_i\beta)$, to the unconditional probability of participation. The term outside of this bracket is the density function of $(y_i - X_i\beta)$. Thus, the bias correction procedure involves scaling the density function of $(y_i - X_i\beta)$ using the ratio of the two probabilities as weights. This procedure yields unbiased estimates for the parameters of the evasion model (the β's), even though the estimates of the parameters of the participation function (the δ's) are unreliable. However, given that we are interested in the former set of estimates, the unreliability of the estimates of δ is no cause for concern.

The Multiple Jurisdiction Issue

An additional complication with the use of state amnesty data for analyzing evasion arises from an important institutional aspect of the overall income tax system in the United States. The income of most U.S. taxpayers is subject to

Wainer (1986), especially the contribution by Heckman and Robb (63–107). To our knowledge, the first application of selectivity correction procedures to a tax compliance problem is by Pitt and Slemrod (1989).

7. In choosing participation variables, one need not be concerned with possible correlation with the evasion variables. In fact, some variables may appear in both the evasion and the participation functions. All that is necessary for identification purposes is that the participation function contains more than just a constant term (see Bloom and Killingsworth 1985). With this procedure, the critical factor is the correlation between the error terms of the evasion and the participation functions.

both federal and state income taxes.[8] In this situation, there is likely to be overlap among the income tax returns that must be filed. Thus, we would expect that the decision regarding what to report on a state income tax return is likely to be affected by what was reported on a federal income tax return, and vice versa.

This interconnection may be due to several factors, some of which can be traced to the structure of the state return. Many state income taxes are piggybacked on the federal tax system. A typical way of doing this is to use Federal Adjusted Gross Income (AGI), with selected modifications, as the income subject to state taxation. Some states taking this approach often require that copies of the federal return be submitted with the state return for verification purposes. In this context, an evader would most likely carry his or her understatement of federal AGI forward to the state income tax return. This can result in state income tax evasion that is strictly caused by the federal evasion decision.

The interconnection between federal and state income tax returns can be more subtle, however. In truth, it may be that the two returns are completed simultaneously as the individual weighs potential costs or benefits associated with compliance at the state level with the corresponding costs or benefits at the federal level. If there is a perceived interdependency between either the costs or benefits of the two systems, the amount of evasion on one tax return may be affected by and affect what is reported on the other return. Such a perceived interdependency could arise from the well-known fact that state and federal tax enforcement agencies have a variety of information-sharing arrangements.

These possibilities suggest that an analysis of the behavior reflected on state tax returns should not be undertaken in isolation from the behavior reflected on the federal return.[9] Exactly how to deal with this, of course, depends on the details of the tax code of the particular state whose amnesty data are employed.

Michigan Income Tax System and Amnesty Program

The Michigan Income Tax

Michigan's income tax system is fairly straightforward and closely linked to the federal system. In fact, the Michigan system is piggybacked on the federal

8. The taxpayer may also be subject to local income taxes as well. However, these taxes are generally less relevant in the present context because they are usually simply payroll taxes where the full amount is withheld. As a result, there is not much to the income reporting issue, and there may not even be a tax return to file.

9. The interdependency is also relevant to the analysis of federal tax evasion, although the effect may be weaker if the direction of causality is primarily from the federal return to the state return.

return such that Michigan residents begin completing their state return by reporting the AGI figure found on their federal returns. Several adjustments to federal AGI are then made to allow for both income that is taxable at the state but not at the federal level and for income that is not taxable in the state of Michigan but is taxable at the federal level.[10] Making these adjustments results in the income subject to tax, from which personal exemptions ($1,500 each), but not itemized deductions, are subtracted to obtain state taxable income.

Michigan Taxable Income was subject to a flat tax rate that varied from 4.60 percent to 6.35 percent during the different tax years covered by this study (1980–85). Two different sets of credits were then deducted from the resulting gross tax figure.[11] Once these credits were removed, any tax payments through withholding or quarterly estimated payments were deducted to determine the balance due or amount of refund.

Given this tax structure, evasion could occur on a return in a number of ways. First, the level of AGI may have been misstated. However, given that this figure was to be taken from the federal return, it seems likely that any evasion here was driven by decisions made when filling out the federal return.[12] Second, the additions to or subtractions from AGI could be misstated. As with AGI, most of this information appears on the federal tax return and its associated schedules. However, since copies of the supplemental federal schedules were not required by the state authorities, it is possible that some independent, state-driven evasion may have occurred at this point.

The other primary possibilities for evading on Michigan income tax returns include overstating the number of exemptions or either type of credit. Of course, one could also have overstated withholding or estimated payment levels, but, given the clear paper trail associated with these items, this seems less likely. Thus, the type of evasion at the state level that seems most likely to

10. The primary adjustments that are added to AGI are interest income received from other states, certain capital gains and other gains, and losses attributable to activity in other states. The primary subtractions from AGI are for interest income from the federal government, military pay or benefits, retirement or pension benefits, certain capital gains, and income attributable to another state.

11. The first set of credits were for income taxes paid to Michigan cities or other states and contributions to Michigan institutions such as universities and libraries. The second set of credits were special allowances for such items as property tax payments, home heating expenditures, and investments in solar energy equipment.

12. The original decision to evade on the federal return could be influenced by opportunities on the state return. We do not consider this possible feedback. Of course, just because this type of evasion is federally driven does not mean that it is not state evasion. In fact, it may be that some state evasion occurs because the individual wants his or her state return to be consistent with his or her federal return. This does suggest, however, that one must look elsewhere for explanations of this form of state evasion behavior.

have occurred is a misstatement of adjustments to AGI, an overstatement of credits from the gross tax bill, or some combination of the two. What makes this activity potentially observable is the existence of a tax amnesty program.

The Michigan Tax Amnesty Program

The Michigan Tax Amnesty Program was fairly conventional.[13] Since it is described in detail elsewhere (see Bowman and Martin 1987 and 1988b; Fisher, Goddeeris, and Young 1989), only a brief summary will be provided here. Michigan Amnesty ran for a limited time, from May 12 through June 30, 1986. Under this program, which was part of a comprehensive overhaul of the state's tax enforcement system, individuals were invited to come forward and report tax deficiencies for any state tax.[14] The carrot used to encourage amnesty filings was that all criminal and civil penalties were waived. The stick was that penalties were to be raised significantly after amnesty expired, and there was to be a dramatic increase in the enforcement effort.[15]

Amnesty was viewed as an unqualified success by the Michigan authorities, as almost $110 million was collected, representing a payback of $55 for every $1 expended on the program. It was recognized that these figures overstated the effectiveness of the program, however, because they included collections of receivables from those who were already known to the tax authorities and from those who would have been identified using normal procedures. As with many other states, Michigan both permitted and encouraged those with known, but currently outstanding, deficiencies to participate. Nevertheless, the Michigan Department of Treasury estimates that about 37 percent of the returns and 41 percent of the revenue came from "original cases" that were not in receivables or otherwise previously known to the department.

Because our essay focuses on income tax evasion, only those who filed for income tax amnesty are of current interest. After eliminating the returns based on known receivables, there were 32,614 returns claiming amnesty for *income* tax deficiencies, which represented 69 percent of the returns filed, and

13. For a comparative survey of the general provisions of various states' amnesty programs, see Mikesell (1986). Summary material also can be found in Dubin, Graetz, and Wilde (1990).

14. The taxes included were income, sales/use, single business, intangibles, inheritance, excise, severance, and public utility property tax. However, almost four-fifths of the revenue collected came from the individual income, single business, and use tax.

15. For details on the increased compliance effort at the state level, see Bowman and Martin (1988a). It should also be pointed out that all amnesty information was forwarded to the IRS.

31 percent of the nonreceivable amnesty revenue. This made income tax filers one of the largest groups of amnesty participants.

To file for income tax amnesty, individuals used the state's standard amended individual income tax form. This form closely follows the Michigan individual income tax return itself. In fact, it requests figures as originally reported on any previously filed return, the changes in any of those figures, and the new, "correct" figure. This makes it quite simple to measure noncompliance. We simply compared the newly reported figures with the originally reported figures.

We have claimed that Michigan's Tax Amnesty Program was conventional in most respects. However, there is one very notable difference from most other states, which has to do with the attention given to advance planning for subsequent research. The Michigan Department of Treasury was more interested in extensively investigating amnesty participants than most other state treasury departments. Toward this end, they created the Michigan Amnesty Data Base, which represents a 10 percent random sample of all amnesty participants. This involved expending over 1,250 hours of labor accumulating, entering, and verifying information submitted by participants.

The original one-in-ten sampling included accounts receivable returns, but these were subsequently discarded, as were a number of returns containing problems that made them unusable. The Amnesty Data Base contained 4,203 nonreceivable returns overall, of which 2,985 or 71 percent pertained to income taxes. Of these, 588 were filed by individuals who were amending a return filed previously, while 2,397 were individuals who had not filed previously. The Michigan Department of Treasury believes that this sample is representative of the population of Michigan State Tax Amnesty filers, while at the same time recognizing that it is not likely to be representative of the population of Michigan income tax evaders as a whole. It is this latter problem we hope to neutralize through the self-selection bias correction procedure described previously.

The Empirical Model and Estimation Results

Specifying an Empirical Model of State Evasion

In our empirical analysis, we are concerned only with income tax amnesty filers. Further, we limit our attention to those who had previously filed and were, therefore, filing amended returns under amnesty.[16] This means that the

16. There are two reasons for limiting attention to the amended return filers. One is theoretical. Nonfilers are examples of corner solution individuals who are normally explicitly ruled out prior to conducting the comparative static analysis that provides the foundation for any

largest possible sample for our analysis would contain 588 observations. However, the sample actually used in this study is considerably smaller.

Prior to carrying out our econometric analysis, we examined the data for internal consistency. This involved recalculating the tax bill and reconciling this with the net balance due on both the original and amended returns of each of these 588 individuals. In the process, we discovered a number of problem observations. For some observations, all or most of the data were missing from one or both returns. In other cases, obvious taxpayer or data entry errors were found. In still others, we were simply unable to replicate the figures on the tax returns by making the required calculations. In a few cases, the figures suggested negative evasion of one form or another.

After removing the observations with these problems, the sample size was reduced to 213 observations. While this loss of observations is regrettable, we believe that by trimming the sample we are reducing the measurement error and thus may be increasing the signal-to-noise ratio in the data. We are unaware of any systematic bias that these omissions might have introduced into the sample, although we recognize that a large sample size would be preferable given our use of the maximum likelihood estimation procedure.

In analyzing the data in this sample, we must address the two issues raised previously, namely, the self-selection bias inherent in the amnesty data and the interdependency between the federal and state tax returns. Regarding the latter, as a first approximation, we assume the process is recursive in that the decision to evade state income taxes follows the decision to evade federal income taxes.

The individual is assumed to decide how much federal income tax he or she wishes to evade, and then to complete a federal tax return accordingly. Then he or she completes a state tax return conditional on what has been reported at the federal level. Thus, we allow for unidirectional causality from the federal evasion decision to the state tax evasion decision, while neglecting the possibility of full simultaneity between the two. In light of both the relative magnitudes of the two tax bills and the way people typically fill out their returns, this is not unreasonable. In any case, this is an improvement over simply ignoring any interdependency on the grounds that we have little or no theoretical guidance as to what to expect.[17]

---

sign expectations. The other reason is tied to measurement and econometrics. One measure of evasion is the amount of income not reported, which in this case is exactly equal to true income. Thus, one might be in the position of wanting to regress income on income. If the measure of evasion is evaded taxes, then one could be regressing this on income and taxes, which is, of course, how evaded taxes was calculated.

17. See, for example, Crane and Nourzad (1990).

Viewing the problem in this way affects how state income tax evasion is measured. Because the Michigan income tax system is so closely tied to the federal system, a significant portion of the evasion that appears on the state return may simply be a carry-through from the federal evasion decision. In other words, a misstatement of federal AGI may be carried forward to the state return for consistency and result in a reduced state tax liability. However, this incidental state level evasion is the result of the federal tax evasion decision and not the decision to evade state income taxes per se and should be netted out.[18]

In order to net out the federally driven state evasion we assume that the AGI figure reported on the state return accurately represents what was filed at the federal level. If this is true, any difference between the amended AGI figure and the AGI figure originally reported must be due to evasion traceable to the federal tax return. This difference is then subtracted from the difference between the taxable income reported on the amended and original state income tax returns. The result is a measure of the misstatement of the additions and subtractions to federal AGI when adjusting it for Michigan tax purposes. This is an income-based measure that is, arguably, purely Michigan-based evasion.

Given the extensive tax credit system that is part of the Michigan tax code, we must also take possible credit overstatement into account. Once again, this is determined by comparing the originally reported figures with those on the amended return. To get a measure of overall evasion, we multiply the misstatement of income by the appropriate tax rate and add the result to the misstated credit figure. This gives an overall measure of Michigan income tax evasion not directly carried forward from the federal tax return.[19]

This evasion measure is to be regressed on a series of independent variables chosen by drawing on the traditional theoretical evasion models, the results of previously empirical work on evasion, and data availability. In principle, we should control for true income, marginal tax rate, probability of detection, and penalty rate. Unfortunately, data availability and institutional considerations limit our options.

To reflect the individual's true income level, we use AGI as reported on the amended return. While a broader measure of income would be preferable, none is available to us. The fact that Michigan is a flat rate tax state means

18. In fact, if this is not done, it would amount to building in a spurious positive relationship between Michigan evasion and true income, one of our independent variables. This will become evident as the empirical model is developed.

19. The measure of credit misstatement is the difference between total credits claimed on the amended and the original returns

that, in any given year, the same tax rate applies to all individuals. Therefore, no marginal tax rate variable can be included in our essentially cross-sectional econometric model of state tax evasion.

The problems identified in the previous section with the compliance policy variables were encountered as expected. The fact that the sample is primarily cross-sectional, coupled with the uniformity of Michigan's penalty rate across individuals during our sample period, means that no penalty rate can be included in the model. In principle, a similar problem should not be present for the probability of detection; subjective assessments of detection probability certainly vary across individuals. Therefore, it is at least conceptually possible to have a different probability for each individual.

In practice, however, reliable measures of subjective probabilities are difficult to obtain. A common alternative in empirical evasion studies has been to use some measure of the objective audit probability as a proxy. Unfortunately, detailed audit figures are very sensitive information from the perspective of the tax authorities and are often not available.

Because of the difficulty with obtaining direct measures of audit activities, we have resorted to controlling for differential probability of detection effects in an indirect manner. Michigan Treasury documents indicate that, prior to the reorganization that followed amnesty, compliance efforts were divided among Treasury offices in nine geographic regions. Since each office had considerable discretion over enforcement efforts in its area, it seems plausible that Michigan audit rates varied by these geographic regions. Therefore, using zip codes, we associate each amnesty filer with one of these nine geographic regions and construct a series of dummy variables that reflect these regions.

In addition to the variables identified by theory, previous empirical evidence suggests that we should also control for demographic characteristics and differences in opportunities for underreporting certain types of income. In this vein, we include dummy variables to reflect married filers and male filers.[20] We also include a dummy variable indicating returns that were prepared by professional tax preparers.[21] Further, in order to reflect differences in the opportunity to underreport, we include a variable measuring the percentage of the overall tax bill that was withheld.

We complete our basic state evasion equation by including one additional

20. The latter, of course, only applies to single filers, because married filers must include an individual of each sex.

21. The expected sign on the professional tax preparer variable is controversial. In fact, in 1987, the IRS held a conference regarding the role of the tax practitioner in promoting tax compliance at which the topic was debated at great length. Complicating the matter further is the fact that this variable may be endogenous.

variable to control for evasion behavior at the federal level. Given our contention that there may be a link between the federal and the state evasion decisions, we believe that some measure of federal evasion must be a part of an analysis of evasion on the state tax return. Ideally, we would use a measure of the full amount of evasion found on the federal tax return. Of course, doing this would require access to the federal tax returns of the individuals in our sample, which, unfortunately, was not available to us. As an alternative, for our measure of evasion on the federal return, we use the difference between the AGI reported on the amnesty return and that on the original state return.[22]

We incorporate federal evasion into our model using a two-step procedure, where federal evasion is first regressed on a series of its determinants, and the predicted value is then included in the state evasion equation. Because our measure of federal evasion contains a disproportionate number of zero values (44 out of 213 observations), the tobit estimation procedure is employed.[23]

It is difficult to form an a priori sign expectation for the coefficient of this variable. The effect will likely depend on whether cheating at the state level is perceived by the evader as a substitute for cheating at the federal level or as a complement to it. In the latter case, one would expect a positive sign for this coefficient, while one would expect a negative sign in the former case.

As with the state evasion model, selection of explanatory variables used in the federal evasion equation is based on a combination of theoretical guidance, past empirical results, and data availability. Two primary variables are true income and the marginal tax rate. To capture the effect of true income, we include measures of AGI and AGI-squared based on the amended return. The quadratic term is included to allow for possible nonlinearities due to both risk aversion and the progressivity of the federal tax system. To capture the direct federal tax rate effect, we include the marginal tax rate that applied to the average taxable income of each individual's AGI class.[24]

Reasonable federal tax compliance variables were more difficult to obtain. In fact, we could come up with no penalty rate variable that was Michigan specific, yet had the necessary variance across individuals. The same held

---

22. Obviously this will not reflect all federal evasion, because it misses any federal evasion taking the form of overstated exemptions, deductions, or credits. However, it is the only measure currently available. In addition, if for some reason there are discrepancies between the AGI on the federal return and the state return, our evasion variable will be measured with error.

23. In principle, a self-selection correction should be applied at this stage as well. To date, we have not been able to obtain estimates using this more complicated procedure.

24. Specifically, we determined the federal AGI class that each individual belonged to using the IRS Statistics of Income—Individual Returns. Next, we calculated the average taxable income for those falling in this particular AGI class. Finally, the marginal tax rate on this average taxable income was determined by consulting the appropriate tax table.

true for a direct measure of the audit rate. However, we do incorporate indirect audit controls by making use of the fact that the IRS categorizes taxpayers into different audit classes based upon return characteristics and subjects these classes to different audit regimes. Based on this, we include dummy variables that loosely categorize our sample individuals into federal audit classes.[25] While it is not clear exactly what we should expect of these variables in terms of sign and significance, it is hoped that their inclusion will be a sufficient control for the differential audit probabilities.

Since the federal evasion decision is also likely to be affected by the opportunities available, we need an additional control for this influence. However, given that we do not have access to the federal returns, no information on federal tax withholding is available. As an alternative, we construct a dummy variable identifying returns of individuals belonging to occupations that tend to have greater opportunities to evade. These include returns of the self-employed, farmers, and salespeople. Finally, we include the two dummies for demographic characteristics discussed earlier—male and married, as well as the dummy reflecting the use of a paid tax preparer. The logic follows that of our earlier discussion.

As discussed previously, our Michigan evasion model cannot be estimated using OLS because the sample is self-selected. In order to apply the maximum likelihood estimation procedure discussed previously, we need to incorporate the participation decision into the likelihood function. This requires identifying factors influencing this decision. There is little formal work to draw on regarding the determinants of amnesty participation. However, recent work using this same Michigan Amnesty Data File by Fisher, Goddeeris, and Young (1989) is helpful.[26] They argue that the decision to participate in amnesty programs is influenced by the perceived increase in the postamnesty penalty and the probability of detection and, to some extent, by nonpecuniary factors such as personal guilt.

As with our evasion equation, there is little we can do with the postamnesty penalty rate because penalties are generally uniform. Therefore, we concentrate on the other factors. The perceived increase in the probability of detection is likely to depend upon what one thinks or expects about the

25. The audit characteristics and classes are as follows. CLASS3: returns with AGI below \$10,000, with farm or self-employment income; CLASS4: returns with AGI between \$10,000 and \$50,000, without farm or self-employment income; CLASS5: returns with AGI between \$10,000 and \$30,000, with farm or self-employment income; CLASS6: returns with AGI greater than \$50,000, but no farm or self-employment income; and CLASS7: returns with AGI greater than \$30,000, with farm or self-employment income. In our model, the default category is returns with AGI less than \$10,000 and no farm or self-employment income.

26. For additional work on amnesty participation, see Andreoni (1988); Leonard and Zeckhauser (1987); Malik and Schwab (1988).

postamnesty compliance effort. We attempt to capture this influence in several ways.

It is widely known that certain types of income such as rents, royalties, and business income are typically underreported with greater frequency than other income. Thus, we might reasonably expect the tax authorities to concentrate their enforcement efforts in these areas. In this case, returns with these types of income will likely receive increased postamnesty scrutiny, and the evaders who filed returns containing these items might reasonably expect their probability of detection to rise.[27] Based on this reasoning, we construct a dummy variable to identify returns with income from these sources.

Another way to partially capture the effects of a perceived increase in the postamnesty compliance effort is suggested by Michigan Department of Treasury documents. These indicate that special attention was to be focused on the returns of professionals who were licensed by the state. Therefore, we define another dummy variable that identifies returns of individuals in occupations that are typically licensed by states.[28]

We also make a crude effort at allowing for possible nonpecuniary influences using an interesting piece of information contained in the Amnesty Data File. The Data Base identifies all returns in the sample that were accompanied by a special letter of explanation concerning amnesty. Including such a letter is curious behavior given that the idea of amnesty is to induce people to come forward in part because there will be no questions asked. It seems somewhat plausible that those feeling the need to provide a special explanation for their participation are individuals who may be experiencing some type of remorse over their behavior. With this in mind, we specify a dummy variable reflecting the presence of such a letter.

On the other hand, the factor that perhaps has the greatest effect on the perceived increase in postamnesty detection probability reflects an influence that is not directly related to the Michigan amnesty program. It is quite likely that the perceived probability of detection at the state level would rise significantly following an IRS audit. Therefore, such individuals would probably be much more likely to participate in a state amnesty program. To control for this effect, we use information in the Amnesty Data Base to construct a dummy variable indicating that the participant was under IRS audit.

To summarize, the participation decision is incorporated into the likeli-

27. This is true regardless of the form the actual evasion took. Note as well that the fact that the preamnesty probability of being audited might have depended on the presence of these two types of income does not undermine our line of reasoning. What we are arguing is that their presence in one's original return has an additional postamnesty effect.

28. The categories we identify with this variable are architecture, medicine/health, law, personal services, and transportation.

hood function using dummy variables representing (1) sources of income that are likely to attract attention, (2) occupational categories that had been targeted for additional scrutiny, (3) unusual behavior that may reflect remorse at having evaded, and (4) the fact that a return was under review by the IRS. Obviously, this specification is rather ad hoc and too simple to completely capture the complex participation decision. However, given the data limitations, we believe this is a reasonable first attempt that we hope can adequately neutralize the bias in our sample.

TABLE 1. Tobit Estimates of Unreported Federal Adjusted Gross Income on Original Returns of Michigan Income Tax Amnesty Participants (FEDEVA)

Variable[a]	Normalized Coefficient	Asymptotic *T*-Ratio	*p*-Value[b]
AGI	0.89769E-05	3.0916	0.00185
AGISQ	−0.37268E-06	−3.1909	0.00130
MTR	0.30711E-01	2.3781	0.01660
OCCUPTN	0.49835	1.9517	0.05048
PREPARE	0.76215	4.2921	0.00002
MALE	0.44382E-01	0.16595	0.86820
MARRIED	0.88319E-01	0.46735	0.64037
CLASS3	−0.28912	−0.34919	0.72693
CLASS4	−0.31495	−0.80268	0.42179
CLASS5	−0.89862	−1.0774	0.28070
CLASS6	−1.2412	−2.2636	0.02339
CLASS7	0.35106	0.46854	0.63915
Constant	−1.1791	−2.7107	0.00673
Squared correlation between observed and predicted values		0.2270	
Log likelihood		−1815.0489	

[a]Variable definitions are as follows.

AGI = Adjusted gross income on amended return
AGISQ = AGI squared
FEDEVA = Underreported federal AGI
MTR = Federal marginal tax rate
OCCUPTN = 1 if occupation = sales, self-employed, or farming; otherwise = 0
MALE = 1 for male taxpayers; otherwise = 0
MARRIED = 1 for married taxpayers; otherwise = 0
PREPARE = 1 if return prepared by a professional preparer; otherwise = 0
CLASS3 = 1 if AGI ≤ \$10,000 with farm or self-employment income; otherwise = 0
CLASS4 = 1 if \$10,000 ≤ AGI ≤ \$50,000 without farm or self-employment income; otherwise = 0
CLASS5 = 1 if \$10,000 ≤ AGI ≤ \$30,000 with farm or self-employment income; otherwise = 0
CLASS6 = 1 if AGI ≥ \$50,000 without farm or self-employment income; otherwise = 0
CLASS7 = 1 if AGI ≥ \$30,000 with farm or self-employment income; otherwise = 0

[b]Marginal significance level, prob $|t| < x$.

The Estimation Results

We begin our review of the estimation results with the tobit estimates for the first stage, which explain the magnitude of the understatement of federal AGI (results shown in table 1). All things considered, reasonable results are obtained. Both AGI and AGI squared are statistically significant, and have a positive-negative sign pattern, which suggests that, other things being equal, evasion rises with increases in true AGI, but at a decreasing rate.

The federal tax rate (MTR) has a statistically significant positive effect on evasion. This is consistent in terms of sign and significance with some previous findings (e.g., Clotfelter 1983; Crane and Nourzad 1986). The coefficient of the occupation dummy variable (OCCUPTN) is also positive and statistically significant. This is as expected, given the widely held view that individuals in these occupations have greater opportunities to evade. In contrast, neither of the demographic variables appears to have any relevance for explaining the level of unreported federal AGI.

The remaining parameter estimates are more difficult to interpret. The significant positive coefficient for the professional tax preparer dummy (PREPARE) could spark some controversy. However, given such complications as the blurred distinction between tax evasion and avoidance and the ability of the taxpayer to shop around for a sympathetic preparer, it is difficult to know what to make of this finding. Along these same lines, a reasonable interpretation for the audit class coefficients is not readily apparent. Thus, we make no attempt to draw compliance policy inferences from these estimated coefficients and remain content to treat them as nothing more than necessary control variables.

Of course, the results shown in table 1, however interesting, are a means to an end rather than an end in themselves. This equation has been estimated primarily to obtain the predicted values of FEDEVA that are then fed into the Michigan evasion estimation that is the main focus of our analysis. The maximum likelihood estimates for Michigan, which allow for the effect of the federal evasion decision and correct for self-selection bias, are reported in table 2.[29]

The predicted value of FEDEVA has a significant positive effect on pure Michigan income tax evasion. This would suggest that state-level evasion is complementary to federal evasion, even when the carry-through effect is

29. Prior to estimation, all continuous variables entering the likelihood function were standardized using the sample means and standard deviations. This was done to improve the convergence properties of the model. OLS results using the same standardized variables are reported in appendix table A1 for comparison purposes.

TABLE 2. Maximum Likelihood Estimates (with Self-Selection Correction) of Michigan Individual Income Taxes Evaded (MICHEVA)

Variable[a]	Coefficient	*T*-Ratio	*p*-Value
FEDEVA	0.284086	3.677	0.00024
AGI	0.410593	2.478	0.01320
PCTWHD	−0.159595	−2.165	0.03041
MALE	−0.410599	−1.242	0.21437
MARRIED	−0.117273	−0.633	0.52676
PREPARE	−0.482466	−2.526	0.01154
MTCLEMENS	−0.016751	−0.091	0.92772
FLINT	−0.338720	−0.616	0.53769
SAGINAW	0.056257	0.131	0.89605
LANSING	−0.125622	−0.320	0.74905
KALAMAZOO	−0.124401	−0.216	0.82882
GRANDRAPI	0.301049	1.250	0.21138
TRAVERSE	0.268905	1.170	0.24216
UP	−0.099677	−0.333	0.73942
Constant1	0.954183	2.707	0.00678
IRS-AUDIT	0.321658	0.815	0.41486
LICENSED	7.609160	0.000	0.99988
GUILT	−0.188707	−0.513	0.60762
RENTROYL	−0.338990	−0.487	0.62603
Constant2	−0.172743	−0.252	0.80118
ζ	0.859215	6.734	0.00000
Squared correlation between observed and predicted values		0.4356	
Log likelihood		−233.7700	

[a]Variable definitions are as follows.

FEDEVA	= Predicted value of FEDEVA (from table 1)
MICHEVA	= Michigan income taxes evaded
PCTWHD	= Percentage of Michigan income tax withheld
MTCLEMENS	= 1 if taxpayer's zip code in Mount Clemens area; otherwise = 0
FLINT	= 1 if taxpayer's zip code in Flint area; otherwise = 0
SAGINAW	= 1 if taxpayer's zip code in Saginaw area; otherwise = 0
LANSING	= 1 if taxpayer's zip code in Lansing area; otherwise = 0
KALAMAZOO	= 1 if taxpayer's zip code in Kalamazoo area; otherwise = 0
GRANDRAPI	= 1 if taxpayer's zip code in Grand Rapids area; otherwise = 0
TRAVERSE	= 1 if taxpayer's zip code in Traverse City area; otherwise = 0
UP	= 1 if taxpayer's zip code in Upper Peninsula; otherwise = 0
IRS-AUDIT	= 1 if taxpayer under IRS audit; otherwise = 0
LICENSED	= 1 if taxpayer's occupation = architecture, medicine, health, law, personal services, transportation; otherwise = 0
RENTROYL	= 1 if rents, royalties, or business income present; otherwise = 0
GUILT	= 1 if a letter of explanation accompanied amended returns; otherwise = 0

All other variables are defined in table 1.

eliminated. In other words, on average, pure state-level evasion increases as federal evasion rises. This also suggests that a careful matching of federal and state tax return data may be an effective compliance policy tactic. A similar conclusion might be drawn regarding back-up withholding provisions, given the significant negative relationship between state-level evasion and the proportion of the tax bill withheld (PCTWHD).

According to the data in table 2, true income (AGI) has a significant positive effect on evasion, as one would expect. On the other hand, the demographic variables perform poorly in the Michigan evasion equation, as neither coefficient achieves statistical significance at conventional levels. As for the geographic region dummy variables, none is individually statistically significant. However, it is hoped that, together, they control for differences in audit rates.

In contrast, the professional tax preparer variable (PREPARE) produces an interesting result; its coefficient is statistically significant but has the opposite sign as in table 1. In other words, it appears that, on average, the use of a professional tax preparer is associated with more evasion at the federal level, but less evasion at the state level. This is a bit difficult to explain. One possibility is that tax preparers recognize a close link between the funding of state government and both their own welfare and that of their clients. Of course, it could also be an indication of shortcomings in model specification or variable measurement. This is certainly a topic for further investigation.

In addition to the evasion function coefficients, the maximum likelihood procedure also provides estimates for the participation parameters (as shown in table 2). But little should be made of these estimates themselves. Recall that the participation variables are included to correct for selection bias, and reliable estimates of the corresponding coefficients are not to be expected (Maddala 1983, 267). It is worth noting, however, that ζ, the correlation coefficient between the error terms of the evasion and participation functions, is quite large and is statistically significant, as would be expected given the self-selected nature of a sample of tax amnesty participants.

Concluding Comments

We have employed a new approach to measuring and empirically analyzing income tax evasion. Using data from the Michigan State Income Tax Amnesty Program, we demonstrated how state amnesty data can be utilized to construct a direct measure of evasion at the individual level. Proper empirical analysis of the evasion behavior embodied in this measure required us to address two problems. First, because the data pertained only to voluntary participants in the state amnesty program, we had to employ self-selection bias correction procedures that take the amnesty participation decision into account. Second, because these data are related to a state that closely links its income tax code to the federal tax system, we had to examine evasion at both levels in order to take the possible interjurisdictional influences into account.

Our analysis indicates that there is a positive linkage from evasion at the federal level to evasion at the state level. In addition, we find that higher income and greater noncompliance opportunity lead to greater evasion at both levels. We also find some support for the proposition that federal marginal tax rates are positively related to federal evasion. Another result, which is somewhat curious, is that the use of a professional tax preparer is associated with more evasion at the federal level, but less evasion at the state level. On the other hand, our results provide no insights into the effects on evasion of either deterrence efforts or demographic characteristics.

The research described here should be of interest for several reasons. Some of the results provide additional evidence regarding the effects of such traditional theoretical determinants of evasion as income and the marginal tax rate. Others confirm the importance of such institutional arrangements as tax withholding as effective compliance policy tools. This latter finding is reinforced by the evidence reported here that state and federal evasion are complementary activities. This suggests that further information sharing and return matching would be a fruitful activity. On the other hand, the conflicting results regarding the role of the tax practitioner are likely to be of value more for the debate they spark than for the results themselves.

Another interesting implication of our research is what it implies about the design and implementation of amnesty programs. We have demonstrated that amnesty data can be useful for analyzing income tax evasion, despite some of the inherent limitations of these data. This would suggest that tax authorities in any jurisdiction who may be contemplating a tax amnesty should give serious consideration to this type of analysis when designing the structure and administration of the program. In hindsight, it is unfortunate that more states did not plan for follow-up analysis and, as a result, much potentially useful data have been destroyed or are not available in a usable form.

This research can be extended and improved in a variety of ways. At the state level, a good place to start is the participation function. Ideally, this decision would be formally modeled in order to identify the relevant explanatory factors more accurately. At the very least, it would be desirable to obtain better measures of the postamnesty penalty and probability variables that are used for our ad hoc participation function. Along the same lines, better treatment of compliance policy instruments in the evasion function itself is needed.

Improvements can also be made in the analysis of evasion at the federal level. Ideally, data from federal returns should be used to get a more complete measure of the extent of federal evasion. Furthermore, this estimation should be done in a way that allows for both the truncation and self-selection bias problems.

Despite this ample room for improvement, we believe that we have produced some interesting results. Equally important, in our opinion, is that we have demonstrated how amnesty data can be used to gain insights into the issue of income tax compliance. We believe this represents a new and potentially fruitful direction for tax compliance analysis that should be given serious attention.

APPENDIX

TABLE A1. Ordinary Least Squares Estimates of Michigan Individual Income Taxes Evaded (MICHEVA)

Variable	Coefficient	*T*-Ratio	*p*-Value
FEDEVA	0.335475	5.012	0.00000
AGI	0.427782	7.310	0.00000
PCTWHD	−0.133573	−2.324	0.02112
MALE	−0.338994	−1.720	0.08696
MARRIED	−0.104177	−0.727	0.46830
PREPARE	−0.538374	−3.791	0.00020
MTCLEMENS	−0.107951	−0.721	0.47190
FLINT	−0.384031	−1.388	0.16679
SAGINAW	−0.006079	−0.022	0.98248
LANSING	−0.207721	−0.884	0.37779
KALAMAZOO	−0.202568	−0.630	0.52911
GRANDRAPI	0.260335	1.303	0.19900
TRAVERSE	0.173662	0.646	0.51918
UP	−0.220065	−0.830	0.40779
Constant	0.557466	2.696	0.00763
Adjusted R^2		0.39446	
SER		0.77813	
$F(14,198)$		10.86420	
Log likelihood		−241.02306	

Note: See table 2 for variable definitions.

REFERENCES

Allingham, Michael G., and Agnar Sandmo. 1972. "Income Tax Evasion: A Theoretical Analysis." *Journal of Public Economics* 1:323–38.

Andreoni, James. 1988. "The Desirability of a Permanent Tax Amnesty." University of Wisconsin at Madison. Typescript.

Bloom, and Killingsworth. 1985. "Correcting for Truncation Bias Caused by a Latent Truncation Variable." *Journal of Econometrics* 27:131–35.

Bowman, Robert A., and Susan W. Martin. 1987. "Michigan Tax Amnesty Report." Michigan Department of Treasury.

Bowman, Robert A., and Susan W. Martin. 1988a. "Enhanced Tax Law Enforcement: A Two-Year Report." Michigan Department of Treasury.

Bowman, Robert A., and Susan W. Martin. 1988b. "Michigan Tax Amnesty Report II." Michigan Department of Treasury.

Clotfelter, Charles T. 1983. "Tax Evasion and Tax Rates: An Analysis of Individual Returns." *Review of Economics and Statistics* 65:363–73.

Crane, Steven E., and Farrokh Nourzad. 1986. "Inflation and Tax Evasion: An Empirical Analysis." *Review of Economics and Statistics* 68:217–23.

Crane, Steven E., and Farrokh Nourzad. 1990. "Tax Rates and Tax Evasion: Evidence From California Amnesty Data." *National Tax Journal* 43:189–200.

Dubin, Jeffrey, Michael A. Graetz, and Louis L. Wilde. 1990. "State Income Tax Amnesties I: Causes." California Institute of Technology. Typescript.

Dubin, Jeffrey, and Louis L. Wilde. 1988. "An Empirical Analysis of Federal Income Tax Auditing and Compliance." *National Tax Journal* 41:61–74.

Fisher, Ronald C., John H. Goddeeris, and James C. Young. 1989. "Participation in Tax Amnesties: The Individual Income Tax." *National Tax Journal* 42:15–28.

Friedland, N., S. Maital, and A. Rutenberg. 1978. "A Simulation Study of Income Tax Evasion." *Journal of Public Economics* 10:107–16.

Geeroms, Hans, and Hendrik Wilmots. 1985. "An Empirical Model of Tax Evasion and Tax Avoidance." *Public Finance/Finances Publiques* 40:190–209.

Graetz, Michael J., Jennifer F. Reinganum, and Louis L. Wilde. 1986. "The Tax Compliance Game: Toward an Interactive Theory of Law Enforcement." *Journal of Law, Economics, and Organization* 39:1–32.

Graetz, Michael J., and Louis L. Wilde. 1985. "The Economics of Tax Compliance: Facts and Fantasy." *National Tax Journal* 38:355–63.

Klepper, Steven, and Daniel Nagin. 1989."The Anatomy of Tax Evasion." *Journal of Law, Economics, and Organization* 5:1–24.

Koskela, Erkki. 1983. "On the Shape of Tax Schedule, the Probability of Detection, and the Penalty Schemes as Deterrents to Tax Evasion." *Public Finance/Finances Publiques* 38:70–80.

Leonard, Herman, and Richard Zeckhauser. 1987. "Amnesty, Enforcement and Tax Policy." In *Tax Policy and the Economy,* ed. Lawrence Summers, 55–85. Cambridge, Mass.: MIT Press.

Maddala, G. S. 1983. *Limited-Dependent and Qualitative Variables in Econometrics.* Cambridge: Cambridge University Press.

Malik, Aran, and Robert Schwab. 1988. "The Economics of Tax Amnesties." University of Maryland. Typescript.

Marchon, Maurice N. 1979. "Tax Avoidance, Progressivity, and Work Effort." *Public Finance/Finances Publiques* 34:453–59.

Mikesell, John L. 1986. "Amnesties for State Tax Evaders: The Nature of and Response to Recent Programs." *National Tax Journal* 39:507–25.

Pencavel, John H. 1979. "A Note on Income Tax Evasion, Labor Supply, and Nonlinear Tax Schedules." *Journal of Public Economics* 12:115–24.

Pitt, Mark M., and Joel Slemrod. 1989. "The Compliance Cost of Itemizing Deductions: Evidence From Individual Tax Returns." *American Economic Review* 79:1224–32.

Reinganum, Jennifer F., and Louis L. Wilde. 1986. "Equilibrium Verification and Reporting Policies in a Model of Tax Compliance." *International Economic Review* 27:739–60.

Reinganum, Jennifer F., and Louis L. Wilde. 1988. "A Note on Enforcement Uncertainty and Taxpayer Compliance." *Quarterly Journal of Economics,* November, 793–98.

Sandmo, Agnar. 1981. "Income Tax Evasion, Labor Supply, and the Equity-Efficiency Trade-off." *Journal of Public Economics* 16:265–88.

Slemrod, Joel. 1985. "An Empirical Test for Tax Evasion." *Review of Economics and Statistics* 67:232–38.

Spicer, Michael W., and L. A. Becker. 1980. "Fiscal Inequity and Tax Evasion: An Experimental Approach." *National Tax Journal* 33:171–75.

Spicer, Michael W., and S. B. Lundstedt. 1976. "Understanding Tax Evasion." *Public Finance/Finances Publiques* 31:295–305.

Tanzi, Vito. 1983. "The Underground Economy in the United States: Annual Estimates, 1930–80." *International Monetary Fund Staff Papers* 30:283–305.

Wainer, Howard, ed. 1986. *Drawing Inferences From Self-Selected Samples.* New York: Springer-Verlag.

Witte, Ann D., and Diane F. Woodbury. 1985. "The Effect of Tax Laws and Tax Administration on Tax Compliance: The Case of the U.S. Individual Income Tax." *National Tax Journal* 38:1–13.

Yitzhaki, Shlomo. 1974. "A Note on Income Tax Evasion. A Theoretical Analysis." *Journal of Public Economics* 3:201–2.

Commentary

C. Y. Cyrus Chu

Since the pioneering work of Allingham and Sandmo, there have been many extensions and elaborations in the theoretical analysis of tax evasion, but empirical studies in this field are relatively rare. One major difficulty in such empirical analysis hinges upon the availability of microdata. Intuitively, studying tax evasion will unavoidably face the problem of the "latent variable" in econometrics. In their essay, the authors try to avoid such an unobservability problem by using tax amnesty data, in which tax evaders "confess" their evasion amount; hence, the latent variable becomes visible. However, the amnesty data set has its own problems. First, people are free to decide whether to join such an amnesty program, so that we have a self-selection problem. Second, the amnesty is for Michigan state income tax only; hence, we have to understand the close connections between federal and state taxes in order to find out the relationship among state tax evasion, federal tax evasion, and state tax amnesty. So, using the amnesty data and solving the related self-selection and federal-state tax connection problems are essentially the basic background of this essay.

The basic econometric setup of Professors Crane and Nourzad is composed of the following three equations.

$$\text{FEDEVA} = f_1(\underset{+}{\text{AGI}}, \underset{-}{\text{AGISQ}}, \underset{+}{\text{MTR}}, \underset{?}{\text{IRSCLASS}}, \underset{?}{\text{MALE}}, \underset{?}{\text{MARRIED}}, \underset{+}{\text{PREPARE}}); \tag{1}$$

$$\text{MICHEVA} = f_2(\underset{+}{\text{AGI}}, \underset{+}{\text{MARRIED}}, \underset{-}{\text{MALE}}, \underset{-}{\text{PCTWHD}}, \underset{-}{\text{PREPARE}}, \underset{+}{\overline{\text{FEDEVA}}}); \tag{2}$$

$$\text{PART} = f_3(\underset{?}{\text{RENTROYL}}, \underset{?}{\text{LICENSED}}, \underset{?}{\text{IRS-AUDIT}}, \underset{?}{\text{GUILT}}). \tag{3}$$

I have placed positive or negative signs below variables to indicate significant positive or negative parameter estimations; the question marks indicate insignificant ones. The abbreviations for variables are the same and will not be repeated here. Equation 1 simply provides an instrumental variable, $\overline{\text{FEDEVA}}$, to solve the error-in-variable problem associated with the original FEDEVA data, which is equal to the difference of the original AGI and the AGI in the amnesty return form. Equation 3 characterizes the selectivity criterion: only those who participate in the amnesty program will appear in the sample point of equation 2. This is where the sample truncation comes from. Overall, the authors provide an interesting and novel empirical attempt to analyze evasion activity. Using amnesty data for a truncated regression is a new approach; the data processing by the authors is quite prudent; and the statistical findings are reasonable. In what follows, I would like to raise a few points or suggestions in hope of making their analysis more satisfactory.

1. In the Michigan Amnesty Data Base, there are 2,985 income tax amnesty cases, among which 588 cases were "amending old returns," and the other 2,397 cases were "new filers" (i.e., they did not file any return originally). The authors consider only the first 588 cases in their empirical analysis. The reason to drop the other 2,397 cases, as they explained, are two: first, nonfilers are corner-solution individuals, and second, without the original income tax return, it is hard to do part of the calculation and regression. I do not think the first argument is relevant empirically; after all, limited dependent variable analyses are designed to tackle the problem of corner solutions. Furthermore, the huge proportion of amnesty participants that are original nonfilers means that this part of the sample contains very important information about amnesty participation, and the empirical results may be very sensitive to these discarded sample points. According to Fisher, Goddeeris, and Young, many of these original nonfilers of Michigan state taxes did file federal tax returns, and had been identified by the Michigan Department of Treasury through computer tape-matching. If the federal tax return data of these nonfilers are available, then the AGI's difference (FEDEVA) can be calculated, and the state tax evasion amount is the amount on the amnesty return. So far as I can see, these data points can be used in equations 1 through 3.
2. The State amnesty program waived all criminal and civil penalties related to the *state* level, but I suppose that the *federal* evasion penal-

ties cannot be waived by the state government. This may explain why a large proportion of the amnesty participants, as the authors pointed out, are not federal tax evaders. But if this is the case, then equation 3 needs to be modified by adding the FEDEVA variable to the arguments of f_3. In other words, FEDEVA may be a reasonable explanatory variable of the amnesty participation decision.

3. As pointed out by Fisher, Goddeeris, and Young, 36 percent of the amnesty participants made payments less than $100. And in Iowa, 73 percent of the participants made payments less than $1,000. This suggests that small amount evaders are likely to join the amnesty program, and, hence, the MICHEVA variable should have been put in the right-hand side of equation 3. Then, clearly, equations 2 and 3 will form a simultaneous equation system, and we have to analyze a bit more sophisticated truncated regression model.
4. The GUILT variable in equation 3 will be 1 if the amnesty participant attached a letter of "explanation," and 0 otherwise. The authors claimed that if there is such a letter, the individual may be experiencing some type of remorse. Although this conjecture may be right, I do not think it is logical to use this remorse variable as an "explanatory" variable for amnesty participation. After all, only amnesty participants could *possibly* submit such letters. So, my suggestion is to drop the GUILT variable in equation 3.

The authors pointed out that, although there clearly exists a selectivity problem, the coefficient of the selectivity-bias adjustment was not significant. The last three previous comments may help to improve such a situation. Finally, I have a point concerning the effectiveness of the amnesty program, but one not directly related to the empirical setup of this essay. The authors pointed out that the amnesty program was viewed as an "unqualified success" by the Michigan authorities. Such "success" was measured by the short-run *additional* tax revenue collected. This seems to imply that we may want to have another "successful" experience in the future. To evaluate whether an amnesty program is successful, in addition to the tax revenue consideration, we have to look at the changes in the deterrent effect of penalties. My suggestion is to set up an econometric model of tax evasion behavior (with either micro- or macrodata) and test whether there is any structural change in the relationship between evading behavior and various deterrent policies (such as the probability of detection and the size of any penalty). Amnesty is certainly a dilution of the penalty. Such a dilution effect will be weak only if it comes as a surprise. The short-run tax revenue increase is not necessarily a success for the amnesty program in the long run.

Can Brute Deterrence Backfire? Perceptions and Attitudes in Taxpayer Compliance

Steven M. Sheffrin
Robert K. Triest

The standard economic model of tax compliance (Allingham and Sandmo 1972) that views compliance as an example of the economics of crime provides a useful starting point for thinking about tax evasion. But in recent years, many scholars have pointed to limitations of this framework. For plausible parameter values, the model substantially underpredicts the number of honest taxpayers (see Skinner and Slemrod 1985). It also does not provide strong predictions about the socioeconomic determinants of evasion. The model does, however, emphasize deterrence, including the severity and certainty of punishment, as an important aspect of the compliance problem.

Another large body of research views tax compliance from sociological and psychological perspectives and emphasizes the effects of social norms and individual attitudes in explaining noncompliance. Kinsey (1988a and 1988b) provides an extensive survey of this work. There has also been experimental research on compliance, often using college students as subjects.

Cowell (1990) provides a convenient review of both the attitudinal and experimental literatures. The survey evidence suggests that individual attitudes and perceptions of the tax system are related to compliance. In particular, there is some evidence that perceived inequities in the tax system are related to noncompliance. Some of the experimental evidence (Spicer and Becker 1980) comes to similar conclusions. However, not all the survey or experimental evidence is conclusive on this point. Mason and Calvin (1984), in an analysis of survey data in Oregon, find that dissatisfaction with the tax system is not directly related to reported noncompliance but changes other attitudes and beliefs. Cowell (1990, 219) reports on experimental evidence

We wish to thank Colin Cameron, Jeff Dubin, Jonathan Feinstein, Jim Poterba, Jon Skinner, and conference participants for helpful comments. Liang Liu and Farshid Mojaver-Hosseini provided excellent research assistance.

that fails to find links between perceived inequities in the system and noncompliance. Other researchers (Kaplan and Reckers 1985), found that beliefs about tax morality were more important than beliefs about the fairness of the tax system. In a similar vein, Song and Yarbrough (1978) found that perceptions of the honesty of others were directly related to the individuals' own tax ethics.

Overall, the evidence does suggest that perceptions of the fairness of the tax system, beliefs about the honesty of others, and perceptions of sanctions from the government probably play some role in compliance behavior. The fact that the evidence is mixed on many of these issues suggests that the responses to surveys or behavior in experimental situations is very sensitive to the precise details of the questions or experimental setups. In this paper, we present our own statistical analysis of the determinants of compliance that we believe is likely to be robust to the precise nuances of the survey. But before presenting our own perspective on these questions, it is worthwhile to ask a more basic question. Suppose our attitudes and perceptions do influence behavior—does this really matter for either policy analysis or policy prescriptions?

A naive economist or deterrence theorist would argue that attitudes could possibly affect compliance behavior but that differences in attitudes should just be treated as any other sort of unexplained heterogeneity in behavior. In other words, one should treat differences in attitudes as random errors in a statistical model. In all empirical work, there are unexplained variations—attitudes toward the tax system are perhaps just another source of randomness and should be treated in the usual fashion.

There are two reasons why we believe this view is incorrect. First, attitudes may be correlated with other variables whose effects on compliance we are interested in estimating. For example, those with a negative attitude toward government may believe the probability of detection is lower than do those who have a less negative attitude. This correlation would result in biased estimation of the coefficient on the probability of detection if attitudes are not controlled for and do have an independent effect on evasion.

Perhaps more important, the naive view ignores the potential for complex interactions between attitudes and compliance. If individual compliance decisions are dependent, in part, on perceptions of aggregate compliance, then the entire nature of the compliance process may differ compared to the situation in which individual attitudes do not affect compliance. Cowell (1990) discusses "epidemic" models in which there are important feedbacks between individual and aggregate compliance behavior.

Suppose, for example, that individuals who do not fully comply with the tax code experience more utility if aggregate noncompliance is higher. Perhaps this is because the guilt or stigma from noncompliance is eased when others are perceived to not comply as well. In this case, the relationship between individual and aggregate noncompliance can cause multiple equilibria. If an individual increases evasion activity, this will raise aggregate noncompliance and have further repercussions in the same direction. The positive complementarity between individual and aggregate decisions in this model is similar to equilibrium search models, such as Diamond's (1984), as both may feature multiple equilibria. When there are multiple equilibria, accidental or incidental factors may influence the aggregate amount of noncompliance in the system.

If attitudes toward the tax system and perceptions of compliance are important determinants of individual compliance decisions, then government decisions and actions could have important indirect effects on outcomes. Indeed, there is the possibility that too much publicity about tax cheating could have inadvertent adverse effects that reduce the morale of honest taxpayers and thereby decrease total compliance.

Similar views were voiced during debates about state and federal tax amnesties. One of the objections to the amnesties was that they could focus too much attention on noncompliance and, thereby, have adverse effects on honest taxpayers. Depending on the magnitude of this effect, overall compliance could decrease. Without an empirical estimate of this effect, however, this argument could not be fully evaluated.

A close examination of attitudes and perceptions may also be useful in the detailed design of compliance measures. For example, there is some evidence that personal experience with audits could actually increase tax resistance (see Spicer and Lundstedt 1976). This could operate through hostility toward more intrusive tax authorities (Strumpel 1969), as documented in the comparisons between West Germany and the United Kingdom (Schmölders 1970). Or, it could also reflect a decrease in the perceived probability of detection (Kinsey and Smith 1987) after a taxpayer reflects on the entire audit process. Our empirical work will examine these issues. Other compliance measures that operate less personally, such as improved computer matching, may be free of these adverse effects.

In this essay, we provide new estimates of the effects of attitudes, perceptions of honesty, and perceived deterrence on tax compliance. The Internal Revenue Service commissioned Louis Harris and Associates to conduct a cross-sectional survey of taxpayers using in-depth group interviews. The Harris survey, conducted in 1987, contains a rich body of information about compliance, attitudes, and economic variables.[1] From this survey, we ana-

1. The Harris survey data were obtained through the Inter-University Consortium for Political and Social Research.

lyzed the responses of 1,444 taxpayers to determine the effects of both attitudes and deterrence on compliance using a statistical methodology that should not be sensitive to minor variations in the questions.

Unlike the studies based on audits, the compliance measure in the Harris survey is based on self-reports. Respondents were asked if they overstated deductions or understated income on their tax returns in the last five years. In our sample, 22 percent reported either one or the other behavior. Researchers have found that the proportion of taxpayers admitting to noncompliance in response to these questions in group interview settings is higher than to similar questions answered through the mail. In the group interview setting, it is possible to reassure individuals that their responses will not be transmitted to the IRS, and experienced interviewers can thus elicit more honest responses.

However, there has been recent work (Elffers, Weigel, and Hessing 1987) that found little connection between self-reports and auditor judgments of noncompliance. One interpretation of this finding is that self-reports are simply not useful. However, as Kinsey (1988b) suggests, there may be real differences of opinion between auditors and taxpayers. For example, in the TCMP audits, a significant proportion of taxpayers make mistakes that overstate their taxable income. Thus, there are presumably also mistakes in the other direction. Auditors would view this behavior as noncompliance, while taxpayers would not. In addition, audits are poor vehicles for uncovering unreported income. If a taxpayer failed to report income that an auditor did not detect, there would again be a discrepancy between auditor judgments and self-reports. Finally, a third source of discrepancy could be disagreements over interpreting the rather complex tax code. Our position is that self-reports do provide useful information, but they must be used with some care for purposes such as estimating revenue losses from noncompliance.[2]

The statistical method we use is based on recent work in the psychometrics literature. In the Harris survey, individuals responded to a very large number of often closely related questions concerning their attitudes toward the tax system. Individuals were typically asked to respond on a scale of 1 to 5 if they strongly disagreed or strongly agreed with particular statements that were often part of a cluster of statements concerning similar topics. Both the large number of questions and the categorical nature of the responses mitigate against simply including all the responses as individual items in a typical regression model. The variables would likely be highly collinear and produce coefficient estimates that would be hard to interpret.

---

2. As discussed in this volume, the Dutch tax compliance system differs sharply from the system in the United States.

Our approach to this problem is to use latent (unobserved) variable techniques. Essentially, we model individuals' underlying attitudes toward the tax system, their perceived probability of detection, and their propensity for noncompliance as latent variables and use the responses to survey questions as indicators of the latent variables. In this framework, the underlying latent variables are related to several indicators, and we typically allow for random noise in the indicators. Since we allow for measurement error in the observed indicators of the latent variables, our method is likely to be robust to minor variations in the phrasing of the questions from which the indicators are derived.

After estimating our statistical model, we use it to explore the significance of possible adverse effects from publicity concerning noncompliance. Adopting an experimental approach, we asked two groups to answer some of the questions on the Harris survey. But before answering the questions, the two groups were given different paragraphs to read. One paragraph emphasized the "tax gap" and noncompliance, while the other emphasized ongoing detection and compliance methods. Differences in responses from the two groups are compared and related to the estimates from our statistical model.

To this point, we have been using the term *attitudes* rather loosely. Following Lewis (1982, 225), we employ the common psychological definition as "learned predispositions to respond in a consistently favorable or unfavorable manner with respect to a given object or set of objects." According to Lewis, there are essentially three views of the relationships between attitudes and behavior. First, attitudes may simply accompany behavior, that is be epiphenomena, and have no useful role in explaining behavior. Second, attitudes may be channels between external stimuli (such as tax rates) and final expressions of behavior but again be largely endogenous phenomena in the system. The third view, which we adopt as a working hypothesis, allows attitudes to have some independent role in determining behavior. According to this view, attitudes are independent causes of behavior and thus merit study if we are to understand behavior fully.

The second section discusses the data and outlines the basic statistical framework (a more detailed treatment of the model is given in the appendix). We present the statistical estimates and analyze the results in the third section. In the fourth section, we turn to the question of the effects of publicity on attitudes and discuss the results of our experimental evidence. The final section discusses the policy implications of our work.

An Econometric Model of Tax Compliance

Our econometric model is a two-equation recursive system. Compliance is modeled as a function of attitudes toward the tax system, the perceived honesty of others, the perceived probability of detection, and a number of socioeconomic characteristics. The perceived probability of detection is modeled as a function of past contact with the IRS. In this section we first describe how the latent variables are constructed, and then outline the specification of our structural model. A more technical exposition of our econometric specification is given in the appendix.

We use two indicators of noncompliance with the tax law, one that measures overstatement of deductions and one that measures underreporting of income. The questions upon which these measures are based are shown in table 1. Note that the questions measure whether the sample member engaged in any tax evasion activity, but do not measure the magnitude of any evasion that did take place. Since both questions were answered on an ordinal, five-point scale, the categorical nature of the variables needs to be taken into account in the econometric analysis.[3]

These variables are treated in two different ways in the econometric estimation. In one specification, underreporting of income and overstatement of deductions are treated as distinct forms of noncompliance. In this specification, the answer to each question is assumed to be generated through the categorization of an underlying continuous random variable. The actual response to the question depends on the range in which the continuous variable falls. For example, if y_{ai} is the continuous variable underlying sample member i's response to the overstatement of deductions question, then a response of "definitely have not" is generated if y_{ai} is less than a threshold value τ_1, while a response of "probably have not" is generated if y_{ai} falls between τ_1 and τ_2.[4]

In the second specification, underreporting of income and overstatement of deductions are treated as indicators of a single latent noncompliance variable. The latent noncompliance variable (η_1) is scaled to have the same mean as the continuous variable generating the responses to the overstatement of deductions question:

$$y_{ai} = \eta_{1i} + \epsilon_{ai} \, , \tag{1}$$

where ϵ_{ai} is a mean zero random variable that can be interpreted as measurement error. The overstatement of deductions variable can thus be interpreted as a "noisy" version of the latent noncompliance variable in this framework.

3. Although the questions were actually answered on a four-point scale, we treated responses off the scale (including refusal) as being between "probably have" and "probably have not." A similar procedure was followed with the other ordinal categorical variables.

4. The responses to the noncompliance questions were reordered such that an increase in one of the underlying continuous variables is associated with an increase in the likelihood of noncompliance.

The underreporting of income variable (y_{bi}) is similarly related to the latent compliance variable, although the scale is allowed to differ:

$$y_{bi} = \lambda_b \eta_{1i} + \epsilon_{bi} , \tag{2}$$

TABLE 1. Survey Questions on Compliance, Attitude, and Perceived Detection

Subject	Response Scale	Survey Question
Compliance	4 point[a]	By the same token, within the past five years or so, do you think you might have overstated any deductions or expenses—like medical, charitable, or business deductions, and so forth—even by *just a small amount?*
		Within the past five years or so, do you think you might have left some reportable income off your federal tax returns—even *just a small amount?*
Attitudes toward compliance and government	6 point[b]	With what things cost these days, it's okay to cut a few corners on your tax form to help make ends meet.
		It's not so wrong to hold back a bit on taxes since the government spends too much anyway.
Perceptions of others' honesty	6 point[b]	Almost every taxpayer would cheat to some extent if he thought he could get away with it.
		The reason the average taxpayer is honest is because he has no choice since his income comes mainly from wages and salary.
Perceived probability of detection	7 point[c]	When people try to cheat by *small* amounts, what do you think are their chances of being caught? Which answer on this card *best* describes their chances of being caught?
		When people try to cheat by *large* amounts, what do you think are their chances of being caught? What answer on this card *best* describes their chances of being caught?
Contact with the IRS	5 point[d]	Within the last three years, have you or has someone you know personally been contacted *by* the IRS, aside from getting a tax form or refund check?
	3 point[e]	Do you personally know anyone who has had difficulties with the IRS concerning their income tax?

[a]4 = definitely have; 1 = definitely have not.
[b]6 = strongly agree; 1 = strongly disagree.
[c]7 = almost certain to be caught; 1 = almost certain not to be caught.
[d]5 = definitely yes; 1 = definitely no.
[e]3 = yes; 2 = not sure; 1 = no.

where ϵ_{bi} represents measurement error. The measurement errors are assumed to be uncorrelated with each other. This specification is equivalent to a very simple confirmatory factor analysis model where the factor loading of y_a on η_1 has been set to one, and the factor loading of y_b on η_1 (λ_b) is to be estimated.

Three other latent variables characterize the structural model. These variables measure attitudes toward the government and the tax system, perceptions of the honesty of others, and the perceived probability of detection.

We utilize two indicators of the respondents' attitudes toward the government and tax code compliance (these questions are also shown in table 1). These questions probe for whether the respondent thinks it is morally acceptable to engage in a limited amount of tax evasion given (*a*) the high cost of living and (*b*) overspending by the government. As with the compliance questions, we specify a simple factor analytic model relating these questions to a single latent attitudinal variable. One would expect that larger (more positive) values of this variable would be associated with an increase in the probability of evasion. The factor loading of the first question is set to one in order to scale the latent variable, while the other factor loading is left free. As before, the measurement errors are assumed to be uncorrelated.

A factor analytic specification is also used to relate two questions probing perceptions of others' honesty to a single latent variable. The latent variable is again scaled by setting the first factor loading to one. Our expectation was that this latent variable would be positively related to noncompliance. Taxpayers who believe that the compliance of others is due mainly to lack of opportunity to evade taxes are more likely to take advantage of such opportunities themselves.

The two perceived probability of detection questions differ only in that the first refers to the probability of being caught for those cheating by a small amount, while the second pertains to those evading on a large scale. A factor analytic model is again specified to relate the responses to these two questions to a single latent probability of detection variable. The factor loading of the first variable is set to one, while the factor loading of the second question is left to be estimated.[5] One would expect the second question's estimated loading to be between zero and one, since the overall chance of being detected when cheating by a large amount is generally thought to be greater than the chance of being caught when cheating by a small amount. The factor loading would need to be a positive fraction in order to reduce the continuous variable underlying responses to the second question to the same scale as the variable underlying the first question.

Two variables, based on the last two questions in table 1, measure the

5. The responses were reordered such that an increase in the latent variable is associated with an increase in the perceived probability of detection.

degree of past contact with the IRS. The first question asks whether either the respondent or an acquaintance has been contacted by the IRS (aside from receiving a tax form or refund check) over the past three years. The second question inquires whether the respondent personally knows anyone who has "had difficulties" with the IRS. Since preliminary attempts at estimation suggested that these could not be treated as indicators of a single latent "contact with the IRS" variable, they are each treated as an ordinal categorical variable generated through a threshold-crossing mechanism by a continuous variable that is measured without error.

In addition to the variables we have described, five socioeconomic characteristics were included in the model, but assumed to be measured without error: household income, the household's marginal tax rate, marital status, a dummy variable set equal to one if the respondent or respondent's spouse had any self-employment income, and a dummy variable set equal to one if the respondent itemized deductions.[6]

The data used to estimate our model is from the 1987 Taxpayer Opinion Survey conducted for the IRS by Louis Harris and Associates (Harris 1988). This survey is based on a national probability sample of adult taxpayers. Out of 2,003 interviews conducted, 1,756 of the respondents were designated as "taxpayers" by the Harris organization on the basis of having filed (or intending to file) a 1985 or 1986 tax return. Of this group, 312 contained missing data on one or more of the variables used in the statistical analysis. This left a subsample of 1,444 observations suitable for use in estimation.

The core of the econometric model consists of two structural equations. The first equation models the latent compliance behavior variable as a linear function of the latent attitude toward government variable, the latent perception of others' honesty variable, the latent probability of detection variable, and the five socioeconomic characteristics that are measured without error. Schematically this can be written as

$$\eta_{1i} = \beta_2\eta_{2i} + \beta_3\eta_{3i} + \beta_4\eta_{4i} + (x_i \cdot \gamma_1) + \zeta_{1i} , \tag{3}$$

where η_1 through η_4 are the latent variables for (respectively) noncompliance, attitudes toward compliance, attitudes regarding honesty, and the perceived

6. Household income is reported only in categorical form in the survey data. Because the bands are fairly narrow, the average of the endpoints of the income bands was used to impute dollar values. In order to impute the household's marginal tax rate, taxable income had to first be imputed. This was done by subtracting estimates of the value of the household's personal exemptions and deductions from household income. The value of deductions was set to the average value within the appropriate published income range if the respondent was an itemizer, equal to the standard deduction otherwise.

probability of detection, x is the vector of socioeconomic characteristics measured without error, and ζ_1 is a mean zero error term. The itemization and self-employment questions serve as indicators of the opportunities for evasion.

A second equation models the perceived probability of detection as a function of past contact with the IRS, contact with someone who has had "difficulties" with the IRS, and the five socioeconomic characteristics.

$$\eta_{4i} = \beta_5 \eta_{5i} + \beta_6 \eta_{6i} + (x_i \cdot \gamma_4) + \zeta_{4i} , \tag{4}$$

where η_5 and η_6 are variables based on the last two questions shown in table 1. The purpose of this equation is to investigate how IRS enforcement efforts affect the perceived probability of detection. Since we are reluctant to use η_5 and η_6 as instruments for η_4 in equation 3, we impose the restriction that ζ_1 and ζ_4 are uncorrelated. This restriction, which implies that the unmeasured determinants of noncompliance are uncorrelated with the unmeasured determinants of the perceived probability of detection, seems more reasonable than the alternative assumption that the contact with the IRS variables (η_5 and η_6) are uncorrelated with the unmeasured determinants of noncompliance.

The primary econometric problem involved in estimating the parameters in equations 3 and 4 is that, instead of directly observing the latent variables, we observe a set of ordinal categorical indicators. Traditional latent variable techniques assume that the joint distribution of the underlying variables is normal and that the indicator variables are continuous. These assumptions are not applicable in our case. Therefore, we draw on some recent advances in the psychometrics literature. Following Muthén (1983 and 1984), we assume that the distribution of the continuous variables underlying the observed categorical variables, conditional on the five socioeconomic variables measured without error, is standard (unit variances) multivariate normal. The values of the underlying continuous variables along with the thresholds determine the responses to the questions. The responses are naturally "ordered" in the data, for example, ranging from "strongly disagree" to "strongly agree." In econometric terms, this would be known as a ten-variate ordered probit specification.

Following Muthén (1984), the estimation was performed in three stages. In the first, ten (one for each ordinal categorical variable) univariate ordered probit regressions were estimated using maximum likelihood techniques. In the second stage, the forty-five conditional correlation coefficients between the ten continuous variables generating the categorical variables were estimated by maximizing the bivariate ordered probit likelihood functions treating the parameters estimated in the first stage as fixed. These two stages provide estimates of all of the moments necessary for determination of the parameters of the structural model. In the last stage, the structural parameters were estimated using a minimum distance estimator to impose the restrictions implied by the model on the correlations and regression coefficients estimated in the first two stages. The parameters estimated in the final stages consist of the factor loadings, coefficients of the structural equations, and the covariance matrix of the latent variables. The calculation of the standard errors takes into account that the population moments were estimated in previous steps. A more complete description of the econometric specification and estimator used is provided in the appendix.

Econometric Results

Table 2 presents the results of the estimation of the factor loadings. Although they are reported separately, the factor loadings were estimated jointly with the parameters whose estimates are shown in tables 3 and 4. Estimates from the specification allowing for two separate noncompliance variables are reported in column one, while column two contains estimates from the single latent noncompliance variable model.

TABLE 2. Estimated Factor Loadings

Latent Variable	Indicator	Two Variable Model	Single Variable Model
Noncompliance	Overstatement of deductions	—[a]	1.00[b]
	Underreporting of income	—[a]	1.15 (.10)
Attitudes toward compliance	Okay to cut corners on tax form	1[b]	1[b]
	Government spends too much	1.02 (.04)	1.01 (.04)
Perception of others' dishonesty	Taxpayers would cheat if they could get away with it	1.00[b]	1.00[b]
	Average taxpayer honest due to lack of opportunity to cheat	0.46 (.06)	0.45 (.06)
Probability of detection	Chance of being caught if cheating by a small amount	1.00[b]	1.00[b]
	Chance of being caught if cheating by a large amount	0.30 (.07)	0.30 (.07)

Note: Figures in parentheses are standard errors.

[a]Factor loadings not estimated. The two noncompliance indicators were treated as separate latent variables.

[b]Factor loading fixed at one.

The estimated parameters are generally of the same sign and magnitude as expected. The factor loadings are all positive, implying that the indicators influence compliance behavior in the same direction as the other indicators that load on the same latent variable. As expected, the perceived probability of detection if cheating by a large amount factor loading is estimated to be between zero and one. The other estimated factor loadings are of reasonable magnitude.

Estimates of the coefficients of the noncompliance equation and standard deviations of the latent variables are reported in table 3. The first two columns

TABLE 3. Noncompliance Equation Estimates

Variable	Overstating Deductions	Underreporting Income	Single Latent Variable
	Structural Coefficients		
Casual attitude toward compliance	.30	.31	.28
	(.04)	(.05)	(.04)
Others' dishonesty	.02	.07	.05
	(.03)	(.03)	(.02)
Probability of detection	−.09	−.12	−.10
	(.04)	(.04)	(.03)
Household income (thousands)	.01	.00	.01
	(.01)	(.01)	(.01)
Marital status (married = 1)	.02	.12	.05
	(.15)	(.13)	(.10)
Itemization status	−.02	−.03	−.03
	(.11)	(.10)	(.08)
Self-employment status	.21	.08	.12
	(.14)	(.14)	(.09)
Marginal tax rate	−1.02	0.75	−0.19
	(1.84)	(1.58)	(1.23)
	Standard Deviations of Latent Variables		
Noncompliance	1.10	1.14	0.41
	(.00)	(.00)	(.00)
Negative attitude toward government	.78		.79
	(.00)		(.00)
Others' dishonesty	1.09		1.12
	(.02)		(.02)
Probability of detection	1.14		1.14
	(.07)		(.07)
χ^2	54.20		66.50
df	33		42

Note: Figures in parentheses are standard errors.

correspond to the specification that allows for two separate forms of noncompliance. In this specification, two sets of structural coefficients are jointly estimated with a single set of factor loadings and the covariance matrix of the latent variables. The third column contains results from the specification treating the two noncompliance variables as indicators of a common latent variable.

The estimated structural coefficients indicate that the perceived probability of detection has a substantial (and statistically significant) deterrent effect on noncompliance. Having a casual attitude toward compliance is associated with a substantially increased likelihood of evasion. As expected, perceiving other taxpayers as complying due only to the lack of opportunity for cheating increases the likelihood of evasion.

The coefficients on the variables measured without error are generally small in magnitude with standard errors large relative to their size. This is surprising, since one would expect the itemization variable to be a good predictor of the overstatement of deductions and the self-employment variable to be a good predictor of underreporting of income. One reason for the relatively small estimated effects may be due to the fact that the compliance questions refer to compliance over the last five years, while the itemization and self-employment variables proxy current tax evasion opportunities. Another factor is that the noncompliance variables measure only whether any underreporting of income or overstating of deductions has occurred, not the extent of the noncompliance. Petty evasion, such as claiming an exemption for a nonexistent child, is given the same weight as larger scale evasion that might require itemization of deductions or receiving self-employment income.

It is interesting to note that the two specifications (the one that combines the two noncompliance indicators and the one that allows separate effects) yield very similar coefficient estimates on the latent variables. While a formal test of whether the two observed noncompliance variables can be combined into a single latent variable is difficult to devise, the determinants of the two forms of noncompliance appear to be very similar.[7]

The results require additional interpretation because of the arbitrary scaling of the indicator variables. While the variances of the indicators were fixed at one for purposes of identification, the variances of the latent variables (conditional on the socioeconomic variables) were estimated along with the

7. Testing is difficult because the two models are not nested. The specification with a single latent noncompliance variable imposes restrictions on the structural coefficients, but allows for measurement error in the indicators of the noncompliance latent variable.

other parameters.[8] In the specification with a single noncompliance variable, the standard deviation of that variable was estimated to be .41, while the standard deviations of the attitude toward government, perception of others' dishonesty, and probability of detection latent variables were .79, 1.12, and 1.14, respectively. These estimated standard deviations can be useful in interpreting the results. For example, a 1.00 standard deviation increase in the probability of detection is estimated to result in a 0.28 standard deviation decrease in the latent noncompliance variable. Similarly, a 1.00 standard deviation increase in the perception of others' dishonesty variable, which might result from an increase in the prevalence of evasion, is estimated to cause a 0.14 standard deviation increase in noncompliance.

What would be the effect of omitting the attitudinal variables on our estimate of the perceived probability of detection coefficient? Omitting the two attitudinal variables in the single noncompliance variable specification results in the perceived probability of detection coefficient increasing in magnitude from −.10 to −.17.[9] Those who view others as dishonest or have a negative attitude toward government tend to view the probability of detection as being lower than do those with more positive attitudes. Omitting the attitudinal variables would lead to unwarranted optimism concerning the efficacy of policies designed to increase the perceived probability of detection.

There has been relatively little research investigating how government policies affect the perceived probability of detection. Table 4 presents estimates of our equation specifying the perceived probability of detection to be a linear function of socioeconomic characteristics, a variable measuring the degree of the respondent's past contact with the IRS, and whether the respondent personally knows someone who experienced difficulties with the IRS. Past contact with the IRS is found to lead to a slight increase in the perceived probability of detection, although we cannot reject the hypothesis that the coefficient is zero at reasonable levels of significance. Surprisingly, personal knowledge of someone with difficulties with the IRS results in a sizable (and statistically significant) decrease in the perceived probability of detection. A possible explanation for this is that taxpayers who are audited or otherwise investigated by the IRS come to the conclusion that it would be relatively easy to successfully "hide" income from the IRS as a result of the experience. This

8. The variances of the latent variables (conditional on the socioeconomic variables) are actually functions of the β coefficients and the covariance matrix of the ζ error terms. The δ method was used to estimate standard errors.

9. In the specification with separate overstating of deductions and underreporting of income equations, the perceived probability of detection coefficients increase in magnitude to −.16 (overstating of deductions equation) and −.23 (underreporting of income equation).

suggests that increasing audit rates may actually have the perverse effect of increasing the level of noncompliance in future years.

Caution should be used in interpreting the perceived probability of detection equation coefficients. Personal knowledge of someone who has had difficulties with the IRS could conceivably be an indicator of noncompliance. If this is the case, then the negative coefficient on this variable may actually be due to the deterrence effect captured in the noncompliance equation.

Our results are similar to those reported by Kinsey (in this volume). She found that vicarious contacts with the IRS through the experience of others could lead to less compliance. In particular, hearing reports of bad behavior by the IRS lowers the perceived fairness of the tax system and reported future compliance. These results are also broadly consistent with those of Kinsey and Smith (1987), who find that having undergone a recent audit leads to a decrease in the probability of future audits.

Table 4 also displays results for the regressions of the other latent variables on the socioeconomic characteristics. As shown in the appendix, these coefficients are estimated jointly with the other parameters discussed thus far. As expected, itemizers are more likely than nonitemizers to both know someone who has had contact with the IRS and to know someone who has had difficulties with the IRS. Those with self-employment income are also more likely to know someone who has had contact with the IRS. Surprisingly, receiving self-employment income is associated with a decrease in the casual

TABLE 4. Model Estimates

Variable	Casual Attitude toward Compliance	Perception of Others' Dishonesty	Perceived Probability of Detection	Contact with the IRS	Difficulties with the IRS
Household income	.00	.00	−.01	.01	.00
(thousands)	(.01)	(.01)	(.01)	(.01)	(.01)
Marital status	−.11	−.15	.02	−.05	−.14
(married = 1)	(.11)	(.11)	(.11)	(.14)	(.18)
Itemization status	−.05	−.05	−.06	.25	.33
(itemizer = 1)	(.09)	(.09)	(.09)	(.10)	(.12)
Self-employment status	−.32	.06	−.13	.36	.13
(self-employed = 1)	(.13)	(.13)	(.12)	(.14)	(.16)
Marginal tax rate	−0.54	−0.35	0.13	−0.47	1.85
	(1.40)	(1.44)	(1.47)	(1.70)	(2.37)
Contact with the IRS	—	—	.04	—	—
			(.04)		
Difficulties with the IRS	—	—	−.22	—	—
			(.05)		

Note: Figures in parentheses are standard errors.

attitude toward compliance latent variable. The other coefficients are not statistically significant.

Orthogonality between the omitted right-hand side variables and the structural equation errors was not imposed in estimating the parameters reported in tables 2 through 4. The hypothesis that the "contact with the IRS" and "difficulties with the IRS" variables are orthogonal to the compliance equation error terms and the "casual attitude toward compliance" and "perception of others' dishonesty" latent variables are orthogonal to the "perceived probability of detection" equation error can be easily rejected.[10] Table 5 presents the estimated coefficients of the noncompliance and perceived probability of detection equations when these exclusion restrictions are relaxed.[11] Although some of the previously excluded variables are statistically significant, the coefficients of the other variables are very close to their previous values. This suggests that omitted variables bias is not a problem.

We prefer the earlier specification over the one shown in table 5, because it seems questionable that the causal ordering runs from the "contact with the IRS" variables directly to noncompliance. The direction of causality could easily run the other way. Further research is needed to estimate a simultaneous equations specification allowing for a more complex causal structure.

To further investigate the sensitivity of our results to our econometric assumptions, we relaxed the assumption of orthogonality between the noncompliance equation error terms and the "perceived probability of detection" error term and instead imposed the assumption that the "contact with the IRS" and "difficulties with the IRS" variables are orthogonal to the noncompliance equation error terms. In both the single and dual noncompliance equation specifications, the attitudinal variables become insignificant and the perceived probability of detection coefficients increase in magnitude to over −.9. As we stated in the previous section, we are reluctant to use the "contact with the IRS" and "difficulties with the IRS" variables as instruments in the noncompliance equations. However, the sensitivity of the results to the identifying restrictions is disturbing. Future work should explore the consequences of using different instruments for the perceived probability of detection.

---

10. Imposing these restrictions increases the value of the minimum distance function (which has a χ^2 distribution under the assumption that the model is correctly specified) to 158.2 (df = 39) for the specification with separate overstating of deductions and underreporting of income equations and to 168.1 (df = 46) for the specification with a single noncompliance equation.

11. Results are shown only for the specification with separate overstating of deductions and underreporting of income equations. Since the reduced-form moment vector implied by the estimated parameters does not change as the variables are added to the structural equations and corresponding orthogonality conditions are imposed, the value of the χ^2-statistic (value of the objective function) also does not change.

Our econometric estimates suggest that caution must be used in implementing policies to increase compliance. Both the direct effect of increased revenue and the indirect effect of changed perceptions of the probability of detection must be considered in evaluating a program that increases the prevalence of audits or other enforcement measures. Our results for the perceived probability of detection equation suggest that the indirect effect of increased enforcement may be to decrease the level of long-run compliance. Further research into how attitudes and perceptions are formed is needed as input into the design of enforcement policies. One step in this direction is documented in the next section, which describes the results of an experiment analyzing the effects of publicity concerning noncompliance and enforcement programs on attitudes and the perceived probability of detection.

Publicity and Attitudes: An Experiment

Attitudes toward the tax system and perceptions of the honesty of others are not formed in a vacuum. Both normal newspaper and television accounts of tax-related matters as well as actions by government officials, especially tax administrators, may influence public perceptions.

TABLE 5. Model Estimates with Exclusion Restrictions Relaxed

Variable	Overstating Deductions	Underreporting Income	Perceived Probability of Detection
Casual attitude toward compliance	.28	.30	−.27
	(.04)	(.04)	(.03)
Others' dishonesty	.01	.07	−.05
	(.03)	(.03)	(.03)
Probability of detection	−.10	−.13	—
	(.04)	(.04)	
Contact with the IRS	.03	.13	.03
	(.05)	(.05)	(.04)
Difficulties with the IRS	.10	.05	−.18
	(.06)	(.06)	(.05)
Household income (thousands)	.01	−.00	−.01
	(.01)	(.01)	(.01)
Marital status (married = 1)	.03	.13	−.01
	(.15)	(.13)	(.11)
Itemization status	−.07	−.08	−.07
	(.11)	(.10)	(.08)
Self-employment status	.19	.02	−.21
	(.14)	(.14)	(.12)
Marginal tax rate	−1.24	0.69	−0.03
	(1.84)	(1.57)	(1.44)

There are many different types of publicity concerning compliance. One popular type is the tax difficulties of famous individuals. Consider the cases of Al Capone, Pete Rose, and Leona Helmsley. How are these cases likely to affect public attitudes?

In the case of Al Capone, his tax difficulties helped place him in jail. The public does not expect notorious criminals to pay taxes on illegal income and, thus, publicity about Capone should not lower tax morale. If anything, the IRS would earn public respect by helping to convict a high-profile criminal.

The Pete Rose case is also not likely to have an adverse affect on tax morality. Rose was convicted of tax evasion on illegal gambling income. While the public may have been disappointed in Rose's overall behavior, they would not expect him to pay taxes on his gambling income just as they would not pay taxes on their own football pool winnings.

The case of Leona Helmsley is more problematic. Her conviction was based on taking business deductions on items for personal use. The average taxpayer does not have the opportunity for this type of activity, although the activity itself would come as no surprise to the average taxpayer. Her case probably would do more detriment to the perceptions of fairness (the system is slanted to the rich) than to general perceptions of overall compliance.

In any case, given the First Amendment and the public delight in the rich and famous, there is little the government can do about tax crimes of famous individuals. The government, and particularly tax administrators, can, however, influence the type of news reporting about overall compliance.

Lewis discussed the role of tax administrators in this context.

> In the past, tax authorities have preferred a low profile, and perhaps for good reason, as their good intentions are often ridiculed by the press and the rest of the media. This low profile has some advantages too, as depersonalized tax officers somehow encourage a perception of fairness, objectivity, and scrupulousness that must be preserved; but it is timely for them to come out from behind their curtain and to take a more subdued but more visible place on stage.
>
> One way in which this could be done would be to publicize successful prosecutions brought against people who have evaded large amounts. This would encourage people to believe that treatment is equitable as well as advertising deterrent effects which would be much more successful than pursuing people who evade small amounts. (Lewis 1982, 180–81)

But is more publicity and a more "visible place on the stage" always desirable?

The single most common news story about tax compliance in the nonbusiness press is the "tax gap" story. By now it should be very familiar since it is common in both newspapers and scholarly articles. For example, on June 18, 1990, an Associated Press story began with a roadside vendor selling a watermelon for cash and a doctor and plumber engaging in a barter transaction. The story then turned to aggregate estimates of the "tax gap" that now hit the $100 billion mark. The overall impression from the story is that tax evasion is rampant.

In contrast, the stories that appear in the business press tend to be less alarmist and more focused. We did a literature search for the 1980s in the *Wall Street Journal* using the code words *tax* and *compliance*. The stories in the *Journal* were much more specific than the "tax gap" stories. Typical stories included discussion of TCMP audits, the proper structure of penalties, one small "tax gap" story highlighting actions of low-income individuals, specific provisions in tax bills, increasing the powers of the IRS through legislation and technology, and the ill-fated withholding on interest and dividends.

It is our view that the "tax gap" stories tend to be alarmist and defeatist and can breed public skepticism. It is well known that estimates of the tax gap are, to put it mildly, somewhat delicate, yet they seem to attract quite a bit of attention. It is perhaps utopian to imagine that the Congress will stop holding hearings whose sole purpose is to gain headlines by dramatizing estimates of uncollected taxes or for presidential candidates to avoid advocating tax increases by pointing to the underground economy. Nonetheless, these actions could potentially damage public confidence. In our opinion, the specific and detailed stories about compliance problems are less likely to have deleterious effects on overall perceptions.

Should the IRS and other tax agencies worry about the nature of the publicity about compliance? To address this question we conducted a simple experiment. We took two groups of students in introductory economics classes and let each answer questions from the Harris survey. Each group read one of the two following statements before answering the questions.[12]

A. The Internal Revenue Service is increasing the resources it is devoting to auditing tax returns and improving tax compliance. New computer systems are being installed and the IRS is improving its ability to use these computers to check for completeness and accuracy of returns. The goal of the IRS is to make sure that all taxpayers, corporations as well as individuals, are paying their fair share of taxes.

B. The Internal Revenue Service announced today that the "tax gap" or

12. The surveys were taken in two large classes in principles. Half of the students in each class were given questionnaire A, and the other half questionnaire B.

> the total of taxes which are due to the IRS but have not been collected has reached over $100 billion. The director of the IRS testified to Congress that the IRS was stepping up its efforts to collect these unpaid taxes. New computer systems are being installed, the director noted, to aid in collecting these funds.

We then analyzed the responses from the two groups to determine if "tax gap" publicity, as opposed to less dramatic publicity, differentially affects attitudes.

Table 6 presents means of the responses to the questions.[13] The scale ranges from 1 for "strongly agree" to 5 for "strongly disagree." The first two questions are those that we previously used as indicators of our "attitude toward government" latent variable. For both of these questions, the mean value of the responses is higher when statement A preceded the questions than when statement B preceded the questions. Reading about the "tax gap" resulted in the students having a more negative attitude toward the tax system and compliance than when they instead read about the Internal Revenue Service's efforts to increase compliance. However, the effect is very small and not statistically significant.

A similar pattern holds for questions 3 and 4, which we previously used as indicators of our "perception of others' dishonesty" latent variable. Students are more likely to view other taxpayers as dishonest after reading about the tax gap than they are when they read about the increased compliance efforts. The magnitude of the differences in the mean responses between the two groups is larger for these two questions than it was for the first two questions.

Reading about the tax gap affects the responses to the last two questions in different ways. Those who read the tax gap statement tended to think there was a smaller chance of being caught if cheating by a small amount than did those who read about the new computer systems, but thought there was a greater chance of being caught if cheating by a large amount. The part of statement B stating that the IRS was "stepping up its efforts to collect these unpaid taxes" probably led those who read this statement to infer that the IRS would be targeting those who were cheating by large amounts. Statement A, by stressing the use of the new computers in checking "for completeness and accuracy of returns," instead led the readers to think it would be difficult to get away with petty evasion.

The third column of table 6 shows the results of ordered probit regres-

13. A question pertaining to the fairness of the tax system was also asked, but is not included in the results shown in table 6.

sions of the categorical response variables (pooling observations from both samples) on a dummy variable that equals one if the sample members read statement B and equals zero if the sample members read statement A. Reading statement B is associated with statistically significant decreases in the perceived honesty of others (questions 3 and 4) and in the perceived probability of detection if cheating by a small amount (question 5). The other ordered probit coefficients are not significant.

The experimental results suggest that publicity concerning the degree of noncompliance and enforcement efforts has the potential for making a large difference in the percentage of the population who choose to evade taxes. Publicizing the "tax gap" increases the degree to which others are viewed as dishonest. Estimates from our latent variables econometric model suggest that this shift in perceived honesty will result in an increase in noncompliance. Publicity emphasizing the modernization of the IRS's computer facilities, rather than the magnitude of the tax gap that is prompting the modernization, leads to an increase in the perceived probability of detection if cheating by a

TABLE 6. Mean Responses to Experimental Survey Questions

Question	Statement A (New Computers)	Statement B (Tax Gap)	Statement B Coefficient
1. With what things cost these days, it's okay to cut a few corners on your tax form to help make ends meet.	3.69 (.09)	3.61 (.08)	−.08 (.12)
2. It's not so wrong to hold back a bit on taxes since the government spends too much anyway.	3.74 (.08)	3.72 (.07)	−.06 (.12)
3. Almost every taxpayer would cheat to some extent if he/she thought he/she could get away with it.	2.52 (.09)	2.25 (.08)	−.26 (.12)
4. The reasons the average taxpayer is honest is because he/she has no choice since his/her income comes mainly from wages and salary.	2.73 (.08)	2.51 (.07)	−.25 (.12)
5. When people try to cheat by small amounts, there is a good chance that they will be caught.	3.23 (.08)	3.44 (.07)	.24 (.12)
6. When people try to cheat by large amounts, there is a good chance that they will be caught.	2.24 (.08)	2.18 (.07)	−.03 (.12)
N	159	165	324

Notes: Figures in parentheses are standard errors. Responses are on a five-point scale with 1 = strongly agree; 5 = strongly disagree.

small amount. Our latent variables model estimates suggest that this will result in a decrease in the prevalence of noncompliance.[14]

Conclusion

Our work provides evidence of the importance of considering taxpayer attitudes and social norms in designing policies to reduce the prevalence of tax evasion. Programs intended to increase compliance may have unintended perverse effects unless their effect on taxpayer attitudes and perceptions are carefully taken into account.

Our latent variable approach to estimating the effects of attitudes and perceived detection probabilities provides a convenient method for reducing the complexity of survey questions into a few key, unobserved variables. Our findings suggest that the effect on compliance from an increase in the perceived probability of detection may be overestimated if attitudes are neglected in the analysis. Statistical bias in the estimated perceived probability coefficient occurs due to omitting the attitudinal variables from the analysis.

Attitudes are important determinants of the evasion decision. Publicity about the existing degree of noncompliance may result in a further increase in noncompliance as taxpayers change their perceptions of social norms. An increase in the budgetary allocation for auditing and enforcement might be counterproductive if widespread publicity about the magnitude of the evasion problem is needed to gain legislative approval for the additional funds.

More generally, tax administrators need to worry about any factors that might shift social norms and perceptions regarding evasion. Increased enforcement efforts might result in a perverse indirect increase in future noncompliance if the enforcement mechanism reveals to the affected taxpayer (and associates) that it is relatively easy to get away with evasion. Some types of enforcement, such as audits, may also negatively affect attitudes by creating an adversarial relationship between the taxpayer and the IRS.

Our analysis suggests that broad, "low-profile" enforcement programs, such as computer matching of income reports and tax returns, may be more desirable than programs that target a narrower group of people (such as

---

14. The factor structure used in the latent variables model is not appropriate for direct application to the experimental data, because the ordered probit coefficients on the statement B dummy variable are of different signs for the two probability of detection questions. We interpret the small (and statistically insignificant) increase in the perceived probability of detection if cheating by a large amount coupled with the large (and statistically significant) decrease in the perceived probability of detection if cheating by a small amount as evidence that publicity regarding the tax gap results in a decrease in the overall perceived probability of detection in our latent variables model.

audits). Broadly based enforcement programs might reduce both the chance of adversarial relationships developing between taxpayers and the IRS, and also the likelihood that taxpayers will lower their estimates of the probability of detection as a result of being affected by the enforcement program.

APPENDIX: DETAILS OF THE ECONOMETRIC SPECIFICATION AND ESTIMATOR

In this appendix, we present the specification of the model with a single noncompliance latent variable in detail. Details of the specification for the version of the model with two noncompliance latent variables are available from the authors. Both variants of the model fall in the class of linear latent variable models with categorical indicators studied by Muthén (1983 and 1984). Bollen (1989) provides a comprehensive survey of similar LISREL-type models. In the exposition below, subscripted symbols refer to scalars and symbols without subscripts are vectors or matrices.

As discussed in the second section, we treat the continuous variables generating the categorical responses to the first eight questions displayed in table 1 (y_a through y_h) as indicators of the four latent variables (η_1 through η_4). The last two questions in table 1 are treated as being generated by continuous variables (y_i and y_j), which are identically equal to the variables that appear in the structural model (η_5 and η_6). We employ a factor analytic specification where each indicator loads on only one latent variable.

$$\begin{bmatrix} y_a \\ y_b \\ y_c \\ y_d \\ y_e \\ y_f \\ y_g \\ y_h \\ y_i \\ y_j \end{bmatrix} = \begin{bmatrix} 1 & 0 & 0 & 0 & 0 & 0 \\ \lambda_b & 0 & 0 & 0 & 0 & 0 \\ 0 & 1 & 0 & 0 & 0 & 0 \\ 0 & \lambda_d & 0 & 0 & 0 & 0 \\ 0 & 0 & 1 & 0 & 0 & 0 \\ 0 & 0 & \lambda_f & 0 & 0 & 0 \\ 0 & 0 & 0 & 1 & 0 & 0 \\ 0 & 0 & 0 & \lambda_h & 0 & 0 \\ 0 & 0 & 0 & 0 & 1 & 0 \\ 0 & 0 & 0 & 0 & 0 & 1 \end{bmatrix} \begin{bmatrix} \eta_1 \\ \eta_2 \\ \eta_3 \\ \eta_4 \\ \eta_5 \\ \eta_6 \end{bmatrix} + \begin{bmatrix} \epsilon_a \\ \epsilon_b \\ \epsilon_c \\ \epsilon_d \\ \epsilon_E \\ \epsilon_f \\ \epsilon_g \\ \epsilon_h \\ 0 \\ 0 \end{bmatrix}, \qquad \text{(A1)}$$

where, as before, the λ's are factor loadings to be estimated and the ϵ's are mean zero measurement errors. We assume that the measurement errors and latent variables are orthogonal ($E(\eta\, \epsilon') = 0$) and that the measurement errors are uncorrelated ($E(\epsilon\, \epsilon') = \theta$, where θ is a matrix with all nondiagonal elements equal to zero). In more compact matrix notation:

$$y = \Lambda\, \eta + \epsilon\,. \qquad \text{(A2)}$$

The latent variables are related to each other and to the socioeconomic characteristics observed without error (x_1 through x_5) by the following equation:

$$\begin{bmatrix} \eta_1 \\ \eta_2 \\ \eta_3 \\ \eta_4 \\ \eta_5 \\ \eta_6 \end{bmatrix} = \begin{bmatrix} 0 & \beta_2 & \beta_3 & \beta_4 & 0 & 0 \\ 0 & 0 & 0 & 0 & 0 & 0 \\ 0 & 0 & 0 & 0 & 0 & 0 \\ 0 & 0 & 0 & 0 & \beta_5 & \beta_6 \\ 0 & 0 & 0 & 0 & 0 & 0 \\ 0 & 0 & 0 & 0 & 0 & 0 \end{bmatrix} \begin{bmatrix} \eta_1 \\ \eta_2 \\ \eta_3 \\ \eta_4 \\ \eta_5 \\ \eta_6 \end{bmatrix}$$

$$+ \begin{bmatrix} \gamma_{11} & \gamma_{12} & \gamma_{13} & \gamma_{14} & \gamma_{15} \\ \gamma_{21} & \gamma_{22} & \gamma_{23} & \gamma_{24} & \gamma_{25} \\ \gamma_{31} & \gamma_{32} & \gamma_{33} & \gamma_{34} & \gamma_{35} \\ \gamma_{41} & \gamma_{42} & \gamma_{43} & \gamma_{44} & \gamma_{45} \\ \gamma_{51} & \gamma_{52} & \gamma_{53} & \gamma_{54} & \gamma_{55} \\ \gamma_{61} & \gamma_{62} & \gamma_{63} & \gamma_{64} & \gamma_{65} \end{bmatrix} \begin{bmatrix} x_1 \\ x_2 \\ x_3 \\ x_4 \\ x_5 \end{bmatrix} + \begin{bmatrix} \zeta_1 \\ \zeta_2 \\ \zeta_3 \\ \zeta_4 \\ \zeta_5 \\ \zeta_6 \end{bmatrix} . \qquad \text{(A3)}$$

Or, in matrix notation,

$$\eta = \beta\,\eta + \Gamma\,\chi + \zeta\,. \qquad \text{(A4)}$$

The errors (ζ) are assumed to have zero means and be uncorrelated with the x variables. The covariances between ζ_1 and ζ_2 through ζ_4, ζ_4 and ζ_5, and ζ_4 and ζ_6 are restricted to be zero. Other elements of the covariance matrix of the ζ's, which is denoted Ψ ($E(\zeta\,\zeta') = \Psi$), are left free. Solving equation A4 for η:

$$\eta = (\mathrm{I} - \beta)^{-1}\,(\Gamma\,x + \zeta)\,. \qquad \text{(A5)}$$

Substituting equation A2 into A5 yields:

$$y = \Lambda\,(\mathrm{I} - \beta)^{-1}\,(\Gamma\,x + \zeta) + \epsilon\,. \qquad \text{(A6)}$$

Thus, the expectation of y given x is

$$E(y|x) = \Lambda\,(\mathrm{I} - \beta)^{-1}\Gamma\,x\,, \qquad \text{(A7)}$$

and the conditional covariance matrix is

$$\mathrm{cov}(y|x) = \Lambda\,(\mathrm{I} - \beta)^{-1}\Psi\,(\mathrm{I} - \beta)'^{-1}\Lambda' + \theta\,. \qquad \text{(A8)}$$

The distribution of y given x is assumed to be multivariate standard normal. Since each of the categorical responses is assumed to be generated by the corresponding y variable falling in a certain range, a multivariate ordered probit model can be used to estimate the conditional means and covariances (of y given x). Since there are ten y variables, estimating all parameters jointly is not computationally feasible. Instead, we first estimate the x variable reduced-form coefficients ($\delta = \Lambda\,(\mathrm{I} - \beta)^{-1}\Gamma$) by running ten univariate ordered probit regressions. Then the elements of the conditional covariance matrix ($\Sigma = \Lambda\,(\mathrm{I} - \beta)^{-1}\Psi\,(\mathrm{I} - \beta)'^{-1}\Lambda'$) are estimated by maximizing the likelihood function of each of the forty-five possible bivariate ordered probit regressions, with the coefficients and category thresholds estimated in the first step treated as constants.

The last step is to estimate the parameters of the structural model (the elements of Λ, β, Γ, and Ψ) by imposing the restrictions implied by the model on the reduced form coefficients and conditional covariances. Let $\hat{s}$ be the vector of estimated reduced form coefficients and covariances, Ω be the vector of parameters of the structural model, and $\sigma(\Omega)$ be the reduced form coefficients and conditional covariances implied by the values of Ω. The elements of Ω are estimated by minimizing the quadratic form

$$[\hat{s} - \sigma(\Omega)]' \, W \, [\hat{s} - \sigma(\Omega)] \; . \tag{A9}$$

Any positive definite weight matrix W will result in a consistent estimator for Ω, but the optimal weighting matrix is the inverse of the covariance matrix of the estimator of s. When W is set equal to this matrix (we set W equal to a consistent estimate of this matrix), the covariance matrix of the estimator of the structural parameters is given by

$$\left[\left(\frac{\partial \sigma}{\partial \Omega}\right)' \, W \left(\frac{\partial \sigma}{\partial \Omega}\right)\right]^{-1} .$$

Chamberlain (1982) provides an exposition of the asymptotic distribution theory for similar minimum distance estimators.

Under the assumption of correct specification, the value of the objective function (eq. A9) has a χ^2-distribution with degrees of freedom equal to the difference between the number of elements in s and the number of elements in Ω. This can be used to conduct an overall test of model validity, although in practice the value of the objective function seems to be used more as an index of the goodness of fit (see Bollen 1989, 256–69).

All stages of the estimation were performed using the GAUSS software package on an IBM-compatible personal computer.

REFERENCES

Allingham, Michael G., and Agmar Sandmo. 1972. "Income Tax Evasion: A Theoretical Analysis." *Journal of Public Economics* 1:323–38.

Bollen, Keneth A. 1989. *Structural Equations with Latent Variables*. New York: Wiley.

Chamberlain, Gary. 1982. "Multivariate Regression Models for Panel Data." *Journal of Econometrics* 18:5–46.

Cowell, Frank A. 1990. *Cheating the Government*. Cambridge, Mass.: MIT Press.

Diamond, Peter. 1984. *A Search Theoretic Approach to the Micro Foundations of Macroeconomics*. Cambridge, Mass.: MIT Press.

Elffers, E., R. H. Weigel, and D. J. Hessing. "The Consequences of Different Strategies for Measuring Tax Evasion Behavior." *Journal of Economic Psychology* 8:311–37.

Harris, Louis, and Associates. 1988. *Taxpayer Opinion Survey: 1987*. U.S. Department of Treasury, Internal Revenue Service, ICPSR 8927.

Kaplan, S. E., and P. M. J. Reckers. 1985. "A Study of Tax Evasion Judgments." *National Tax Journal* 38:97–102.

Kinsey, Karyl A. 1988a. "Survey Data on Compliance: A Compendium and Review." American Bar Association Working Paper 8716. Chicago: American Bar Association.

Kinsey, Karyl A. 1988b. "Theories and Models of Tax Cheating." American Bar Association Working Paper 8717. Chicago: American Bar Association.

Kinsey, Karyl A., and Kent Smith. 1987. "Income Tax Cheating: Opportunities, Preferences, and Sanctions." American Bar Foundation. Mimeo.

Lewis, A. 1982. *The Psychology of Taxation*. Oxford: Martin Robertson.

Mason, R., and L. D. Calvin. 1984. "Public Confidence and Admitted Tax Evasion." *National Tax Journal* 37:489–96.

Muthén, Bengt. 1983. "Latent Variable Structural Equation Modeling with Categorical Data." *Journal of Econometrics* 22:43–65.

Muthén, Bengt. 1984. "A General Structural Model with Dichotomous, Ordered Categorical and Continuous Latent Variable Indicators." *Psychometrica* 49:115–31.

Schmölders, G. 1970. "Survey Research in Public Finance: A Behavioral Approach to Fiscal Policy." *Public Finance* 25:300–306.

Skinner, Jonathan, and Joel Slemrod. 1985. "An Economic Perspective on Tax Evasion." *National Tax Journal* 38:345–53.

Song, Young-dahl, and Tinsley E. Yarbrough. 1978. "Tax Ethics and Taxpayer Attitudes: A Survey." *Public Administration Review* 38:442–52.

Spicer, M. W., and S. B. Lundstedt. 1976. "Understanding Tax Evasion." *Public Finance* 31:295–305.

Spicer, M. W., and L. A. Becker, 1980. "Fiscal Inequity and Tax Evasion—An Experimental Approach." *National Tax Journal* 33:171–75.

Strumpel, B. 1969. "The Contribution of Survey Research to Public Finance." In *Quantitative Analysis in Public Finance,* ed. A. T. Peacock, 13–32. New York: Praeger.

Commentary

Jeffrey A. Dubin

The essay by Sheffrin and Triest attempts to demonstrate an empirical connection between attitudes and perceptions and taxpayer compliance. While economists have historically spent little time studying attitudes (taking underlying preferences as exogenous), there has been considerable convergence between psychologists, sociologists, and economists in the last decade. This includes the common methodologies of psychometrics and econometrics in the areas of model identification and errors in variables. Economists have also begun to collect and analyze direct attitudinal information, including the consumer sentiment survey conducted at the Michigan Survey Research Center and the study of surveys designed to elicit the value of environmental resources.

My comments regarding the current essay can be divided into two parts. The first part addresses the econometric specification and the second the results from the analysis. The key to the specification is the relationship of an indicator of noncompliance and a latent noncompliance variable. This relationship between indicators and latent factors is at the heart of the LISREL or MIMIC modeling methods.

Sheffrin and Triest adopt a variant of the usual psychometric approach because some of the indicators themselves are not observed. Instead, a categorical measure is provided by the respondent that is assumed to reflect the strength or magnitude of the indicators. This method is attributed to Muthén (1984), but really finds its roots in such earlier work as Bock and Lieberman (1970). While the model of Sheffrin and Triest relates noncompliance to attitudes toward the government, perceptions of the honesty of others, and the perceived probability of detection, I will limit my remarks to the treatment of the perceived probability of detection. In order to examine the sensibility of the specification I will adopt a simplifying notation.

Let

w = vector of tax return attributes,
z = vector of individual attributes,
p^* = perceived detection rate (latent),

p = indicator of perceived audit rate,
a^* = compliance consciousness (latent),
a = vector of compliance consciousness indicators,
u^* = utility of noncompliance (latent indicator), and
d = revealed noncompliance with $d = 1$ indicating noncompliance and $d = 0$ indicating compliance.

The relationship between latent variables and the underlying exogenous variables is given by

$$a^* = z\Gamma_0 + \xi_0 , \tag{1}$$

and

$$p^* = w\Gamma_1 + \xi_1 . \tag{2}$$

The relationship between indicators and latent variables is given by

$$a = a^*\Pi_0 + \nu_0 , \tag{3}$$

and

$$p = p^*\Pi_1 + \nu_1 , \tag{4}$$

where Π_j are the so-called factor loadings. The relationship between the latent indicator u^* and the other latent variables is assumed to be

$$u^* = p^*\beta_1 + a^*\beta_2 + z\gamma + \epsilon. \tag{5}$$

The system of equations 1 through 5 closely parallels the model employed by Sheffrin and Triest. In a traditional LISREL framework, indicators are related to u^* by equations similar to equations 3 and 4. In contrast, Muthén's approach assumes that the outcome d categorizes the event $u^* > 0$.[1] Under appropriate assumptions, this system is identifiable and can be estimated using the method given in Muthén (1984).

My first comment is that the linear framework that is adopted in Sheffrin and Triest's analysis does not allow plausible interactions. In keeping with the

1. This structure is consistent with the random utility maximization of McFadden (1981), where u^* is given the interpretation of direct utility that is deterministic to the individual (but unobserved to the analyst). This interpretation is not, however, required for my subsequent comments.

extant theory, whether the detection rate is high or low may be irrelevant for taxpayers who are "compliant conscious," that is, taxpayers for whom a^* is large. It would then appear that the perceived detection rate should enter the model as an interaction. An alternative specification supposes that one's attitudes regarding compliance modify the responsiveness of the audit effect. Suppose instead that

$$u^* = p^*(\beta_1 + \beta_2 a^*) + z\gamma + \epsilon \,. \tag{6}$$

If it is assumed that p^* and a^* are normally distributed, then this model is not a simple probit unless the coefficient β_2 is identically zero. In this case, the Muthén framework is inappropriate. Can the structural model given by equation 6 be estimated? The answer to this is yes, if we move away from the two-level structure of latent variables adopted by Muthén. Assume a simple probit or logit specification wherein

$$Q = \text{Prob}[d = 1] = G[p^*\alpha + z\gamma] \tag{7}$$

where $a = (\beta_1 + \beta_2 a^*)$ and G is the cumulative distribution function for either the normal or the logit. Using equations 3 and 4 we can determine the conditional distribution of $x^* = (a^*,p^*)$ given $x = (a,p)$. It is then possible to estimate

$$E(Q) = \int G[p^*\alpha + z\gamma] f[x^*|x] d\chi^* \,. \tag{8}$$

Finally, a method of moments approach can be used to compare $E(Q)$ with the observed compliance outcome d.

While it is difficult to know how the results of Sheffrin and Triest would change under this proposed alternative specification, it is also unclear that the specification, as presented by them, should be accepted. Indeed, while their model is clearly identified, it is, in fact, overidentified. This should be clear since eleven indicators are related to six latent factors. Latent variable models permit tests of the overidentifying restrictions, and these tests could be conducted in their analysis.

Turning to the results themselves, the authors find that the perceived probability of detection is a significant deterrent of noncompliance. Also, it is found that knowledge of someone who has had difficulties with the IRS results in a significant decrease in the perceived probability of detection. The authors conclude that increasing audit rates may actually have the perverse effect of increasing noncompliance. This is a provocative result, but I think also premature.

The survey question at issue relates to detection and there is no established link between the examination rate and the detection rate. The survey question asks about the chances of being caught when people cheat by a *large* or by a *small* amount. Is this detection or selection? Does it say anything about the effect of audits as distinct from their effectiveness? Finally, I suspect that the reported relationship between perceived detection and knowledge of others with difficulties with the IRS is a missing interaction with income or tax status.

Regarding the second half of the essay, I see no conflict with either the advertisement of the tax gap or the threat of increased use of computers, since both appear to increase the perceived detection rates (at least for large amounts of underreported income). However, such advertisements may increase the perception of greater wrongdoing and, therefore, lead more individuals to not comply. While this may be a valid inference, it only underscores the fact that credible threats are crucially important. Thus, it does little good to talk about the severity of the tax compliance problem absent a presentation of the potential solution.

In sum, the essay by Sheffrin and Triest nicely sets the stage for a more detailed examination of the attitudes regarding audit rates and detection rates and the interaction of these variables with other structural effects. A natural extension of this research would analyze survey data of this kind linked over time. Alternatively, the addition of external contextual variables (such as district-level audit rates) to this study would be extremely helpful, permitting a clearer modeling of the relevant factors that condition the unobserved latent effects.

REFERENCES

Bock, R., and M. Lieberman. 1970. "Fitting a Response Model for *n* Dichotomously Scored Items." *Psychometrika* 35:179–97.

Muthén, B. 1984. "A General Structural Equation Model with Dichotomous, Ordered Categorical, and Continuous Latent Variable Indicators." *Psychometrika* 49:115–32.

McFadden, D. 1981. "Econometric Models of Probabilistic Choice." In *Structural Analysis of Discrete Data with Econometric Application,* ed. Charles F. Manski and Daniel McFadden, 198–272. Cambridge, Mass.: MIT Press.

Reciprocity and Fairness: Positive Incentives for Tax Compliance ✓

Kent W. Smith

Introduction

Deterrence engendered by the efficient detection and punishment of infractions is only one aspect of most enforcement and regulatory programs. Empirically, there is usually a subtle balance between detection and punishment on the one hand, and positive assistance and encouragement on the other. This mixture of strategies has been found in several studies of the police (Bittner 1967 and 1970; Black and Reiss 1967; Muir 1977) and regulatory agencies (e.g., Bardach and Kagan 1982; Braithwaite 1985; Hawkins 1984). Many of these researchers have also come to the conclusion that a balance of strategies often produces more compliance more efficiently than does either strategy alone, an argument that has been formalized by Scholz (1984), building on Axelrod's research on evolutionary game theory (1984).

Control and punishment tempered by cooperation and assistance may be particularly appropriate for taxpaying and other regulatory areas in which the law prescribes complex and burdensome behaviors that are not in the short-term self-interest of the individuals or other entities under regulation, and in which monitoring and detection of noncompliance is relatively weak (see Smith and Kinsey 1985). In the United States, however, the traditional legislative and administrative response to problems of noncompliance has been some combination of more "bright-line" statutes and regulations, increased penalties, and increased monitoring and control. In the last few years, though, there has been a noticeable shift toward a more balanced set of strategies in the

I am indebted to Loretta Stalans for her collaboration in developing some of the ideas behind the analyses presented here. I thank Richard Lempert for his cogent discussion of the essay at the conference, and John Braithwaite and Tom Tyler for their insightful and helpful comments and suggestions on related analyses. The data used here were made available to social science researchers by the Internal Revenue Service.

Internal Revenue Service, with an increased emphasis on quality, "customer" service, and reasonable and fair treatment of taxpayers.

There are at least four reasons for this change of focus. First is the belief that the government has an ethical responsibility to assist taxpayers in meeting their tax reporting obligations, particularly given the increasing complexity of the tax system. Second is a growing clarity of the limits of detection and negative sanctions (see, e.g., Internal Revenue Service 1990). There is also a concern by some that the public's confidence in and support for the federal tax system is deteriorating to the point that the viability of the system may be endangered, although this trend may be part of a more general trend toward disaffection from government and other large entities (see Lipset and Schneider 1983). Finally, many tax administrators believe that improving the responsiveness and fairness of tax administration will have a positive, long-term effect on compliance.

This essay examines some of the bases for this fourth argument. The research on the balanced strategies of police and other regulatory agencies suggests that responsiveness and fairness in tax administration should provide positive incentives for compliance without detracting from the deterrent effect of enforcement efforts. However, there is very little specific evidence about the effects of such positive incentives on tax compliance. In the next section, I review some of the theoretical reasons to expect such an effect, building on recent social psychological research. I then introduce some survey data and explain the variables that can be used to test some effects suggested by the theoretical arguments. The fourth section outlines the hypothesized effects and presents the results of the statistical analysis. Some concluding observations are in the final section.

Theoretical Considerations

The data I use allow us to examine two related aspects of what tax administrators can offer taxpayers: responsive and helpful service (the term *responsive* is suggested by Bardach and Kagan 1982) and procedural fairness (Leventhal 1980; Lind and Tyler 1988; Tyler 1990a and 1990b). Both involve evaluations of the process of tax administration, but the dimensions of evaluation are different. The concept of procedural fairness, if not the precise term, appears in the literature on disputes and civilians' encounters with authorities and in the literature on regulatory agencies. It concerns such questions as how much opportunity individuals (or other entities) have to tell their side of an issue, how hard the authorities try to be fair to individuals, how correctable decisions are, and how equitably and consistently individuals are treated (see Tyler 1988). Responsive and helpful service is a separate but related concept that appears primarily in the regulatory literature. It relates more to the administrative aspects of tax and other regulatory laws and focuses on the willingness and ability of the authorities to help individuals solve the problems they encounter when trying to comply with the laws. Failures of responsive service leads to complaints of ineptness, inefficiency, lack of interest or concern, and "bureaucratic" indifference. Fairness becomes a salient dimension of evaluation primarily when decisions about individuals are made by authorities, when the treatments of different individuals are compared, or when regulations and statutes are themselves being evaluated. Many of the problems taxpayers bring to tax administrators do not invoke evaluations of fairness, but there is still a desire for responsive and helpful service.

Responsive service and procedural fairness are both positive incentives in the broad sense that they are positive actions by administrators toward taxpayers that are, among other things, intended to increase compliance. They are not directly linked to specific acts of compliance in the way that promised rewards for compliance are. Rather, the link of the positive incentive to the behavior is indirect. The positive actions by administrators are intended to increase taxpayers' positive attitudes and commitments to the tax system and taxpaying. The assumption is that these positive attitudes and commitments will, in turn, increase the likelihood of compliant behaviors (see Smith and Stalans 1991). In the remainder of this section, I explore some of the social psychological reasons for expecting responsiveness and procedural justice to lead indirectly to reciprocating compliance by the taxpayer.[1]

The Norm of Reciprocity

One of the strongest social psychological reasons for expecting that positive behaviors by administrators toward taxpayers will increase the likelihood of compliance is the strong tendency for humans to try to reciprocate, in kind, behaviors directed toward them (see, e.g., Cialdini 1984 and 1989). The response of reciprocating behavior appears to be such a fundamental principle of human behavior that Gouldner (1960) referred to a cross-societal "norm" of reciprocity: a norm both in the sense of a universal regularity and a moral responsibility.

Much research across a wide range of applied areas demonstrates that reciprocation is a powerful mode of persuasion (for reviews, see Axelrod 1984; Cialdini 1984). In two computer simulations, Axelrod (1984) demonstrated that the reciprocity rule was better than more complex or punitive rules at obtaining cooperation from the other player (see also Scholz 1984). Regan

1. Much of the discussion in this section is drawn from Smith and Stalans (1991). The dynamics I am exploring are normatively based ones and complement Scholz's analysis of self-interested cooperative strategies (1984).

(1971) has experimentally shown that reciprocity is likely to occur even when the initiator was disliked. There is also evidence that the reciprocity norm holds for concessions (see Cialdini 1984 for a review). The reciprocity norm evokes an obligation for individuals to make a concession to someone who has made a concession to them. Thus, cycles of antagonism between the tax administrator and the taxpayer might begin to be broken by a positive concession by the administrator.

There are two cautions, however, about extending this social psychological research to the relationship between the tax administration system and the individual taxpayer. Both are empirical questions that require careful study. First, much of the research on reciprocity has involved the inducement of quite specific and simple behaviors, such as the purchase of an item or the returning of a favor. Does this research also apply to such ongoing, complex, and burdensome behaviors as taxpaying? Empirical studies of other regulatory regimes suggest that it may (see especially Bardach and Kagan 1982; Braithwaite 1985), but the relevance of much of the laboratory research needs to be explored. Second, most of the research and examples of effective inducements of reciprocity have focused on the behavior between individuals or other, more-or-less equal entities. The picture is less clear for the interaction between individuals and such large, impersonal entities as the state.

Legitimacy and Allegiance to Authority

Tyler's recent research (1990a and 1990b) provides support for the importance of allegiance to authority and the perceived legitimacy of authority in citizens' compliance decisions about everyday laws. He argues that legitimacy and allegiance are affected by citizens' perceptions of how the authorities treat them and others, and that legitimacy and allegiance, in turn, affect compliance. Thus, people who perceive that government authorities make an effort to be fair and to treat them respectfully tend to assign greater legitimacy to the authorities and be more compliant than those with more negative perceptions of government authorities.

Tyler's research continues a cumulative body of research indicating that people's perceptions of how they and others like them are treated by the authorities strongly affect their evaluations of authorities and their willingness to cooperate with them (see, e.g., Lind and Tyler 1988; Tyler, Casper, and Fisher 1989; Tyler and McGraw 1986). People want fair, respectful, and dignified treatment from authorities. In many instances they are more concerned about whether their views are heard by authorities than about whether their views affect authorities' decisions (for a review, see Tyler and McGraw 1986; see also Bardach and Kagan 1982). Research suggests that these perceptions of what has come to be known as procedural justice affect attitudes and behavior independently of the objective outcomes of encounters with authorities (see Tyler 1990a and 1990b).

The Effects of Responsive Service and Procedural Fairness

The reciprocity and legitimacy arguments both lead to the proposition that tax authorities' responsive, respectful, and fair treatment of taxpayers tends to foster respect for and cooperation with the tax system. This proposition is perhaps clearer and almost self-evident if it is stated in negative terms: Authorities' unresponsive, disrespectful, and unfair treatment of taxpayers fosters disrespect for and rebellion against tax authorities and tax laws—also a form of reciprocation in kind.

Responsive service and procedural fairness as positive treatments by tax authorities can have both direct and indirect effects on taxpayers' compliance behavior. Positive actions by authorities toward taxpayers may be reciprocated by compliant actions on a simple tit-for-tat basis, a direct effect on taxpayers' actions that is not mediated by normative or legitimating processes. However, reciprocity also appears to be a basic, normative obligation in many social situations, and positive treatments by authorities may also engender in taxpayers a more general normative commitment to compliance, particularly if the taxpayers believe that the authorities normally and routinely act positively toward taxpayers. Furthermore, responsiveness and procedural fairness are generally viewed as normatively appropriate actions by government officials. The response of individuals to them in the long run is probably a normative one as well. The research on legitimacy and allegiance also suggests that responsiveness and procedural fairness primarily affect compliance indirectly by increasing perceptions of legitimacy and feelings of allegiance, which are normative aspects of decision making. Tyler (1990b), for example, found that procedural fairness had an indirect effect on compliance through legitimacy.

The strength of the direct effects on compliance of responsive service and procedural fairness probably depends upon how much personal experience taxpayers have had with the tax authorities. Those who have had significant personal contacts with the tax authorities may reciprocate positive actions on a tit-for-tat basis while also developing a more generalized normative response. Those who have not had much personal contact develop their perceptions of how tax authorities treat taxpayers from what they know about the experiences of others and from their more general concepts of the tax system and of how government officials treat citizens. Because these perceptions are typically less specific than are personal experiences, their effects on compliance are likely to be primarily indirect ones through generalized normative commitments and allegiance.[2] In a general sample of U.S. taxpayers, such as the one I examine here, there will be a relatively small number of personal contacts with tax authorities for more-than-routine information seeking about obtaining and completing tax forms. Consequently, we should expect to find a predominance of indirect, rather than direct, effects in these data.

The distinction I am making about who is affected by the authorities' positive actions is akin to that between specific and general deterrence. The processes by which responsive service and procedural fairness affect the future behavior of those to whom the actions were directed are probably not the same as the processes by which they affect the behaviors of other taxpayers, just as the processes underlying specific and general deterrence are not the same.

I argued earlier that responsive, quality service and procedural fairness are related but distinct components of individuals' evaluations of tax administrators. The data presented in the next section certainly are consistent with this distinction. A relevant question, therefore, is whether the two have different effects on compliance attitudes and behavior. If the primary, lasting effect of positive actions by the authorities is on taxpayers' normative commitment to compliance, then it is reasonable to expect that the more normatively based of the two components has the stronger effect on normative commitments. Thus, I would predict that the perception of procedural fairness probably has the stronger effect on normative commitment and, indirectly, on compliance.

In fact, the two components may be cumulative in such regulatory areas as tax administration, in the sense that responsive service may be viewed by many as a precondition for procedural fairness in decision making and the administration of the laws. An agency that cannot provide responsive service in solving problems about following the laws is not going to be able to enforce the laws in a procedurally fair and equitable manner. It is reasonable to expect, consequently, that perceptions of procedural fairness are an intervening variable between perceptions of responsive service and normative commitment. Indeed, in encounters focusing primarily on enforcement, judicial decision making, or other forms of dispute resolution, the two aspects of procedural evaluation are probably less distinguishable because the evaluative focus is so clearly on fairness. They are distinguishable in tax and certain other regulatory areas because so many encounters with authorities involve administrative problems of reconciling accounts and records and of interpreting and following complex and ambiguous record-keeping and reporting requirements.

---

2. I am indebted to Richard Lempert for stimulating this line of reasoning about the conditions under which there may be direct effects of positive treatment on compliance.

There is another issue of some theoretical and practical importance about these positive incentives for compliance. If a balance of strategies emphasizing both positive incentives and the detection and punishment of noncompliance is to be effective, then the two strategies must symbiotically reinforce each other, rather than detract from each other. There is a danger that an organization that emphasizes responsive service and procedural fairness may be perceived as ineffective in detecting noncompliance and "soft" on violators. On the other hand, quality service and fair procedures may contribute to an overall aura of effectiveness in all aspects of the agency's operations. Certainly it can be argued that fair procedures should generally lead to fair outcomes in which the guilty are detected and treated appropriately, just as are the innocent. Whether the relationship between the two strategies is one of symbiosis or antibiosis may well be a matter of finding the proper balance between the strategies. Determining if a proper balance has been reached for a particular agency in a particular set of circumstances is probably an empirical question at this stage of our theoretical development. One issue I examine statistically in this essay, therefore, is whether perceptions of responsive service and procedural fairness positively or negatively affect deterrence perceptions.

The Survey Data and Variables

Survey Respondents

The data are drawn from a national survey of taxpayers conducted for the Internal Revenue Service by Louis Harris and Associates, Inc. In-person interviews were conducted with 1,756 recent tax filers during July and August 1987 (Harris 1988). For my analysis, I excluded 183 respondents (10.4 percent) because of missing data on key behavioral variables, an excessive number of missing answers, or inconsistent answers.

The compliance measure in my analysis is the self-reported likelihood of underreporting income during the past five years, as I will discuss subsequently. I am also including information on compliance contacts by the IRS to see what effect they have had on perceptions of the IRS. To make the statistical analysis tractable, I needed to eliminate possible feedback from the underreporting of income to enforcement contacts by the IRS. Those respondents who indicated that they might have omitted some income were asked which types of income might have been omitted. Using this information and the year in which the respondents were last audited, I eliminated another 15 respondents who (1) reported receiving a notice because of information-report matching or who had been audited during the previous four years (a conservative number given the lag time of most audits), and (2) whose possible underreporting of income in the past five years might have generated the enforcement contacts.[3]

For the remaining sample of 1,558 respondents, two approaches were used for the inevitable missing values. For the background and demographic variables, missing values were replaced by a sequence of regression estimates. For the attitudinal items, including perceptions of the IRS, means were substituted for missing values.[4] The sample was weighted to represent the population of tax filers, using the proportional weights provided by Harris and Associates. The weighted sample size was set equal to the unweighted one.

Measurement of Variables

Responsive Service and Procedural Fairness

At various points in the survey, there were several questions about perceptions of the IRS. After eliminating those with high proportions of missing data and low correlations with the other questions about the IRS, I formed two scales, based on a factor analysis and the substantive focus of this essay.[5] Because the items in each attitudinal scale were answered on the same response scale, the value of a scale for a particular respondent was calculated simply as the mean of that respondent's answers to the constituent items.

Responsive Service

The first scale, which I have labeled "Responsive Service," contains five questions about how the respondents rate various aspects of the IRS "compared to other financial institutions that handle money and accounts, like banks" and two questions comparing the IRS to "other federal government agencies that have contact with the public." The respondents were asked to

3. The issue of possible feedback from underreporting income to enforcement activity is whether or not the self-reported possibility of omitting certain types of income could have caused the particular enforcement activities. An audit undertaken for some other reason that also detected the self-reported omitted income would not create a problem of nonrecursivity.

4. As a rough test of the substantive significance of the pattern of missing data, I included in the regression analyses a count of the number of items that were missing and estimated. It was not significant and was not included in the final regressions reported here. Further details about the variables and the data preparation methods are available upon request.

5. The factor analysis of fifteen variables produced three factors with eigenvalues greater than 1, that together accounted for 63.9 percent of the items' variances. After rotation, three distinct clusters of variables emerged: the two scales used here and one focusing specifically on the quality of taxpayer service assistance. The pattern of correlations between this third scale and the other variables in the analysis were similar to those for responsive service and procedural fairness, but considerably smaller. In the preliminary regression analyses, it had no effects on other variables net those of procedural fairness; therefore, I have not included it here.

rate the IRS on a scale from 1 for much worse to 9 for much better. The five items comparing the IRS to other financial institutions are:

Helpfulness of staff (mean = 4.7; SD = 1.7),
Willingness to solve problems (4.8; 1.7),
Efficiency at handling paperwork (4.8; 1.6),
How well the staff are trained (4.9; 1.6), and
Honesty of the staff (5.3; 1.4).

The two items comparing the IRS to other federal agencies are

Helpfulness of staff (5.2; 1.5), and
Willingness to solve problems (5.2; 1.5).

Cronbach's α for the additive scale is .91. The scale has a mean of 4.97 and a standard deviation of 1.27.

Procedural Fairness

The second scale, concerning the procedural fairness of the IRS, is based on four items answered on a six-point scale from strongly disagree to strongly agree.

I am confident that the IRS would never try to take more money from me than they should (mean = 3.8; SD = 1.5),
IRS procedures and practices are fair and reasonable ones that respect the rights of taxpayers (3.7; 1.4),
IRS employees have an unusual amount of honesty and integrity (3.8; 1.2), and
You can depend on the IRS to keep accurate tax records (4.1; 1.4).

The last item substantively makes sense as part of this scale because many disputes with the IRS that lead to taxpayers' perceptions of unfair treatment involve disagreements about records and accounts, particularly for those who pay estimated taxes or have employees. Cronbach's α for this scale is .77 with a mean of 3.87 and standard deviation of 1.07.

The two scales have a zero-order correlation of .47. There are some cautionary notes about these scales. First, the items that loaded on a particular factor were drawn from the same general set of questions, so there is no doubt of some instrumentation effect in the high inter-item correlations, although I believe the scales are also substantively quite coherent and interpretable. Second, the proportions of missing data for the items forming the responsive service scale were the highest of all the variables in the analyses, ranging up to 19 percent. The conservative means-substitution procedure consequently has probably considerably attenuated this scale's correlations with other variables.

Enforcement Contacts by IRS

Respondents were asked if they had ever been audited by the IRS and if they had ever received a notice that they may have underreported some income (presumably through information-return matching). Those who indicated that they had had such enforcement contacts were asked if they had to pay more, less, or the same amount of tax as a result of the last contact of each type. Because this part of the analysis is somewhat exploratory and not theoretically driven, I formed several alternative indices of enforcement contact and empirically selected the one that had the highest and most consistent zero-order correlations with the other variables in the analysis.[6] The index that appeared to be the strongest was a simple count of the number of types of contacts the respondents had received, ranging from 0 to 2. Perhaps the perceived breadth and effectiveness of IRS enforcement are enhanced by having experienced more than one type of enforcement contact. In the sample for this analysis, 83.1 percent reported no contacts of either type; 14.0 percent, one type of contact; and 2.9 percent, both types of contacts.

Structural Opportunity

As a general concept, *structural opportunity* for an action refers to those structural characteristics of an individual's social, economic, and physical situation that increase the likelihood that the individual can successfully execute the action. Several researchers (Kagan 1989b; Klepper and Nagin 1989; Long and Swingen 1988; Smith 1990; Smith and Kinsey 1987; Stalans, Smith, and Kinsey 1989) analyzing tax noncompliance have emphasized the importance of the social and economic characteristics of a noncompliant action that affect its likely success. Opportunity has also been emphasized in some research on white-collar and corporate crime (e.g., Smigel and Ross

6. Among the indices I explored were dummy variables for each type of contact; 3-point scales for each type (with 0 = no contact, 1 = a contact but no extra tax, and 2 = a contact and extra tax); a combined dummy variable for either or both contacts; a three-point index equaling the maximum of the corresponding indices for the two types of contacts; and the count of the types of contacts. The patterns of correlations for all of the indices were generally the same, and the quantitative differences were relatively small. Because the associations were driven largely by the 83.1 percent of the respondents who reported neither type of contact, the possible deterrent effect of having to pay more tax versus that of having to pay no additional tax because of a contact was probably swamped. As Kinsey has argued in this volume, such effects must be explored with more focused subsamples.

1970) and juvenile delinquency (see Cloward and Ohlin 1960). It both has a direct effect on noncompliance, net those of both normative and deterrence factors, and increases the effects of the other factors (an interaction or specification effect; see, especially, Smith 1990; Stalans, Smith, and Kinsey 1989).

Cohen and colleagues (e.g., Cohen and Land 1987; Cohen and Machalek 1988) have provided the fullest analytical development of the concept in studies of predatory property crimes. They focus on the presence of suitable targets and the absence of effective guardians. For noncompliance with tax laws and many regulatory laws, where there are no specific victims and generally only one guardian protecting against violations, opportunity for successful noncompliance focuses on the current situation of the potential offender and reduces to the ability of the administrator of the laws to detect and punish the noncompliance, in this case underreporting income.

Those respondents (and spouses for the married respondents) who received any form of income during 1986 that was not required to be reported to the Internal Revenue Service by third parties (apart from the de minimus limits for savings accounts and the like) were coded as having higher opportunity for successfully underreporting income (55 percent). All others were placed in the lower opportunity category (45 percent). In the statistical analysis, structural opportunity is captured by a dummy variable for higher opportunity and is labeled "Higher Opportunity" in the figures and tables.

General Attitudes about the Tax System and Government

More specific attitudes about and perceptions of the IRS may be shaped, in part, by people's general attitudes about the tax system and the federal government. Three frequently mentioned general attitudes concern the fairness of the tax system, the complexity of the tax system, and general confidence in government officials (see Lipset and Schneider 1983). Unfortunately, the survey did not have several good items tapping each of these attitudes, so I must be content with more limited one- or two-item measures.

Fairness of the Tax System

The one item I will use to tap the general perceived fairness of the federal income tax system is, "How do you feel about the federal income tax system as it applies to the 1986 tax return—do you feel it is quite fair to most people, or reasonably fair, or somewhat unfair, or quite unfair to most people?" The answers were coded from 1 for "quite unfair" to 4 for "quite fair." The mean response was 2.6, with a standard deviation of .86.[7]

7. The other item tapping fairness was a Likert-type item, "The present tax system benefits the rich and is unfair to the ordinary working man or woman." The correlation between these two

Complexity of the Tax System

Two items formed a reasonably consistent scale of perceived complexity with a Cronbach's α of .70. The first item was asked in the context of requesting information from the IRS. Respondents were asked to rate the information on a six-point scale from "difficult to understand" (6) to "easy to understand" (1; mean = 3.8; SD = 1.6). The second item was "How complicated do you think our federal income tax laws and rules are for your particular income situation?" which also was on a scale from 1 for "not at all complicated/ very easy to understand" to 6 for "extremely complicated/ very difficult to understand" (mean = 4.1, SD = 1.56). The mean of the combined complexity scale is 4.0, with a standard deviation of 1.3.

Confidence in Government Officials

Again, there was only one item in the survey to tap the respondents' general sense of confidence in government officials or, put negatively, disaffection from them. Respondents evaluated the statement, "Public officials can usually be trusted to do what's right," on a four-point scale from 1 for "strongly disagree" to 4 for "strongly agree" (mean = 2.37, SD = .91).

Perceived Likelihood of Detection

There were two questions about the perceived likelihood of detection, conditional on noncompliance. One concerned cheating by large amounts; the other, by small amounts. The wording was "When people try to cheat by large/small amounts, what do you think are their chances of being caught?" answered on a seven-point scale ranging from 1 for "almost certain not to be caught" to 7 for "almost certain to be caught." The middle three values were anchored by "40 percent chance," "50-50 chance," and "60 percent chance." The mean responses for the large cheaters' and small cheaters' items were 4.8 and 3.9 respectively; the standard deviations were both 1.6.

Information about the detection risks for small cheaters is likely to be transmitted primarily through interpersonal communication channels, while information about large cheaters' being caught is more likely to be obtained from mass media sources (see Mason 1987; Stalans, Kinsey, and Smith 1991). Most people who intentionally underreport some income probably consider themselves relatively small cheaters, and earlier analyses of these data (Smith 1990) suggest that the question about the likelihood of small cheaters being caught may be a reasonable proxy for a more specific question about the conditional likelihood of the respondents themselves being caught. Thus, my

items was only .185, precluding a two-item scale. I chose the one described in the text because it was the more general of the two and because it had stronger zero-order associations with the other variables in the analysis.

expectation is that the effect on either attitudes or behavior of the perceived likelihood of large cheaters' being caught is probably an indirect one through the perceived likelihood that small cheaters will be caught. I am keeping both variables in the analysis to explore how general attitudes and the two positive-incentive items affect detection perceptions.[8]

Normative Acceptability of Underreporting Income

One set of questions was introduced by "People feel differently about reporting certain financial transactions on their income tax return." Respondents used a six-point scale from 1 for "not at all acceptable" to 6 for "perfectly acceptable" to evaluate four items about not reporting various types of income.[9] The mean response for each respondent forms an internally consistent scale (Cronbach's $\alpha = 0.76$) of the acceptability of underreporting income. This scale measures normative evaluations of underreporting income without linking them to any particular set of justifications and, consequently, may tap realistic norms better than would items making such linkages (see Smith 1990).

Underreporting Income

The respondents were asked about the probability that they underreported income during the past five years (four-point scale from "Definitely have not" [1] to "Definitely have" [4]): "Within the past five years or so, do you think you might have left some reportable income off your federal tax returns—even *just a minor amount?*" The probability form of the question was considered less threatening, and it also reflects the uncertainty that might arise from incomplete records or questions about what is taxable income. Of the respondents in the analysis, 73.3 percent reported that they definitely had not underreported income in the last five years; 10.9 percent, that they probably

8. I also initially explored a third deterrence-related variable, the perceived likelihood that the respondent's own 1986 tax return would be audited. Its highest zero-order correlation with the other variables in the analysis, 161, was with the contact index. It had no net effect on either normative acceptability or underreporting behavior. One problem with this question is that it does not ask about the likelihood of detection conditional upon noncompliance. Another reason this after-the-fact detection question has very little systematic association with other variables may be that the tendency for people to consider themselves relatively invulnerable and in control of their own destinies (see Perloff and Fetzer 1986; Tyler 1984) counterbalances the deterrence processes. Those who intentionally underreport income may well minimize the likelihood of detection, particularly after the noncompliance has occurred.

9. The items were (1) "trading or exchanging goods or services with a friend or neighbor and not reporting it" (mean = 4.42), (2) "reporting your main income fully, but not including some small outside income" (mean = 2.96), (3) "being paid in cash for a job and then not reporting it" (mean = 2.76), and (4) "not reporting some earnings from investments or interest that the government would not be able to find out about" (mean = 2.16).

had not; 11.5 percent, that they probably had; and 4.3 percent, that they definitely had. These answers are naturally biased downward, although they are not entirely inconsistent with available enforcement data.[10] An analysis of residuals from the initial regression analyses indicated that the natural log of this variable should be used.[11] The mean of the transformed variable is 0.26 with a standard deviation of 0.45.

Using information on noncompliance during the past five years can pose difficulties in interpreting the causal order of the relationship between the noncompliance measure and normative commitments. I am assuming that the norms are of longer duration and causally prior to the noncompliance behavior in the past five years. Some patterns in the data support this assumption. As already noted, the measure of normative commitment I am using is an index of the acceptability of underreporting income. If this acceptability norm had been developed recently as an after-the-fact justification for recent noncompliance, then one would expect it also to be associated with the structural conditions that foster noncompliance by the respondents and others they know. There is, however, virtually no correlation (0.036) between the measure of structural opportunity and normative commitment.[12]

As Greenberg (1981) and Paternoster et al. (1983) have noted, there may also be a problem of causal order between noncompliance during the past five years and my measure of the perceived likelihood of detection: the perceived likelihood of detection may have been developed, in part, from the experience of successful or unsuccessful underreporting in the past. Again, the patterns of association in the data suggest that this is not a problem. If there were a causal effect from underreporting to the perceived likelihood that small cheat-

---

10. In intensive Internal Revenue Service audits of a weighted probability sample of individual returns for 1982, 59 percent had no unreported income and 73 percent had no more than $50 of net unreported income of all types (tabulations prepared by the IRS for the author).

11. In another analysis of these data focusing only on regression equations for underreporting income (Smith 1990), the analysis of residuals indicated that the perceived likelihood that small cheaters would be caught should also be logged, although the differences were relatively small. In the current analyses, such a transformation was not indicated for the other equations involving this variable. To maintain consistency across equations, I have elected to use the initial form of the small cheater's item throughout these analyses.

12. In a survey of Minnesota taxpayers, we have found that normative commitments concerning noncompliance are related to structural opportunity, suggesting occupationally and financially structured subcultures that are more likely to condone noncompliance (see Stalans, Smith, and Kinsey 1989). Such an association, however, does not exist in this national sample. From the point of view of improving noncompliance, this fact can be read in either a "half-full" or "half-empty" manner. On the national level, there does not appear to be a reinforcing confluence of opportunity and normative acceptance. On the other hand, there appear to be many taxpayers with normative inclinations toward noncompliance waiting for the opportunity to arise.

ers are caught, then there should also be an association between the perception item and the structural factors affecting noncompliance. However, there is no significant net effect of structural opportunity on the perception item even though structural opportunity has the strongest effect on underreporting, as measured by t-values. By the same token, this lack of association between structural opportunity and the measure of perceived likelihood of detection underscores the fact that this general perception item is only a proxy for a respondent-specific measure that is also conditional upon noncompliance. Being forced to use this proxy may be reducing specification bias, but it is also probably giving a lower-bound estimate of the deterrence effect.

Control Variables

Finally, I included five demographic variables: age, coded in years (mean = 45.6; SD = 16.9); a dummy variable for females, coded 0 for males and 1 for females (50 percent female); a dummy variable for single marital status (17 percent single); years of education (mean = 12.9; SD = 2.8); and the respondent's (plus spouse's, if married) 1986 pretax income (mean = $27,200; SD = $20,300). To avoid regression coefficients starting several places to the right of the decimal point, age and income were both divided by ten for the analyses. I am using these demographic variables as control variables serving as proxies for clusters of other social psychological or contextual variables lying outside the theoretical purview of this essay.

Models and Results

How the Respondents Think the IRS Could Improve Compliance

Before turning to an examination of the relationships suggested by the theoretical analysis, it is instructive to consider briefly what the respondents themselves believe the IRS could do to improve compliance. As I noted earlier, the traditional legislative response to problems of noncompliance has been to mandate or urge greater enforcement activities and larger penalties. The public appears to favor a more balanced set of strategies.

Toward the end of the survey, after questions both on service and assistance and on enforcement activities and penalties, the respondents were asked to evaluate "some ways that might help the IRS do a better job of collecting the tax money that is owed to the country." They were given eight initiatives to evaluate on a scale from 1 for "not at all effective" to 6 for "extremely effective." Five of the initiatives received mean evaluations of 4.0

TABLE 1. Mean Evaluations of Selected Methods of Collecting Taxes Better, Overall and by Perceived Fairness and Complexity of Tax System

Groupings	Simplify System	Increase Likelihood Caught	More Help and Assistance	Publicize Penalties	Increase Penalties
Overall Means	5.14	4.85	4.74	4.59	4.49
Fairness	***	*	NS	*	***
Quite unfair	5.34	4.72	4.70	4.48	4.28
Somewhat unfair	5.21	4.86	4.72	4.56	4.54
Somewhat fair	5.05	4.86	4.75	4.60	4.50
Quite fair	4.92	5.12	4.84	4.94	4.94
Complexity	***	**	*	*	***
Low	4.79	5.05	4.63	4.86	4.74
Medium	5.02	4.90	4.67	4.57	4.58
High	5.40	4.73	4.85	4.54	4.33
Weighted N^a	1,507	1,501	1,524	1,537	1,492

Note: Responses range from 1 = not at all effective to 6 = extremely effective; NS = not significant at p = .05.

[a]Missing cases answered "Not sure."

$*p \leq .05$. $**p \leq .01$. $***p \leq .001$.

or greater, as shown in the first row of table 1.[13] The respondents believed that simplifying "the whole tax collection system" is the most effective initiative, followed by increasing the likelihood of being caught. Closely behind this deterrence-oriented initiative is one focusing on positive, responsive service, offering "more help and assistance to taxpayers." The last two focus again on punishments, reminding people about the penalties for tax evasion and increasing the penalties.

The data shown in table 1 also suggest that people's evaluations of the current tax system affect their evaluations of what could be done to improve compliance. The second set of groupings breaks down the evaluations of the alternative initiatives by the respondents' perceptions of the fairness of the current tax system. Those who believe the current tax system is generally fair tend to emphasize detection and punishment (it is only the "bad" guys who are cheating), while those who believe the system is unfair emphasize simplifying the system and increasing positive service. Likewise, in the last set of groupings, those who believe the current system is not very complex see less need to change the system or offer service than do those who view the current

13. The three receiving mean evaluations less than 4.0 were (1) "remind people that it's patriotic to pay taxes," (2) "pay rewards to people whose information leads to uncovering and conviction of tax evasion," and (3) "making sure that the names of those who have been fined or jailed for tax reasons appear in the newspapers."

system as being very complex. The former again emphasize detection and punishment while the latter emphasize simplification and service. I should note, however, that these differences, while statistically discernible, are matters of relative emphasis. The means in every row of table 1 still suggest a preference for a balance of strategies.

The Predicted Model and Statistical Estimation Procedures

Figure 1 pictorially presents the relationships among the substantive variables that are suggested by the theoretical discussion in the second section. For reasons that I shall explain in a moment, the scale of responsive service is not included in figure 1. To complete the system of relationships and specify what additional variables should be in the equations, I have also included some other effects suggested by related research. In specifying the hypothesized effects, I have adopted the general assumption that more specific attitudes and perceptions are affected by the more general ones. This assumption is probably appropriate, especially for the vast majority of the respondents who have had very little personal experience with federal tax authorities. As I noted previously, their perceptions of the responsiveness and procedural fairness of the IRS are developed from what they know about the experiences of others and from their more general conceptions of the tax system and of how government officials treat citizens. There is little question that specific, salient experiences are often generalized and help form more general attitudes. However, I think it is appropriate to assume that the dominant direction of influence among attitudes and expectations is typically from the general to the specific, particularly if there have not been personal experiences related to the topic of the specific attitude. Certainly this direction of effect is assumed in much of survey research.

Procedural Fairness

I expect that the perceived procedural fairness of the IRS is related to the more general attitudes about complexity, fairness, and trust in public officials. I also expect that perceptions of procedural fairness are affected by experiences with IRS enforcement contacts, although I have no theoretical expectations about the direction of that effect (hence the question mark for the arrow from "contacted by IRS" to "IRS procedural fairness").

Likelihood of Detection Variables

The likelihood of catching small cheaters should also be positively affected by having had enforcement contacts by the IRS, presuming that those contacts, once made, are generally effective in detecting noncompliance. The argument

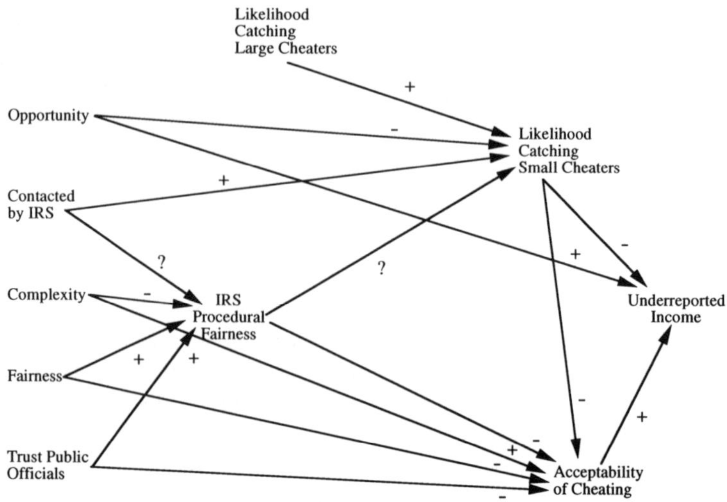

Fig. 1. Hypothesized relationships among substantive variables

is that most intentional noncompliers consider themselves noncomplying by relatively small amounts, and that enforcement activities directed toward their noncompliance should affect perceptions of the likelihood that cheating by those same relatively small amounts will be detected. There are probably fewer clear reasons to expect that personal experience with enforcement contacts will affect perceptions that large cheaters are likely to be caught. One possible argument for such an effect would be that being contacted personally by the IRS leads people to believe that those who cheat by large amounts are even more likely to be detected. To explore this possibility and the often-cited trickle-down effect from the perceived detection of large cheaters to the perceived detection of small cheaters, I have included the likelihood of catching large cheaters in the model.

I have noted that procedural fairness might affect deterrence perceptions, but that the direction was an empirical question. Again, I am predicting that procedural fairness will have a direct effect on the perceived likelihood of catching small cheaters, but I am not predicting the direction of that effect. Prior research (see, e.g., Mason 1990; Stalans, Kinsey, and Smith 1991; Stalans, Smith, and Kinsey 1989) indicates that information about the detection of small cheaters is primarily derived from interpersonal communication, and that the networks for these communications are related to occupations or types of financial arrangements. Consequently, I have included an effect from "higher opportunity" to the "perceived likelihood for small cheaters".

Acceptability of Underreporting

Perhaps the central hypothesis derived from the preceding theoretical discussion is that procedural fairness should have a strong negative effect on the normative acceptability of cheating. A great deal of research and everyday speculation suggests that the acceptability of cheating should also be affected by the general complexity, fairness, and trust variables. Perhaps less common is the prediction that the likelihood of catching small cheaters will also decrease the normative acceptability of cheating. The laws governing taxpaying are not rooted in basic cultural values about the proper behavior between individuals. Rather, they are rooted in the needs of the state and the obligations of citizens to the state (see Smith 1990; Smith and Kinsey 1987). Citizens, consequently, are more likely to take their taxpaying obligations seriously if they perceive that the state does also. A primary indicator of the state's interest is its concern with detecting and punishing noncompliance. Such arguments about the boundary-setting functions of detecting and punishing deviance have a long tradition, tracing back at least to Durkheim ([1926] 1964), but researchers have given them relatively little attention in recent years because of the tendency to treat deterrence and normative commitment as competing models of decision making, rather than as complementary ones.

Underreporting Income

The final variable in the model shown in figure 1 is the self-report of the likelihood of having underreported income during the past five years. This part of the model has already been explored (see Smith 1990), and I will not devote much attention to it here if only the predicted effects are statistically discernible. I am including it to explore whether procedural fairness and the other variables in this expanded model have direct effects on underreported income net those of opportunity, likelihood of catching small cheaters, and the acceptability of cheating.

Estimation Procedures

As I have explained, I have eliminated from the sample the few respondents whose self-reported underreporting may have led to enforcement contacts. With their omission, the model is recursive and can be estimated by ordinary least squares regression.[14] In exploring the model for each dependent vari-

14. Because of the relatively low reliability and validity of some of the exogenous variables, I elected to use single-equation, rather than full-information, estimation procedures. With full-information procedures such as LISREL, these variables' biases and instabilities would have affected the estimation of all equations in the system. With single-equation OLS estimation, their effects on the coefficients of other variables are limited to the equations in which they appear.

able, I first entered the effects predicted by the theory (as summarized in fig. 1). I then allowed the other, prior variables and the demographic control variables to enter the equation if their effects were statistically discernible. The final equations reported here include only those variables whose effects were discernible at the .05 level or lower (two-tailed).

The Effects of Responsive Service

I have not included responsive service in the model because my predictions of the intervening nature of procedural fairness were strongly supported. Responsive service has a strong, positive effect on perceptions of procedural fairness, but it has no effects on other variables net those of procedural fairness. When procedural fairness is removed from the models and replaced by responsive service, its effects are generally the same as those of procedural fairness, but weaker. With two exceptions, the variables that affect responsive service also affect procedural fairness when response service is removed from the equation. The two exceptions are income and higher opportunity: these two variables appear in the equation for responsive service, but their indirect effects on procedural fairness through responsive service are not statistically discernible as direct effects in the equation for procedural fairness without responsive service (see table 2). In sum, responsive service appears to be a very important factor affecting perceptions of procedural fairness, perhaps almost a precondition; but the effect of these two positive incentives on other variables is entirely through perceptions of procedural fairness.[15]

The Final Estimated Model

Table 2 presents the unstandardized regression coefficients and the model statistics for the final set of equations. The dependent variables form the columns of the table with the independent variables forming the rows. Because of the recursive nature of the model, the lower left portion of the table

---

Similarly, by using OLS, the possible measurement problems with self-reported underreporting are restricted to the one equation involving the variable. Adding adjustments for attenuation due to measurement error would not have solved the problem for full-information procedures.

15. I should note that this conclusion is based upon a combination of theoretical and statistical conditions. The statistics alone are also consistent with a spurious relationship between responsiveness and the variables that appear to be dependent upon procedural fairness. In this alternative, the relationship between responsiveness and procedural fairness could be either a noncausal association or a causal effect from procedural fairness to responsiveness. As I discussed in the second section, I think a convincing argument can be made that responsiveness is a precondition for procedural fairness in regulatory areas. In specifying an equation, this relationship is captured by an effect of responsiveness on procedural fairness.

from the row for procedural fairness down is, of course, blank. The statistical results largely support the predictions from the theoretical discussion and previous research. The unexpected findings are primarily in the equations for the two deterrence variables. For ready comparison with figure 1, I have summarized the estimated effects among the substantive variables in figure 2. In this section I shall make a few comments about each equation, in the order they appear in the columns of table 2.

TABLE 2. Ordinary Least Squares Regression Coefficients in Estimated Models for Endogenous Variables (weighted data)

	Dependent Variables				
Independent Variable	IRS Procedural Fairness	Likelihood Large Caught	Likelihood Small Caught	Acceptable to Underreport	Log of Likelihood Underreported
Demographic					
Age (in 10 years)	.114***	—	.180***	−.173***	−.034***
Female	.121*	.200*	.336***	−.216**	−.072**
Single	.146*	.236*	—	—	—
Education (in years)	−.046***	.033*	−.045**	—	—
Income (in $10,000s)	—	—	−.101***	−.034*	−.013*
Background					
Contacted by IRS	−.152**	.265**	—	—	—
Higher opportunity	—	—	—	—	.123***
General attitudes					
Trust officials	.294***	—	—	—	—
Tax system fair	.158***	.113*	—	−.098*	.024*
Tax system complex	−.103***	—	—	—	—
Opinion about IRS					
Procedural fairness		.208***	.089*	−.166***	—
Detection perceptions					
Likelihood large cheaters caught			.304***	—	—
Likelihood small cheaters caught				−.134***	−.034***
Normative orientation					
Acceptability of underreporting					.066***
Constant	3.214	4.005	1.979	5.457	0.292
Adjusted R^2	.179	.038	.189	.126	.130
F-value	43.57	11.37	61.44	38.49	34.14
df	8,1549	6,1551	6,1551	6,1551	7,1550
p	<.001	<.001	<.001	<.001	<.001

Note: N = 1,558.
*$p \leq .05$, two-tailed. **$p \leq .01$, two-tailed. ***$p \leq .001$, two-tailed.

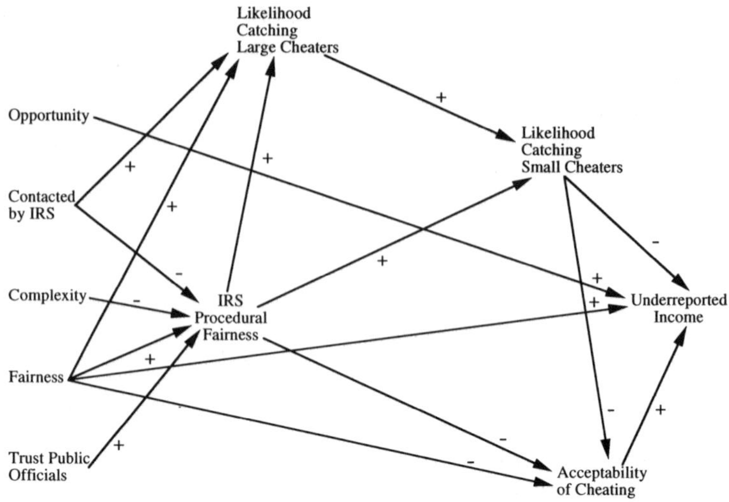

Fig. 2. Substantive relationships in the estimated model

Procedural Fairness

As predicted, the three general attitudes affect the more specific perception of the procedural fairness of the IRS. In terms of *t*-values, the two largest effects are those of trust in public officials and age, followed by those for fairness and complexity. Experience with IRS enforcement contacts has a smaller, but discernible, negative effect. In this general sample of taxpayers with only a minority having had any enforcement contacts, experience with IRS enforcement does not appear to enhance the perception of procedural fairness.

Likelihood that Large Cheaters Are Caught

Counter to my expectations, experience with enforcement seems to primarily increase the perceived likelihood that *large* cheaters will be caught. Contact experience does not have a discernible effect on the perceived likelihood that small cheaters will be caught. This lack of effect exists even with the likelihood for large cheaters removed from the equation. The positive effect of the fairness of the tax system on the likelihood for large cheaters being caught suggests that detecting and punishing gross violations of the law is considered to be part of a fair tax system. This same dynamic may explain the unexpected positive effect of procedural fairness on the perceived detection of large cheaters. Only 4 percent of the variance for this variable is explained by the variables in this analysis. As I noted previously, perceptions about the detection of large cheaters are probably developed primarily through the mass media. Exposure and attention to such communications appears to be largely unrelated to the variables included here.

Likelihood that Small Cheaters Are Caught

There are other aspects of the equation for the perceived likelihood that smaller cheaters will be caught that are somewhat surprising, in addition to the lack of an effect for experience with enforcement contacts. As expected, there is a strong trickle-down effect from the perceived likelihood for large cheaters, but the perceptions do not appear in this sample to be related to structural opportunity. This lack of effect may be because structural opportunity is respondent-specific, while the perceived likelihood item refers to small cheaters in general. Procedural fairness does have a positive effect, but it is much smaller than its effect on the likelihoods for large cheaters. Perhaps procedural fairness, and the reasonableness and flexibility associated with it, is more consistent with high likelihoods of catching large cheaters than with high likelihoods of catching small cheaters.

Acceptability of Underreporting

The predictions about the variables affecting the normative acceptability of underreporting, on the other hand, are largely supported by the data. In terms of *t*-values, the two largest effects in the equation, after those for age and gender, are those for procedural fairness and the perceived likelihood that small cheaters will be caught. Of the three general attitude variables, only the fairness of the tax system has a discernible direct effect on the acceptability of underreporting. That effect is in the predicted direction, as are the indirect effects of complexity and trust in officials.

Underreporting Income

Finally, the equation for underreporting income is almost exactly as expected. The one surprise is the positive direct effect of the fairness of the tax system. There are two reasons I am hesitant to make much of this counterintuitive effect. First, its probability against the null hypothesis of zero effect is almost exactly .05, the lowest for any effect in table 2. Second, this measure of the fairness of the tax system is based on only one question, the opening question in the survey. Its reliability and, perhaps, its validity are therefore considerably less than one would hope for. The indirect effects of this measure of fairness are in the expected direction, and I think speculation about this marginal direct effect should held in abeyance to see if it is confirmed by better measures of tax system fairness. Also, the effects of the other variables in the equation for underreporting income are virtually unchanged when this measure of the fairness of the tax system is removed. As I have noted, there is a much more extensive exploration of the equation for the likelihood of having underreported income in Smith (1990).

Concluding Observations

There are several intriguing findings that may foster speculation and, I hope, further research. Rather than cataloging them, I want to focus on a few main points by way of conclusion. The data presented here, while far from conclusive, clearly support the argument that responsive service and procedural fairness are positive incentives that affect normative commitments to tax compliance. At the same time, they appear to reinforce perceptions of effective enforcement programs. These cross-sectional data, however, tell us much less about how perceptions of responsiveness and procedural fairness are formed in such regulatory arenas as tax administration, apart from raising questions about the effects of past and perhaps current enforcement contacts. More research of different types now needs to be done to explore how these perceptions are formed, particularly by the direct actions of tax administrators, and how they are changed once formed. My theoretical analysis highlighted reciprocity and the legitimacy of (and allegiance to) authorities. I think these are probably among the more important dynamics of the process, but the data did not explore them directly. Rather, they tested outcome relationships predicted by them.

Further research should be attuned to some potentially important distinctions among taxpayers and among analytical concepts. As I have noted, the specific and general effects of positive treatments probably involve difference processes, just as do specific and general deterrence. Of the taxpayers who have not had significant personal contacts with tax administrators, only some have formed clear perceptions of the authorities' responsiveness and procedural fairness. The processes by which they have formed those perceptions are probably different than those for taxpayers who have had personal contacts with tax authorities. What are the differences in these processes, and do the perceptions formed through these specific and general processes have different consequences for attitudes, normative commitments, and behavior?

With respect to analytical concepts, is the distinction between responsive service and procedural fairness a meaningful distinction? I have suggested that a substantive argument can be made for the distinction, at least in regulatory arenas, and it appears in the factor analysis of items in the survey I have used here. If responsive service and procedural fairness are separable concepts, then researchers should explore the relationships between them and try to disentangle their determinants and effects. The distinction is consistent with the work by Tyler (1986) on the importance of procedural fairness in organizational settings, but our contrasting findings about the relationships between these two types of evaluations indicate the need for more theoretical and empirical research.

Another major theme these findings reinforce is that deterrence and normative commitment are, indeed, often symbiotic and complementary strategies. Administrators and the public seem to recognize this fact. As researchers we need to do more to develop theoretical models, research designs, and statistical analyses that integrate them in a theoretically coherent way rather than choosing to focus on one or the other, or simply placing them in the same statistical equation to compete with each other.

Finally, more comparative and cross-national work needs to be done on how responsive service and procedural fairness affect attitudes and behavior. Most of the current work on the factors affecting taxpaying attitudes and behavior that is being cited by U.S. researchers is being done in the United States. It is consequently embedded in a particular set of cultural expectations for and perceptions of how laws and regulations are and should be administered and enforced. Robert Kagan (1990; see also Kagan 1989a) has recently argued that the "adversarial legalism" of the United States stands at one end of a multidimensional continuum of existing policy-making and regulatory processes and regimes. This overarching cultural environment of complex regulations and confrontational administration may make it particularly difficult for any particular agency to affect citizens' perceptions of it, much less change citizens' attitudes and behaviors toward it and the laws it is required to enforce. On the other hand, the cultural environment may be a background against which slight movements in other directions on the continuum may stand out in sharp and effective contrast—movements that might be lost in other policy-making and administrative cultures. If our goal is to strive for general models and theories whose ranges of application can be tested and specified, then we need to expand research on taxpaying and its interaction with tax administration beyond the United States to a range of other countries.

REFERENCES

Axelrod, R. 1984. *The Evolution of Cooperation*. New York: Basic Books.

Bardach, E., and R. A. Kagan. 1982. *Going by the Book: The Problem of Regulatory Unreasonableness*. Philadelphia: Temple University Press.

Bittner, E. 1967. "The Police on Skid-Row. A Study of Peace Keeping." *American Sociological Review* 32:699–715.

Bittner, E. 1970. *The Functions of the Police in Modern Society*. Chevy Case, Md.: National Institute of Mental Health.

Black, D., and A. J. Reiss. 1967. "Patterns of Behavior in Police and Citizen Transactions." In *Studies of Crime and Law Enforcement in Major Metropolitan Areas,* vol. 2, *Field Surveys,* pt. 3, sec. 1. Washington, D.C.: President's Commission on Law Enforcement and Administration of Justice.

Braithwaite, J. 1985. *To Punish or Persuade: Enforcement of Coal Mine Safety.* Albany: State University of New York Press.

Cialdini, R. B. 1984. *Influence: The New Psychology of Modern Persuasion.* New York: Quill.

Cialdini, R. B. 1989. "Social Motivations to Comply: Norms, Values, and Principles." In *Taxpayer Compliance,* vol. 2, *Social Science Perspectives,* ed. J. A. Roth and J. T. Scholz, 220–227. Philadelphia: University of Pennsylvania Press.

Cloward, R. A., and L. Ohlin. 1960. *Delinquency and Opportunity.* New York: Free Press.

Cohen, L. E., and K. C. Land. 1987. "Sociological Positivism and the Explanation of Criminality." In *Positive Criminology,* ed. M. R. Gottfredson and T. Hirschi, 45–55. Beverly Hills, Calif.: Sage.

Cohen, L. E., and R. Machalek. 1988. "A General Theory of Expropriative Crime: An Evolutionary Ecological Approach." *American Journal of Sociology* 94:465–501.

Durkheim, E. [1926] 1964. *The Division of Labor in Society.* Trans. George Simpson. New York: Free Press.

Gouldner, A. W. 1960. "The Norm of Reciprocity: A Preliminary Statement." *American Sociological Review* 25:161–78.

Greenberg, D. R. 1981. "Methodological Issues in Survey Research on the Inhibition of Crime." *Journal of Criminal Law and Criminology* 72:1094–1101.

Harris, Louis, and Associates, Inc. 1988. *1987 Taxpayer Opinion Survey.* Internal Revenue Service Document 7292. Washington, D.C.: Internal Revenue Service.

Hawkins, K. 1984. *Environment and Enforcement: Regulation and the Social Definition of Pollution.* Oxford: Clarendon Press.

Internal Revenue Service. 1990. *Income Tax Compliance Research: Net Tax Gap and Remittance Gap Estimates (Supplement to Publication 7285).* Publication 1415. Washington, D.C.: Internal Revenue Service.

Kagan, R. A. 1989a. "Editor's Introduction: Understanding Regulatory Enforcement." *Law and Policy* 11:89–119.

Kagan, R. A. 1989b. "On the Visibility of Income Tax Law Violations." In *Taxpayer Compliance,* vol. 2, *Social Science Perspectives,* ed. J. A. Roth and J. T. Scholz, 76–125. Philadelphia: University of Pennsylvania Press.

Kagan, R. A. 1990. "Adversarial Legalism and American Government." Paper presented at the annual meeting of the Law and Society Association, Berkeley, Calif.

Klepper, S., and D. Nagin. 1989. "The Anatomy of Tax Evasion." *Journal of Law, Economics and Organization* 5:1–24.

Leventhall, G. S. 1980. "What Should Be Done with Equity Theory? New Approaches to the Study of Fairness in Social Relationships." In *Social Exchange: Advances in Theory and Research,* ed. K. Gergen, M. Greenbert, and R. Willis, 27–55. New York: Plenum Press.

Lind, E. A., and T. R. Tyler. 1988. *The Social Psychology of Procedural Justice.* New York: Plenum Press.

Lipset, S. M., and W. Schneider. 1983. *The Confidence Gap: Business, Labor, and Government in the Public Mind.* New York: Free Press.

Long, S. B., and J. A. Swingen. 1988. "The Impact of Legal Complexity and Opportunity on Taxpayer Compliance." Paper presented at the invitational conference on tax research, Internal Revenue Service, Washington, D.C.

Mason, R. 1987. "A Communication Model of Taxpayer Honesty." *Law and Policy* 9:246–58.

Muir, W. K., Jr. 1977. *Police: Streetcorner Politicians.* Chicago: University of Chicago Press.

Paternoster, R., L. E. Satzman, G. P. Waldo, and T. G. Chiricos. 1983. "Perceived Risk and Social Control: Do Sanctions Really Deter?" *Law and Society Review* 17:457–79.

Perloff, L. S., and B. K. Fetzer. 1986. "Self-Other Judgments and Perceived Vulnerability to Victimization." *Journal of Personality and Social Psychology* 50:502–10.

Regan, D. T. 1971. "Effects of a Favor and Liking on Compliance." *Journal of Experimental Social Psychology* 7:627–39.

Scholz, J. T. 1984. "Cooperation, Deterrence, and the Ecology of Regulatory Enforcement." *Law and Society Review* 18:179–224.

Smigel, E. O., and H. L. Ross, eds. 1970. *Crimes Against Bureaucracy.* New York: Van Nostrand Reinhold Co.

Smith, K. W. 1990. "Integrating Three Perspectives on Noncompliance: A Sequential Decision Model." *Criminal Justice and Behavior* 17:350–69.

Smith, K. W., and K. A. Kinsey. 1985. "Cooperation and Control: Strategies and Tactics for Tax Examination." *Tax Administration Review* 2:13–29.

Smith, K. W., and K. A. Kinsey. 1987. "Understanding Taxpaying Behavior: A Conceptual Framework with Implications for Research." *Law and Society Review* 21:639–63.

Smith, K. W., and L. J. Stalans. 1991. "Encouraging Tax Compliance with Positive Incentives: A Conceptual Framework and Research Directions." *Law and Policy* 13:35–53.

Stalans, L. J., K. A. Kinsey, and K. W. Smith. 1991. "Listening to Different Voices: Formation of Sanction Beliefs and Taxpaying Norms." *Journal of Applied Social Psychology* 21:119–38.

Stalans, L. J., K. W. Smith, and K. A. Kinsey. 1989. "When Do We Think about Detection? Structural Opportunity and Taxpaying Behavior." *Law and Social Inquiry* 14:481–503.

Tyler, T. R. 1984. "The Assessment of Social Risk: Integrating Personal Victimization Experience and Socially Transmitted Information about Crime." *Journal of Social Issues* 40:27–38.

Tyler, T. R. 1986. "When Does Procedural Justice Matter in Organizational Settings?" *Research on Negotiations in Organizations* 1:7–23.

Tyler, T. R. 1988. "What Is Procedural Justice? Criteria Used by Citizens to Assess the Fairness of Legal Procedures." *Law and Society Review* 22:103–35.

Tyler, T. R. 1990a. "Justice, Self-Interest, and the Legitimacy of Legal and Political

Authority." In *Beyond Self-Interest,* ed. J. J. Mansbridge, 171–79. Chicago: University of Chicago Press.

Tyler, T. R. 1990b. *Why People Obey the Law.* New Haven: Yale University Press.

Tyler, T. R., J. D. Casper, and B. Fisher. 1989. "Maintaining Allegiance Toward Political Authorities: The Role of Prior Attitudes and the Use of Fair Procedures." *American Journal of Political Science* 33:629–52.

Tyler, T. R., and K. M. McGraw. 1986. "Ideology and the Interpretation of Personal Experience: Procedural Justice and Political Quiescence." *Journal of Social Issues* 42:115–28.

Commentary

Richard Lempert

In reading the essays for this conference, I was reminded of the first conference dealing with tax compliance that I attended about five years ago. On the one hand, I am struck by the differences and the way in which the work I read for this conference is an improvement on what I read then. The essays today are more interesting, intelligent, and methodologically sophisticated. Indeed, it is not just the statistical methods that are more adequate; there are new and interesting sets of data. There are, for example, the diaries that John Carrol persuaded a sample of taxpayers to keep during the tax season and TCMP microdata that several researchers have been able to employ. Just as important is the progress I see in creative, plausible theorizing. No longer are most explanations for compliance confined to simple deterrence models. Instead, more and more researchers, like Kent Smith whose essay I shall turn to shortly, are positing different mechanisms of compliance and providing more textured accounts of why people do or do not pay their taxes.

Yet it is these very advances that lead to an "on the other hand" that is discouraging. For despite the inherent interest of this set of conference essays, I leave them feeling that I know little if anything more about the dynamics of tax compliance than I knew leaving a similar conference five years before. The reason for this, I think, is that our methods for data analysis and our theories of explanation have far surpassed the quality of the data, even the new kinds of data, that compliance researchers have to work with.

Perhaps the most frustrating kind of data to analyze is the kind of data that Kent Smith uses in the essay I have been asked to comment on; that is, data from someone else's survey. In working with survey data collected by another researcher with a different research agenda, one always wishes that certain questions were phrased in a different way, that response categories were different, or that different questions were asked. While I do not intend my comments to be largely methodological criticisms, I can imagine some of the frustrations Kent must have felt. At places this shows. For example, at several points, Kent notes the likely unreliability and possible invalidity of certain theoretically important concepts that are measured by only one or two items, and ultimately his decision about how best to derive his model is affected by this consideration.

I am particularly troubled about the way in which the ultimate dependent variable in this study, underreported income, is measured in the data that Kent used. The dependent variable consists of respondents' answers to the question: "Within the past five years or so, do you think that you might have left some reportable income off your federal tax returns—even a minor amount?" Respondents' answers were confined to a four-point scale ranging from 1 = "definitely have not" to 4 = "definitely have." Putting aside the question of what to make of the four-point scale (I have the nagging feeling that the second choice, which is "probably have not," is a denial equivalent to "I am only slightly pregnant"), I have other problems with this measure. The first is that, in encouraging respondents to mention even minor amounts of omitted income, the question encourages respondents to mention small items unintentionally left off the tax return, such as an omission that a respondent only realizes when he or she fills out, without omission, a subsequent year's tax return and compares that return with the one for the prior year. If an omission was actually inadvertent, it is unlikely to have been affected by the theoretically crucial independent variables.

My second problem with this variable, and one that is more troublesome, is that the question asks for admissions of noncompliant behavior that extend back five years or a bit more. Yet the questions that are used to form the independent variable ask for views as of the time of the survey. Thus, current conditions and attitudes are used to explain prior, perhaps quite a bit prior, behavior. Kent is aware of the general problem and specifically addresses it in connection with his normative commitment and perceived likelihood of detection variables. For example, Kent explicitly assumes that norms are longstanding (at least five years) and presents data on a low correlation with structural opportunity that are consistent with, but by no means prove, the hypothesis that normative commitment is a cause of, rather than a rationalization for, underreported income. A similar argument is made to justify treating a respondent's current perceived likelihood of detection as reflecting beliefs that are causally prior to the underreporting of any income during the past five years. But other variables may be affected as well. For example, one of the biggest surprises in the final model is an unexpected and counterintuitive path between a belief that the tax system is fair and underreported income. Perhaps one should not make much of this finding for the reasons Kent gives, but it is interesting to note that the positive relationship is less counterintuitive if underreported income is the causally prior variable. Those who have underreported in the past may be more likely than those who have reported everything to currently feel that the amount of taxes they pay, and hence the system that demands that payment level, is fair. Alternatively those who have underreported may now feel the system is fairer because they, like the rich people they read about, have loopholes they can take advantage of.

In my view, Kent's theoretical ideas are of higher quality than the data he has available to test them with. Indeed, I think they represent an important contribution to how to conceptualize mechanisms of tax compliance. Tax compliance models have usually emphasized the costs of compliance, such as the costs of coping with complexity (see, e.g., Slemrod 1989) or the costs of noncompliance, which encompass the kinds of costs captured in deterrence models (see, e.g., Klepper and Nagin 1989), although some creative researchers have experimented with the incentive effects of rewards (see, e.g., Thibaut, Friedland, and Walker 1974). The procedural justice literature on which Kent draws is replete with findings of the power of fair procedures to affect attitudes and even behavior—findings that are often counterintuitive, given the assumptions of various rational choice models and a view that, as rational actors, people seek to maximize objective outcomes.

For example, people who come to traffic court to protest tickets and have their cases dismissed when called have won a complete victory and do not even have to spend time presenting a defense. Yet Tyler reports that such people are often angry and think less of the court because, although they have won, they have not been given a chance to tell their stories (see Lind and Tyler 1988). In another study, individuals' evaluations of encounters with the courts and the police over such minor matters as traffic tickets and misdemeanors turned less on the outcomes they received than on their evaluations of the fairness with which they were treated (see Tyler 1984). Indeed, not only were judgments of procedural fairness more important to the evaluation of the court than the absolute outcomes the parties received, procedural fairness judgments were also more important than actual outcomes relative to both the outcomes others were perceived to receive and the outcomes respondents expected before their cases were heard. Even when outcomes may be quite severe, as in felony cases, it appears that procedural justice judgments have a more substantial direct effect on judgments of outcome satisfaction (see Casper, Tyler, and Fischer 1988) and outcome fairness (see Landis and Goodstein 1986) than the sentence received. In the Casper, Tyler, and Fischer and Landis and Goodstein studies, sentence severity is only one of a number of factors that affect procedural justice judgments, and its effects are entirely indirect. Finally, McEwen and Maimen (1984) found that compliance with small claims court judgments was greater when the judgments resulted from mediation than when they resulted from adjudication—a result they attributed to the fact that, in mediation, parties consent to judgment.

Thus, I think that Kent identifies an issue worth exploring when he suggests that a sense of procedural fairness will enhance compliance with tax obligations, but this raises the question of what the IRS can do to enhance perceptions of procedural fairness. Probably the strongest and most powerful factor that leads to judgments of fair procedure is "voice," the ability to state one's case or tell a story to a decision maker. Thibaut and Walker (1975) focused on the importance of voice in their path-breaking research on procedural justice, and numerous researchers have confirmed this aspect of their results since then. Indeed, voice appears to matter not just in settings where one expects to be allowed to state a case—such as a judicial trial—but also in settings where a right to be heard may not be expected, such as worker promotion or job assignment decisions (see Earley and Lind 1987; Kanfer et al. 1987; Lissak 1983). And voice is related not just to abstract judgments of fairness, but also to performance levels (see Earley 1984).

But how are taxpayers to be given "voice"? Except in an audit, the taxpayer has no real chance to tell a story to the IRS. Indeed, the most effective mode of tax collecting—income withholding—allows taxpayers to speak only after income has been taken from them and the issue is a refund. Taxpayers do fill out returns and, in this sense, have a chance to speak, but the returns are designed to elicit a limited range of information. They are not designed to give taxpayers an opportunity to tell their own stories of why they should not be required to pay certain amounts. And even if tax returns were altered so that they provided the taxpayer an opportunity to speak to the government (an experiment well worth doing), there might be no effect, for the taxpayer could never be sure that a decision maker would listen.

Other forms of process control, such as consenting to judgments in small claims courts (McEwen and Maimen 1984), also seem to affect compliance with legal obligations. But it appears unlikely that the IRS will allow taxpayers any more process control than the situation demands. Indeed, such recent changes in the tax law as income reporting and the obligation to secure social security numbers for children are likely to diminish whatever sense of control taxpayers have and, at the same time, appear likely to increase tax payments. This may be because process control only affects compliance when other organizational guarantees of compliance are impractical at best.

A third ingredient that is important to fairness judgments, at least when people deal with such authorities as the police or the courts, is official politeness and respect for rights. This may be why, in Kent's data, the responsiveness scale was so strongly related to the procedural justice measure. IRS actions to increase the agency's apparent respect for rights and politeness involve less fundamental changes in the tax collection system than actions that increase taxpayer voice or process control and so seem a more viable way for the IRS to attempt to enhance perceived fairness. Indeed, attempts to improve politeness and respect for rights is worthwhile, regardless of the salutary effects this may have on tax compliance. If, however, the concern is tax compliance and if a sense of being treated respectfully affects not just fairness perceptions but also taxpaying behavior, there remains the question of whether these effects occur only when the taxpayer has personally experienced respectful treatment or whether second-hand information, acquired by word of mouth or through the press, is sufficient to trigger a "tax amenable" response. If tax compliance is the goal, a "politeness and respect strategy" should differ depending on the mechanism involved.

It is also not clear that greater respect for the IRS and a greater sense that IRS procedures are fair will translate into more cooperative taxpaying behavior. Interestingly, in Kent's data there is no direct effect from procedural fairness judgments of the IRS to underreported income. Indeed, it may be that the ideas that form the theoretical motivation for Kent's work, the norm of reciprocity and the ideas of legitimacy and allegiance to authority, do not justify focusing on IRS actions at all. The IRS is, after all, not collecting money for itself; it is an agency of the federal government acting on behalf of that government. It may well be that taxpayers' attitudes toward the federal government dwarf any compliance effects that might be attributed to attitudes toward the IRS.

Here, a natural experiment commends itself. In the first half of the 1991 taxpaying season, the United States fought and won the most popular war in recent memory. The president's popularity reached an all-time high and faith in the governmental institutions increased as well. A comparison of taxpaying behavior in 1990 and 1991 could be quite revealing. The date of payment might also matter, with the expectation being that those who paid their taxes in the heady days following the cease-fire would be most compliant relative to their former years' returns and (depending on what future polls may show) that those paying by the April 15 deadline are more compliant relative to their past behavior than those who took three- and six-month extensions. Indeed, to the extent that extensions reflect an unwillingness to pay in the first instance, one would predict that the proportion of taxpayers requesting extensions, net of those who have been in the Persian Gulf, will decrease in 1991.

If tax compliance increases with general government approval, it will, of course, not mean that efforts by the IRS to increase its perceived procedural fairness will be ineffective in enhancing tax compliance or, indeed, that such efforts will be less effective than changes in perceptions of the federal government. Whether the kinds of effects that Kent predicts exist and what their magnitude is remain empirical questions. If my proposed experiment shows an effect, there may be more rather than less reason to actively pursue the path that Kent has started on, for some of the theoretical underpinnings of Kent's venture will be confirmed in a different setting.

In conclusion, I believe that we should be grateful to Kent for calling our attention to the potential importance that reciprocity, legitimacy, and procedural fairness have for tax compliance. I believe that Kent's theoretical ideas are sound, and in certain areas that do not concern tax compliance they are well supported by empirical research. At the same time, I do not find the implications of these ideas for IRS action or taxpaying behavior clear. It might be, for example, that IRS efforts to increase taxpayer voice or process control will require changes in tax collection methods, like income withholding, that have far greater compliance returns than those that enhanced fairness judgments and greater legitimacy could produce. Or it may be that judgments of the IRS's fairness are unimportant to taxpaying behavior because, to the extent that reciprocity and legitimacy are forces for tax compliance, the attitudes that count are attitudes toward the federal government in general and not specific attitudes toward the government's tax collection agency. (It is possible that attitudes toward the IRS affect attitudes toward the federal government in general, but we do not now know that such an effect exists.) Kent's research does show effects of IRS procedural fairness judgments, and these effects are indirectly related to Kent's measure of underreported income. However, for reasons I have mentioned, I do not think that Kent's data allow a very good test of his theories. Thus, I conclude that further research is needed. The theories that Kent draws on are well enough supported that it is plausible to suppose that they have the kinds of effects on tax compliance that Kent posits.

REFERENCES

Casper, J. D., T. R. Tyler, and B. Fischer. 1988. "Procedural Justice in Felony Cases." *Law and Society Review* 22:483–507.

Early, P. C. 1984. "Informational Mechanisms of Participation Influencing Goal Acceptance, Satisfaction, and Performance." Ph.D. diss., University of Illinois, Champaign.

Early, P. C., and E. A. Lind. 1987. "Procedural Justice and Participation in Task Selection: The Role of Control in Mediating Justice Judgments." *Journal of Personality and Social Psychology* 52:1148–60.

Kanfer, R., J. Sawyer, P. C. Earley, and E. A. Lind. 1987. "Participation in Task Evaluation Procedures: The Effects of Influential Opinion Expression and Knowledge of Evaluative Criteria on Attitudes and Performance." *Social Justice Research* 1:235–49.

Klepper, Steven, and Daniel Nagin. 1989. "The Criminal Deterrence Literature: Implications for Research on Taxpayer Compliance." In *Taxpayer Compliance,* ed. Jeffrey A. Roth and John T. Scholz, 2:126–55. Philadelphia: University of Pennsylvania Press.

Landis, J. M., and L. Goodstein. 1986. "When Is Justice Fair." *American Bar Foundation Research Journal* 1986:675–708.

Lind, E. Allan, and Tom R. Tyler. 1988. *The Social Psychology of Procedural Justice*. New York: Plenum Press.

Lissak, R. I. 1983. "Procedural Fairness: How Employees Evaluate Procedures." Ph.D. diss., University of Illinois, Champaign.

McEwen, C. A., and R. J. Maiman. 1984. "Mediation in Small Claims Court: Achieving Compliance Through Consent." *Law and Society Review* 18:11–49.

Slemrod, Joel. 1989. "Complexity, Compliance Costs, and Tax Evasion." In *Taxpayer Compliance,* ed. Jeffrey A. Roth and John T. Scholz, 2:156–81. Philadelphia: University of Pennsylvania Press.

Thibaut, J., N. Friedland, and L. Walker. 1974. "Compliance With Rules: Some Social Determinants." *Journal of Personality and Social Psychology* 30:792–801.

Thibaut, J., and L. Walker. 1975. *Procedural Justice: A Psychological Analysis*. Hillsdale, N.J.: Erlbaum.

Tyler, Tom R. 1984. "The Role of Perceived Justice in Defendant's Evaluations of Their Courtroom Experience." *Law and Society Review* 18:51–74.

Deterrence and Alienation Effects of IRS Enforcement: An Analysis of Survey Data

Karyl A. Kinsey

Strümpel (1969) formalizes the results of a multinational study of tax enforcement and tax compliance conducted nearly three decades ago into a simple, three-variable model. In that model, the concept of "rigidity of assessment" captures aspects of tax enforcement that reflect a deterrence model of social control. Strümpel argues that enforcement techniques emphasizing detection and punishment have two opposing effects on tax compliance. The first is the expected deterrent effect: the fear of getting caught and the severity of sanctions motivate taxpayers to comply with the law. However, the retroactive, confrontational, and coercive aspects of a deterrence approach to law enforcement also have an indirect, negative effect by alienating taxpayers and lowering their willingness to comply voluntarily with the law. Lower willingness to comply may lead to active efforts to evade taxes illegally, as well as to such other forms of tax resistance as aggressive legal avoidance, increased use of appeals processes, and political lobbying to muzzle the tax agency.

Strümpel's model anticipates and cogently summarizes the major themes of more recent research on regulatory and tax law enforcement (see Bardach and Kagan 1982; Braithwaite 1985; Hawkins 1984; Levi 1988; Long 1981; Scholz 1984; Smith and Kinsey 1985). These studies emphasize the difficulty of adequately articulating and applying uniform legal standards to the multiplicity of fact situations experienced by those subject to regulation. They emphasize the difficulty of developing unambiguous and consensual definitions, standards, and even terminologies of compliance. They emphasize the limits of enforceability in the face of organized resistance to legal authority. And they emphasize the importance of law enforcers being seen as reasonable bargaining partners, capable and willing to moderate or renegotiate government expectations when citizens face excessively high costs of compliance.

This research was supported by grant SES-8711961 from the Law and Social Science Program of the National Science Foundation. My thanks to Alan Plumley, John Scholz, Joel Slemrod, Kent Smith, and Loretta Stalans for comments and suggestions.

The multinational study described by Strümpel focused on the tax enforcement experiences of business owners and self-employed professionals, while the regulatory literature focuses on businesses and corporations. The generality of this model beyond business samples to individual taxpayers is open to question. Corporate executives, business owners, and entrepreneurs often endorse an ideology of free-market capitalism that may predispose them toward negative evaluations of government regulation and control. The financial stakes of tax enforcement are often higher for business returns, which intensifies potential conflicts of interest and provides incentives for each side to resolve legal and evidentiary ambiguities in their own favor (see Dubin, Graetz, and Wilde 1987; Graetz and Wilde 1985). In addition, efforts by tax enforcers to maximize yields from enforcement resources may lead business taxpayers to believe they are being singled out for scrutiny, while the errors and evasions of taxpayers with lower incomes escape detection and punishment.

Differences in the legal and tax situations of ordinary taxpayers may also serve to weaken the strength of relationships among legal sanctions, willingness to comply voluntarily, and compliance behavior. Taxpayers with labor income tend to file simpler tax returns and face lower compliance costs than those with business or investment income (see Long and Swingen 1989; Slemrod and Sorum 1984). Determinations of noncompliance may, therefore, be more straightforward and unproblematic for most individual taxpayers, weakening the likelihood that a deterrence strategy of law enforcement would produce conflict and the development of antagonistic attitudes toward law enforcers. Even when individual taxpayers believe that tax enforcers have been unfair or excessively punitive, limited opportunities and resources for successful noncompliance may weaken the effects of willingness to cooperate on actual compliance behavior (see Kinsey 1986; Stalans, Smith, and Kinsey 1989).

Regulatory and tax law enforcement agencies in the United States tend to rely primarily on a deterrence model of law enforcement (see Bardach and Kagan 1982; Braithwaite 1985; Hawkins 1984). Not surprisingly, studies of compliance with the U.S. individual income tax have focused on testing deterrence predictions (Kinsey 1986; Klepper and Nagin 1989b; Roth, Scholz, and Witte 1989). Overall, evidence suggests at least modest support among individual taxpayers for the first prediction of Strümpel's model, that increasing the probability of sanctions for past acts of noncompliance will deter future noncompliance behavior. At the aggregate level, studies of official data find evidence of deterrent effects, although these effects are difficult to estimate due to the endogeneity of enforcement efforts (see Crane and Nourzad 1985 and 1987; Dubin, Graetz, and Wilde 1987; Graetz, Reinganum, and Wilde 1986; Klepper and Nagin 1989a, 1989b, 1989c; Witte and Woodbury

1985). Likewise, survey studies find support for key cognitive and behavioral assumptions of the deterrence model. Objective opportunities for successful noncompliance shape subjective evaluations of detection risk (see Klepper and Nagin 1989c; Stalans, Smith, and Kinsey 1989). Subjective risk perceptions, in turn, shape future intentions to cheat on taxes (see Grasmick and Bursik 1990; Smith 1990; Stalans, Smith, and Kinsey 1989; Tittle 1980).

Evidence for the second part of Strümpel's model, that a deterrence approach to law enforcement affects willingness to comply voluntarily, has not been the subject of contemporary tax research. Studies conducted in other sociolegal settings, though, find that ordinary citizens react strongly to their perceptions of the procedures used and the decisions made by governmental authorities (see Katz et al. 1975; Lind and Tyler 1988; Tyler 1990; Tyler, Casper, and Fisher 1989). In a panel study, Tyler (1990) found that the perceived unfairness of experiences with the police and other legal authorities affects subsequent self-reports of illegal behavior. While tax studies have focused, with mixed results, on the effects of fairness perceptions on compliance (see Mason and Calvin 1984; Scott and Grasmick 1981; Spicer and Lundstedt 1976; Warneryd and Walerud 1982), the effects of law enforcement on fairness perceptions have not received much attention. In a recent study of audited taxpayers, though, McGraw (1989) found that the perceived fairness of audit procedures shapes attitudes toward tax authorities.

Although the relationship between enforcement contacts and the willingness to comply voluntarily is unclear, several studies find that individual taxpayers and tax enforcers often disagree about determinations of noncompliance in specific instances. Hessing, Elffers, and Weigel (1988) found no correspondence between official determinations of tax cheating and taxpayer admissions of noncompliance. Similarly low levels of correspondence occur between taxpayer reports of the financial outcomes of IRS enforcement contacts and their admissions of past noncompliance (see Kinsey 1988). Some of these discrepancies reflect successful tax evasion among taxpayers with opportunities to underreport income (see Kinsey 1988; Klepper and Nagin 1989a). But a substantial proportion of taxpayers who pay the government additional taxes, interest, and penalties as a consequence of enforcement contact remain unpersuaded—or at least unwilling to admit—that their tax returns were noncompliant. When asked directly, 33 percent of the taxpayers in a national survey who reported past audits asserted that the examiner's report at the end of the audit was at least partially wrong (see Harris 1987).

My study uses cross-sectional survey data to examine the adequacy of Strümpel's model among ordinary taxpayers, focusing in particular on the effects of enforcement contacts on sanction perceptions, the perceived fairness of tax laws, and future intentions of noncompliance. Ideally, the question of enforcement effects would be studied using a research design in which tax returns are assigned randomly to enforcement contact and control group conditions. This would allow the effects of the enforcement contacts themselves to be isolated from the potentially confounding effects of taxpayer characteristics that shape IRS decisions to initiate an enforcement contact. This methodology is not available, however. In the absence of random assignment, it is important to control statistically for financial and background characteristics of taxpayers that may confound the relationship between enforcement contacts and taxpayer reactions to law enforcement efforts. The initial part of my analysis will focus on describing the relationship between selected taxpayer characteristics and exposure to IRS enforcement efforts. These characteristics will in turn serve as control variables for the remainder of the analysis.

At this point, it is worth noting two strategic advantages to using sample survey data to examine the effects of tax law enforcement contacts. First, it is possible to obtain independent estimates of the specific and general effects of enforcement contacts (see Blumstein, Cohen, and Nagin 1978). Respondents were asked not only to describe their own personal contacts with the IRS, but were also asked to describe the reactions of other people they know who were contacted by the IRS for enforcement purposes. The analysis of personal contact experiences examines the specific effects of tax law enforcement on individuals. The analysis of vicarious contacts allows an evaluation of the potential ripple effects of enforcement that are central to models of general deterrence. Further, a comparison of respondents' descriptions of personal and vicarious enforcement experiences will point to potential biases in the diffusion of information about tax enforcement as it filters through the population (see Geerken and Gove 1975; Mason 1987; Stalans, Kinsey, and Smith 1991).

Second, juxtaposing self-reports of admitted past noncompliance with the financial results of personal enforcement outcomes will allow deterrent effects to be distinguished from experiential learning effects (see Paternoster et al. 1982 and 1983). Experiential interpretations of the relationship between legal sanctions and behavior argue that people start out with unrealistically high expectations about the likelihood of detection and punishment if they were to disobey the law. Over time, offenders who are not detected and punished by legal authorities adjust their sanction perceptions downward to a more realistic understanding of the limitations of law enforcement. In other words, it is not so much that perceived sanctions increase compliance behavior, but that noncompliance behavior decreases sanction perceptions.

In Kinsey (1986), I argued that experiential learning effects are more likely for underreported income than overstated deductions, because the burden of proof for detecting underreported income is on the IRS. In later qualitative interviews, though, I have noticed that the few taxpayers and tax practitioners who boast about misleading the IRS tend to describe more instances involving overstated deductions than underreported income. These data will allow a closer and more systematic analysis of potential differences in experiential learning effects for overstated deductions and underreported income.

Cross-sectional surveys of illegal behavior, however, suffer from serious limitations, in particular the problem of establishing causality and the problem of biases in self-reports of sensitive behavior. It is not possible to eliminate these problems completely, but the analysis will attempt to minimize their effects by using admitted past noncompliance as an independent variable. Doing so straightens out the timeline assumed by the deterrence model (see Grasmick and Bursik 1990). This allows a better opportunity to examine whether IRS enforcement contacts produce changes in current sanction perceptions and anticipated behavior, as opposed to the expected continuation of past habits and standing decisions (see Carroll 1987; Smith and Kinsey 1987).

In addition, including admissions of past noncompliance in regression equations for future intentions reduces the likelihood of biased estimation resulting from nonrandom error in self-reported noncompliance. If one assumes that past admissions share the same biases as future intentions, then including past admissions as an independent variable will yield better estimates, because any shared correlation between other independent variables and measurement error in self-reported noncompliance will have been controlled.

Data Collection

In the winter of 1988, the Minnesota Center for Survey Research conducted a statewide telephone survey of adult taxpayers on behalf of the American Bar Foundation. The selection of respondents to interview occurred in two stages. First, a household was randomly selected using random-digit dialing, and then a respondent was selected from within the household. To be selected, an individual must have filed a federal income tax return in the past three years and must have either personally filled out the tax return or worked directly with a paid preparer in completing the return. When more than one person in a household met these criteria, the individual with the most recent birthday was selected for interview. The response rate to the survey was 71 percent, and a total of 1,202 interviews were conducted.

Two different survey forms were used in the survey to control for potential order effects within four sets of questions, including two sets on sanction perceptions. Random starts were also used for lists of questions about tax deductions and sources of income. Questions about enforcement contacts were placed near the end of the questionnaire; this placement probably reduced errors of recall because the respondent had already answered questions about sources of tax information, past tax deductions, sources of income, and noncompliance with the law.

Personal Enforcement Contact

All respondents were asked if they or their spouse had been contacted by the IRS within the past three years about possible problems with their tax returns. A total of 177 (15 percent) of the respondents indicated enforcement contact. Several follow-up questions were asked about these contacts, including the type of contact, the financial outcome, perceptions of the thoroughness of the exam, the perceived legal correctness of the outcome, and the perceived willingness of IRS employees to listen to the taxpayer's explanation of what happened on the return. Due to the small case base ($N = 177$) of respondents reporting enforcement contacts by the IRS, my analysis will cover all types of enforcement contacts rather than try to develop separate estimates for different IRS enforcement programs.

Vicarious Enforcement Contact

All respondents were also asked how many other people they knew who had been contacted by the IRS in the past three years about possible problems on their tax returns. Half (52 percent) indicated they did not know anyone else contacted by the IRS, 18 percent knew one other person, 13 percent knew two, and 16 percent knew three or more people contacted by the IRS. Those who knew others were asked a series of follow-up questions about what they were told by the person with whom they had talked most about their enforcement contact. The wording of most of these follow-up questions is identical to those asked of respondents who had been personally contacted.

Admitted Past Noncompliance

A series of eight questions asked if respondents had claimed particular deductions, credits, and exemptions on tax returns in the last three years. For each one claimed, respondents were then asked if they might have overstated it on federal tax returns, even by just a small amount. Response alternatives were "(1) definitely have not, (2) probably have not, (3) probably have, and (4) definitely have." A measure of the likelihood of past overstating of deductions was constructed by taking the maximum value of items with valid responses. In addition, respondents were asked how many times in the past three years they had overstated deductions, including any deductions not mentioned in the earlier list. The likelihood and frequency measures were averaged to form a scale of past overstating of deductions (Cronbach's $\alpha = .75$).[1]

Twelve questions were asked about sources of income received by respondents and their spouses in the past three years. For each income source received, respondents were then asked the likelihood that they might have underreported this income on tax returns, using the same format as the deduction questions. The self-reported frequency of underreporting in the past three years was also ascertained. The resulting likelihood and frequency measures of underreporting income were averaged to form a scale of past underreporting of income (Cronbach's $\alpha = .79$).

Perceptions of Formal Sanctions

Three types of legal sanction perceptions were measured in the survey: the perceived likelihood that the respondent's tax returns will be examined by the IRS, the perceived certainty of detection if the respondent cheated on taxes, and a measure of perceived severity to the respondent if the IRS detected noncompliance.

Three questions covered the perceived likelihood that the IRS would examine the respondent's tax return within the next three years. One asked if IRS computers would check over the return to see if it should be audited, another asked if information on the return would be compared to other information about income the IRS receives, and the third asked if the respondent's tax return would be audited. These responses were averaged to form a scale of the likelihood of an IRS examination (Cronbach's $\alpha = .78$).[2]

Four questions focused on the perceived likelihood of detection by the IRS if the respondent did not comply with tax laws. Two concerned the underreporting of income and two covered overstating deductions, and specific dollar amounts of $500 and $1,000 were varied for each type of noncompliance. Responses were averaged to form a scale of the perceived probability of detection for noncompliance (Cronbach's $\alpha = .92$).

Comparisons of the relative effects of IRS enforcement contacts on exam certainty and detection certainty will provide another indicator of the possibility of experiential effects. The correlation between these two measures of sanction perceptions is only .15 ($p < .001$), indicating that perceptions of

1. Cronbach's α is a measure of the internal consistency of a summary scale. It ranges in value from 0 through 1, with higher values indicating greater reliability of measurement.

2. Each of these items had a fairly substantial proportion (9–11 percent) of missing values. Only 5 percent, however, failed to answer all three items. To reduce attrition in sample size, this and other scales are constructed using any items with valid responses, even if that means the scale is based on responses to only one item.

exam certainty and perceptions of detection certainty are distinctive constructs.

Perceived severity of legal sanctions is measured by a single item asking how big of a problem it would be if the IRS detected noncompliance on the respondent's tax returns. Over half (57 percent) of the respondents indicated it would be a large problem, 18 percent indicated it would be a moderate problem, 16 percent a small problem, and 8 percent said it would be no problem at all if the IRS detected noncompliance on their tax returns.

Perceived Fairness of Tax Laws

At the beginning of the interview, respondents were asked if they agreed with two statements regarding the fairness of tax laws. One referred to taxpayers in general and the other to taxpayers in the respondents' income situation. Response alternatives ranged from strongly disagree (1) to strongly agree (4). These questions were averaged to form a scale of the perceived fairness of tax laws (Cronbach's α = .66).

Likelihood of Future Cheating

Respondents were asked two questions about the likelihood of future noncompliance on federal tax returns in the next three years. One question focused on underreporting income, while the other asked about overstating deductions and expenses on future returns. Four response alternatives were available, ranging from very unlikely (1) to very likely (4). The two items were averaged to form a scale of the likelihood of future noncompliance (Cronbach's α = .69).

Control Variables

Age and sex are controlled because previous research indicates these variables may be related to both noncompliance and sanction perceptions (see Grasmick, Finlay, and Glaser 1984; Thurman, St. John, and Riggs 1984; Tittle 1980). Income, avoidance efforts, and opportunity for underreporting income are included to serve as crude indicators of potential IRS enforcement selection criteria. Tax information seeking is included to control for individual differences in knowledge and interest in tax issues among taxpayers, which should affect the likelihood of vicarious enforcement contacts.

The likelihood the respondent would feel guilty for cheating is included as a control variable for two reasons. First, it serves as a potential indirect indicator of past noncompliance and, as such, supplements the self-reported measures of admitted noncompliance. Second, guilt feelings are positively correlated with perceptions of legal sanctions, suggesting the need to differentiate cognitions about the sanctions supplied by law enforcers from self-sanctioning provided by personal conscience (see Grasmick and Bursik 1990).[3]

Legal avoidance is measured by a single question asking how much time the respondent spent in the past year actively exploring different ways to reduce income taxes. Opportunity is a dichotomous variable indicating if the respondent received income that is not subject to full information reporting to the IRS (see Kinsey 1986; Klepper and Nagin 1989a; Stalans, Smith, and Kinsey 1989). Guilt feelings are measured as the mean of two questions about the likelihood the respondent would feel guilty if he or she underreported income or overstated deductions (Cronbach's $\alpha = .89$). Tax information seeking is the average amount (Cronbach's $\alpha = .68$) of tax information received by the respondent from nine types of information sources (see Stalans, Kinsey, and Smith 1991).

Results

Reports of the results will be divided into two sections. The first section focuses on descriptive analyses of the characteristics of taxpayers reporting personal and vicarious enforcement contacts by the IRS and their descriptions of these contacts. The second section will focus on testing the effects of enforcement contact experiences on current sanction perceptions, the perceived fairness of tax laws, and future intentions to cheat on taxes.

Descriptive Analyses of Enforcement Contacts

Table 1 reports the results of descriptive analyses of the relationships between control variables, admitted past noncompliance, and IRS enforcement contact experiences. Personal enforcement contacts are analyzed using logistic regression, while the number of vicarious contacts are analyzed using Ordinary Least Squares (OLS) regression.

It is not possible to evaluate precisely how representative contacts reported by the survey respondents are of IRS enforcement contacts with Minnesota taxpayers. However, the characteristics of respondents with personal contact experiences are generally consistent with national statistics of examination coverage reported in table 7 of the IRS *Annual Report* (Internal

3. Guilt feelings could arguably be considered an indicator of the willingness to comply and, thus, endogenous to my analysis. However, the processes described in Strümpel (1969) and in studies of regulatory enforcement seem more descriptive of norm neutralization, the justification of otherwise disapproved acts (see Mason and Calvin 1984; Thurman, St. John, and Riggs 1984), than of changes in core moral values.

TABLE 1. Characteristics of Respondents Experiencing Personal and Vicarious Enforcement Contacts (unstandardized coefficients)

	Personal Contact[a]	Number of Vicarious Contacts[b]
Admitted past noncompliance		
Underreported income	.30**	−.05
Overstated deductions	.11	.14*
Controls		
Legal avoidance effort	.24*	.13**
Tax information seeking	−.10	.32***
Log income	.45**	.23***
Opportunity	.55**	.18**
Feel guilty if cheated	−.05	.00
Female	−.24	−.10
Age	.12	−.08***
R^2	NA	.11

Note: NA = not applicable.
[a]Logistic regression analysis.
[b]OLS regression analysis.
*$p < .05$. **$p < .01$. ***$p < .001$.

Revenue Service 1987). According to those statistics, examination rates are generally higher for high-income returns, more complex returns, and returns with self-employment or farm income. Similarly, high-income respondents, respondents who avoid taxes legally (which increases complexity), and respondents with opportunities for noncompliance (which includes self-employment and farm income) are more likely to report IRS enforcement contacts.

The success of the IRS in selecting noncompliers for enforcement action is also suggested by the preponderance of contacted respondents who admit past underreporting of income on tax returns. However, admissions of past overstated deductions are not related to personal enforcement contacts. This suggests that the IRS experiences greater success in identifying returns with potential problems of underreported income than returns with overstated deductions.

As expected, those who seek information about taxes from a variety of sources are more likely to have come into contact with other people who have been subject to IRS enforcement efforts. The effects of income, avoidance effort, and opportunity on knowing others contacted by the IRS are similar to those observed for personal contact experience. In a further analysis (not reported in table 1), personal contact experience was added to the equation for vicarious contacts. Even though personal contact is itself related to knowing others contacted by the IRS ($\beta = .26, p < .01$), including it does not change the results for other variables. Taken together, these findings suggest the active exchange of information about IRS enforcement efforts among networks of taxpayers in audit classes having higher examination rates (see also Stalans, Kinsey, and Smith 1991).

Table 2 presents respondent reports of the reasons the IRS contacted them about their tax returns in the past three years. Their responses reflect the mix of enforcement programs within the IRS, including Service Center identifications of math errors, notices produced by income information-matching programs, audits and requests for documentation of deductions, and efforts to collect back taxes. Open-ended responses to the "other" category primarily concern compliance with reporting requirements and the use of appropriate forms.

Some respondents indicated multiple reasons for contact, presumably because a contact involved multiple issues or they were contacted more than once. In order to maximize information about direct examinations of tax returns, follow-up questions were included that focus on the first type of contact listed in table 2 that the respondent experienced. The second column in the table reports the distribution of the referent contacts for which respondents provided more detailed descriptions and evaluations. These frequencies indicate that 61 percent of the referent contacts involve some form of examination of the return. When math errors are included, 79 percent are cases involving the determination of tax liability.

Table 3 compares descriptions and evaluations of IRS performance made by those personally contacted by the IRS with reports by those with vicarious contacts of what they heard about the IRS from other taxpayers. For each group, the first column reports the frequencies of all responses, while the second column eliminates missing values when reporting frequency distributions.

TABLE 2. Respondent Reports of Reasons for Enforcement Contact by the IRS (in percentages)

	Reasons for Contact by IRS	Referent Contact for Follow-up Questions
To audit tax return	22	22
To ask about income IRS thought had not been reported	38	29
To question deductions	22	10
To collect back taxes	34	9
To correct a math error	37	18
Other	19	13

Notes: $N = 177$. Percentages total more than 100 percent because some respondents reported more than one reason for IRS contact.

TABLE 3. Tax Outcomes and Evaluations of IRS Performance, by Type of Enforcement Contact (in percentages)

	Personal Contacts[a]		Vicarious Contacts[b]	
	All Responses	Valid Responses	All Responses	Valid Responses
Financial outcome				
Paid more	47	51	54	64
No change	30	33	21	25
Money back	15	16	10	12
In process/DK	8	—	14	—
Thoroughness of exam				
Looked at all problem areas	59	74	31	76
Overlooked some problem areas	21	26	10	24
DK/Not mentioned	20	—	59	—
Legal correctness				
Taxpayer paid more than legally owed	12	13	22	27
Taxpayer paid less than legally owed	3	3	5	6
Amount about right	77	84	55	67
In process/DK	8	—	17	—
IRS willingness to listen				
Very willing	43	62	16	21
Somewhat willing	16	23	33	41
Somewhat unwilling	3	5	16	20
Very unwilling	7	11	15	19
DK/Not mentioned	30	—	20	—

[a]$N = 177$.
[b]$N = 577$.

The distribution of financial outcomes reported by respondents with personal enforcement contacts seems low relative to IRS national statistics on examination outcomes. Only 51 percent of those with valid responses indicate they paid more taxes, while 33 percent indicate no change, and 16 percent said they got money back. This is likely due to people who paid small amounts of additional taxes classifying themselves in the "no change" category. When outcomes for math errors are examined separately, the results approximate the 50-50 split between receiving refunds and paying more that one would expect for random calculation errors.

Comparisons of personal and vicarious contact experiences suggest that opinions about the fairness of IRS enforcement contacts are more likely to be communicated to other taxpayers than information about detection risks. Almost 60 percent of those with vicarious contacts indicated no mention of the thoroughness of the audit, while only 20 percent of those with personal contacts did not have an opinion. When restricted to valid responses, the distributions of thoroughness evaluations for personal and vicarious reports are virtually identical. About three-fourths indicate the IRS looked at all parts of the return where there might have been problems, while the remaining one-fourth indicate the IRS overlooked some part of the return that was problematic.

For the most part, taxpayers with personal experiences of IRS enforcement contacts favorably rate the fairness of their encounter with the IRS. Of those giving valid responses, 84 percent thought the outcome was legally correct, and only 13 percent thought the IRS got more money from them than it was legally entitled to. Evaluations of procedural fairness were also quite positive; 85 percent of those with valid responses indicate the IRS employees who handled their case were willing to listen to explanations of what happened. One-third of those with personal contacts did not rate willingness to listen, which probably reflects a lack of interaction between themselves and individual IRS employees.

The reports of vicarious contacts present a different picture of IRS fairness. People who negatively evaluate their experience with the IRS appear more likely to tell other taxpayers about it than those with positive or neutral evaluations. Of cases with valid responses, more than one-fourth of the vicarious reports—twice the proportion of personal contacts—involve instances in which the contacted person believed the IRS got more money than it was legally entitled to claim. Even stronger differences occur for ratings of the willingness of IRS employees to listen to taxpayer explanations. About 40 percent of vicarious reports involve assertions that IRS employees were unwilling to listen, compared to only 16 percent for personal contacts. These results indicate the importance of extending the analysis of general (ripple) and specific effects of enforcement to include fairness evaluations as well as sanction perceptions.

Effects of Enforcement

The analysis of enforcement effects begins with a series of parallel OLS analyses of the effects of IRS contacts on five variables tapping key aspects of the Strümpel model. The strategy of this analysis is to begin by testing whether personal and vicarious contacts increase sanction perceptions (the deterrence hypothesis) and decrease fairness perceptions (the alienation hypothesis). In addition, the net effects of contacts on future intentions will be examined. A later analysis will examine the mediating effects of sanction perceptions and fairness perceptions between enforcement contacts and future intentions.

My analysis will begin by examining the effects of a simple dummy variable coding of personal contact experience and the number of vicarious contacts on the dependent variables. It is important, though, to go beyond the sheer fact of enforcement contact to examine whether discrete features of enforcement contacts shape sanction perceptions, evaluations of fairness, and future intentions to cheat. This will be done by constructing dummy variables that classify contacts in terms of their financial outcomes and respondent evaluations of the legal correctness of IRS decisions to assess additional taxes. The deterrence hypothesis would predict that additional tax assessments should increase the perceived certainty of detection, while the alienation hypothesis predicts that beliefs that additional taxes are legally incorrect should decrease evaluations of tax system fairness.

In all analyses, the reference group for dummy variable codings of personal contact experiences will be taxpayers who have not been contacted by the IRS about potential problems with their tax returns. The reference group for dummy variables describing vicarious enforcement experiences will be taxpayers who indicated they did not know anyone who had been contacted by the IRS. In other words, respondents who were personally contacted by the IRS are being compared to those who were not contacted, and those with vicarious enforcement contacts will be compared with those who have not heard about IRS contacts from other people.

Table 4 reports the first part of the analysis, which focuses on the simple fact of personal and vicarious enforcement contacts. These results indicate

TABLE 4. Effects of Enforcement Contacts on Perceived Sanctions, Fairness, and Future Intentions (unstandardized OLS coefficients)

	Exam Certainty	Detection Certainty	Problem if Caught	Fairness of Tax Laws	Likelihood of Future Cheating
Enforcement contact					
Personal contact	.44***	.24**	−.16*	−.10†	−.10**
Vicarious contact	.07**	.05†	.02	−.04**	.00
Admitted past noncompliance					
Underreported income	−.05	−.07	−.01	−.01	.29***
Overstated deductions	.05	−.12*	.00	.02	.30***
Controls					
Legal avoidance effort	.12**	.05	−.03	.01	−.03
Tax information seeking	.17**	.01	.02	−.03	.04
Log income	.20***	−.17***	−.11*	−.06*	−.05*
Opportunity	.14*	−.09	.04	.02	.02
Feel guilty if cheated	.00	.30***	.28***	.05**	−.12***
Female	.00	.15*	.19**	−.13***	−.04
Age	.00	.00	−.09***	−.02	−.04***
R^2	.14	.13	.12	.03	.49

†$p < .10$. *$p < .05$. **$p < .01$. ***$p < .001$.

that both personal and vicarious enforcement contacts increase the perceived likelihood of examination by the IRS and, to a lesser degree, the perceived certainty of detection for noncompliance. The results also show a tendency for personal contacts to somewhat decrease taxpayer perceptions of fairness, but this effect is only of borderline significance. The results for future intentions indicate that the net effect of personal contact experiences is greater anticipated compliance with the law.

These results suggest that personal enforcement contacts primarily have a deterrent effect, with only weak evidence of alienation from the tax system. The results for vicarious contacts, in contrast, indicate greater support for the alienation hypothesis of enforcement effects than for deterrence effects. The effect of vicarious contacts on detection certainty are of only borderline significance, and vicarious contacts significantly lower the perceived fairness of tax laws. Vicarious contacts, however, do not in and of themselves affect future intentions of noncompliance.

The results shown in table 4 also suggest experiential effects for both the perceived certainty of detection and the perceived severity of sanctions. Respondents with personal contacts are less likely than those not contacted to believe it would be a problem if the IRS detected noncompliance on their returns. Likewise, the effects of personal contacts on perceived certainty are weaker for both personal and vicarious contact experiences than those observed for the likelihood of examination. Furthermore, self-reports of past overstated deductions have significant negative effects on detection certainty, even though they have a nonsignificant, positive effect on examination likelihood.

Table 5 shows the results of analyses examining whether the financial outcomes of personal and vicarious enforcement experiences affect the five dependent variables. Fifteen cases of personal contacts are coded as missing values for this analysis because enforcement outcomes were still unresolved or the respondent did not remember the outcome. The results shown in table 5 indicate that the negative effects of vicarious contacts on fairness perceptions are concentrated among those respondents who have talked with taxpayers who paid more taxes. A borderline significant trend for the opposite effect is observed for personal contacts. Those who did not pay more tend to have lower fairness perceptions, perhaps reflecting annoyance at having to convince the IRS that their returns were compliant.

The financial outcomes of personal contacts do not condition the previously observed experiential effect for perceived severity. Results from qualitative interviews suggest the experiential effect for perceived severity may be concentrated among taxpayers undergoing their first enforcement contact. Auditors and tax practitioners report that people are often nervous and scared initially, but end up finding the experience less intimidating than expected.

TABLE 5. Effects of Enforcement Contact, by Financial Outcome (unstandardized OLS coefficients)

	Exam Certainty	Detection Certainty	Problem if Caught	Fairness of Tax Laws	Likelihood of Future Cheating
Outcome of personal contact					
Paid more	.43***	.36**	−.18	−.08	−.17**
Did not pay more	.41***	.15	−.15	−.13†	−.03
Outcome of vicarious contact					
Other taxpayer paid more	.09	.09	.04	−.12**	:04
Other did not pay more	.11	.09	.08	−.05	.00
Outcome unknown	.07	−.05	.02	.03	−.07
Admitted past noncompliance					
Underreported income	−.05	−.08*	−.02	.00	.29***
Overstated deductions	.05	−.10*	.00	.02	.30***
Controls					
Legal avoidance effort	.12**	.06	−.03	.01	−.03
Tax information seeking	.19**	.00	.01	−.03	.03
Log income	.21***	−.16***	−.11*	−.06	−.05*
Opportunity	.14*	−.07	.04	.02	.03
Feel guilty if cheated	.00	.30***	.28***	.06**	−.12***
Female	.00	.14*	.18**	−.13***	−.04
Age	.00	.00	−.09***	−.02	−.04***
R^2	.13	.14	.12	.02	.48

†$p < .10$. *$p < .05$. **$p < .01$. ***$p < .001$.

The survey questionnaire did not ask about earlier contacts, so it is not possible to test this hypothesis directly. However, it is consistent with the finding that older respondents perceive fewer problems, since older respondents are more likely to be repeat players with previous enforcement contacts.

Several pieces of evidence in the Minnesota data suggest substantial experiential effects among contacted taxpayers for the perceived certainty of detection. To begin, admitted past noncompliers are no more likely to pay additional taxes than respondents who deny noncompliance. The zero-order correlation between paying more taxes and past underreporting of income is only .05 for respondents with personal contacts, while that for overstating deductions is −.06.[4] In addition, as table 5 shows, admissions of past noncompliance have significant negative effects on current perceptions of detection certainty. Moreover, contact outcomes show a different pattern of effects for perceived certainty of detection than for perceived likelihood of examina-

4. These results replicate those of two previous studies that found low to nonexistent correlations between self-reports of noncompliance and the financial outcomes of tax enforcement contacts (see Hessing, Elffers, and Weigel 1988; Kinsey 1988).

tion. Those who paid more taxes and those who did not are equally likely to expect future examination of their tax returns. But only those assessed additional taxes by the IRS perceive a higher likelihood that any noncompliance would be detected. Not surprisingly, these respondents are also more likely to plan to file fully compliant returns in the future.

If past tax cheaters have indeed escaped detection, then admissions of past noncompliance should interact with contact outcomes to shape the perceived certainty of detection. This hypothesis was tested in two ANCOVA analyses, one that included a single measure of past noncompliance and another that included separate measures for overstating deductions and underreporting income. In these analyses, admissions of noncompliance are dichotomized according to whether the respondent completely denies past noncompliance or admits even a remote possibility of having failed to comply. By this standard, 30 percent of the respondents are classified as possibly noncompliant for income reporting, 32 percent are classified as possibly noncompliant on deduction claims, and 44 percent are classified as possibly noncompliant for both measures. The covariates in the analysis include vicarious contact experiences as well as control variables.

When the combined measure is used, past noncompliance interacts with personal contact outcomes to shape the perceived certainty of detection ($F = 3.932$, $p < .05$). The results of the analysis with the two separate noncompliance measures indicates that overstating deductions dominates this effect, although its interaction term with financial outcomes reaches only a borderline level of significance ($F = 3.307$, $p < .08$). Table 6 describes the

TABLE 6. Effects of Personal Contacts on Perceived Certainty of Detection by Past Admitted Noncompliance

	Fully Compliant	Admits Only Underreporting	Admits Only Overstating	Admits Both Types
Correlation of financial outcome with detection certainty	−.07	.19	.50**	.30*
N	69	26	22	42
Mean detection certainty by contact status				
Contacted, paid more	3.28	3.07	3.27	3.03
N	30	17	12	22
Contacted, did not pay more	3.39	2.69	2.25	2.45
N	39	9	10	20
Not contacted by IRS	3.05	2.90	2.87	2.70
N	563	119	148	156

$^{*}p < .05$. $^{**}p < .01$.

nature of the interactions in more detail, with respondents classified according to whether they admit both, either, or neither of the two types of past noncompliance. As the first part of the table shows, the dummy variable for paying more taxes is significantly related to perceived detection certainty only for the two categories involving admissions of overstating deductions.

The lower panel of table 6 presents the average perceived certainty of detection for all respondents, classified by admitted past noncompliance and personal enforcement contact status. These results reveal both deterrence and experiential effects among taxpayers admitting past noncompliance. In all three categories of past noncompliance, taxpayers assessed additional taxes had higher sanction perceptions than uncontacted taxpayers, while those who were not assessed more taxes had lower sanction perceptions than uncontacted taxpayers. The strongest deterrent effect, but also the strongest experiential effect, occurs among taxpayers who admit past overstated deductions but not underreported income. No evidence of experiential effects is found among fully compliant taxpayers; for these respondents, IRS enforcement contacts increase the perceived likelihood of detection regardless of whether the respondent paid more taxes.

Table 7 shows a further expansion of the analysis of enforcement contacts by subdividing outcomes involving the payment of additional taxes by whether the respondent believes the IRS was legally entitled to the additional taxes resulting from the contact. Even though the number of cases (19) involving personal contacts is small, it is apparent that the difference in the perceived legal correctness of personal contact outcomes does not alter the conclusions of earlier analyses. Taxpayers contacted by the IRS are less likely to plan future noncompliance even when they paid additional taxes that they believe were incorrectly assessed by the IRS.

The results for vicarious enforcement contacts are quite different. Taxpayer beliefs that the IRS forces others to pay more than they legally owe not only decrease the perceived fairness of tax laws, but also increase future intentions to cheat on taxes. Although those hearing assertions of unfair IRS treatment perceive a higher likelihood that the IRS will examine their own returns, this does not translate into significantly greater perceptions of detection certainty. Further analysis suggests these respondents may have a reasonable basis for believing they can escape detection in the face of higher exam likelihoods: the effects of vicarious reports of incorrect tax assessments on future intentions are concentrated almost entirely among taxpayers with opportunities to escape detection for underreporting income.

The previous analyses demonstrate at least partial support for the deterrence and alienation hypotheses of enforcement effects predicted by Strümpel. However, the analysis of future intentions thus far has not provided a complete test of the model. Strümpel predicts not only that enforcement contacts

TABLE 7. Effects of Enforcement Contact by Financial Outcome and Perceived Legality (unstandardized OLS coefficients)

	Exam Certainty	Detection Certainty	Problem if Caught	Fairness of Tax Laws	Likelihood of Future Cheating
Personal contact					
Paid more than legally owed[a]	.27	.41†	−.19	−.20	−.19†
Paid right amount/less/DK	.46***	.35**	−.19	−.04	−.17**
Did not pay more	.40***	.15	−.16	−.05	−.05
Vicarious contact					
Other paid more than legally owed	.20*	.06	.17†	−.26***	.14**
Other paid right amount/less/DK	.04	.10	−.03	−.06	.00
Other did not pay more	.12	.09	.08	−.11	.00
Outcome unknown	.07	−.05	.02	−.07	.03
Admitted past noncompliance					
Underreported income	.06	−.08*	−.02	.00	.29***
Overstated deductions	.05	−.10*	.00	.02	.29***
Controls					
Legal avoidance effort	.12**	.06	−.02	.00	−.03
Tax information seeking	.19**	.00	.02	−.03	.04
Log income	.21***	−.16***	−.12*	−.05	−.05*
Opportunity	.14*	−.07	.04	.02	.03
Feel guilty if cheated	.01	.30***	.28***	.12**	−.06**
Female	.00	.14*	.18**	−.13***	−.04
Age	.00	.00	−.09***	−.03*	−.04***
R^2	.13	.14	.12	.03	.49

[a]$N = 19$.
†$p < .10$. *$p < .05$. **$p < .01$. ***$p < .001$.

will shape sanction and fairness perceptions, but also that these perceptions, in turn, will affect future behavior. It is at this point that the model runs into some trouble. When the perceptual variables are included in the equation for future intentions, the results for the enforcement contact variables remain unchanged, and the sanction and fairness perception variables show null effects on future intentions.

The lack of mediating effects of fairness perceptions is likely due to problems of measurement. The fairness questions asked of all respondents do not focus specifically on tax law enforcement. Instead, these questions ask for general evaluations of the fairness of tax laws, when questions focusing on the perceived fairness of the IRS's enforcement of tax laws would have been more appropriate for this analysis. The question on legal correctness, in contrast, focuses specifically on evaluations of the IRS's performance. It is not surprising that this question, asked only of those reporting contacts, has direct effects on future intentions rather than being mediated by the general fairness questions asked of all respondents.

The lack of mediating effects of sanction perceptions between the financial outcomes of enforcement and future noncompliance intentions is more troublesome. It suggests the possibility that other mechanisms, such as education, may account for the effects of contact outcomes on future intentions. However, simply adding sanction perceptions to the equation of future intentions fails to take into account substantial differences in the initial vantage points of different taxpayers. Other essays in this volume note that enforcement variables have little effect on the compliance attitudes and behaviors of honest taxpayers. Increasing the sanction perceptions of compliers can only reinforce, not change, prior standing decisions to comply with the law (see Carroll 1987). This suggests that any effects of sanction perceptions on future intentions will occur primarily among respondents admitting past noncompliance.

Table 8 reports the results of separate analyses, for admitted past compliers and noncompliers, of the mediating effects of sanction perceptions between enforcement experiences and future intentions. In addition, another analysis (not reported in table 8) included interaction terms of past noncompliance with each independent variable to test if observed differences in effect sizes between compliers and noncompliers are statistically significant.

The results shown in table 8 indicate that the effects of enforcement contacts are concentrated among those admitting past noncompliance. Furthermore, the results indicate that the effects of IRS enforcement reflect the operation of specific deterrence more than experiential learning effects. In the first equation for noncompliance, which excludes sanction perceptions and general fairness evaluations, the results show that past noncompliers who are assessed more taxes by the IRS plan to comply more in the future. In contrast, those who did not pay more taxes do not evidence any changes in the likelihood of future cheating. This suggests that successful enforcement efforts by the IRS deter future noncompliance among previously noncompliant taxpayers, while unsuccessful enforcement mainly reinforces the prior standing decision of tax cheaters to not comply.[5]

The results of the second equation, which includes the sanction perception and general fairness measures, also point to a deterrence explanation of enforcement contact effects. Once sanction perceptions are added, the effect of paying more taxes on future intentions drops to nonsignificance, while

5. This analysis, however, focuses only on the likelihood of future noncompliance and does not test the effects of sanction perceptions on the frequency or dollar amounts that might be involved in future noncompliance.

TABLE 8. Effects of Perceptual Variables on Future Intentions by Admitted Past Noncompliance (unstandardized OLS coefficients)

	Denies Past Noncompliance		Admits Past Noncompliance	
	Equation 1	Equation 2	Equation 1[a]	Equation 2[a]
Personal contact				
Paid more	−.02	−.03	−.19*	−.16
Did not pay more	−.03	−.03	.02	.02
Vicarious contact				
Other paid more than legally owed	.14**	.15**	.25*	.28**
Other paid right amount/less/DK	.03	.02	.04	.04
Other did not pay more	.00	.01	.00	.00
Outcome unknown	.00	−.01	−.16	−.16
Controls				
Legal avoidance effort	−.02	−.02	−.02	−.02
Tax information seeking	.02	.02	.08	.08
Log income	−.02	−.02	−.05	−.06
Opportunity	−.01	−.02	.29***	.28***
Feel guilty if cheated	−.08***	−.08***	−.21***	−.19***
Female	−.02	−.02	−.11†	−.09
Age	−.03**	−.03**	−.10***	−.10***
Perceptions				
Exam certainty	—	.00	—	.00
Detection certainty	—	.01	—	−.08*
Problem if caught	—	−.01	—	.00
Fairness of tax laws	—	.03	—	.05
R^2	.06	.06	.22	.23

[a]Equation 1 excludes and Equation 2 includes sanction perceptions and general fairness evaluations.
†$p < .10$. *$p < .05$. **$p < .01$. ***$p < .001$.

perceptions of detection certainty significantly affect future intentions. The results of the interaction analysis indicate the observed differences between past compliers and noncompliers in the effects of perceived certainty on future intentions are statistically significant ($t = -2.698$, $p < .001$). Even though enforcement contacts increase exam certainty and lower perceived severity, neither exam certainty nor severity affect future intentions of noncompliance.

The results for compliers also indicate that neither personal enforcement contacts nor sanction perceptions affect the compliance intentions of those who deny past noncompliance. Honest taxpayers also appear unresponsive to the temptations of opportunity, even though opportunity is strongly related to future intentions among admitted past cheaters. The differences in opportunity effects between past compliers and noncompliers is statistically significant ($t = 4.392$, $p < .0001$), as are the observed differences in the effects of age ($t =$

$-.3.169$, $p < .01$) and guilt feelings ($t = -3.474$, $p < .001$). The strong effect of guilt on future intentions among past noncompliers provides support for the argument that noncompliance sometimes involves the short-term neutralization of internalized norms and values (see n. 3).

The effects for vicarious reports of unfair tax assessments indicate that support for the alienation hypothesis occurs among those who deny past noncompliance as well as those admitting past acts of noncompliance. The results among past noncompliers appear somewhat stronger, but the difference in effects is not statistically significant. These results indicate that the diffusion among the general population of stories about unfair IRS enforcement may influence previously honest taxpayers to join the ranks of noncompliers.

Discussion

The results of my study suggest support for both elements of Strümpel's model among individual taxpayers. The results, however, also suggest different routes for each of the basic elements of the model. Deterrence effects appear to be specific in nature and heavily dependent on the effectiveness of the IRS in actually detecting noncompliance. Previously noncompliant respondents who have personally paid additional taxes as a consequence of an IRS enforcement contact not only perceive a greater certainty of detection, but also are more likely to intend to comply on future returns. Previously noncompliant taxpayers who are not assessed additional taxes lower their perceptions of certainty and plan to continue past habits of noncompliance.

Restricting the analysis to only enforcement contacts involving the examination of returns does not materially change the pattern of results or conclusions of the more inclusive analysis. Further analysis, though, suggests that specific deterrent effects are concentrated among respondents contacted by the IRS about underreported income. In that analysis, dummy codes for the reasons for IRS contact were substituted for the personal contact variable. The results indicate that contacts about underreported income increase the perceived certainty of detection and decrease the likelihood of future noncompliance. Contacts involving audits or the documentation of deductions, in contrast, have no effect on either the perceived certainty of detection or future intentions.

These and other results suggest that the IRS is more successful at detecting unreported income than overstated deductions. While unreported income is difficult to detect, both the IRS and tax researchers have been able to use information about the taxpayer's occupation, work setting, and major sources of income as reasonably effective guides for identifying where unreported income is most likely to be found. Fewer guideposts are available for deductions, and the necessity of relying on the taxpayer's own records to substantiate most deductions may even produce perverse outcomes during enforcement contacts. People who will lie on a tax return would not likely hesitate to fabricate false or misleading documentation to avoid additional assessments by IRS enforcers examining their return. On the other hand, reasonably honest people may sometimes "guesstimate" their deductible expenses, but are less likely to submit fraudulent documentation to the IRS to substantiate those claims.

While the net effects of personal IRS contacts appear to be improved compliance, the results for vicarious contacts suggest little support for general deterrence effects. Instead, taxpayers appear to hear from other taxpayers more about the fairness of enforcement contacts than the IRS's effectiveness in detecting noncompliance. Moreover, respondents hearing vicarious reports are more likely to hear stories about arbitrary decisions or rude treatment than evaluations by respondents of their own contacts with the IRS would suggest. Hearing such reports of apparently unjust law enforcement lowers the perceived fairness of income tax laws and increases future intentions of noncompliance. These effects are concentrated among individuals who have opportunities to cheat on their taxes and escape detection.

Why do vicarious reports show alienation effects, even though most taxpayers are satisfied with their own contact experiences? And why is there so little support for general deterrence when there is fairly clear support for specific deterrence? It is likely that several factors serve to bias the transmission of information about tax enforcement away from the subject of enforcement effectiveness and toward fairness judgments.[6] First, the minority of taxpayers who think the IRS treated them unfairly may vent their anger by talking in more detail and to more people than taxpayers who evaluate the IRS's performance more favorably. In addition, taxpayers who agree with IRS assertions that their tax returns were noncompliant may be reluctant or feel ashamed to talk about the results of their contacts with others. If they do talk about the contact, they may attempt to save face and minimize their own culpability by criticizing the IRS's performance. The result would be that information about IRS effectiveness and fairness in detecting noncompliance either stops with the taxpayer involved or becomes distorted, while information about apparent injustices is communicated more readily.

6. It should be noted that just-world theory offers a different perspective than the one discussed here on the direction of biases in fairness evaluations. Lerner (1980) argues that most people tend to discount information that would otherwise lead them to perceive themselves as victims of injustice. This perspective suggests that the personal contact reports underestimate actual levels of IRS misconduct in administrating tax laws. There is some evidence, however, that the assumptions of just-world theory may not apply to the federal income tax system. In most surveys, large majorities of respondents routinely evaluate their personal tax burdens as distributively unfair (see Kinsey, Grasmick, and Smith, in press).

In addition, the legally mandated confidentiality of most income tax violations means that tax officials cannot release or publicize the results of routine tax cases the way police departments can regarding such routine violations as drunk driving and shoplifting. This eliminates an important mechanism for transmitting information about enforcement effectiveness, and (in effect) leaves detected noncompliers with almost complete control over who will find out about their enforcement contact and what they will hear (see Kinsey 1986). This also means that the IRS may be unable to state its side of the story in cases where taxpayers go public with accusations of agency misconduct in the handling of their cases.

The selective nature of information communicated about the IRS in vicarious reports and the effects of negative reports on the future intentions of other taxpayers are particularly sobering. Taxpayers are more likely to hear vicarious accounts of enforcement contacts by the IRS than to be contacted personally. This suggests the possibility that, in the aggregate, the alienating effects of vicarious reports about IRS enforcement generate more acts of noncompliance than personal contacts deter. This possibility merits closer examination in future studies of the effects of IRS enforcement efforts.

REFERENCES

Bardach, E., and R. Kagan. 1982. *Going by the Book: The Problem of Regulatory Unreasonableness.* Philadelphia: Temple University Press.

Blumstein, A., J. Cohen, and D. Nagin, eds. 1978. *Deterrence and Incapacitation: Estimating the Effects of Criminal Sanctions on Crime Rates.* Washington, D.C.: National Academy of Sciences.

Braithwaite, J. 1985. *To Punish or Persuade? The Enforcement of Coal Mine Safety.* Albany: State University of New York Press.

Carroll, J. S. 1987. "Compliance with the Law: A Decision-Making Approach to Taxpaying." *Law and Human Behavior* 11:319–35.

Crane, S. E., and F. Nourzad. 1985. "Time Value of Money and Income Tax Evasion under Risk-Averse Behavior: Theoretical Analysis and Empirical Evidence." *Public Finance* 3:381–94.

Crane, S. E., and F. Nourzad. 1987. "On the Treatment of Income Tax Rates in Empirical Analysis of Tax Evasion." *Kyklos* 40:338–48.

Dubin, J. A., M. J. Graetz, and L. L. Wilde. 1987. "The Effect of Tax and Audit Rates on Compliance with the Federal Income Tax, 1977–85." Social Science Working Paper no. 638. California Institute of Technology. Photocopy.

Geerken, M. R., and W. R. Gove. 1975. "Deterrence: Some Theoretical Considerations." *Law and Society Review* 9:497–513.

Graetz, M. J., J. F. Reinganum, and L. L. Wilde. 1986. "The Tax Compliance Game: Toward an Interactive Theory of Law Enforcement." *Journal of Law, Economics, and Organization* 2:1–32.

Graetz, M. J., and L. L. Wilde. 1985. "The Economics of Tax Compliance: Fact and Fantasy." *National Tax Journal* 38:355–63.

Grasmick, H. G., and R. J. Bursik, Jr. 1990. "Conscience, Significant Others, and Rational Choice: Extending the Deterrence Model." *Law and Society Review* 24:837–62.

Grasmick, H. G., N. J. Finlay, and D. L. Glaser. 1984. "Labor Force Participation, Sex Role Attitudes, and Female Crime: Evidence from a Survey of Adults." *Social Science Quarterly* 65:703–18.

Harris, Louis, and Associates, Inc. 1987. *Taxpayer Survey.* Washington, D.C.: Internal Revenue Service.

Hawkins, K. 1984. *Environment and Enforcement: Regulation and the Social Definition of Pollution.* Oxford: Clarendon Press.

Hessing, D. J., H. Elffers, and R. H. Weigel. 1988. "Exploring the Limits of Self-Reports and Reasoned Action: An Investigation of the Psychology of Tax Evasion Behavior." *Journal of Personality and Social Psychology* 54:405–18.

Internal Revenue Service. 1987. *Internal Revenue Service Annual Report, 1987.* Washington, D.C.: Internal Revenue Service.

Katz, D., B. A. Gutek, R. L. Kahn, and E. Barton. 1975. *Bureaucratic Encounters.* Ann Arbor, Mich.: Survey Research Center, Institute for Social Research.

Kinsey, K. A. 1986. "Theories and Models of Tax Cheating." *Criminal Justice Abstracts* 18:403–85.

Kinsey, K. A. 1988. "Measurement Bias or Honest Disagreement? Problems of Validating Measures of Tax Evasion." American Bar Foundation Working Paper no. 8810. Chicago: American Bar Foundation.

Kinsey, K. A., H. G. Grasmick, and K. W. Smith (in press). "Framing Justice: Taxpayer Evaluations of Personal Tax Burdens." *Law and Society Review,* forthcoming.

Klepper, S., and D. Nagin. 1989a. "The Anatomy of Tax Evasion." *Journal of Law, Economics, and Organizations* 5:1–24.

Klepper, S., and D. Nagin. 1989b. "The Criminal Deterrence Literature: Implications for Research on Taxpayer Compliance." In *Taxpayer Compliance: Social Science Perspectives,* ed. J. Roth and J. Scholz, 126–155. Philadelphia: University of Pennsylvania Press.

Klepper, S., and D. Nagin. 1989c. "Tax Compliance and Perceptions of the Risks of Detection and Criminal Prosecution." *Law and Society Review* 23:209–40.

Lerner, M. J. 1980. *The Belief in a Just World: A Fundamental Delusion.* New York: Plenum Press.

Levi, M. 1988. *Of Rule and Revenue.* Berkeley: University of California Press.

Lind, E. A., and T. R. Tyler. 1988. *The Social Psychology of Procedural Justice.* New York: Plenum Press.

Long, S. B. 1981. "Social Control in the Civil Law: The Case of Income Tax Enforcement." In *Law and Deviance,* ed. H. L. Ross, 185–214. Beverly Hills: Sage.

Long, S. B., and J. A. Swingen. 1989. "The Role of Legal Complexity in Shaping Taxpayer Compliance." In *Lawyers on Psychology and Psychologists on Law,* ed. P. Koppen and D. J. Hessing, 127–46. Amsterdam: Swets and Seitlinger.

Long, S., and J. Swingen. 1988. "Complexity, Opportunity, and Compliance." Paper presented at the annual meeting of the Law and Society Association, Vail, Colo.

Mason, R. 1987. "A Communication Model of Taxpayer Honesty." *Law and Policy* 9:246–58.

Mason, R. G., and L. D. Calvin. 1984. "Public Confidence and Admitted Tax Evasion." *National Tax Journal* 47:489–96.

McGraw, K. M. 1989. "The Influence of Fairness and Outcomes on Evaluations of Tax Experience." Paper presented at the annual meeting of the Law and Society Association, Madison, Wis.

Nagin, D. 1978. "General Deterrence: A Review of the Empirical Evidence." In *Deterrence and Incapacitation: Estimating the Effects of Criminal Sanctions on Crime Rates,* ed. A. Blumstein, J. Cohen, and D. Nagin, 95–139. Washington, D.C.: National Academy of Science.

Paternoster, R., L. E. Saltzman, G. P. Waldo, and T. G. Chiricos. 1982. "Causal Ordering in Deterrence Research: An Examination of the Perceptions-Behavior Relationship." In *Deterrence Reconsidered,* ed. J. Hagan, 55–70. Beverly Hills: Sage.

Paternoster, R., L. E. Saltzman, G. P. Waldo, and T. G. Chiricos. 1983. "Perceived Risk and Social Control: Do Sanctions Really Deter?" *Law and Society Review* 17:457–79.

Roth, J. A., J. T. Scholz, and A. D. Witte. 1989. *Taxpayer Compliance,* vol. 1, *An Agenda for Research.* Philadelphia: University of Pennsylvania Press.

Scholz, J. T. 1984. "Voluntary Compliance and Regulatory Enforcement." *Law and Policy* 6:385–404.

Scott, W. J., and H. G. Grasmick. 1981. "Deterrence and Income Tax Cheating: Testing Interaction Hypotheses in Utilitarian Theories." *Journal of Applied Behavioral Science* 17:395–408.

Slemrod, J., and N. Sorum. 1984. "The Compliance Cost of the U.S. Individual Income Tax System." *National Tax Journal* 37:461–74.

Smith, K. W. 1990. "Integrating Three Perspectives on Noncompliance: A Sequential Decision Model." *Criminal Justice and Behavior* 17:350–69.

Smith, K. W., and K. A. Kinsey. 1985. "Cooperation and Control: Strategies and Tactics for Tax Examination." *Tax Administration Review* 2:13–30.

Smith, K. W., and K. A. Kinsey. 1987. "Understanding Taxpaying Behavior: A Conceptual Framework with Implications for Research." *Law and Society Review* 21:639–63.

Spicer, M. W., and S. B. Lundstedt. 1976. "Understanding Tax Evasion." *Public Finance* 31:295–305.

Stalans, L. J., K. A. Kinsey, and K. W. Smith. 1991. "Listening to Different Voices: Formation of Sanction Beliefs and Taxpaying Norms." *Journal of Applied Social Psychology* 21(2):119–38.

Stalans, L. J., K. W. Smith, and K. A. Kinsey. 1989. "When Do We Think about Detection? Structural Opportunity and Taxpaying Behavior." *Law and Social Inquiry* 14:481–503.

Strümpel, B. 1969. "The Contribution of Survey Research to Public Finance." In

Quantitative Analysis in Public Finance, ed. A. T. Peacock, 13–32. New York: Praeger.

Thurman, Q. C., C. St. John, and L. Riggs. 1984. "Neutralization and the Tax Evasion Decision: How Effective Would a Moral Appeal Be in Improving Compliance with Tax Laws?" *Law and Policy* 6:309–27.

Tittle, Charles R. 1980. *Sanctions and Social Deviance: The Question of Deterrence.* New York: Praeger.

Tyler, T. R. 1990. *Why People Obey the Law.* New Haven: Yale University Press.

Tyler, T. R., J. D. Casper, and B. Fisher. 1989. "Maintaining Allegiance toward Political Authorities: The Role of Prior Attitudes and thc Use of Fair Procedures." *American Journal of Political Science* 33:612–28.

Warneryd, K. E., and B. Walerud. 1982. "Taxes and Economic Behavior: Some Interview Data on Tax Evasion in Sweden." *Journal of Economic Psychology* 2:187–211.

Witte, A. D., and D. F. Woodbury. 1985. "The Effect of Tax Laws and Tax Administration on Tax Compliance: The Case of the U.S. Individual Income Tax." *National Tax Journal* 38:1–13.

Commentary

Alan H. Plumley

I should preface my remarks by owning up to one of my biases: I do not put much stock in opinion surveys, especially ones that try to get honest answers from people about their *behavior,* especially about their *future* behavior, especially when the questions ask about possible *illegal* behavior, especially when the respondents could reasonably believe that their participation is not *anonymous,* especially when 29 percent of those contacted choose not to participate. Indeed, in her essay, Kinsey cited evidence that taxpayers' admissions of their noncompliance do not correspond well with official determinations. I am not surprised. Nor did the essay change my bias. Having said that, however, I must admit that Kinsey does make useful observations and poses useful questions about the indirect effect of IRS enforcement activities. In my discussion, I will highlight what I consider to be the most important of these and point out some possible problems and alternate interpretations of the data and results.

First, I think the survey and Kinsey's analysis are very clever in separating the two components of what we in the IRS refer to as the "indirect effect" of enforcement: (1) the change in voluntary compliance exhibited in subsequent years by those who *have* been contacted for enforcement purposes (which we call the "subsequent-year effect," as in the Erard essay, and which Kinsey calls the "specific effects" of "personal contact"); and (2) the change in voluntary compliance exhibited by those who have *not* been contacted directly, but who form perceptions of the likelihood and severity of enforcement through indirect means—such as from others who *have* been contacted directly. We call this the "ripple effect," and Kinsey calls it the "general effect" of "vicarious contact."

This brings to mind a recurring problem. It often gets confusing when people use different terms for the same thing or mean different things by the same word or expression—an inevitable problem when people from several disciplines discuss the same issues from different perspectives or traditions. I suggest that we develop a common vocabulary for discussing these concepts. As a first step to help standardize some of our terminology, we included a fairly exhaustive glossary of compliance and enforcement terms in a report we recently published (Publication 1501, *Evaluation of the IRS System of Projecting Enforcement Revenue*). If this helps the rest of the research community, we would be pleased. If any of you would like to add to this glossary or rephrase any of the current listings, we would be happy to hear from you.

Back to the study's design. I believe that the American Bar Foundation's survey was better than Kinsey acknowledges. She suggests that, "ideally, the question of enforcement effects would be studied using a research design in which tax returns are assigned randomly to enforcement contact and control group conditions." I think not. We do not want to know how taxpayers respond to *random* enforcement contacts; we want to know how they respond to the *actual* enforcement environment. In that environment, taxpayers are not selected randomly, but because the IRS believes it very likely that they have been noncompliant. This is a significant distinction if deterrence plays any role at all in taxpayers' thinking; taxpayers are assumed to respond to their perceived risk of getting caught and facing some perceived set of consequences. Therefore, if we were to perform a controlled experiment that is relevant to the actual enforcement environment, it could not be based on a random sample of returns from the entire population; it would have to be representative of those who are actually contacted (i.e., those who the IRS believes are the most noncompliant). The control group would also have to be representative of that subpopulation (in order to control for perceptions of the likelihood of being audited). In fact, the "test" in such a design would not be the enforcement contact itself (since that is common to all returns in the subpopulation), but rather the *lack* of such a contact. This forgoing of typical enforcement opportunities is what makes such a study infeasible, or at least inadvisable. The ABF survey avoided this problem by taking a random sample from the population and collecting data on enforcement contacts that had *already* taken place. By statistically controlling for various potential differences between those contacted by the IRS and those who were not, Kinsey's study is much more appropriate than any controlled experiment.

The most useful aspect of the survey, however, was that it also asked questions about "vicarious" enforcement contacts—getting at the "ripple effect." By making this distinction, Kinsey's results suggest that while both personal and vicarious contacts increase taxpayers' certainty of being examined in the future and their certainty that noncompliance will be detected, both of these effects are much stronger for the personal contact, as one might expect. However, the results suggest that while there is a modest positive subsequent-year effect (i.e., personal contacts improve compliance by lowering one's likelihood of future cheating), there is *no* discernible ripple effect overall—the only significant exception to this being a *negative* ripple effect (i.e., an *increase* in the likelihood of future cheating) when the vicarious contact resulted in the other taxpayer paying more than he or she thought he or she legally owed. Given the fact that empirical evidence is accumulating from other studies (such as Beron, Tauchen, and Witte in this volume) that there is a *positive* ripple effect, I attribute the results here to the weaknesses of the opinion data. Even if the subsequent-year effect is more pronounced than the ripple effect for the typical taxpayer, the importance of the ripple effect is that it presumably is exhibited by many *more* taxpayers (because the vicarious contacts are multiplied), perhaps resulting in a greater impact in the aggregate.

Two other significant findings do seem believable, but have unequal importance. First, the reported likelihood of future noncompliance seems to be determined most by admissions of past noncompliance. This seems believable both because people are not likely to change their behavior too quickly and because those who say they are likely to "cheat" in the future are likely to be the very same ones who are willing to admit to past noncompliance. Although this finding is significant, it seems not to be very important. In contrast, the finding that personal enforcement contacts have the effect of reducing one's fear of the consequences of future contacts does seem important. Kinsey speculates—correctly, I think—that much of the fear that taxpayers have about the IRS is unwarranted, and that many of them realize that after experiencing an enforcement contact. Survey and anecdotal evidence suggests that what taxpayers fear most about the prospect of being audited is the audit experience itself—not the financial consequences. Perhaps this is reflected in these results. It may also help explain the seemingly counterintuitive result that this reduction in fear is not accompanied by a greater willingness to be noncompliant. (Alternatively, it may be that this tendency is not observed because it is overwhelmed by the deterrent effect of an increased certainty of being contacted and of having noncompliance found when contacted.)

By the way, this latter finding—that the net effect of enforcement contacts is to *increase* a taxpayer's certainty of having noncompliance detected—raises some interesting issues. Some have speculated that audits would have the *opposite* effect—an experiential effect—since the experience would alert taxpayers to the fact that examiners are not omniscient and cannot detect all noncompliance. I think one reason that the deterrence effect predominates here is that the enforcement contacts experienced by those in the sample are mostly not audits in the usual sense; in fact, fewer than one-fourth were audits. Contacts arising from the matching of information documents or from math error checking have a much higher likelihood of detecting the noncompliance or errors at which they are targeted. It is not too surprising that these respondents perceived a greater likelihood of detection, now that they have been contacted. But it would not be appropriate, in my opinion, to generalize this finding to audits—at least not on the basis of this analysis. An additional reason for this caution is that taxpayers who realize that their audit did not detect significant amounts of noncompliance will probably not be as honest about the IRS's detection capabilities as those whose noncompliance was completely detected. This is another example of the weaknesses of behavioral surveys.

Remembering that the enforcement contacts represented in the sample are generally not audits helps us to understand another finding, I believe. One of the significant results highlighted in table 1 is that enforcement contacts are significantly related to underreporting income, but not to overstating deductions. I believe that this is mostly attributable to the large number of respondents who had been contacted by the document matching program concerning underreported income specifically. The results Kinsey obtained (not tabulated) when she included dummy codes for the reasons for IRS contact corroborate my conclusion. Since contacts about underreported income mostly arise from the document-matching program (which is very effective in identifying noncompliance), it is not surprising to find that these contacts increase the perceived certainty of detection and decrease the likelihood of future noncompliance. We should not infer from this, however, that traditional audits are equally effective deterrents with respect to unreported income. Audits are much more effective at detecting overstated deductions than underreported income. It is simple to question a deduction, placing the burden of proof on the taxpayer. It is much harder for an auditor to track down evidence of unreported income, where the burden of proof is on the auditor. I do not believe that very many taxpayers falsify documentation in order to justify their overstated deductions during an audit; such blatant fraud would not be too hard to detect. Rather, I believe that most taxpayers who overstate their deductions simply stretch the truth as they file their returns, hoping they will not be audited. This is an interesting controversy, however, and I hope that further research sheds more light on the relative frequency and magnitudes of these two forms of noncompliance.

Finally, I would like to offer some general suggestions concerning the analysis and presentation. First, it would have been more helpful to have had more information about the types of analysis and actual model specifications—even if in an appendix. Also, it seems to me that, for some of the analyses, it would have been appropriate to check for possible endogeneity of some of the explanatory variables. For example, legal avoidance and tax information seeking are probably influenced by one's certainty of being examined just as much as they help to explain that certainty.

All in all, however, I feel that the survey and Kinsey's essay have made useful contributions to our understanding of the impact of enforcement contacts on voluntary compliance. Chief among them, perhaps, is the effort to separate the two components of the indirect effect of enforcement: the ripple effect and the subsequent-year effect. My main reservation is that the data are probably too biased to support convincing results.

Does Deterrence Deter? Measuring the Effect of Deterrence on Tax Compliance in Field Studies and Experimental Studies

Dick J. Hessing, Henk Elffers, Henry S. J. Robben, and Paul Webley

Why do people evade taxes? Becker (1968) argues that people become criminals not because their motivations are different from others but because their analyses of costs and benefits differ. Applied to the tax situation, this argument treats people as rational, amoral decision makers whose aim is simply to maximize utility. The classic model (Allingham and Sandmo 1972) assumes that behavior is influenced by factors such as the tax rate (which determines the benefits of evasion) and the penalties for fraud and the probability of detection (which determine the costs).

This model produces generally unsurprising predictions. For instance, an increase in the penalty rate and an increase in the probability of detection both result in more income being declared. But, simultaneously, with penalties on tax evaded rather than income concealed and decreasing absolute risk aversion, the model predicts that evasion *decreases* when the tax rate rises. The model is not quite as simple as has sometimes been claimed; in addition to allowing predictions like the latter one, Allingham and Sandmo incorporate a nonmonetary variable, reputation, and the notion of risk aversion into their model as well as briefly exploring the dynamic case. Here the predictions are also fairly commonplace, for example, in a dynamic model where discovery of evasion leads to auditing of past tax returns, income declarations increase as the years go by.

The classic model predicts that both probability of detection and the severity of penalties will affect evasion; if detection is likely and penalties severe, people will be more compliant. Kinsey's 1984 review suggests that for criminal behavior in general, penalties are less a deterrent than the probability of being caught, and this pattern is also found in the literature on tax com-

The authors gratefully acknowledge helpful comments from Richard M. Bird.

pliance. The evidence that fear of detection is a deterrent is mixed. Mason and Calvin (1978) report that, in their survey study, the highest correlation with admitted evasion was the perceived probability of not being caught. Many studies have found that evaders and participants in the underground economy perceive a lower probability of detection than others (e.g., Grasmick and Scott 1982; Scott and Grasmick 1981; Van Eck and Kazemier 1988; Vogel 1974), while people generally overestimate the chance of being audited. Using IRS records from 1969, Dubin and Wilde (1988) also found that audits had a deterrent effect. Two additional studies using TCMP data do not support this notion. Long (1980) used a classic deterrence econometric feedback model and TCMP data aggregated at the IRS district level. The estimated deterrent effect of audits was demonstrated to be explainable by bias introduced through random sampling error. A second, later study using individual-level TCMP panel data showed little specific deterrent effect of an audit (Long and Schwartz 1987).

This raises the question of what influences people's perceptions of the probability of detection. To explore this issue, Klepper and Nagin (1989) presented individuals with a series of detailed scenarios about a hypothetical taxpayer. They found that age and the itemization of deductions were associated with perceiving lower probabilities of detection overall, but, more interestingly, perceived probabilities of detection varied according to the nature of the specific declaration made. So, for example, detection was seen as less likely for income not subject to third-party reporting and more likely if tax was evaded on a large proportion of an item (e.g., a charitable deduction).

Although the evidence that heavier penalties produce more compliance than lighter penalties is limited, it is undoubtedly the case that fines and other punishments are, to a certain extent, deterrents. Some researchers have argued that, above a certain threshold of probability of detection, a mild penalty is as effective a deterrent as a heavy one (see Friedland 1982), though Jackson and Jones (1985) found that, when the probability of detection was low (less than 4 percent), people were sensitive to the size of the penalty. Witte and Woodbury (1985) found that there was a relationship between the severity of sanctions and compliance, but only for a specific group of taxpayers (those who had high incomes and were self-employed). This suggests that we need to know much more about individual differences in the personal perceptions and personal consequences of penalties.

Given the current mild sanctions and low probability of detection, this kind of approach would predict that virtually everyone should be evading tax (see Smith and Kinsey 1987); in other words, we should not be asking "why do people evade taxes" but, rather, "why do people pay them" (see Alm, McClelland, and Schulze 1989).

In this essay, we review a series of field studies and experiments we have performed with an emphasis on studying deterrence. Given the limitations of space, we will not be able to give detailed descriptions of these studies and we have to refer the reader to the original studies for details.

The First Field Study

Elffers, Weigel, and Hessing (1987) carried out a study to combine self-reported and official data at an individual level. With the help of the Dutch Ministry of Finance and using a complicated methodology to guarantee confidentiality, they used a contrast-group design: two carefully audited groups of individuals were selected from a sample of 3,500. One group had made accurate returns for two consecutive years, the other had not complied, in the eye of the tax assessor, for two consecutive years. The tax returns were not drawn from a random sample, but from two separate pools; one a group of taxpayers for whom no additional taxes or corrections had been assessed during the course of the normal auditing procedure for 1981 and 1982, the other a group whose returns had been corrected and unpaid back taxes had been collected. The returns were scrutinized by two tax inspectors, and only cases where noncompliance was clearly fraudulent and substantial (over F 500, approximately $250) were retained in the "tax evader" category. Those returns that required no corrections after the two independent reviews were retained in the nonevader category. There were 342 individuals in each group. This contrast group design guarantees that both groups consist of clear cases.

The anonymity of the respondents was carefully protected. The tax authorities sent the individuals' names, addresses, and coded tax return details to a notary and sent the individuals a letter asking them if they would like to take part in the research. Those wishing to participate replied to the notary, who then released the names and addresses (but not the tax return details) to the researchers. During the interview, respondents noted their answers on a separate form that was sent to the notary. He then coupled the coded tax return details with the respondent's data, removed names and addresses, and sent the complete data to the researchers. Finally, the tax authorities revealed the decoding key for the tax returns. All of this ensured that at no time did the authorities, the notary, or the researcher know all three chunks of information about an individual (i.e., identification, tax evasion status, and interview data).

This cumbersome procedure led to a rather low response rate (23 percent overall), but there are good reasons for believing the participants to be reasonably representative of the original categories. First, those individuals who were finally revealed to be evaders were nearly as likely to participate as the nonevaders (21 percent compared to 25 percent). Second, the average amount of money evaded did not differ significantly between those evaders who participated and those who did not.

Three measures were used to assess the fear of punishment.

a. *Perceived certainty of punishment.* Respondents used five-point scales to rate the likelihood of apprehension if they were to illegally reduce their income tax liabilities by F 500 or F 5,000. The two ratings were summed such that high scores reflected a greater perceived certainty of detection.
b. *Perceived severity of punishment.* Respondents also rated the severity of the penalties for both types of tax evasion. High scores on this two-item measure indicated that the respondent judged the penalties to be severe.
c. *Perceived risk index.* In order to assess the combined influence of the first two variables, the certainty of punishment ratings were multiplied by the severity of punishment ratings for each pair of questions and the two products were summed. High scores on this index, therefore, reflected higher perceived risk in terms of both the certainty and severity of anticipated punishments.

Although this type of procedure has been recommended elsewhere (see Grasmick and Green 1980; Scott and Grasmick 1981), it should be noted that the nonsignificant correlation obtained between the "certainty" and "severity" measures ($r = .04$, $p > .10$) suggests that perceptions of these two characteristics of legal sanctions are empirically separable.

Despite safeguarding respondents' anonymity (which should have minimized the effect of impression management), the results showed that documented and self-reported tax evasion did not correspond at all. The correlation between self-reported evasion and documented evasion over two years was .06, and −.03 for the relation between self-reported evasion and the amount of taxes paid back over two years. There were inconsistencies between the self-reported tax evasion and official data in 45 percent of the cases. As might be expected, this discrepancy was less in the nonevader group, where 25 percent reported some misrepresentation of income or deductions, than in the evader group, where 69 percent denied evading taxes in either year. Evasion was usually denied even by the most flagrant evaders: among those whose audits resulted in corrections of more than a thousand guilders (approximately $500) in both 1981 and 1982, more than 70 percent denied misrepresenting income or deductions in either year.

This noncorrespondence resulted in a rather striking pattern: the variables that were correlated with self-reported tax evasion were not the same variables that were correlated with actual tax evasion behavior. In particular, the perceived certainty of punishment was significantly correlated with self-reported behavior ($r = -.27$, $p < .001$) and not with actual behavior ($r = .03$, NS). The perceived severity of punishment did not relate significantly with either behavior ($r = -.07$ and $-.09$, both NS). The perceived risk index again correlated significantly with self-reported behavior ($r = -.30$, $p < .001$) and not with actual behavior ($r = .02$, NS).

The self-presentation perspective can be used in interpreting these findings: the items used to assess both the deterrence variables and the self-reports explicitly referenced the tax evasion issue. Thus, they may have inadvertently cued respondents to report an internally consistent self-presentation. Respondents who acknowledged misrepresentation may have tended to report low deterrence perceptions as partial justifications for their evasion. Denials of evasion may have provoked a similarly consistent "packaging" of related cognitions, regardless of the relationship of such norms to actual past behavior (see Elffers, Weigel, and Hessing 1987).

Two Experimental Studies

Although interesting from the theoretical and methodological points of view, combining data from self-reports and official records is not an easy option. On the contrary, the confidentiality restrictions make the procedure cumbersome, which, in turn, leads to considerable subject attrition. Even more crucial is the fact that the active cooperation of the tax authorities is essential. So there is a need for alternative ways of gathering data on tax evasion. Experimental approaches are one possibility.

The experimental approach to tax evasion was pioneered by Friedland, Maital, and Rutenberg (1978). The experiments discussed here are an improvement of their technique and involved embedding tax decisions within a small business simulation. In such a simulation, participants had to imagine that they were a shopkeeper running a small supermarket for a couple of years. Each year consisted of several periods. In each period subjects had to make a number of financial decisions (on investment, on advertising, on the pricing of their goods) and, at the end of each year, they had to prepare a tax return and pay taxes on the amount declared. To make their tax declaration, subjects entered their income and taxable deductions directly into the computer, followed by a pause while the declaration was "sent off" for auditing. The subjects were not told of the focus of the experiment on tax evasion. Subjects performed their tasks individually and received no rewards, except a bottle of wine for all subjects after the experiment was finished (for an extensive description, see Webley et al. 1991).

In the first study, a random sample from the local telephone directory was made of telephone numbers starting with a preselected code. Then a letter was sent inviting the recipient to participate in an economic behavior research project involving microcomputers. Of 291 persons contacted, 22 women and 50 men agreed to participate, a response rate of just under 25 percent. The subjects were between 21 and 71 years old, with an average age of 40. All subjects were tested individually.

Two between-group factors were employed in the study: the period in which the tax return was audited and the type and nature of social comparison (the results of which will not be discussed here). During the simulation, each subject was audited once; the audit occurred either in the first, fourth, seventh, or eleventh period. The dependent measures were (*a*) the overall frequency of underdeclaring and the overall percentage of income declared, and (*b*) the frequency of underdeclaring and the percentage of income declared in each of the years of the simulation. After the simulation, the subjects completed a questionnaire measuring sociodemographics, attitudes, norms, and personality attributes.

The data obtained in the simulation were analyzed with the period in which the audit occurred as the between-group factor and comparison and the overall frequency of underdeclaring and overall percentage of income declared as dependent measures. The experience of having been audited did not have any influence on subsequent behavior in the experiment. Significant correlations were obtained for several personality attributes and evasion behavior in the experiment in a pattern similar to that of the first field study.

In the second experiment, eighty-eight undergraduate students participated, sixty-eight men and twenty women, most taking economics as their main subject. Various alterations were made to the manipulations of the deterrence variable. In this study, the audit variable was replaced by an opportunity variable to represent different levels of deterrence. For the high-deterrence condition, a set of three tax deductible items was randomly drawn for each individual subject from the set of six itemizable deductions arranged for the low-deterrence condition. Moreover, deterrence was made salient by a message immediately before the tax declaration. For the high-deterrence condition, it said that most of the customers paid in checks, which would be cleared through the company's back account, thus leaving traces by which the tax authorities could easily investigate the real business income. In contrast, those in the low-deterrence condition were told their income derived mainly from cash receipts, which would be very difficult to verify by the revenue authorities. For a rationale, one can think of the visibility of income as a deterrent to incorrectly completing tax forms (Kagan 1989, 81–82).

Deduction fraud was more prevalent than income fraud (37 cases vs. 26 cases). The deterrent manipulation proved partly successful, as significant effects were found for the amount evaded but not for the frequency of evasion.

The Social Security Study

The method used in this study paralleled the one used in the first field study on tax evasion (Elffers, Weigel, and Hessing 1987). In this study (Hessing, Elffers, and Robben 1990) three groups were used in a contrast-group design: (1) respondents for whom no suspicions were raised on possible abuse of their unemployment benefit; (2) respondents on social security caught for fraud; and (3) a control group of respondents from the general population.

More than 1,000 respondents were originally approached. Of these, 209 were never reached, 126 refused to cooperate, and 460 never responded at all; 345 respondents were willing to cooperate (30 percent) and 145 were eventually interviewed (14 percent of the original sample). In the interview group, 51 respondents had no fraud history, 45 respondents had committed fraud, and 49 respondents were from the control group. To guard the confidentiality, the interviewers were unaware of the fraud/social security status of the respondents during the interview. At the outset of the interview, respondents were asked whether they were on social security or not, in order to ask him or her the appropriate questions. Eighty respondents out of 96 "admitted" they were receiving social security and 16 denied receiving benefits.

Although we do not assume that the probability of being caught when engaging in social security fraud is higher than in the case of tax evasion, the relationship between officially measured and self-reported behavior was satisfactory ($r = .60, p < .01$). It seems that social security fraud is clearer—for all parties involved, including the researchers—than tax evasion. More people deny fraud than the actually established instances of no fraud; forty-nine versus forty-three. Five respondents admitted fraud while they were thought to be "clean," and eleven respondents denied fraud while they have actually been caught committing fraud.

As can be expected from the correlation between self-reported and officially measured behavior, there were not many (significant) differences between both data sets. Certainty of punishment correlated $-.37$ with officially measured behavior and $-.29$ with self-reported behavior (both $p < .01$). Severity of punishment correlated .21 and .29 ($p < .01$), respectively.

Those who had committed fraud reported a higher certainty and a higher severity than both the "clean" group and the control group. Also, when certainty and severity ratings were multiplied to create an index, they showed higher scores on this index, reflecting a stronger perceived deterrence for the fraud group. The experience of having been caught seems to be the most likely explanation for this difference. They seem to be more aware of the threat of being caught, but they certainly do not intend to be influenced by it. They reported that they would not refrain from fraud, even if detection and punishment were increased.

The Second Field Study

In the Dutch tax system, every single tax form is checked every year. This audit process is flexible and the quality and depth of the process is left to the individual assessing tax inspector, varying from a quick glance to a full-scale audit. In general, there are five levels of checking, depending on the complexity and absolute level of the income concerned. The average time it takes to check a single tax form lies—depending on the level on which the tax form is checked—between thirteen and forty-one minutes. "Clean" tax forms (tax forms that do not need a correction) take sixteen minutes, tax forms on which corrections are possible but not applied take twenty minutes, while it takes an average of twenty-seven minutes to check a form on which a correction will be applied. And, of course, the more corrections applied, the longer it takes to check: twenty-seven minutes for one to five corrections and an average of eighty-eight minutes if more than five corrections are applied.

The Dutch tax system does not really have a strong deterrent to evading (from an economic point of view). When a tax form is found to be incorrect, the tax inspector simply corrects the tax form and collects the tax associated with it. That is, if necessary, he or she corrects the amount that the taxpayer should have declared. This is done whether it is a matter of a positive correction (the declared income should have been higher) or a negative correction (the declared income should have been lower). The question of willful evasion of taxes does not enter the process at this stage. If the (positive) correction takes place during the normal processing of the tax form, there is no possibility of administering a fine. In fact, a punishment is only possible when, after the tax form has been processed and cleared, new information comes to the attention of the tax inspector that gives him or her reason to correct the amount declared after all and when there are enough grounds to suspect an intention to evade taxes. In such a case, the inspector can administer a penalty ranging from 25 percent to 100 percent of the taxes that should have been paid on the amount not declared originally. However, this fine can only be administered when it was not possible for the tax inspector to have such knowledge during the routine processing of the tax form.

This observation study was performed in 1988, again with the complete cooperation of the Ministry of Finance. The tax forms of 918 taxpayers made up the central part of this study. These tax forms contained a random sample of the normal workload of six tax inspectorates in the southern part of the Netherlands. The 918 tax forms were checked like any other tax form with two important differences: (1) the tax inspector was asked to do the checking while orally describing his or her considerations, and (2) the inspector was asked—when applying a correction—to differentiate between corrections for errors or mistakes and corrections for intentional evasion. These considerations and decisions were then recorded on a coding form by a trained observer.

The central behavior in question concerned the 1986 tax year (the official data for this tax year were available in 1988). Out of the original sample of 918 respondents, 220 respondents were interviewed about their past fiscal behavior over 1983 to 1986 with an almost identical setup as used in the first field study. From this sample, 120 respondents also took part in a simulation experiment similar to the one described previously. On this group of respondents, the data consist, therefore, of a behavioral outcome measure over 1986, a self-reported measure over 1984 to 1986, the perceived deterrence as measured in 1989, and, finally, the behavioral simulation measure as assessed in 1989.

Three Behavioral Measures

According to the assessment 27 (12.3 percent) of the 220 taxpayers had evaded taxes in 1986. During the interview, 196 of them answered the question whether they had evaded taxes: 35 (17.9 percent) admitted tax evasion and 161 denied having evaded taxes. Thirty-one (25.8 percent) of the 120 taxpayers who took part in the simulation study evaded taxes during the simulation. We expected that the correlations between these behaviors would show the following pattern: no (significant) correlations between self-reported evasion and the behavioral outcome measure and low correlations between self-reported behavior and behavior in the simulation and, finally, high correlations between the behavioral outcome measure and the behavioral simulation measure (see Elffers, Weigel, and Hessing 1987; Webley et al. 1991). The results proved our expectations partly right and partly wrong: the self-reported measure correlated −.11 and −.02 with the behavioral outcome measure and the behavioral simulation measure, and the correlation between the behavioral outcome measure and the behavioral simulation measure was also −.02 (for a discussion of these results, see Elffers 1991; Robben 1991).

Corrections for Errors or Mistakes and Corrections for Evasion

Although many taxpayers receive a correction on their declared income every year, very few of them are corrected for suspected evasion: 28.4 percent received one correction in three years, 14.0 percent two corrections in three years, and 7.3 percent received a correction each year. For suspicion of evasion, the results were 8.5 percent, 3.9 percent, and 1.0 percent. When a taxpayer is corrected for suspected evasion, there is an increased chance that he or she will be corrected for evasion again in the following year. Of the 3 percent of the taxpayers who were not corrected for evasion during the

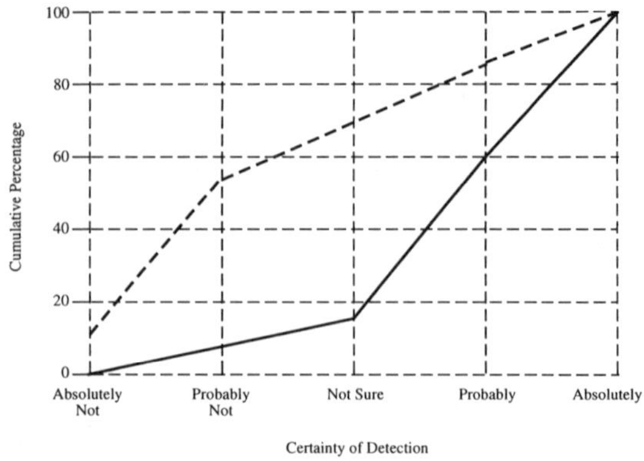

Fig. 1. Cumulative distribution of the certainty of detection. (N = 220; --- = undercompliance of F 500;— = undercompliance of F 5,000.)

period from 1983 to 1985, only 3 percent received a correction for evasion in 1986. Of the taxpayers who were corrected once for evading taxes during that period, 6 percent were corrected for suspected evasion in 1986. And, finally, for those taxpayers who were corrected two or three times in those years, the proportion was 28.2 percent.

Perceived Deterrence

Although deterrence in the Netherlands is perhaps relatively mild compared to deterrence in such other countries as the United Kingdom and the United States, the Dutch taxpayers still believe that evading taxes is a risky act (see fig. 1 and table 1). Furthermore, the respondents perceived a higher certainty for larger evasions and a higher certainty for false deductions. They seem to realize that the detection of false deductions is much easier than the detection of unreported income. A similar difference can be observed in table 2: taxpayers believe that larger evasions will receive more severe punishments.

Detected Evasion and Subsequent Perceived Deterrence

The experience of detected evasion did change—though inconsistently—the subsequent perceptions of deterrence (see tables 2 and 3). While the experi-

TABLE 1. Perceived Severity of Punishment for Evading

Amount Evaded	Just Pay Taxes	Including 50 Percent Fine	Including 100 Percent Fine	Including 200 Percent Fine
F 500	61	25	14	—
F 5,000	32	37	29	3

Note: N = 220.

TABLE 2. Corrections for Errors or Mistakes and Evasion and Subsequent Perceived Deterrence (F 500)

		Certainty of Detection					
		Unreported Income		False Deductions		Severity	
	N	*X*	SD	*X*	SD	*X*	SD
Not corrected	107	2.78	1.15	2.84	1.00	1.54	.69
Corrected for errors or mistakes	80	2.88	1.27	2.92	1.25	1.53	.76
Corrected for evasion	31	2.35	0.91	2.77	1.09	1.48	.77
F(*df*)		2.29/2		.23/2		.08/2	

$^{*}p < .05$.

ence of detection had no effects on the perceived certainty and perceived severity for evading F 500, the effects were significant for evading F 5,000: those who had been corrected (without suspicion of intentional evasion) showed a higher perceived certainty of punishment.

Perceived Deterrence and Fraud Behavior in the Simulation Experiment

Between the act of evasion in the simulation experiment and the perceived deterrence on tax evasion (both measured in 1989, in the same research setting), we could not observe significant relations (see table 4).

Deterrence and Self-Reported Behavior

To assess the impact of the experience of having been corrected for either errors or mistakes or for evasion, we asked those respondents who could remember having been corrected in the past three years ($N = 90$): "Did you

TABLE 3. Corrections for Errors or Mistakes and Evasion and Subsequent Perceived Deterrence (F 5,000)

		Certainty of Detection					
		Unreported Income		False Deductions		Severity	
	N	*X*	SD	*X*	SD	*X*	SD
Not corrected	107	4.03	.99	4.09	.87	2.04	.78
Corrected for errors or mistakes	80	4.36	.73	4.39	.59	1.99	.93
Corrected for evasion	31	4.06	.63	4.16	.64	2.07	.89
F(*df*)		3.69*/2		3.71*/2		.12/2	

$^{*}p < .05$.

TABLE 4. Perceived Deterrence and Evasion in the Simulation

Deterrence	Amount Evaded in Experiment
Certainty of punishment	
F 500 not reported income	−.03
F 500 false deductions	−.13
Severity of punishment	
F 500 evasion	−.00
Certainty of punishment	
F 5,000 not reported income	.15
F 5,000 false deductions	.14
Severity of punishment	
F 5,000 evasion	.04

Note: $N = 118$.

willfully try to evade taxes?" The number of times one had been corrected for mistakes or errors in the past three years was unrelated to the intentional act of evasion ($r = .02$, NS). Also, the number of times one had been caught evading in the past was unrelated to the intentional act of evasion ($r = -.04$, NS).

Experienced Deterrence and the Effect on Subsequent Behavior

Although Dutch taxpayers believe that tax evasion will be detected and punished, these perceptions did not have any influence on the evasion behavior in the simulation experiment or on self-reported, real-life behavior. We now come to the final analyses: the relationships between being corrected for evasion and the effect on subsequent behavior.

The remarkable observation is that, when a taxpayer is corrected for evasion, there is a very good chance that he or she will be corrected again for suspected evasion in the next year and the year after that. The average correlation between correction in one year and corrections in subsequent years for intentional evasion is .32, $p < .001$ (see table 5).

Figure 2 shows the occurrence of noncompliance and evasion for three groups of taxpayers: taxpayers whose forms were unchallenged, taxpayers whose forms were corrected for error(s), and taxpayers who were corrected for evading taxes.

Discussion

The studies we have discussed all point to more or less the same conclusion. In the first field study, the certainty of punishment and the severity of punish-

TABLE 5. Correlations between Detected Evasion and Subsequent Evasion, 1983–86

	Caught Evading		
Caught Evading	1984	1985	1986
1983	.31*	.28*	.13*
1984	—	.36*	.12*
1985	—	—	.30*

Note: $N = 785$.
$*p < .001$.

ment were unrelated to the behavioral outcome measure, but showed significant correlations with self-reported behavior. In two subsequent experiments, the effects of deterrence were rather mixed. Then, in the social security study, a different picture emerged. Reasonably strong correlations were ascertained between having committed fraud and perceived deterrence. However, we could also determine that the experience of deterrence did not alter intentions to commit fraud in the future, but did lower the trust one had in the effectiveness of (alternative) deterrence measures. Finally, in our recent field study—where we were able to combine behavioral outcome measures with self-reported behavior and behavioral simulation measures—the results were again negative. Perceived deterrence was not influenced by the experience of deterrence, nor did perceived deterrence have any influence on each of the three behaviors in question. However, those taxpayers who had been cor-

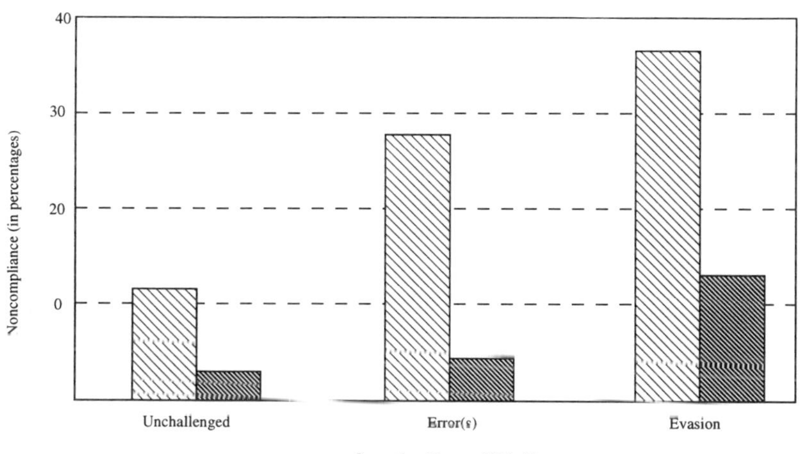

Fig. 2. Recurrence of evasion in 1986. (*N* = 785; ▧ = noncompliance; ▩ = evasion.)

rected for mistakes or errors in the past did have a higher perceived certainty of being punished.

These observations lead to the following tentative conclusions. There are probably three groups of taxpayers: (1) taxpayers who never evade taxes and accordingly hardly ever receive corrections on their tax forms; (2) taxpayers who will try to evade now and then; and (3) taxpayers who will often try to evade (habitual evaders). When the first group is corrected for errors, mistakes, or mistaken evasion, their perceived deterrence increases. Nonevaders do not need deterrence to keep them from evading, or, alternatively, a small measure of deterrence is enough to keep them from doing so. For the second and third groups, deterrence does not seem to have any effect. If there is an effect of deterrence on evasion, it is in the wrong direction. They either are not impressed by the effect of deterrence, or they intend to recover the losses resulting from deterrence. All in all, we believe that these data give us little reason to put much faith in the deterrent effect of deterrence and we still have to face the question: Why do people pay taxes?

REFERENCES

Allingham, M. G., and A. Sandmo. 1972. "Income Tax Evasion: A Theoretical Analysis." *Journal of Public Economics* 1:323–38.

Alm, J., G. M. McClelland, and W. D. Schulze. 1989. "Why Do People Pay Taxes?" Paper presented at the annual meeting of the Law and Society Association, Madison, Wis.

Becker, G. S. 1968. "Crime and Punishment: An Economic Approach." *Journal of Political Economy* 76:169–217.

Dubin, J. A., and L. L. Wilde. 1988. "An Empirical Analysis of Federal Income Tax Auditing and Compliance." *National Tax Journal* 41:61–74.

Elffers, H. 1991. *Income Tax Evasion: Theory and Measurement.* Deventer: Kluwer.

Elffers, H., R. H. Weigel, and D. J. Hessing. 1987. "The Consequences of Different Strategies for Measuring Tax Evasion Behavior." *Journal of Economic Psychology* 8:311–37.

Friedland, N. 1982. "A Note on Tax Evasion as a Function of the Quality of Information about the Magnitude and Credibility of Threatened Fines: Some Preliminary Research." *Journal of Applied Social Psychology* 12:54–59.

Friedland, N., S. Maital, and A. Rutenberg. 1978. "A Simulation Study of Income Tax Evasion." *Journal of Public Economics* 10:107–16.

Grasmick, H. G., and D. E. Green. 1980. "Legal Punishment, Social Disapproval and Internalization as Inhibitors of Illegal Behavior." *Journal of Criminal Law and Criminology* 71:325–35.

Grasmick, H. G., and W. J. Scott. 1982. "Tax Evasion and Mechanisms of Social Control: A Comparison with Grand and Petty Theft." *Journal of Economic Psychology* 2:213–30.

Hessing, D. J., H. Elffers, and H. S. J. Robben. 1990. "De psychologie van de WW-fraudeur" (The psychology of social security fraud). In *Sociale-zekerheidsfraude: Juridische, economische en psychologische aspecten van fraude in het sociale zekerheidsstelsel* (Social security fraud: Legal, economic, and psychological aspects of fraud in the social security system), ed. D. J. Hessing and H. P. A. M. van Arendonk, 191–245. Deventer: Kluwer.

Hessing, D. J., K. A. Kinsey, H. Elffers, and R. H. Weigel. 1988. "Tax Evasion Research: Measurement Strategies and Theoretical Models." In *Handbook of Economic Psychology,* ed. W. F. van Raaij, G. M. van Veldhoven, and K. E. Warneryd, 516–37. Dordrecht: Kluwer.

Jackson, B., and S. Jones. 1985. "Salience of Tax Evasion Penalties versus Detection Risk." *Journal of the American Taxation Association* (Spring): 7–17.

Kagan, R. A. 1989. "On the Visibility of Income Tax Law Violations." In *Taxpayer Compliance,* vol. 2, *Social Science Perspectives,* ed. J. A. Roth and J. T. Scholz, 76–125. Philadelphia: University of Pennsylvania Press.

Kinsey, K. A. 1984. "Theories and Models of Tax Cheating." Taxpayer Compliance Project Working Paper 84-2. Chicago: American Bar Foundation.

Klepper, S., and D. Nagin. 1989. "Tax Compliance and Perceptions of the Risks of Detection and Criminal Prosecution." *Law and Society Review* 23:209–40.

Long, S. B. 1980. *The Internal Revenue Service: Measuring Tax Offenses and Enforcement Response.* Washington, D.C.: U.S. Government Printing Office.

Long, S. B., and R. D. Schwartz. 1987. "The Impact of IRS Audits on Taxpayer Compliance: A Field Experiment in Specific Deterrence." Paper presented at the annual meeting of the Law and Society Association, Washington, D.C.

Mason, R., and L. D. Calvin. 1978. "A Study of Admitted Tax Evasion." *Law and Society Review* 13:73–89.

Robben, H. S. J. 1991. *A Behavioral Simulation and Documented Behavior Approach to Income Tax Evasion.* Deventer: Kluwer.

Scott, W. J., and H. G. Grasmick. 1981. "Deterrence and Income Tax Cheating: Testing Interaction Hypotheses in Utilitarian Theories." *Journal of Applied Behavioral Science* 17:395–408.

Smith, K. W., and K. A. Kinsey. 1987. "Understanding Taxpaying Behavior: A Conceptual Framework with Implications for Research." *Law and Society Review* 21:639–63.

Van Eck, R., and B. Kazemier. 1988. "Features of the Hidden Economy in the Netherlands." *Review of Income and Wealth* 34:251–73.

Vogel, J. 1974. "Taxation and Public Opinion in Sweden: An Interpretation of Recent Survey Data." *National Tax Journal* 27:499–513.

Webley, P., H. S. J. Robben, H. Elffers, and D. J. Hessing. 1991. *Tax Evasion: The Experimental Approach.* Cambridge: Cambridge University Press.

Witte, A. D., and D. F. Woodbury. 1985. "The Effect of Tax Laws and Tax Administration on Tax Compliance: The Case of the U.S. Individual Income Tax." *National Tax Journal* 38:1–13.

Commentary

Richard Bird

I found this essay both interesting and frustrating. It is interesting because it reports on an impressive series of field studies and experiments. It is even more interesting because it provides a potentially illuminating contrast to the overwhelming reliance on U.S. data in this field. And it is especially interesting because the authors draw some striking conclusions from their analyses. They themselves particularly emphasize that their results cast substantial doubts on the deterrent effect of deterrence. I do not mind seeing one more nail driven, however tentatively, into the coffin of the simple deterrence model, but what I personally found more interesting is their other, more tentative, conclusion, namely, that there are probably three groups of taxpayers—the honest, the crooked, and the rest. I find this interesting because it accords with my own intuitions about the nature of tax evasion and what can and should be done about it.

Before developing that thought a bit, however, let me explain why I found this essay frustrating. It is frustrating on two different levels, both of which I suspect may be explained by the fact that the authors are attempting to condense a vast amount of work in a very few pages. By my count, three forthcoming books are summarized here, in addition to three already published articles (one in Dutch). No doubt the inadequate description of the studies reported can be more than fully explained by this heroic condensation. The same may well be true of the second level of frustration I have, namely, at the important questions that do not seem to have been asked. Curiously, the authors themselves initially note that one of these questions—"why do people pay taxes?"—is likely to be both more interesting and relevant than its converse; so far as I can tell, however, they never again consider this question.

Let me go through a few issues, more or less in the order in which they came up in reading the essay. First, in reporting on the first field study, the authors stress the lack of correlation between documented and self-reported tax evasion. Their explanations lean toward cognitive explanations of why self-reported evasion may differ from the official version. One problem with this approach is that we have no idea of the probability that evaders are actually caught. As explained later in the essay, the official data on which the authors rely are not really audit data (let alone "full audit" data of the TCMP type) at all. I see no reason why we should presume the official numbers measure "true income" and attempt to rationalize self-reported discrepancies: the self-reports may be more accurate. Another problem is that we are given no idea of what a Dutch tax administrator might consider to be "evasion."

Second, I found the highly condensed summary of the two experimental studies particularly frustrating both because, in principle, it is refreshing to see experimental academics working with someone other than the usual student subjects and because the idea of embedding tax decisions within a more general small business simulation seems a potentially promising one. Indeed, it would be interesting to develop this role-playing approach to tax enforcement further, explaining, for example, the effects of varying particular "norms" on compliance and of tying taxation to the provision of desired public goods. Unfortunately, I came out of this account not even clear about whether the first experiment was run for two, two-period years or three, four-period years. I also have no idea if the subjects knew the study had a tax evasion focus, whether they were rewarded for their participation, or whether any reward they may have received was related to their behavior. I was also left in the dark about what "personality attributes" were related to what evasion behavior. Nor do I have a clear idea, from this account, whether the investigators modeled the tax evasion decision as a two-stage process—the first stage being the decision to evade or not and the second stage being the decision about how much to evade. The final result reported for the students suggests it was, but the presentation of a lumped dependent measure for the other group suggests it was not. Or was it different in the two studies? Moreover, since, as far as I can make out, each subject seems to have been treated individually, it appears no information on the influence on behavior of the perceived behavior of others was obtained. If so, this seems particularly unfortunate because, as Frank Cowell has said, "No tax evader is an island, entire of itself." Much evidence suggests that the perceived relative size of the two extreme groups mentioned earlier may be a significant influence on the size (and perhaps the behavior) of the critical middle group.

Two final points may also be made about these experiments. First, while I regret that the opportunity to test whether students are a "representative" group was apparently missed by running a different experiment on them, it is particularly frustrating to be told of what looks to be a very useful "opportunity" variable (payment by cash vs. check) used in the student experiment, but given no idea at all of the outcome of this experiment. Second, because the experiments clearly had a small business focus and the conclusions of these studies are compared to those of the field studies, are we to infer that the field studies, too, were of such self-employed individuals, that is, that everyone studied had the same opportunity to evade in the sense that their income, or most of it, was not subject to withholding?

Third, perhaps refreshingly, I have no great problem with the social security study, except to note that, obviously, its inclusion casts doubt on the hypothesis about the population of the field studies just cited since the social security recipients studied are presumably mainly unemployed workers—although, again, I have to guess about this. In any case, the greater coincidence of self-reported and official evasion in this simpler case could perhaps be interpreted to support both of the doubts mentioned earlier about the interpretation of the field study. First, it is clearer to both official and citizen in the social security case what the rules are and when they are broken. And, second, "real" evaders are more likely to be caught by officials. The main frustration I have to record here is that we are given no idea of what is meant by new (or alternative) deterrence measures: it is impossible to follow the authors' brief discussion of this point. Finally, I assume the fraud studied here involves the improper receipt of transfers: one would think this might involve a different sort of evasion behavior than nonreporting of taxable income. Is the behavior of a confidence trickster who actively defrauds you of your money the same as that of a waiter who pockets the wallet you left on your seat?

Fourth, the brief description of the Dutch tax administration in this essay both cries out for more elaboration and suggests how important it is to be absolutely clear about what we are comparing before we engage in comparative studies. Schmolders long ago pointed out that British tax administration is very different from German tax administration, and the nature and perhaps scale of tax evasion in each country partially reflects these administrative differences. Dutch tax administration is equally clearly very different from U.S. tax administration, and those who would compare the results of these studies with the many U.S. studies must surely take these differences into account. Whether or not tax administrations, so to speak, get the evaders they deserve, it would be useful to have more information on the Dutch system than we are given here. For example, if all returns are checked manually (as appears to be the case), are there any prior selection criteria (e.g., by reported income sources) applied at all, or is each case considered independently each year? By the same inspector? What is the ratio of positive to negative corrections? If it is true, as we seem to be told here, that penalties can be applied only in the absence of new information that could not have been known to the inspector at the time of the initial processing, and if there is no other audit process giving rise to "audit trails," then it would seem the only way anyone would ever get caught would be if a disgruntled employee or competitor informed on him or her—or there is some sort of information-matching system about which we are not told. If the former is the case, then most of the corrections would seem to be either simply arithmetical errors or, perhaps more probably, mistaken (or at least questionable) interpretations of the law, and not evasion (as usually understood) at all. Nonetheless, we are told that the inspectors can tell evasion when they see it: how, with this sort of system? Do they apply industry norms, cross-reference value-added and income tax returns, or depend, as I have suggested, on informers? The little we are told just whets the appetite for a clearer discussion of what is being called evasion in all these studies.

Finally, with respect to the second field study reported by the authors, unfortunately once again some crucial pieces of information are missing from this highly condensed account. The missing items range from the trivial—what number of cases is reported in tables 1 and 2 and why are there only 218 in tables 3 and 4—to the critical—in which experiment did the 120 (of the 220, of the 413, of the 918) take part? The same question about the relation between self-reported and officially recorded evasion comes up. Perhaps the most interesting, and strongest, finding in this study, however, is that those who evade (and get caught) in one year are likely to evade (and get caught) in subsequent years. These are presumably the Bad Hats in the taxpaying population, those who always cheat, whether they are caught or not.

The introduction of these villainous characters returns me, in a roundabout way, to where I began, with the Good, the Bad, and the Indecisive. As I noted, the authors also emphasize that their studies suggest there are three such groups. It is not entirely clear from what is presented here, however, why they emphasize that deterrence affects the noncongenitally honest adversely, if at all. Moreover, as already mentioned, nowhere do they say anything relevant to the question of why the Good Guys pay: are they indeed congenitally honest? If so, how did they get that way, and is the spread of this gene open to policy manipulation? Or does their compliance reflect, instead, a lack of opportunity or the simple certainty of the tax as it affects them? Finally, if a Good Guy has an unpleasant experience with the tax authorities (e.g., being labeled a cheat), some authors have suggested he or she may be more likely to cheat because he or she will now perceive the system as unfair (as, e.g., the work of Strümpel suggests). There seems to be no evidence of this in the Dutch case, which, if true, is interesting. More generally, what would the effects be of rewarding "good" taxpayers, for example, in some monetary way, or by the Medal of Honesty, or whatever?

As for the Bad Guys, is tax cheating like buying lottery tickets or drinking or smoking? That is, are these addicted evaders? If so, how did they get that way, and can their numbers be reduced in any operational way? Finally, and I think most important, do the relative numbers of these two extremes—or, more accurately, public perceptions of their numbers—affect the behavior of the thundering herd in the middle? And, if so, can the authorities manipulate perceptions in any significant fashion (e.g., by stressing that most people are honest; by punishing the guilty, especially perhaps the guilty rich, visibly; by going out of their way to be pleasant to taxpayers with whom they come into contact; and by stressing all the good things done with the money collected)? These would seem to be some of the questions that need to be much more carefully studied with respect to tax compliance if the sort of intensive work and effort underlying this essay is to bear fruition in the form of improved public policy.

Deterrence and Beyond: Toward a Kinder, Gentler IRS

James Alm, Betty Jackson, and Michael McKee

Traditional methods for increasing tax compliance have emphasized greater probabilities of detection and more severe penalties on evasion. However, because there are factors other than detection and punishment that affect individual compliance decisions, there are numerous compliance strategies available to governments. For example, there is some evidence from psychology that rewards may be more effective than punishments for eliminating undesired behavior and for motivating desired behavior, so that positive inducements for honest taxpayers may be a useful tool for increasing tax compliance. Further, the recognition that taxes are necessary to finance government expenditures may play a significant role in many individuals' compliance decisions, and both the ways in which taxes are spent and the manner in which these decisions are made may also affect compliance. There is also some theoretical speculation that taxpayer uncertainty about tax and enforcement policies can increase tax compliance. In the face of such uncertainty, it is argued, a rational individual may well increase his or her compliance. The existence of these and other factors suggests that governments may be able to affect tax compliance through channels other than greater fines and audits. However, the impact of these various strategies is not known.[1]

This essay reports the results of new laboratory experiments that investigate the effects of increased enforcement efforts and positive inducements on tax compliance; we also summarize the results of some previous experiments

We received many helpful comments from the participants at the conference. Joel Slemrod, in particular, provided several suggestions that have materially improved both the content and the presentation of the essay. The Peat Marwick Main Foundation provided financial support for this research.

1. There are, of course, other factors that both affect compliance and that are (potentially) influenced by government actions. Gordon (1988) suggests that morality and stigma costs may explain compliance. Psychologists argue that social norms and perceptions of fairness affect the compliance decision. Machina (1983) and Kahneman and Tversky (1979) argue that individuals either can show great sensitivity to or can overweight low probabilities, so that they may pay more taxes than implied by expected utility theory. These elements are not considered here.

on the impacts of uncertainty and of the public sector decision process on compliance.[2] In the laboratory setting, subjects are faced with a typical compliance decision: they receive income, they pay taxes on income voluntarily reported, and they face a chance that underreported income will be detected and penalized. Various policies are introduced, and their impacts on compliance are investigated. For example, enforcement efforts are examined by changing the probability of detection and the penalty on unreported taxes, and positive inducements are introduced as various schemes by which honest taxpayers are rewarded, either as individuals or as a group.

The experimental results indicate that each strategy can increase compliance, at least to a degree. Greater enforcement efforts raise compliance; however, given the likely range in which these tools can be varied, there are significant limits on the degree to which greater penalties or greater audit rates can be relied upon to improve compliance. Positive inducements can also be effective devices for inducing tax compliance. Compared to a no-reward case, tax compliance is significantly greater when compliant individuals are eligible for a lottery, when they receive an immediate, fixed reward, or when their future chances of detection decline; the introduction of a public good financed by the taxes of all individuals also significantly increases compliance. Uncertain policies affect compliance, although not always in a positive way. When there is no apparent benefit from tax payments, uncertainty always increases individual compliance. However, when individuals receive an obvious benefit from their tax payments, uncertainty always has the opposite effect on compliance. Finally, the level of compliance increases when taxpayers perceive that they have greater input to the social processes that allocate their tax payments. In short, governments should pursue a variety of approaches that go beyond simple deterrence in order to achieve their desired degree of tax compliance.

The next section discusses several factors that may enter into the individual compliance decision. The experimental design is presented in the third section. The fourth section reports the results of the new experiments and the previous experiments; the summary and conclusions are in the fifth section.

Factors in the Compliance Decision

In this section, we discuss various factors that may explain why people pay taxes. These theories are then used to motivate the various compliance strategies that governments can pursue.

The traditional economic explanation for tax compliance derives from the economics-of-crime approach of Becker (1968) that was first applied to

2. The experimental results on uncertainty and fiscal institutions are discussed in more detail in Alm, Jackson, and (McKee 1991 and n.d.).

compliance by Allingham and Sandmo (1972).[3] Here, an individual is assumed to maximize the expected utility of the evasion gamble, weighing the certain benefits of successful evasion against the risky prospect of detection and punishment. The sole factor that motivates any compliance is the fear of getting caught and penalized; in fact, if the expected penalty rate is less than the tax rate on reported income, then a rational individual will not report any income. There is some empirical evidence that compliance is affected by detection and punishment, at least to a degree.[4] However, most of this evidence is based on estimates of aggregate responses. Detailed information on individual responses to enforcement actions is seldom available.[5] Laboratory methods allow the generation of such information on individual responses.

It is, however, important to recognize that detection and punishment cannot explain the compliance behavior of all individuals. The percentage of tax returns that are subject to detailed audit is quite small in most countries, and penalties are seldom more than a fraction of unpaid taxes. As argued by Graetz and Wilde (1985) and Skinner and Slemrod (1985), a purely economic analysis of the evasion gamble suggests that most individuals would evade if they were purely rational, since it is unlikely that cheaters would be caught and penalized. However, compliance in many countries remains relatively high.[6] Additional factors must play a role—perhaps a dominant one—in tax compliance.

Another element in compliance decisions is suggested by fiscal exchange theory. Compliance may be motivated by the presence of government expenditures; that is, individuals may pay taxes because they value the goods provided by government and they recognize that their payments may be necessary both to help finance the goods and to get others to contribute.

There is a large and growing literature that supports the notion that compliance depends, in part, on the use of tax revenues. Some of this work looks at voluntary contributions to public goods.[7] Other work looks directly at

3. For a survey of this literature, see Cowell (1990).

4. See Dubin and Wilde 1988; Witte and Woodbury (1985).

5. See, however, Alm, Bahl, and Murray (1990) for estimates of the compliance impact of income tax rates, payroll benefits, the probability of detection, and the penalty on unpaid taxes using microdata on individual workers in Jamaica.

6. For example, the Internal Revenue Service estimates that voluntary compliance in the United States exceeds 80 percent in recent years (see Internal Revenue Service 1988). In a related vein, the "underground economy" is generally estimated to constitute only 2 to 10 percent of the gross national product of most industrialized economies; for a discussion of this evidence, see Cowell (1990).

7. See, for example, the theoretical work of Taylor (1976), Axelrod (1984), and Palfrey and Rosenthal (1984), and the experimental work of Brubaker (1982), Rapoport (1985), Bagnoli and McKee (1991), and Bagnoli, Ben-David, and McKee (n.d.). For contrary experimental results, see Isaac, McCue, and Plott (1985); Isaac, Walker, and Thomas (1984); Kim and Walker (1984). Dawes and Thaler (1988) survey much of this literature.

the impact of government expenditures upon compliance.[8] Both strands often conclude that individuals pay more as the benefit from their contributions increases. However, the nature of the individual responses is still somewhat unclear and controversial.

Compliance behavior may also be affected by taxpayer uncertainty about enforcement and tax policies. There are numerous sources of this uncertainty: a tax code that is increasingly complex and frequently changed, the lack of uniform training of government auditors, taxpayer ignorance of the factors that lead to a tax audit or to a prison sentence, or merely the discussion of potential changes in tax policies. In the face of such uncertainty, a rational individual may well report more income than he or she otherwise would.

To illustrate, suppose that a taxpayer becomes more uncertain about, say, the amount of underreported income that will be discovered by government auditors. This increased risk raises the cost of evasion while leaving the return to reported income unchanged, and an individual can lower his or her exposure to risk by complying more fully with the tax code. As shown in theoretical work by Alm (1988), Scotchmer and Slemrod (1989), and Beck and Jung (1989), an individual who maximizes the expected utility of the evasion gamble will often report more income.

As yet, there is little evidence to support this conclusion. Further, this result is derived from models that do not consider government expenditures. Ignoring the expenditure side of the fiscal exchange means that individual compliance decisions can be treated as independent across individuals, so that each need consider only his or her own behavior. However, when taxes are used to provide public goods, behavior becomes interdependent, and individuals' responses to greater fiscal uncertainty need not be the same as when they receive nothing for their taxes. For example, Sandler, Sterbenz, and Posnett (1987) show that increased uncertainty about group contributions to a public good may lower an individual's contributions. Also, the results of Isaac, Schmidtz, and Walker (1989) imply that uncertainty about the imposition of costs on free riders will lead to lower voluntary contributions to a public good.

Another factor that may affect compliance behavior is the presence of positive inducements for those individuals found to be compliant. There is an enormous psychology literature that concludes that rewards can be more effective than punishments for eliminating undesired behavior and for motivating desired behavior.[9] However, the potential effects of positive inducements upon tax compliance behavior have not been examined.[10]

---

8. See Alm, Jackson, and McKee (1991); Alm, McClelland, and Schulze (n.d.); Becker, Buchner, and Sleeking (1987); Cowell and Gordon (1988).

9. See, for example, Nuttin and Greenwald (1968); Postman (1947); Skinner (1953); Thorndike (1911).

10. See, however, Falkinger and Walther (1991) for a theoretical analysis of the impact of rewards on compliance.

A final factor in the compliance decision is the process by which public expenditure decisions are made. There is some speculation that individuals will be more likely to pay their taxes if they have a voice in the allocation and decision process; government decisions that are imposed are unlikely to generate such feelings of participation.[11] Individual perceptions of the desirability of the tax allocations also seem likely to affect compliance. If individuals are strongly in favor of specific government expenditures—and if they know that others share their feelings—then they may be more likely to pay their taxes, even when they have no say in the decision process.[12] However, the effects of these dimensions of fiscal exchange are controversial.

There are many other factors that affect compliance: social norms, morality, perceptions of fairness, the presence of tax practitioners, peer group pressures, overweighting of the actual chances of audit, and so on. In fact, Internal Revenue Service (1978) lists over sixty factors that, it believes, determine compliance. It is, perhaps, useful to start with enforcement as a strategy for increasing compliance, but government approaches should not end there.

However, the impact of these various factors is not yet known. This is due, in large part, to the difficulty of obtaining information on individual responses to policy changes. The next section outlines the experimental design that generates such information.

Experimental Design

We use laboratory experimental methods to examine the impact of various government policies on compliance. The laboratory has been found to be a useful device for investigating individual behavior because it allows considerable control over the incentives and the institutional setting that face subjects (see Plott 1987; Smith 1982). The absence of controlled field data—and the small chance that such data will soon be available—makes it likely that laboratory methods offer the best opportunity to investigate the individual behavioral responses to government policies.

The laboratory economy replicates the basic structure of the voluntary income reporting and tax assessment system of the United States. Individuals receive income, they pay taxes on income voluntarily reported, they face a probability of audit, and they pay a penalty on taxes not disclosed if they are detected cheating. Into this setting various policy options are introduced, and compliance is compared in the absence and in the presence of the specific policy.

11. See, for example, Kidder and McEwen (1989); Pommerehne and Weck-Hanneman (1989).

12. See Spicer and Lundstedt (1976) for evidence that reported tax evasion is related to the benefits received from taxes. Contrary evidence is presented in Westat (1980).

In each laboratory session, the subjects are organized in a group of five individuals, and each subject is assigned an identification number. The subjects are told that the session will last an unknown number of periods, called rounds; the actual number of rounds is predetermined and equals twenty-five. Each person is given an initial endowment of ten tokens, and is told that accumulated tokens will be redeemed for cash at the end of the session at a fixed, announced conversion rate. At the beginning of each round, each subject is also given an income in tokens. The amount is randomly drawn from the interval of 2.00 to 3.00 tokens in increments of 0.25, and the amount is known only to the individual. The subject is asked to declare his or her income, which is taxed at the announced rate of 30 percent.

An individual pays no taxes on unreported income. However, each subject faces a probability in each round that evasion will be detected by an audit, at which point he or she must pay all unpaid taxes for the current and the previous four rounds, plus a fine equal to some multiple of the unpaid taxes.[13] The audit process follows the purely random audit procedure utilized by the Internal Revenue Service in its Taxpayer Compliance Measurement Program. The audit selection is performed using a bingo cage that contains one numbered ball for each subject plus additional balls that determine the overall probability of audit. After all individuals have reported their incomes and paid their taxes in a round, up to one person is chosen for an audit in that round by randomly drawing one ball with replacement from the bingo cage. Balls are placed in and drawn from the cage in full view of the subjects.

Subjects are volunteers from principles of economics classes and have no prior experience in the experimental setting being investigated.[14] Each session is replicated with three different groups of five subjects, all run concurrently in the laboratory. All sessions begin with the instructions being read aloud while the subjects follow along on their own copies.[15] Five practice rounds

13. The use of an audit procedure that goes back as far as four periods from the current period is meant both to capture the nature of the potential catastrophic loss that faces an audited individual and to reflect the institutional reality that the Internal Revenue Service can engage in extended back audits if fraud is discovered.

14. The use of student subjects is nearly universal in experimental economics. Availability and cost play a role in this practice. More important, properly designed experiments evaluate individual decision making, and there is no reason to doubt that students have access to the same cognitive processes as nonstudents. Those studies comparing student and nonstudent responses have generally found no significant differences (see Plott 1987 for further discussion and examples).

15. The instructions for the base case session are in the appendix, and those for the other treatments are available upon request. An important feature of the experimental design is that the instructions use "neutral" terminology; that is, all references to taxes, audits, declared income, and the like are replaced with such neutral words as *contributions, checks, disclosed income,* and so on. It is a basic tenet of the experimental paradigm that neutral terms be given in instructions in order to avoid context effects (see Plott 1987; Smith 1982 for further discussion of this issue). We use tax terminology for ease of exposition in the text.

are given, and any questions are answered. The full e
Each session lasts approximately one hour, and each
between $15 and $25, with the amount depending upo
mance in the experiment. The experiments are conducted
Economics and Psychology at the University of Colora
facility is equipped with a dedicated MicroVAX compute
nals, with one terminal serving as a monitor. All subject
and recorded on the computer, and all calculations are mac

Several sessions are conducted, and their features a ...arized in table 1. In the base case session (S1), the tax rate on declared income is 0.30, the probability of audit is 0.04,[16] and the fine rate on detected evasion of unpaid taxes is 1.00.[17] Individuals receive nothing for their tax payments in the base case session. This treatment provides a baseline that allows comparison of results when changes in the values of the fiscal parameters are made. The other sessions introduce penalty changes, audit rate changes, and positive inducements. Results are also summarized from previously conducted sessions in which fiscal uncertainty is introduced and in which institutional changes are made.

Note that it is possible to calculate a measure of the expected value of the compliance gamble for each session. For example, in the base case session, an increase of 1 token in declared income lowers (certain) income by the tax rate on declared income (0.30), but raises (expected) income by the product of the probability of detection (0.185),[18] the total penalty on unpaid taxes (2),[19] and the tax rate on income (0.30). The expected value therefore equals −0.189. The expected values for the other sessions can be calculated in a similar manner, and are reported in table 1.

These calculations indicate that the optimal individual strategy for a risk-neutral individual in all sessions is to report zero income, since the expected value of 1 additional token of declared income is always negative. More generally, optimal individual decisions for any linear payoff function will tend to exhibit all-or-none behavior; that is, individuals will either report all in-

16. Recall that each session is replicated with three different groups of five subjects. These replications are run concurrently in the laboratory, so that the three groups of five subjects are in the laboratory at the same time. The audit selection is conducted by placing twenty-five balls numbered 1 through 25 in a bingo cage. If a ball numbered 1 through 15 is drawn, then the subject with that identification number is audited; if a ball numbered 16 through 25 is drawn, then no one is audited. The ball is returned to the bingo cage before the start of the next round.

17. Note that this fine rate means that individuals pay back taxes plus a penalty equal to back taxes if they are caught cheating.

18. This probability is a compound probability, since unreported income in a single period may be detected with probability 0.04 in that current period and with probability 0.04 in each of the next four periods. The total probability of detection therefore equals $[1 - (0.96)^5]$, or 0.185.

19. Recall that the penalty on unpaid taxes in the base case session equals unpaid taxes plus a penalty equal to unpaid taxes. The effective penalty on unpaid taxes therefore equals 2.00.

TABLE 1. Experimental Design

Session	Audit Rate	Fine Rate	Tax Rate	Positive Inducement	Expected Value
S1. Base case	0.04	1	0.30	None	−0.189
			Enforcement Sessions		
S2. Audit decrease	0.02	1	0.30	None	−0.242
S3. Audit increase	0.06	1	0.30	None	−0.140
S4. Fine decrease	0.04	0	0.30	None	−0.245
S5. Fine increase	0.04	2	0.30	None	−0.134
			Positive Inducement Sessions		
S6. Lottery	0.04	1	0.30	$^1/_{25}$ probability of winning 50 tokens	−0.109
S7. Fixed reward	0.04	1	0.30	2 tokens	−0.109
S8. Audit reduction	0.04	1	0.30	Reduction in audit rate to 0.027 and to 0.013	−0.186
S9. Public good	0.04	1	0.30	Public good	−0.069

Note: The experimental design of those sessions that examine fiscal uncertainty and institutional factors is discussed in Alm, Jackson, and McKee 1991 and n.d.

come or no income. As discussed subsequently, there is substantial (though not complete) experimental evidence of such all-or-none behavior; however, there is also more compliance than is suggested by a risk-neutral strategy.

Enforcement Sessions

Four different treatments are conducted here. In two sessions, the audit rate is varied. The single-period audit rate is lowered from the level of 0.04 in the base case to 0.02 in S2; in S3 the audit rate is increased to 0.06. Sessions S4 and S5 introduce changes in the fine or penalty rate on underreported taxes. In S4, the fine rate is lowered from 1 in the base case treatment to 0, so that an audited subject pays only unpaid taxes, while in S5 it is raised to 2. For all four sessions, the levels of the other parameters are maintained at their base case values.

Positive Inducement Sessions

Four alternative forms of positive inducements are examined. In the lottery treatment (S5), subjects who are checked and found to be fully compliant for the current and the previous four rounds are entered in a lottery in which the chances of winning are 1 in 25. The lottery prize is set at 50 tokens, or an amount roughly equal to the average earnings of a subject for the entire session. The lottery is conducted at the end of the session, and, if won by a subject, the prize is added to the subject's final balance. In the fixed reward session (S7), a subject audited and found to be fully compliant receives an immediate reward of 2 tokens.[20] In the audit reduction session (S8), an individual found to be compliant has the future probability of audit reduced from 0.04 to 0.027 on the first occurrence of an audit, and from 0.027 to 0.013 on the second occurrence; an individual who is audited but noncompliant has the future audit probability remain at 0.04.[21] The last session (S9, or the public good session) examines the impact on compliance of the introduction of a public good, financed by the taxes of all five group members. The public good is created by summing the taxes collected from the group in a given period, multiplying this total by 2 to reflect the consumers' surplus generated by the public good, and then dividing the amount equally among the five people in the group.

---

20. Note that the fixed reward equals the expected value of the lottery.

21. The audit reduction occurs as follows. If an audited individual fully complies, then his or her drawn ball is retained, and an unnumbered ball is put back into the bingo cage in order to keep the probability of audit unchanged for the other subjects. If an audited individual is not compliant, then his or her ball is replaced in the bingo cage. Note that, in these sessions, three sets of balls numbered 1 through 25 are initially placed in the bingo cage.

Previous Work

The basic experimental setting can also be used to examine the effects of additional factors on individual tax compliance behavior. For example, Alm, Jackson, and McKee (n.d.) introduce fiscal uncertainty by applying a mean-preserving spread to a single variable of interest, and the subjects are forced to make their compliance decisions before knowing the realized value of the random variable. They analyze uncertainty about the probability of audit, the fine rate, and the tax rate; all sessions are run twice, with and without the public good. Alm, Jackson, and McKee (1991) also investigate the role of fiscal institutions in tax compliance. They compare compliance when subjects decide, by majority vote, on the use of their tax payments with compliance when the identical choice is imposed on them; they also compare compliance when the level of popular support for the use of the taxes varies. These previous results are briefly summarized here.

Experimental Results

The new results are summarized in table 2 and figures 1 and 2. Comparisons are made using the average compliance rate for each session. The average compliance rate equals the ratio of declared income to actual income averaged across all five subjects in a group, all three replications of each group, and all twenty-five rounds in each replication.[22]

Note that the average compliance rate in the base case, session S1 (0.332), exceeds the zero level predicted by a risk-neutral version of expected utility theory.[23] The average compliance rates by round in S1 are fairly constant over time (see fig. 1). In addition, the frequency distribution of the individual subject compliance rates is generally consistent with all-or-none

22. Note that, for each session, there are 375 individual observations, or five subjects times three replications times twenty-five rounds. These individual subject data are available upon request. All tests are based upon difference-of-means tests for the round-by-round compliance rates, which require that the data on average compliance rates be normally distributed and that the observations be independent. Independence is achieved by averaging the individual compliance rates in a given round across all five subjects in a group and all three (independent) replications of each treatment; this procedure generates twenty-five round observations on the average compliance rate in a given session. Normality of these twenty-five observations is tested using the Bowman-Shelton statistic. For all treatments, the assumption of a normal distribution cannot be rejected.

23. This level of compliance is roughly comparable to average compliance rates estimated by the Internal Revenue Service for those income return items that are not subject to source withholding or that require interpretations of complex regulations (e.g., tips, proprietors' incomes, and Schedule E income). Estimated compliance rates for return items subject to withholding or information reporting generally exceed 90 percent (see Internal Revenue Service 1988).

TABLE 2. Experimental Results

Session	Average Compliance Rate
S1. Base case	0.332
	Enforcement Sessions
S2. Audit decrease	0.317
S3. Audit increase	0.376
S4. Fine decrease	0.321
S5. Fine increase	0.365
	Positive Inducement Sessions
S6. Lottery	0.513
S7. Fixed reward	0.448
S8. Audit reduction	0.369
S9. Public good	0.374

Note: The experimental results for those sessions that examine fiscal uncertainty and institutional factors are discussed in Alm, Jackson, and McKee 1991 and n.d.

behavior (see fig. 2), with nearly two-thirds of the observations at the extremes, although there are clearly more observations at full compliance than predicted by risk-neutral expected utility theory. Inspection of the individual subject data demonstrates that within-subject behavior is quite consistent throughout the sessions. For example, in the base case, ten of the fifteen

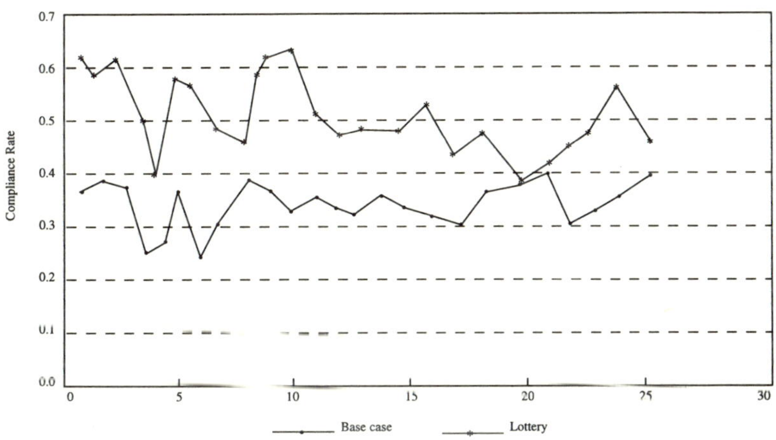

Fig. 1. Average compliance rates, base case versus lottery

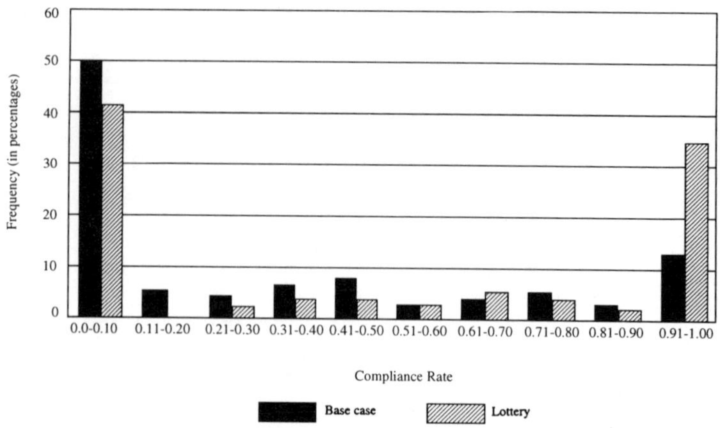

Fig. 2. Frequency of compliance rates, base case versus lottery

subjects have virtually the same compliance rates across the twenty-five rounds of the session. This result suggests that subjects generally determine their best strategy and then repeat this behavior throughout the session.

Enforcement Sessions

Consider first the introduction of enforcement changes. In S2, the audit rate is lowered from its value of 0.04 in the base case to 0.02; in S3, the audit rate is raised to 0.06. The impact of these changes on the average compliance rate is consistent with the standard expected utility model of compliance; that is, compliance falls when the probability of audit falls, and rises when the audit rate increases. However, the differences in compliance rates across these sessions are not large. Compliance in S2 falls only to 0.317, a decline from the base case that is not statistically significant. Compliance in S3 increases to 0.376. Although the difference between this and the base case compliance rate is statistically significant, the numerical difference is not large.[24] Because the probabilities in all cases are quite low, it may well be that the changes in the audit rates, though large in relative terms, are not large enough in absolute terms to attract much response from the subjects.

Similar results occur in the fine sessions, S4 and S5. The reduction in the fine rate from one in the base case to zero in S4 lowers the average compliance rate to 0.321, but the effect is nonsignificant. Increasing the fine rate raises

24. The calculated t-statistic is 2.55. The critical value with $df = 48$ is 2.40, $p = .01$, one-tailed, and is 1.68, $p = .05$, one-tailed.

compliance to 0.365. Again, although the difference between S5 and S1 is statistically significant (t-statistic = 2.36), the difference is not numerically large.

Note that the expected value of reporting one additional token is approximately the same for reductions in enforcement (S2 and S4), and for increases in enforcement (S3 and S5). The experimental results are consistent with these rankings. There is no statistical difference between S2-S4 and between S3-S5.

Positive Inducement Sessions

As suggested by the theoretical analysis of Falkinger and Walther (1991), the experimental results indicate that positive inducements have a significant and positive impact on compliance, although the magnitude varies somewhat. The lottery session (S6) has the largest effect on compliance, increasing the average compliance rate from 0.332 in the base case to 0.513 (t-statistic = 11.20). Compliance is higher in every round of the lottery session than in the base case, although there is a slight tendency for lottery compliance to decline over time, due perhaps to the remoteness (at the end of twenty-five rounds) of the lottery (see fig. 1). Compliance also increases significantly with the fixed reward session (S7), from 0.332 in the base case to 0.448 (t-statistic = 5.43). As with the lottery session, however, there is some tendency for compliance to decline in the latter rounds of S7. Note that the compliance rate in the lottery session is significantly higher than in the fixed reward session, even though their expected values are identical. Rewarding compliant individuals with an audit rate reduction (S8) also increases compliance from 0.332 in the base case to 0.369 (t-statistic = 2.53), although the effect here is not as large as for the other positive inducement sessions. It may be that the reduction in probabilities is too small to have a major impact upon compliance, or that the low audit rates lead subjects to dismiss the chances of audit entirely. Still, the difference between the base case and the audit reduction sessions tends to increase in the latter rounds of the sessions. Finally, S9 provides evidence that individuals pay taxes, in part, because they recognize that payment is necessary to receive government goods. The introduction of a public good in S9 has a positive impact upon compliance, increasing the average compliance rate from 0.332 in the base case to 0.374 in S9 (t-statistic = 2.29). However, the increase in the public good session is not as large as in the lottery or the fixed reward sessions, even though the expected value of S9 exceeds the expected values in S6 and S7.

These results suggest that positive inducements can have a significant impact upon compliance. However, these rewards must be both immediate and salient to have a numerically significant effect, and their impacts depend, in part, on how individuals weight the probability of winning the prize. For example, although the expected value of the public good session is the largest of the positive inducement sessions, it is the lottery that has the largest actual impact in these sessions, a result consistent with casual empirical evidence that a large prize with a low probability of success is more attractive than a smaller, more certain prize. In addition, a lottery may be more effective if given at more frequent intervals. A greater lottery prize, fixed reward, or future audit reduction may also encourage more compliance. Indeed, emphasizing that taxes are necessary to receive government services may be an effective tool for getting individuals to pay their taxes.

Note that an individual can qualify for a reward only by complying fully. Positive inducements, therefore, increase compliance primarily by altering the frequency of extreme behaviors, shifting individuals from very low to very high compliance rates (see fig. 2).

Previous Work

The introduction of fiscal uncertainty has significant effects upon compliance, effects that depend markedly on the presence or the absence of a public good. As discussed in more detail in Alm, Jackson, and McKee (n.d.), greater uncertainty about the audit rate, the fine rate, or the tax rate always raises compliance when there is no public good. However, the introduction of uncertainty in the presence of a public good always lowers compliance. In all cases, the differences are statistically significant.

The contrasting results for these sessions occur because the presence of the public good complicates the individual decision calculus. When individuals receive nothing for their tax payments, each subject makes the compliance decision independently of the choices of others. However, when individuals receive a public good whose size depends upon the contributions of all taxpayers, these decisions become interdependent, and each individual must determine both his or her response to uncertainty and the responses of others. As suggested in Sandler, Sterbenz, and Posnett (1987) and Isaac, Schmidtz, and Walker (1989), greater uncertainty may well lower contributions to a public good.

The manner in which group decisions are made and the level of popular support for the public goods over which these decisions are made also have significant effects on compliance. Alm, Jackson, and McKee (1991) report that compliance is significantly greater when subjects choose (by majority vote) the use of their taxes than when the identical result is imposed upon them. They also find that compliance is higher when the vote is decisive than when the vote is close, so that individuals are more likely to pay their taxes when they know that the program they select enjoys widespread approval. Not surprisingly, Alm, Jackson, and McKee (1991) find that compliance is significantly reduced by the imposition of an unpopular program. In fact, compliance is lower with an imposed, unpopular public good than in the complete absence of any public good. These results suggest that governments can encourage individuals to pay more in taxes by ensuring that individuals feel that they have a say in the decision process and by spending taxes in ways consistent with the preferences of the citizens.

Conclusions

Experimental evidence indicates that there are a variety of strategies that governments can pursue to increase tax compliance. Greater efforts to detect and to penalize tax evaders will increase compliance, although the effects may not be large if the size of the enforcement changes are not perceived by individuals as significant. Positive inducements can also be an effective tool for increasing compliance. Average compliance increases significantly when individuals receive something in exchange for their taxes and when individuals found to be compliant are rewarded in some way. The introduction of uncertainty—intentional or not—affects compliance; however, the direction depends upon the presence or absence of a public good. Finally, individuals are more likely to comply when faced with government expenditures that they select themselves and that they know enjoy the approval of their fellow citizens.

Like any applied work, these results should be viewed with some caution. They are based upon somewhat artificial laboratory experiments, they are derived from student subjects, they use small samples, and, in several cases, the effects on compliance are not large. Still, the results should not be dismissed lightly. No field data exist at present to examine many of the issues here, and it is unlikely that such data will soon be available. Further, there is an extensive—and growing—literature that argues convincingly that experimental results can contribute significantly to policy debates, as long as some conditions are met: the payoffs to subjects must be salient, better subject decisions must yield higher payoffs, the decision costs must be commensurate with the payoffs, and the experimental setting must capture the essential properties of the naturally occurring setting that is the object of investigation.[25] Laboratory methods may offer the only opportunity to investigate the behavioral responses to policy changes.

More broadly, there are numerous other factors that are thought to affect the compliance decisions of individuals, so there are additional strategies that governments can pursue. Governments can introduce a tax amnesty, in which individuals have the opportunity to pay previously unpaid taxes without being

25. See, for example, Plott (1987); Smith (1982).

subject to the penalties and prosecution that the discovery of evasion normally brings.[26] They can attempt to influence individuals' notions of fairness and of taxpayer obligations. Governments can alter the level and distribution of tax rates and tax burdens. They can change the procedures that determine how returns are selected for audit. In short, enforcement is important in maintaining and increasing tax compliance. However, there are numerous other policies available to governments, and they should pursue a range of approaches in order to achieve the desired level of tax compliance.

APPENDIX

Instructions

Introduction

This is an experiment in the economics of decision making. Several research organizations have provided funds for this research. Read the instructions carefully. If you follow them and make good decisions, you may earn a considerable amount of money that will be paid to you in cash at the end of the session.

Organization

You have been organized into groups of five persons. Each group will consist of the same five persons for the duration of the session. The specific identities of the other persons in your group will not be revealed to you. You may not communicate with anyone else in the room during the session.

The session will last for several rounds. In each round, you will be required to make a decision and your total earnings will depend on these decisions. At the beginning of the session you will be given a quantity of tokens. You will have the opportunity to add to these tokens in each round, and, at the end of the session, the tokens you have accumulated will be converted to cash at the rate of four tokens per dollar.

Each round will proceed as follows. You will be given a new quantity of tokens. The exact quantity you and the others in your group receive will be randomly drawn by the computer from the range 2.00 to 3.00 tokens in increments of 0.25 tokens. All values are equally likely and only you will know the quantity you have received. You have the choice of keeping your tokens or disclosing them. You will pay 30 percent of the tokens you disclose. You may disclose all or part of the tokens you receive. For example, if you receive 2.00 tokens and disclose 1.40 tokens, you will pay 0.42 tokens (0.30 times 1.4).

After everyone has disclosed his or her tokens, up to one person may be selected

26. See Alm, McKee, and Beck (1990) for an experimental analysis of the effects of a tax amnesty on long-run compliance.

for a check. In this check, the computer will compare the person's true quantities of tokens for the current round and the previous four rounds with the actual levels disclosed. If you are checked, any tokens received but not disclosed in the current and previous four rounds will be discovered. You will pay the shortfall that is discovered and an additional shortfall penalty. In this session, the shortfall penalty rate is set at one—you pay the shortfall plus an amount equal to the shortfall. In the above example, you would pay .36 additional tokens, that is, the shortfall of .6 times the rate of .3 plus the fine of .18. The computer will calculate the shortfall payment and subtract it from your balance.

The procedure for selecting the person for a check is as follows. Each person has an ID number that appears on your computer screen and these go from 1 through 15. In the bingo cage are balls numbered 1 through 25. After everyone has disclosed his or her tokens, a ball will be drawn from the cage. If the number on the ball is from 1 through 15, the person with that ID will be checked. If the number is from 16 through 25, no one will be checked in that round. The ball will be returned to the cage prior to the start of the next round. Each person will have a 1 in 25 (or 4 percent) chance of being checked in each round.

We will begin with five practice rounds to familiarize you with the payment, disclosure, and check processes. In these practice rounds, the process will be as described above. At the end of the five practice rounds, your balance will be reset to 10.00 tokens as the binding or real rounds begin.

Are there any questions? Let us begin with the practice rounds.

REFERENCES

Allingham, Michael G., and Agnar Sandmo. 1972. "Income Tax Evasion: A Theoretical Analysis." *Journal of Public Economics* 1:323–38.

Alm, James. 1988. "Uncertain Tax Policies, Individual Behavior, and Welfare." *American Economic Review* 78:237–45.

Alm, James, Roy Bahl, and Matthew N. Murray. 1990. "Tax Structure and Tax Compliance." *Review of Economics and Statistics* 72:603–13.

Alm, James, Betty R. Jackson, and Michael McKee. 1991. "Fiscal Exchange, Collective Decision Institutions, and Tax Compliance." University of Colorado at Boulder Working Paper. Typescript.

Alm, James, Betty R. Jackson, and Michael McKee. N.d. "Institutional Uncertainty and Taxpayer Compliance." *American Economic Review.* Forthcoming.

Alm, James, Gary H. McClelland, and William D. Schulze. N.d. "Why Do People Pay Taxes?" *Journal of Public Economics.* Forthcoming.

Alm, James, Michael McKee, and William Beck. 1990. "Amazing Grace: Tax Amnesties and Compliance." *National Tax Journal* 43:23–37.

Axelrod, Robert M. 1984. *The Evolution of Cooperation.* New York: Basic Books.

Bagnoli, Mark, and Michael McKee. 1991. "Voluntary Contribution Games: Efficient Private Provision of Public Goods." *Economic Inquiry* 29:351–66.

Bagnoli, Mark, Shaul Ben-David, and Michael McKee. N.d. "Voluntary Provision of

Public Goods: The Multiple Unit Case." *Journal of Public Economics*. Forthcoming.

Beck, Paul, and Woon-Oh Jung. 1989. "An Economic Model of Taxpayer Compliance under Uncertainty." *Journal of Accounting and Public Policy* 1:1–27.

Becker, Gary S. 1968. "Crime and Punishment: An Economic Approach." *Journal of Political Economy* 76:169–217.

Becker, Winfried, Heinz-Jurgen Buchner, and Simon Sleeking. 1987. "The Impact of Public Transfer Expenditures on Tax Evasion." *Journal of Public Economics* 34:243–52.

Brubaker, Earl. 1982. "Sixty-eight Percent Free Revelation and Thirty-two Percent Free Ride? Demand Disclosure under Varying Conditions on Exclusion." In *Research in Experimental Economics,* ed. Vernon L. Smith, 2:151–66. Greenwich, Conn.: JAI Press.

Cowell, Frank A. 1990. *Cheating the Government*. Cambridge, Mass.: MIT Press.

Cowell, Frank A., and James P. F. Gordon. 1988. "Unwillingness to Pay: Tax Evasion and Public Good Provision." *Journal of Public Economics* 26:305–21.

Dawes, Robyn, and Richard Thaler. 1988. "Anomalies: Cooperation." *Journal of Economic Perspectives* 2:187–98.

Dubin, Jeffrey A., and Louis L. Wilde. 1988. "An Empirical Analysis of Federal Income Tax Auditing and Compliance." *National Tax Journal* 41:61–74.

Falkinger, Josef, and Herbert Walther. 1991. "Rewards versus Penalties: On a New Policy Against Tax Evasion." *Public Finance Quarterly* 19:67–79.

Gordon, James P. F. 1988. "Individual Morality and Reputation Costs as Deterrents to Tax Evasion." *European Economic Review* 32:797–805.

Graetz, Michael J., and Louis L. Wilde. 1985. "The Economics of Tax Compliance: Fact and Fantasy." *National Tax Journal* 38:355–63.

Internal Revenue Service. 1978. *A Dictionary of Compliance Factors*. Washington, D.C.: U.S. Government Printing Office.

Internal Revenue Service. 1988. *Income Tax Compliance Research: Gross Tax Gap Estimates and Projections for 1973–1992*. Washington, D.C.: Department of the Treasury.

Isaac, R. Mark, Kenneth F. McCue, and Charles R. Plott. 1985. "Public Goods Provision in an Experimental Environment." *Journal of Public Economics* 26:51–74.

Isaac, R. Mark, D. Schmidtz, and James M. Walker. 1989. "The Assurance Problem in Laboratory Markets." *Public Choice* 62:217–36.

Isaac, R. Mark, James M. Walker, and Susan H. Thomas. 1984. "Divergent Evidence on Free-riding: An Experimental Examination of Possible Explanations." *Public Choice* 43:113–49.

Kahneman, Daniel, and Amos Tversky. 1979. "Prospect Theory: An Analysis of Decision under Risk." *Econometrica* 47:263–91.

Kidder, Robert, and Craig McEwen. 1989. "Taxpaying Behavior in Social Context: A Tentative Typology of Tax Compliance and Noncompliance." In *Taxpayer Compliance,* vol. 2, *Social Science Perspectives,* ed. Jeffrey A. Roth and John T. Scholz, 47–75. Philadelphia: University of Pennsylvania Press.

Kim, Oliver, and Mark Walker. 1984. "The Free Rider Problem: Experimental Evidence." *Public Choice* 43:3–24.

Machina, Mark. 1983. "Generalized Expected Utility Analysis and the Nature of Observed Violations of the Independence Axiom." In *Foundations of Utility and Risk Theory with Applications*, ed. Bernt Stigum and Fred Wenstop, 263–95. Dordrecht: D. Reidel.

Machina, Mark. 1987. "Choice Under Uncertainty: Problems Solved and Unsolved." *Journal of Economic Perspectives* 1:121–54.

Nuttin, Joseph, and Anthony G. Greenwald. 1968. *Reward and Punishment in Human Learning*. New York: Academic Press.

Palfrey, Thomas, and Howard Rosenthal. 1984. "Participation and the Provision of Discrete Public Goods." *Journal of Public Economics* 24:171–93.

Plott, Charles R. 1987. "Dimensions of Parallelism: Some Policy Applications of Experimental Methods." In *Laboratory Experimentation in Economics: Six Points of View*, ed. Alvin E. Roth, 193–219. New York: Cambridge University Press.

Pommerehne, Werner, and H. Weck-Hanneman. 1989. "Tax Rates, Tax Administration, and Income Tax Evasion in Switzerland." University of Saarland, Saarbrucken, Discussion Paper no. B8904. Typescript.

Postman, Leo. 1947. "The History and Present Status of the Law of Effect." *Psychological Bulletin* 44:489–563.

Rapaport, Amnon. 1985. "Provision of Public Goods and the MCS Experimental Paradigm." *American Political Science Review* 79:148–55.

Sandler, Todd, Frederic P. Sterbenz, and John Posnett. 1987. "Free Riding and Uncertainty." *European Economic Review* 31:1605–17.

Scotchmer, Suzanne, and Joel Slemrod. 1989. "Randomness in Tax Enforcement." *Journal of Public Economics* 38:17–32.

Skinner, B. F. 1953. *Science and Human Behavior*. New York: Macmillan.

Skinner, Jonathan, and Joel Slemrod. 1985. "An Economic Perspective on Tax Evasion." *National Tax Journal* 38:345–53.

Smith, Vernon L. 1982. "Microeconomic Systems as an Experimental Science." *American Economic Review* 72:923–55.

Spicer, Michael W., and S. B. Lundstedt. 1976. "Understanding Tax Evasion." *Public Finance/Finances Publiques* 31:295–305.

Taylor, Michael. 1976. *Anarchy and Cooperation*. New York: Wiley.

Thorndike, Edward Lee. 1911. *Animal Intelligence*. New York: Macmillan.

Westat. 1980. *Individual Income Tax Compliance Factors Study: Qualitative Research Results*. Rockville, Md.: Westat, Inc.

Witte, Ann D., and Diane F. Woodbury. 1985. "The Effect of Tax Laws and Tax Administration on Tax Compliance: The Case of the U.S. Individual Income Tax." *National Tax Journal* 38:1–14

Commentary

Julie H. Collins

I commend the authors for extending their experimental analysis of tax compliance decisions past the threshold of simply investigating the economic effects of enforcement. Their point is well taken that a purely economic analysis that considers only the traditional enforcement variables—audit probability and fines—suggests that evasion would be much more pervasive than it actually is in most countries. Additional economic, as well as noneconomic, factors must be examined to understand the empirical phenomenon of tax compliance. Based on a plethora of psychological literature concluding that rewards can be more effective than punishments for eliminating undesired behavior and for motivating desired behavior, Alm, Jackson, and McKee add positive inducements to their experimental analysis. Thus, in addition to examining the effects of altering audit probabilities and fines, they examine the effects of the following positive inducements: lottery, fixed reward, audit reduction, and public good.

The expected value of compliance, however, differed across the experimental sessions, and neutral terminology was utilized in each session. This made it difficult to disentangle the effect of a particular enforcement or inducement mechanism from the variable cost of compliance. For instance, while compliance was higher in the positive inducement sessions than in the enforcement sessions, the expected costs of compliance were smaller in these sessions. It would have been interesting to provide an enforcement and positive inducement comparison with equivalent expected values to determine whether positive rewards tend to dominate punishment when the economic reward to noncompliance remains constant. There were two positive inducement conditions with equivalent expected values—lottery and fixed reward. It was interesting to note that the lottery inducement dominated the fixed reward.

The results of the public good inducement were disappointing. The expected cost of compliance was lower in this condition than in any other treatment. However, the compliance level (0.374) does not seem practically different from the base condition compliance level (0.332). This difference is significant statistically in this study. However, the variance of the means across the twenty-five rounds is quite low in all conditions. Thus, statistical significance is found with very little differences in means across conditions. In general the authors are careful not to overstate their findings. However, given the low cost of compliance in this condition, the neutral terminology, and the weakness of this result, the authors' conclusion that evidence is provided that individuals pay taxes, in part, because they recognize that payment is necessary to receive government goods may not be justified.

The authors find that compliance in the lottery condition declines slightly over time and indicate that this is perhaps due to the remoteness (at the end of twenty-five rounds) of the lottery. It seems that the salience of the lottery should be increasing as the experiment progresses. Were subjects allowed to enter the lottery more than once, increasing their chances of winning to 0.08 or 0.12? If not, then once they became eligible for the lottery, we would expect compliance to decline in subsequent rounds.

Compliance was greater with the audit reduction positive inducement (0.369) than with the base condition (0.332). The difference in the two conditions increased in the later rounds of the sessions. In the audit reduction condition, a subject audited and found to be compliant had the future probability of audit reduced from 0.04 to 0.027 on the first occurrence, and from 0.027 to 0.013 on the second occurrence. This strategy may increase compliance until the first audit. After the first audit, if the subject is clean, compliance may increase even more as the subject is seeking the second audit reduction. Thus, one may not find a subsequent major decline in compliance due to the audit reduction until subjects are audited twice. It would be interesting to examine the behavior of subjects conditional on the number of previous audits and perhaps to extend the horizon of this condition to observe more and more subjects after they had been audited twice.

The subjects received income at the beginning of each round of the experimental sessions. The subjects were informed that there were five possible income levels ranging from 2.00 to 3.00 tokens in increments of 0.25. A subject's actual income was determined in each of the twenty-five rounds by a random draw. It would be interesting to analyze compliance conditional on the income draw. Did the income draw affect the propensity to cheat?

As a concluding thought, one aspect of positive inducements that is not captured in this experiment may be useful to consider in future work. For taxpayers who do not view taxes as an economic game and feel a "moral obligation" to comply, do positive inducements have a negative effect on compliance over time? In other words, when the government offers rewards such as these, is it a negative inducement to some subgroups of taxpayers? Psychological measures that capture the taxpaying responsibility of individuals could be incorporated. Then comparisons of compliance behavior of subjects scoring high and low on such a dimension both before and after a positive inducement system is implemented would be a fruitful extension of this work.

The Construction of Compliance and the Challenge for Control: The Limits of Noncompliance Research

Doreen McBarnet

Tax research has been dominated by the issue of noncompliance. Deterring noncompliance and securing compliance may, however, not be enough; compliance, far from being a solution to revenue problems, may itself pose a major problem for tax policy and enforcement. Compliance is not a simple concept that can remain a taken-for-granted backdrop to the study of *noncompliance*. It is, itself, a social and legal construct. This essay draws on the findings of an empirical research project on tax avoidance to argue that the research agenda must move beyond its preoccupation with noncompliance and confront the problematic nature and the practical and theoretical challenge of compliance itself.[1]

Compliance as Taxpayer Strategy

Compliance constitutes a policy and enforcement problem when it becomes not an *end,* the declared objective of those making and enforcing law, but a *means,* employed by those subject to the law, of defeating that objective.[2] The different strategies used by regulatory agents in enforcing laws or securing compliance have been the subject of a number of research studies (e.g., Bardach and Kagan 1982; Hawkins 1984). Less attention has been paid to the range of strategies employed by those subject to the law in resisting it.

Some people may positively accept law imposed on them on consensual

1. The research on which this essay is based was conducted with Dr. Graham Mansfield. I should like to thank the Economic and Social Research Council, who provided the initial funds for embarking on research on tax avoidance (award numbers E0625033 and R000231235), and the Jacob Burns Fund for Socio-legal Research, which has provided support for continuing and developing work in this area.

2. Law can, of course, also be symbolic.

grounds or receive it passively, doing nothing to resist it; but others do not.[3] Tax is rarely welcome. Faced with an unwelcome legal imposition, several active responses are possible. The first is noncompliance; one can simply break or ignore the law, hope not to be caught, or prepare covering accounts in case of investigation. The second is compromise; one can negotiate with those enforcing the law over the meaning or applicability of the law and make a deal on how it is going to be enforced in this particular case. This is common practice in British tax negotiations. The third is compliance. But complying with the law does not necessarily mean capitulating to its unwelcome aspects. On the contrary, it may mean challenging enforcement by approaching compliance not as compliance in substance, but merely as compliance in form; compliance is not a simple concept, but subject to differential social and legal constructions. Legal requirements may be complied with to the letter, but in a minimalist way that prevents the declared objectives of law from being achieved—what might be termed "formal" or "mere compliance." Or legal rules may be approached and transformed, through lateral thinking, into positive routes for tax avoidance via what we might call "creative compliance."

Opting for the strategy of compliance in form is not just a matter of an outraged response to "regulatory unreasonableness" (Bardach and Kagan 1982) or "nitpicking" enforcers (Braithwaite 1985, 100). Nor is it a matter of resorting to procedural defense as a response to the enforcement initiatives of regulators, as in Mann's study of defenses in white collar crime (Mann 1985). It can also reflect an active strategy of "preemptive legalism" (McBarnet 1991). The initiative comes from the regulated. Law is used creatively, treated not as an imposition beyond control but as a material to be worked on and transformed to suit one's own interests. The research on which this essay is based explored taxpayer and tax practitioner strategies in using the law and its institutions to escape tax impositions while nonetheless complying—or constructing compliance—with the strict requirements of legal rules.

The strategy of compliance in form achieves two things. If successful, it allows taxpayers to escape tax; in that it is just like successful noncompliance. But at the same time, whether successful in that first goal or not, it allows them to escape any risk of stigma or penalty. Compliance in form contains the bonus of providing immunity from the risks inherent in noncompliance.

Where a strategy of compliance in form is undertaken by the regulated, any equation of legal compliance with policy effectiveness breaks down. The failure of law to meet its objectives is not the product of noncompliance with legal requirements. On the contrary, law is complied with to the letter; yet the declared objectives of the law are still not achieved. Compliance, therefore,

3. Resistance implies intentional action. Noncompliance is also used to include unintentional failure to meet legal requirements; my concern is, however, with deliberate strategy.

becomes not a measure of the success of legal policy. On the contrary, compliance becomes the problem.

Yet research on regulation, and more specifically on tax, has traditionally turned little attention to the matter of empirically probing *how* the compliant comply. The research on which this essay is based sought to remedy this by treating compliance as a social and legal construct and by explicitly shifting the focus from noncompliance with tax law to legal tax *avoidance*. The focus shifted in social location, too, from the tax population at large to an elite subsection, referred to by interviewees as "high net worth" individuals, and from personal taxpayers alone to large corporations. If compliance is a social and legal construct, compliance in the hands of economic elites, constructed with the resources of major law firms at their disposal, might be very different from that of the bulk of the population.

The study explored the operation of tax avoidance and the role of tax practitioners via in-depth interviews with accountants and lawyers in major firms, financiers, consultants, and Revenue officers; via courtroom observations of key cases; and via documentary and legal analysis. It began with the premise that concern with securing compliance as a matter of enforcement policy, and focusing on noncompliance as a matter of research policy, were not enough. The boundary between compliance and noncompliance itself required research and analysis. What is the difference between compliance and noncompliance? How is compliance socially and legally constructed? Just a few findings are reviewed below. They suggest that neither enforcement nor research can limit themselves to the issues raised by noncompliance, that the regulatory problem posed by *compliance* raises fundamental issues about the nature, structure, and limits of legal control that also have to be addressed.

Noncompliance and Compliance in Form: Tax Evasion and Tax Avoidance

What is the difference between noncompliant activity and activity that is merely compliant in form? In Britain, a clear distinction is drawn in law and enforcement practice between tax evasion and tax avoidance. Tax evasion and tax avoidance are both designed to escape the payment of tax. Both are complex terms covering a range of activities on a spectrum from the lawful to the fraudulent. Tax evasion is illegal, subject to civil or criminal penalties. Some attempts at tax avoidance fail in the civil courts; some of those may be seen as an abuse of law. But much tax avoidance is accepted as lawful. Indeed, the use of legal techniques to avoid tax has been upheld repeatedly in the courts as not only lawful, but as a right, an entitlement, even (in the context of company directors' obligations vis-à-vis shareholders) as a duty. While tax evasion is therefore legally defined as noncompliant activity, successful tax avoidance is within the law. Legal textbooks in Britain refer repeatedly to the "sharp distinction" between tax evasion and tax avoidance. What is the difference, empirically and conceptually, between them?

The answer from the law books is that tax evasion is characterized by deceit, misrepresentation, and concealment. Tax evasion might involve deliberately understating profits or other income with the intent to escape tax, deliberately overstating expenses, fabrication of invoices, or making false claims to allowances. It would be fraudulent to give a false description of the legal status of a payment or person or to deliberately fail to disclose income.

Yet tax *avoidance* schemes and devices have been constructed and used routinely by large companies, banks, and the stock market; by nationalized industries; and by "high net worth" individuals to achieve just these ends by legal means. Such devices have involved charging of the same interest costs against profits twice; the artificial creation of losses, not actually sustained, to set against capital gains, or of expenses to set against profits; transferring allowances from a taxpayer who would be entitled to them but cannot use them to offset against tax to a taxpayer for whom they were not intended; legal laundering of interest into tax-free capital gains, or of capital assets into revenue expenses. I have analyzed some of the techniques for achieving these ends elsewhere (see McBarnet 1988). A wide range of schemes is explored in the research project as a whole. No one example can demonstrate all the types and nuances of avoidance techniques, but perhaps the U.S./U.K. example of the "Delaware Link" scheme may give some flavor of what can be involved.

In 1985, according to U.K. Inland Revenue estimates, £700 million per year in double-charged interest ($1.4 million at current exchange rates) was set against the profits of multinational companies to escape taxes due. Without legislation, the Inland Revenue stated that there was not a thing it could do to prevent it. How can companies quite deliberately double charge interest, that is, charge one interest bill twice over, yet comply with the law? If it is done by falsifying documents to produce two bills when only one has actually been paid, or by passing expenses, incurred by one taxpayer and used to offset tax, to another to do the same, it is illegal evasion. But it could, via the "Delaware Link" scheme, be done legally.

The trick here was a clever use of jurisdictional loopholes between different countries. In this case, there was a clash of legal definitions on company residency between the United States and the United Kingdom that the scheme exploited. The U.S. definition depended on where the company was registered. The U.K. test was a matter of where the company's management and control were exercised. A company could, therefore, be registered in the United States, usually in Delaware, with its particularly favorable company laws—hence the name—but be managed from the United Kingdom, and so meet the requirements for residency in both countries. Being defined as resident means a company is subject to that country's tax regime.

However, double tax treaties stop double charging of tax on the same income. In the Delaware link scheme, dual residency, immune from double tax, was nonetheless used for the opposite purpose, to use one set of expenses to escape tax twice.

Dual-resident companies were set up and used by multinational groups specifically and deliberately to create expenses that could be claimed in both jurisdictions by borrowing money from one of the other companies in the same group, thus creating interest payments as an expense. The tax allowance value of the expenses could be used, under group relief provisions, to offset against profits in the rest of the group—but it would be used twice, once in the United States, once in the United Kingdom.

Artificiality permeated the device. The money borrowed would not necessarily be used for any commercial purpose. The dual-resident company might borrow to acquire a company already owned by another member of the group. "It would have been more palatable if it had involved real fresh investment as opposed to just shunting debt around the group to restructure it for tax avoidance," said one Inland Revenue officer interviewed. It was important that the dual-resident company did not have taxable profits itself or the interest would simply be set against those, instead of being used twice for the rest of the group. The money to pay for the interest would therefore be carefully injected into the dual-resident company in a form that did not give rise to taxable profits. Indeed, a *double* dual-resident structure might be used to separate interest going out from dividends coming in.

Of course the interest that created the double-charged expense would be paid to another company in the group and tax might be payable on it as income. Indeed, internal movements of money within a group would, without tax avoidance devices, be likely to simply cancel each other out. In this case, however, even if tax was paid on the interest received from the dual-resident company, the double charging of the interest in the two countries meant a bonus because tax would only be paid once, but expenses would be charged twice. Not content with this bonus, however, some corporate tax planners created structures that not only allowed double charging of the interest as expense, but avoided tax on the interest received as income altogether. This might be done by using a conduit company in a tax haven. The Inland Revenue stated that it did not, in practice, receive tax from the interest payment income. The group might therefore achieve double tax relief on an artificial interest charge that was itself received free of tax.

Expenses were thus manufactured and double charged to offset against taxes due. But the scheme was not evasion, just clever avoidance. It did not break the law; it used the law. The group complied with the rules of both United Kingdom and United States tax laws and, in doing so, quite legally charged the same expenses twice. The device was not simply latching onto an exemption deliberately created as a matter of policy. Politics may have entered the scene when the United States and United Kingdom authorities had to face up to who should do something about it, with frantic attempts to assess who was likely to lose most, if not in tax, then in attracting international business. But it would be difficult to suggest that this means of escaping tax originated in intended policy. Nor was it simply a matter of slipping into an accidental but convenient loophole. Highly complex and artificial structures and transactions were contrived in order to fully exploit the opportunity that the gap between jurisdictions presented. The loophole was stretched far beyond its immediate scope by creative legal engineering. But no rules were broken, no transactions were hidden, no fraudulent claims or misrepresentations made. On the contrary, part of the reason for the rise in the use of the device between 1983 and 1985 (from fifty companies claiming £400—$800 million—in relief to nearly double) was the public statement by a reluctant Inland Revenue that it was, in the present state of the law, quite lawful. What the multinational companies involved were doing was not prohibited by law; on the contrary, the device was constructed *from* the law. They had not broken the law, but worked creatively on its fabric and turned it to their advantage.

What this demonstrates is that there is more than one way to defeat the goals of the revenue department and escape tax. Taxpayers—or, more accurately, *some* taxpayers, those with the opportunity and necessary resources—do not need to resort to noncompliance to escape taxes they are unwilling to pay. Taxpayer activity based on compliance in form can escape tax impositions just as readily as out-and-out noncompliance. Such examples, however, would not show up in research that treated legal avoidance as beyond its ambit. To focus only on noncompliance and exclude compliance in form may be to delude ourselves on the scale of the problem facing regulation.

To divide the taxpaying world into only the black-and-white categories of compliant and noncompliant without distinguishing compliance in substance from compliance in form might be misleading in another way. Given the inequalities of scope for legal avoidance activities, more readily available to big business and "high net worth" individuals than to the generality of wage earners, we may provide a picture of the social distribution of compliance that distorts reality. Projected tax revenues may be undermined not just by the noncompliance of the population in general, but also by the activities of those sectors of society with the resources to construct compliance in form while still escaping tax.

Constructing Compliance

Compliance is a construct, and one reason for focusing on tax avoidance was to probe the process by which activity is labeled avoidance or evasion, compliance or noncompliance.

There may be gray areas around the boundaries of lawful and unlawful behavior that can be obscured by accepting "permissible" activities at face value. Our research suggested that some schemes presented as examples of clever legal avoidance in fact relied, at some point or another, on *noncompliance,* not only in the sense of relying on "specious legal arguments" (Roth, Scholz, and Witte 1989, 22), but in the sense of simple nondisclosure or misrepresentation. One complex deal, for example, depended for part of its tax efficiency on neglecting to disclose the "sensitive" element of the transaction (which would have made it fall outside the safety net of lawful avoidance) to the revenue department and hoping the department would not spot it. What are presented as legal avoidance schemes may obscure a "dark figure" of noncompliance.

Whether or not a tax avoidance device is permissible under statute is a matter of decision making by the Inland Revenue or Internal Revenue Service and, ultimately, the judiciary. In the Delaware Link example, the Inland Revenue agreed that the scheme was within the law as it currently stood. But what the law means and how it applies can be subject to argument and can be affected or preempted by strategies employed by taxpayers and tax practitioners.

This is not simply a matter of some applications of law being ambiguous (see Kinsey 1987; Roth, Scholz, and Witte 1989). "Ambiguity" is not necessarily a quality inherent in particular areas of application of law. It may also be the product of strategy and process. Taxpayers and practitioners opting to negotiate tax liability may strive to present an image of law as uncertain and unclear, with the "correct" application ambiguous. Revenue officials keen to settle may agree. However, a quite different image might have been presented if the strategy selected was legalistic avoidance, compliance in form. The law would then be claimed as certain; as certain and favorable to the taxpayer; and revenue officials would be presented with a challenge to take the case all the way to final appeal if they disagreed.

Our research found a number of techniques for manipulating and claiming the certainty of rules. Graetz, Reinganum, and Wilde, in a neat turn of phrase, have referred to the use of lawyers' opinions as "fraud insurance" (1985). We found not only that lawyers' opinions were used to justify the nonpayment of tax *and* nondisclosure of transactions that might result in tax, but that taxpayers and practitioners "shopped around" a number of lawyers until they received an opinion that suited, and "managed" the opinions they received through prior discussions to ensure the "right questions," as one solicitor put it, were framed: "if your instructions are properly drafted you shouldn't get a surprise."[4] Taxpayers opting for a strategy of compliance in

4. See McBarnet (1991) for data and more detailed discussion.

form might also go to considerable lengths to control the definition of the legal form with which they would comply. If challenged they might fail; the enforcers' definition of the meaning or applicability of legal rules might prevail. But one point of the strategy was that the transaction, in its endorsed-by-lawyers form, could be treated by the taxpayer as not taxable. It might, therefore, be not declared at all, or not in a recognizably taxable form. The revenue department might never have the opportunity to challenge.

Compliance is socially constructed through information management. In the United Kingdom, a clear line is drawn in law and practice between what is liable to be treated as deliberate evasion and what is avoidance or a mistake. The line is disclosure; if all the relevant information is disclosed, the attempt to escape tax, even if not accepted, will not be treated as evasion. This line is manipulated. Practitioners operate techniques of "nondisclosing disclosure" to ensure that they disclose enough to stay on the right side of the compliance-noncompliance boundary but present the information in a way that obscures its relevance.

Accountants and lawyers interviewed revealed a number of techniques of "nondisclosing disclosure" in routine use. These techniques, described in more detail elsewhere (see McBarnet 1991), ranged through burying key information on page 195 of a 300-page document and leaving tax inspectors to spot its significance if they could, spreading significant points (which only take on relevance when read together) between pages 12, 119, and 164, or hiding crucial facts in a welter of irrelevances in the "extended disclosure approach." Full disclosure can, in fact, hide rather than reveal. One may lay false trails: "Presentation is all important: how a return strikes an inspector in the first instance can easily send him in the wrong direction." One may use words with care. Accountants would "redescribe" the activities outlined by their client in a more innocuous form. "I say don't use these words in the accounts, use these, they're less likely to excite the inspector." Or "It'll be an uphill battle for me if you describe it like that. Try this." Attention might be directed from a big issue to a little one: "leave something for the Inland Revenue to find." By one means or another, information is presented in ways that will not attract tax simply because it will not attract attention. The disclosure rules are not breached, but they are complied with in a way that does not effectively disclose tax-relevant information.

In a number of ways, then, the labels "legal avoidance" rather than "illegal evasion," or "compliance" rather than "noncompliance," are constructs, the product of a process of not just enforcer labeling but taxpayer and tax practitioner manipulation. The line between noncompliant behavior, requiring research, and behavior that is within the law and therefore beyond research, cannot simply be taken for granted. The process by which the labels are achieved requires study. To opt out of researching the boundary between compliance and noncompliance and what lies beyond is to ignore the process by which that boundary is managed.

Limits on Research or Limits in the Law?

There is another reason for extending research beyond noncompliance to compliance. In neglecting to confront the problem posed by compliance, we may also be neglecting fundamental challenges for policy, enforcement, and for sociolegal theory. In defining legally compliant activity as beyond the limits of research, we may be obscuring rather than highlighting a real problem of limits in the law and in the possibility of effective legal intervention.

To define activities as lawful is, in effect, to define them as beyond the legitimate intervention of regulation. If the legal limits on regulators are accepted as setting limits on research too, then we might never ask how limits can be enforced on enforcers, what it means to stay on the right side of the legal line that says no-go to enforcement. This has been touched on already at a microlevel in the preceding section on the construction of compliance, but there are more structural issues involved too.

What distinguishes tax evasion from tax avoidance? The answer I have suggested elsewhere is: it's not what you do but the way that you do it (see McBarnet 1992). Tax evasion methods simply ignore or break the law; tax avoidance devices use the methods of law to neutralize its impact. Law, in short, is not only an instrument of regulation but a means of escaping regulation. What does this suggest about regulation through law?

Law is, in its *structure*—not just in specific substantive laws—complex, multifaceted, and contradictory. Within the concept of law, we can distinguish the ideology of law (as in the rule of law); legal ideology (ideas expressed in law); legal policy (the purpose of law); legal content (the actual wording of statutes and cases); legal forms and institutions; legal and quasi-legal professions; and legal techniques. These elements do not necessarily work in harmony; one can be used to counter another. That they are *used* is an important point to stress. We are not discussing here deterministic structures but ideologies and forms that can be actively utilized. Law should be seen as a raw material to be worked on,[5] and, in tax avoidance, what we are seeing is tax practitioners working on the law to circumvent regulation and create legal advantages for their clients that were not necessarily intended. Compliance in form is possible because structural contradictions in law can be exploited. Legal techniques can be used to work on the content of statutes and cases to produce a method literally complying with the words of the law while nonetheless defeating its purpose. This is done in a way that meets the require-

5. See McBarnet (1984) for discussion.

ments of the forms and procedures of law, may even use the institutions of law for endorsement, and is justified by the ideology of the rule of law.

The ideology of the rule of law legitimizes compliance in form. The rhetoric of the rule of law requires that citizens should be governed by law, not by the whim of governors. Law should be known to those citizens and prestated, not retrospective. This, of course, assumes a degree of certainty in the content of law that may be elusive.[6] It may be elusive because the content of law cannot include every possible variant that it is intended to cover, or would be intended to cover if it had been foreseen. Indeed one of the reasons every variant cannot be foreseen is that a good deal of legal creativity is invested in finding a variant, however outlandish, that has not been foreseen. The feasibility of law that is not in some sense retrospective has also been questioned (see Graetz 1977). But the rhetoric of the rule of law can be a powerful political tool, as we shall see.

Faced with the problem of compliance in form, one answer is to regulate through laws that allow wide discretion to impose compliance in substance instead, disallowing activities that comply only in form. This approach is exemplified in the United States in a line of cases, from *Gregory v. Helvering* (1935) on. Yet recent British experience, charted in our research, suggests there may be limits to this approach, limits imposed by utilizing the ideology of the rule of law.

After years of judicial decisions dominated by literalism and formalism, by routine acceptance of compliance in form, the substance-over-form approach was used in relation to tax avoidance in *Ramsay* (1981) and *Furniss v. Dawson* (1984), which looked through the form of transactions in a tax avoidance device to their underlying purpose of circumventing the law. This "new approach," however, also provoked powerful criticism, including a coordinated lobby of the accountancy and legal professions. The substance-over-form approach has, in fact, since been retreated from in *Craven v. White* (1988) (see Mansfield 1989) and *Shepherd v. News International* (1989), and there has been a drift back to rules, to compliance in form, and to avoidance.

Ramsay and *Furniss* stimulated a vociferous lobby against judicial policy-making, post hoc decisions, and the uncertainty of substance over form, not just from the accounting and legal professions but more generally. Letters in the press described the "new approach" as "usurping the authority of Parliament," "infringing the provisions of the European Convention for the Protection of Human Rights" (*Financial Times,* July 5, 1984), and as a "clear infringement of individual freedom" (*Times* (London), March 3, 1984). What

6. However, a "working certainty" may sometimes be achieved in practice. See McBarnet and Whelan (1991).

was being invoked was the ideology of the rule of law, no mere sociological or political abstraction but a very powerful political tool.[7]

What the U.K. experience would suggest is that there may be limits in the possibility of effective control, regulation, or policy implementation through law. Structural contradictions in law are reflected in the constant discourse of dilemma over how law should operate—through specificity or through generality.[8] In either case, the ideology of the rule of law can be brought in to criticize or undermine it. If law is specific, it becomes a recipe book for avoidance, for circumvention by carefully defining activities to fall outside its ambit but stay within the bounds of legality. If it is general, it necessarily operates with wide discretion and is subject to the image or reality of arbitrariness. In the first case, compliance in form is facilitated by the ideology of the rule of law; in the second case, attempts to control compliance in form are obstructed by invoking the rule of law.

The ideology of the rule of law, as a dominant theme in the legitimation of the democratic state, provides a powerful ideological tool for lobbying against the substance-over-form approach. In the area of taxation in particular, the rhetoric of "no taxation without representation" underlines rule of law arguments against judicial lawmaking (in an area constitutionally reserved for the legislature) and post hoc decision making in general. Ideology can be used to draw politically resonant limits on what can be done as law. Political lobbies can be ignored, of course, and precedent is flexible enough for judges to justify discretion. But there may also be limits in how far down this road regulation can go in the face of articulate opposition and maintain its legitimacy; how far, in short, law can go and still be seen as law.

Conclusion: Putting Tax Avoidance on the Research Agenda

Noncompliance raises many major issues for policy and for theory. But there is a real danger: in concentrating attention on noncompliance, the constructed and problematic nature of compliance will be overlooked, and wider issues—the role of tax practitioners in undermining declared tax policy; the different routes available to rich and poor, individuals and corporations, for escaping tax; the possible limits of the law—will be ignored. Legal tax avoidance, taking us into just these issues, should therefore be recognized as a key topic for research and analysis too.

---

7. On a more day-to-day level the ideology of precedent may also be used to construct working rules. See McBarnet and Whelan (1991).

8. See McBarnet and Whelan (1991 and 1992) for a discussion of this discourse of dilemma in the context of the regulation of financial reporting more generally.

Yet legal tax avoidance is not high on the agenda for tax research. The recent report of the Panel on Taxpayer Compliance Research, set up at the request of the IRS by the Committee on Research on Law Enforcement and the Administration of Justice, explicitly excludes from its definition of noncompliance "the structuring of one's financial affairs within the law so as to reduce taxes, perhaps in ways that were not intended by lawmakers," in short, legal tax avoidance (Roth, Scholz, and Witte 1989, 2). In consequence, tax avoidance is also excluded from its review of the issues, and from its agenda for research. Our research, however, suggests there are dangers in too readily accepting that noncompliance is a subject fit for research and compliance is not, quite simply because these definitions are constructs that may themselves be manipulated. We must be wary of setting artificial limits on research.

Roth, Scholz, and Witte suggest that "greater knowledge about the relationships between tax practitioners and taxpayer compliance could offer one of the most promising areas for improving compliance . . . to the extent that practitioners can be encouraged to foster compliance in their clients, enforcement resources could be concentrated on the most problematic areas" (1989, 178). Here again, the problematic nature of compliance must be taken into account. The potential role of tax practitioners in securing more effective enforcement depends on what kind of compliance they foster. Our own study in the United Kingdom, focused as it was on tax avoidance, highlighted the role of practitioners in securing compliance in form rather than compliance in substance, undermining rather than bolstering enforcement. Indeed, this might be inherent in the structural role of professional practitioners. Insofar as it is their job to interpret, apply, and work with the "raw material" of the law as best they can in their clients' interests, legally avoiding tax can be seen as a professional duty. The role of the professions contributes to the structural scope for legal avoidance. The cost of professional advice, in turn, affects any differential distribution of noncompliance, compliance in substance, and compliance in form between social classes and between individuals and corporations.

Studying tax avoidance, exploring the structures that make it possible and legitimize it, raises basic questions about the limits of tax enforcement and the limits of regulation through law. Avoidance poses a different kind of problem from noncompliance and, perhaps, a more fundamental one. Evasion and gray areas play on problems of enforcement, but avoidance plays on structural problems in law. How do you enforce law that has not been breached? How do you throw the book at taxpayers who are already playing the game by the book? There are many questions on noncompliance that call for study, but research must also go further. For the research and policy communities to opt for concentrating attention on *noncompliance* may be to blind themselves to the fact that compliance, too, can pose a major, and perhaps even more intractable, problem.

REFERENCES

Bardach, E., and R. A. Kagan. 1982. *Going by the Book: The Problems of Regulatory Unreasonableness*. Philadelphia: Temple University Press.

Braithwaite, J. 1985. *To Punish or Persuade?* New York: State University of New York Press.

Graetz, M. 1977. "Legal Transitions: The Case of Retroactivity in Income Tax Revision." *University of Pennsylvania Law Review* vol. 126:47–87.

Graetz, M. J., J. Reinganum, and L. Wilde. 1985. "The Tax Compliance Game." Mimeo.

Hawkins, K. 1984. *Environment and Enforcement*. Oxford: Clarendon Press.

Kinsey, K. 1987. "The Social Dynamics of Tax Encounters." American Bar Foundation. Mimeo.

McBarnet, D. 1984. "Legal Form and Legal Actors." *International Journal of the Sociology of Law* 12:231–38.

McBarnet, D. 1988. "Law, Policy, and Legal Avoidance: Can Law Effectively Implement Egalitarian Policies?" *Journal of Law and Society* 15:113–21.

McBarnet, D. 1992. "It's Not What You Do but the Way That You Do It: Tax Evasion, Tax Avoidance, and the Boundaries of Deviance." In *Unravelling Criminal Justice: Eleven British Studies,* ed. D. Downes, 267–68. London: Macmillan.

McBarnet, D. 1991. "Whiter than White Collar Crime: Tax, Fraud Insurance, and the Management of Stigma." *British Journal of Sociology* 42:323–44.

McBarnet, D., and C. J. Whelan. 1991. "The Elusive Spirit of the Law: Formalism and the Struggle for Legal Control." *Modern Law Review* 54:848–73.

McBarnet, D., and C. J. Whelan. 1992. "Regulating Accounting: Limits in the Law." In *Accounting and the Law,* ed. M. Bromwich and A. Hopwood, 99–111. Englewood Cliffs, N.J.: Prentice-Hall.

Mann, K. 1985. *Defending White Collar Crime*. New Haven: Yale University Press.

Mansfield, G. 1989. "The New Approach to Tax Avoidance." *British Tax Review* no. 1: 5–19.

Roth, J., J. Scholz, and A. D. Witte. 1989. *Taxpayer Compliance*. Philadelphia: University of Pennsylvania Press.

CASES

Craven v. White. 1988. STC 476.

Furniss v. Dawson. 1984. 2 WLR 226.

Gregory v. Helvering. 1935. 55 S Ct 266.

Ramsay (WT) Ltd. v. IRC. 1981. 2 WLR 449.

Shephord v. News International Plc. 1989. CD TLR (30 June).

Commentary

Daniel Nagin

This essay grapples with a number of important and thorny issues of business tax compliance. My comments focus on two such issues.

The first involves Dr. McBarnet's distinction between compliance with policy versus compliance with rules. My understanding of this distinction is as follows. Compliance with policy refers to a situation where the regulator and regulatee attempt to come to an accommodation via negotiation and conciliation. The objective of such mediation is not to win conformance with the letter of the law but rather the spirit of the law. By spirit, I understand Dr. McBarnet to mean the underlying rationale or policy objective that prompted the passage of the law or promulgation of the regulation.

An example might involve a negotiation between an environmental agency and an industrial firm on the mechanisms and timetable for reducing pollution discharges. Suppose that the business recognizes and freely acknowledges that its discharges exceed legislated levels and indicates a genuine desire to conform to standards. Notwithstanding, they are able to demonstrate that meeting the letter of the law would be financially ruinous.

While I am no expert on environmental regulation, this is the sort of situation where it is entirely conceivable that a responsible regulator and responsible business could negotiate an arrangement that meets the underlying policy objectives of the law. I say this because there is a broadly shared consensus in our society on the underlying objectives of environmental regulations—protecting the health and welfare of human beings and, to a lesser extent, plants and animals. To be sure, there are strong disagreements about specifics—what chemicals are dangerous and at what levels and so forth—but this should not obscure the fact that there are many responsible companies that take seriously the ethical obligation to their employees and society at large not to poison the workplace and the environment.

Let me turn now to the concept of compliance with rules. Here, the relationship between the regulator and the regulatee is adversarial. Issues of contention revolve around whether the regulatee has conformed to the letter, not the spirit, of the law. Dr. McBarnet argues that the compliance with rules regime typifies the relationship between tax agencies and business taxpayers, particularly large business taxpayers. From my own experience as a tax administrator, I have no fundamental disagreement with this generalization. I would observe, however, that I cannot imagine how the relationship could be otherwise. Unlike environmental protection or workplace safety issues, there are generally no strong ethical issues at stake in the tax laws. In the United States and England, we do not hold to the principle that what does not clearly belong to the individual belongs to the state. As such, commonly shared normative positions cannot be referenced as a basis for the sort of mediation that typifies the compliance with policy regime.

Let me illustrate this conclusion with an example. Pennsylvania has a business tax called the Capital Stock and Franchise Tax. Assets committed to manufacturing and processing are exempt from this tax. Let me give you a taste of the sorts of legal disputes that have arisen concerning eligibility for the manufacturing and processing exemption: Is a machine's foundation subject to the exemption? Does production of ice cream constitute manufacturing or processing? Is a computer used both for regulating manufacturing processes and also for administrative purposes exempt? If yes, what proportion? Is a forklift used both on the manufacturing floor and the inventory operation exempt?

The manufacturing exemption is illustrative of innumerable provisions in federal, state, and local tax codes. These provisions share a number of common characteristics. First, millions of dollars turn on technical interpretations of the statute. Second, these technical provisions are not grounded in any well-defined and widely understood policy objectives. To be sure, when the manufacturing exemption was enacted, the purpose was to encourage and promote manufacturing in Pennsylvania but you can rest assured that the legislative record provides absolutely no guidance on the sorts of technical issues that I previously enumerated. Third, as I previously indicated, technical provisions in the tax law are generally not designed to protect any widely shared community standard. In short, what is involved is big bucks and technical minutia. There are no compelling moral issues at stake, just money. In these circumstances, it seems to me an adversarial, compliance-with-rule regime is inevitable.

Dr. McBarnet also argues that tax avoidance poses a different kind of problem from noncompliance and, perhaps, a more fundamental one. I believe this conclusion should be qualified by "depending on what problem one is studying." If one is concerned, for example, with the equitable distribution of the tax burden, I believe the issue of tax avoidance should somehow be addressed, although I am not quite sure how. On the other hand, if one's primary focus of concern is understanding why and under what circumstances individuals or institutions are willing to incur the hazards of not complying with legal requirements, then so-called tax avoidance is only relevant to the extent that it shapes the compliance decision. As Dr. McBarnet emphasizes, tax avoidance is perfectly legal and, thus, not directly relevant to many questions that are important in their own right. Some examples include: How does the threat of detection and punishment shape the decision to conform or not conform to a legal standard? How do norms and community standards influence compliance decisions? What factors shape perceptions of the costs and benefits of illegal behavior?

There is, however, an impure form of tax avoidance that I believe should receive far more attention in compliance research and the compliance policy domain. What I have in mind are tax avoidance strategies that do not unequivocally meet the letter of the law. Such schemes involve reporting strategies built on untested legal ground. Stated differently, they are reporting strategies grounded, at least in part, in legal ambiguity. Some have suggested that tax understatements stemming from such reporting strategies are somehow not noncompliance. I believe this position is wrong. Noncompliance is, ultimately, whatever the IRS and the courts say it is. The contention that noncompliant reporting decisions based on legal ambiguity are somehow not noncompliance has diverted attention from such important questions as: how does legal ambiguity shape reporting decisions? As a matter of public policy, how should reporting positions grounded in legal ambiguity that are ultimately determined to be noncompliant be penalized, if at all?

As I stated at the outset, the essay tackles some very difficult questions in largely uncharted research territory—business tax noncompliance. While I have some real concerns about certain of Dr. McBarnet's arguments, her work represents a valuable first step.

Contributors

James Alm
Department of Economics
University of Colorado

Kurt J. Beron
School of Social Sciences
University of Texas at Dallas

Richard Bird
Department of Economics
University of Toronto

John S. Carroll
Sloan School of Management
Massachusetts Institute of Technology

C. Y. Cyrus Chu
The Institute of Economics
Academia Sinica (Taipei)

Julie H. Collins
School of Business
University of North Carolina

Steven E. Crane
Department of Economics
Marquette University

Jeffrey A. Dubin
Division of Humanities and Social Sciences
California Institute of Technology

Henk Elffers
Department of Social Sciences
Erasmus University, Rotterdam

Brian Erard
Department of Economics
University of Toronto

Jonathan S. Feinstein
Graduate School of Business
Stanford University

Dick J. Hessing
Department of Social Sciences
Erasmus University, Rotterdam

Betty Jackson
Accounting Department
University of Colorado

Karyl A. Kinsey
American Bar Foundation

Richard Lempert
School of Law
University of Michigan

Susan B. Long
School of Management
Syracuse University

Jeffrey K. MacKie-Mason
Department of Economics
University of Michigan

Doreen McBarnet
Centre for Socio-Legal Studies
Oxford University

Kathleen M. McGraw
Department of Political Science
State University of New York at Stony Brook

Michael McKee
Department of Economics
University of Colorado

Silvia A. Madeo
School of Business Administration
University of Missouri at St. Louis

Daniel Nagin
School of Urban and Public Affairs
Carnegie-Mellon University

Farrokh Nourzad
Department of Economics
Marquette University

Alan H. Plumley
Research Division
Internal Revenue Service

Eric M. Rice
The World Bank

Henry S. J. Robben
Department of Economic Psychology
Erasmus University, Rotterdam

John T. Scholz
Department of Political Science
State University of New York at Stony Brook

Steven M. Sheffrin
Department of Economics
University of California–Davis

Joel Slemrod
School of Business Administration
University of Michigan

Kent W. Smith
American Bar Foundation

Marco R. Steenbergen
Department of Political Science
State University of New York at Stony Brook

Eugene Steuerle
Urban Institute
Washington, D.C.

Helen V. Tauchen
Department of Economics
University of North Carolina

Robert K. Triest
Department of Economics
University of California–Davis

Paul Webley
Department of Psychology
University of Exeter

Ann Dryden Witte
Department of Economics
Wellesley College

Index